W9-CGZ-031

THE TOE BONE
AND THE TOOTH

Other titles by the same author:

Secrets of the Talking Jaguar
Long Life, Honey in the Heart

Martín Prechtel

THE TOE BONE
AND THE TOOTH

Thorsons

With the prominent exception of Gaspar Culan, Stanley Rother, Gustavo
Rodas and Nicolas Chiviliu, who are all deceased, different proper
names have been used in the text out of courtesy to the living.
None of the place names have been altered.

Thorsons
An Imprint of HarperCollins*Publishers*
77-85 Fulham Palace Road,
Hammersmith, London W6 8JB

The Thorsons website address is:
www.thorsons.com

TM

and *Thorsons* are trademarks of
HarperCollins*Publishers* Ltd

First published by Thorsons 2002

1 3 5 7 9 10 8 6 4 2

Cover illustration and all interior illustrations by Martín Prechtel

A catalogue record of this book
is available from the British Library

ISBN 0-00-714267-6

Printed and bound in Great Britain by
Creative Print & Design (Wales), Ebbw Vale

DEDICATION

·

TO

THE DEER-EYED DAUGHTER OF THE MOUNTAIN,
THE MOTHER OF THE GREAT DIVERSITY

AND

TO

all those peoples, plants and animals who have been and
continue to be forcibly uprooted, rerouted, relocated, corralled, cut,
branded, burnt out, burned down, burnt up, crushed, eradicated or driven
from their homes in infinite diasporas of all types, to live where they may
be unwelcome, while still trying to keep alive their seed capsules of cultural
memory in hopes to regrow a home again. May their descendants be
carved by the inherited grief of their ancestral loss to become feeders
of what is holy in the ground, dedicated to something bigger than
their need for justice and the pursuit of revenge.

In memory of four men who died in love with something bigger than
themselves: Gaspar Culan, Stanley Rother, Gustavo Rodas and Nicolas
Chiviliu Tacaxoy.

TABLE OF CONTENTS

ACKNOWLEDGEMENTS

After living the story, knowledge and events that now reside inside this book, I carried them for years, gathered together like a painful, holy seed, so tightly clutched inside my closed hand that the seed itself took on the form of an angry fist. This went on so long that what I held became geologically compressed by the overwhelming weight of loneliness that the seed was gradually petrified into what held it, becoming one and the same with the stone of my unopened hand.

Because of that, though widely requested, this book could not be pried from my hands and was never to be written. I was yet too raw, too tender, still overly immersed in what had happened, loyally "saving" the unopened hand that was killing me. My teachers had wanted me to plant my seed, not to keep my seeds forever as seeds. But how could I do it, when the people around me had no respect for what I was planting in their ground? So, my fist stayed closed and would have done so forever until the rest of me had followed it into stone, if it had not been for the air-clearing symphony of my curly-headed wife-to-be's persistent cooing, who is herself a magical horse made of trumpeter swans, migrating cranes and the tidy, mica-dusted fur from the hind feet of wild mice, whose flute-like sound melted the stone and sang the fisted seed out of the ground and into flower in the untroubled breeze of her beauty and loyal friendship.

Who could have known that the opening of the hand was greater than the secret it was holding and that after its lifetime of holding a secret that the receiving hand would become the greatest secret that it held? That gift-woman sent from the Deer-eyed Mother of Life knew, that genius woman knew.

For all that, to her alone among humans goes the greatest gift, if I had one big enough to give, which is not to mention the several thousand hours she spent in back-snapping, brain-curdling, dedicated labor and patient, uncompromising wrangling with typing, papers, personalities and logistics, along with her genius understanding of what it is I write.

For all of that I give a toast of protection, admiration and love to my curly-headed wife, Hanna Keller. Thank you.

Thanks as well to all the people who read, love and understand my books and a greater thanks to those who at first do not understand and read them over and over again, even after they do.

My express gratitude to all the following friends, supporters, allies, towns, tribes, groups and nations, because all of us in one way or another are living out this tale:

Best friends poet Robert Bly and Ruth; Wick Fisher and family; Marianne Lust; Deborah Lubar; Mira Verner-Lust; Tom Verner; Shivam O'Brien; Diane Miller and family; Annie Spenser; Mark Goodwin; Nicolas Ostler; Nick and Manda Clements; Marc Rylance; Clair Van Campen and family; all the actors at the Shakespeare's Globe in London; Jimmy Holden at HarperCollins; the publishing team at Thorsons; Greg Brandenburgh; William Ayot; Tom Keller and family; Lois and Bill Steinhauser and family; George Prechtel, John Prechtel; Jorge and Santiago Prechtel; Jeff Harbour and family; David Abram and family; Enhtur Ayush; Marilyn Bacon and family; Deborah Felmeth and Mouawia Bouzo; Guy Jean and Violette; Craig Ungerman and Camille Benjamin; Jeanene McNeil and family and friends; all the attendees of the Ojo Caliente Writer's Retreat and the Love Letters to the Flowering Earth Conferences; the people of Ojo Caliente, Duranes, Gavilan, New Mexico, especially Mayordomo Celestino Lucero and family; the people of El Rito, especially Robert Alire and family; Donald Alire and family; Levi Romero; Vincete Griego; guitarist Pedro Cortes; Michele Ward; Richard Seidman and Rachael Resch; Judyth Hill; all the participants in the UK and Europe in the New Sap in the Old Tree conference; all those friends and supporters in the United Kingdom, Africa, India, Balkans, Columbia, Mongolia, Canada, Czech Republic, France, Italy, Syria, Turkey, Japan, Southeast Asia, Nicaragua, Peru, Mexico, San Salvador, Honduras, Israel, Spain, Germany, Finland, Ireland; all the supporters, book stores and friends in the US, in particular those in Arizona, Vermont, Oregon, Northern California, Alabama, Colorado, New Mexico, Minnesota, the Carolinas, New York State and Michigan; to name just a few.

For all the stories of all the tribal and village people of the world, the world couldn't survive without you.

For all the diverse peoples and the beautiful land of Guatemala, in particular the ancient Tzutujil and the newest generation of Tzutujil once again interested in their immense culture and in their valuable indigenous root. *Utzlaj jie achinaq chiwa xix majun tnmastaj i tzij, ojerlaj cholic tzij. Matiosh chiwa xix ix conjilaal.*

For the story herself and my divination bundle where she speaks, without which I would not have existed, and of course for anyone I may have forgotten.

Kiil utziil
Utzlaj bey
Utzlaj colo´
Nimlaj taq Kaslimaal
Majun lovlo´
Oxlajuj matioxiil.

THEIR ARMS OUTSTRETCHED
INTO THE NIGHT

After the terrible massacre of December 1991, resulting in the long-awaited removal of all the soldiers that had been permanently bivouacked in Santiago Atitlan for eight years, in the early spring of 1992 I returned for the very first time in just as many years to Guatemala and Santiago Atitlan.

I was met outside the airport by five teenage Atiteco boys who had still been young children when I'd left the village. In a little yellow Japanese pickup with the back window missing and the truck bed piled high with *cum* and *q´oq´*, or Mayan squashes, covered with a canvas, these young men had come to fetch me and drive me the 90 kilometers to the lakeside.

They wanted me to sit up front with the driver while the rest stood in the back, until we were due to pass an army or police roadblock, for which they had me burrow under the squashes and canvas with three of them seated on top during the inspection, by which ruse we were able to clear all seven checkpoints on the hot Pacific coast before the steep climb past Patuluul, the Land of Zapotes, up to the cool highlands and on to the Mother Lake, Lake Atitlan. At that particular time, from there to the village, the road would be left unpatrolled.

When we entered the first profusion of volcanic hills and forests, the driver stopped the truck while one of the young fellows in the back, a distant relative of mine through my children's Tzutujil grandmother, inquired of me if it were true that I knew the story of The Toe Bone and the Tooth and if so could I tell it to them from here on out as we drove.

The landscape we were driving through was the story and we had to proceed mighty gradually, stopping very often, to allow me to tell the whole tale, pointing out all the places, rocks, rivers, trees, volcanoes, animals and so on as we passed them. Certain mountains that we circumnavigated were actually part of a different story to which they forced me to jump as well, only to return back to The Toe Bone and the Tooth after rounding the bend back into our original story.

I suddenly recollected how the last time I'd been on this road, I'd been telling the same tale, albeit headed in the opposite direction into exile with my little family. From the look on their enraptured faces, that alternated between a surprised thrill and embarrassment, I wondered if any of these attentive Tzutujil youth knew what came next at each stage of this powerful old story of their ancestors. I found myself asking them at intervals in the telling of the tale, "You remember, don't you?" None of them did.

At one point, just before getting to the southeastern corner of the Mother Waters of Lake Atitlan, I got lost as well, the story didn't match the land and I recognized nothing. I stopped speaking.

For these boys this road had always been this way, for me it was out of the story, an unknown thing. Amazed at my confusion the boys explained that an earthquake, several floods and an intense forest fire had rerouted the river, reorganized and tumbled down two mountains. The road now slowly edged around a slope of yellow dust and fast-growing gravilea trees, swinging 200 yards west to what had been, in my time, pure air above a deep ravine.

Another of the boys yelled to us, "This must've been where the Mountain God threw down the hills and tried to burn the Raggedy Boy. The mountain was angry for all our tearing up the ground."

In the interim of my absence all these young men, either through their families, as war orphans, or by themselves, had been coerced by political circumstance into becoming protestant Christians, who expressly prohibited the old stories and any proximity with people who might know them. As a result none of the young people truly knew their own people's "Big" stories such as The Toe Bone and the Tooth, but all had heard about them on the sly.

Though they didn't know the tales, here in one telling they were already inside the story, remembering what had recently happened as part of what had always happened for thousands of years for the land and for their people. What was indigenous in them was still alive and ready to listen to the likes of me from far away who'd spent his life married to the meaning of their stories, which became my stories, stories that had been demonized by missionaries who came from the land in which I now lived.

Arriving at the edge of the village at two in the morning on Wednesday, ten hours later than expected, we were an emotionally charged and exuberant crowd of men as we unloaded one of the boy's squashes at his house at the bottom of the hill at Chinimya. Far off but coming toward us, in the night we heard the shuffling of a hundred bare feet on stones, the squeaking of sandals, the muffled hum of men and women walking behind the roar and squeal of the big village drum played by my old comrade Aqoquix, and a new flute man.

This was a part of the ongoing ritual of initiation for young people that always coincided with the ecstatic and exuberant Mayanized Catholic Holy Week. On this night, every year for hundreds of years, the old people and initiating chiefs had come to meet the young men, right here at the northern shore of the village, who would have just returned from the wild mountains on the south side of the bay. It was here on this day, every year, in the dark under the almost full moon that the boys, in high spirits, would paddle with great speed in a rousing return in several thirty-person canoes filled to overflowing with great bundles of evergreen branches trailing in the moon-lit water.

I had been in charge of this whole year-long ceremonial and involved in various capacities with it every year that I'd lived in the village. But initiation rituals ceased the year before I'd fled the town, from this exact spot, less than a decade previously. Hope and emotion wrestled in me until I noticed that the drum and flute player should have gone with the boys in the canoes.

When they saw me, the whole entourage of old timers stopped moving, the drum and flute ceased and every one of them looked down the hill. The Najbey Quej, my old friend the "First Deer" yelled, *"Nix atet arja rilaj a Martín?"*

"Could that be you, Old Martín?"

"Hie Tidta´, anen niniga."

"Truly old brother parent, it's me alright."

"Natrsaga a goural naban, katjo wavie, jo ncosmaja."

"How come you're so lazy? Get over here and let's get to work."

I was only forty-one, but they'd called me Old Martín since I was twenty-two. Tearful and hysterical when we had parted years before, now my elegant and enduring old comrades welcomed me back home as if I'd just returned from an extended pee among the rocks. They welcomed me by letting me know that they hadn't let me go. I was remembered. As far as they were concerned, no matter how far I roamed or what we'd had to do to survive, I was still in the story with them and had never actually left the village.

Marching with the old folks again we arrived at the lake edge where I expected to see the initiate youth of this huge Mayan town, their mentors, their chiefs, their branches and their long, loaded, hand-carved log canoes beached on the soggy shore; but none were to be seen, nor would they be.

No one expected them for there were no longer any initiations. But the old people with their headcloths over their shoulders, their hands outstretched into the night toward the Mother Waters and her mother, the Grandmother Moon, commenced to speak the exact old words of ritual remembrance as if the initiate boys had actually been standing there.

"It's good to see your faces again,

It's good to feel your breath again.

We the eight hundred shimmering

Forgetters, the big trees and big vines
Do not forget you, our new
Fruit, whose seeds will
Be our remembrance planted in the
Deep humus of our passing.
We do not forget you,
We do not abandon you.
Yesterday and the day before
When we saw... "

For those who'd been inside these old-time initiations it was easy to imagine the tired boys standing there with the branches strapped on their back, dancing to our words under their loads, swinging in the lake breeze. Now the village did ritual after ritual to what couldn't reply or be seen by those that had never seen it before.

After that only one half of the rituals could be done, but these were carried out so assiduously that the following generations assumed by going through the motions they were doing the whole thing. Fifty percent of what was holy and necessary was missing. Those dedicated old beauties were the last generation to know the difference.

How much of the many religious and spiritual approaches in the world are extravagant, later outgrowths of the tiny, treasured bits that displaced people, overrun or driven to disperse from their homelands, could carry in their arms as they fled, leaving the greater portion of their Big Stories, rituals and understandings still waiting in the long-lost ground of their origination?

Are most of the allegorized, dogmatized, literalized, sanitized, boring, overly historified rituals and written stories, only jealously guarded fragments of a pushed-aside indigenous intactness which all people, in this increasingly displaced world, have hidden somewhere in their bones as an unremembered legacy in which an intact living story still waits to come into view?

For, if, as my old Tzutujil friends used to go on about, our human bodies are actually the Earth itself, then somewhere inside this earth-body our homelands still await our return; inner homelands in whose soil our indigenous souls lie ready like seeds; seeds whose DNA are the Big culturally intact Stories; seeds that have waited for thousands of years for the spiritual climate to shift enough to where the tears of our human grief about the day we finally remember the overwhelming magnitude of our diverse, earth-oriented cultural losses could moisten the seeds of our Big Stories, causing our indigenous memories to sprout again into well-rooted trees of remembrance upon whose branches a never-before-seen-fruit, a new possibility for humans on Earth might come into sight, remembered beyond its own recollecting into a time beyond the already known and limited imagination of the age.

Some stories however, like The Toe Bone and the Tooth, sometimes refuse to wait in the ground like seeds and, without the old rituals where they used to live out their lives, they show up in the most unexpected places: under bridges, in wars, at the job, on the street hitchhiking, living out that Big Story in extraordinary ways inside the lives of ordinary people anywhere, who like refugees learn to live any way they can away from their homelands.

The Earth itself never stops talking out its Big Story, it is the people who stop listening. The Big Story needs the Earth to hear its tale and the people need the story to be on the Earth. But that means we have to have good open ears to listen. The indigenous soul hiding inside us has just such ears.

This book is an account of the old Tzutujil mythology of The Toe Bone and the Tooth as it lived itself out in my own life, a life spent trying to keep the story alive and remembered, when the spiritual landscape of the Tzutujil Maya it was born from was dismembered by the troops of the same syndrome of cultural amnesia that has caused all the diasporas of the world.

This book is not only about Mayans or Guatemala, Americans, America or the English; it is about how long it takes to become a human being. It seems to say that humans are most useful to the Universe when they are blessing, especially when the unblessed become the blessers and when humans give their gifts to what they can't see; when they turn the failure and grief of their losses into life-giving beauty and when they are in love.

The Toe Bone and the Tooth is a love story and I give it as a gift to all those that love, especially to those with arms outstretched in the night, who having given all they had left, speak alone to what they would have loved and hearing only in reply the moon upon the water, begin to sing, hoping the real one might appear.

PADRE'S
REVOLUTION

Gaspar Culan the younger didn't believe the sun was a God: The sun was not "Our Father." He didn't believe that the forested volcanic mountains surrounding his village were palatial worlds inside of which whole families of Gods, lineages of deities, danced, dreamt, worked and wept in villages of magical animals and speaking trees, whose weather warriors equipped with assorted lightning held thunderous feasts and could make the earth quake by cracking their knuckles.

Neither was the earth a sky for another world beneath, nor was it alive at all; its springs and ponds were not the bodies of holy Mother Gods, whose children of trees and grasses they suckled into ripe ages, who then wept for them in river floods and torrential storms of maternal grief in the eternal knowledge, well understood but never accepted, of their constant obligation and joy at giving birth to every plant and creature on this flowering Earth only to watch them disappear, devoured into the starving maws of other of her children.

To him jaguars were not the form taken by the curious God of the center of the world when coming to catch a glimpse of the Rain Gods' creation: the human.

Nobody knew why or when it was or how it happened that Gaspar Culan the younger, grandson of a long line of ancient royal Mayans, shamans, famous weavers and merchant magicians, woke up one morning at an early age and saw the world as a ragged patch of lifeless stone and human hatred.

Perhaps because every day he saw the unpatched rips and holes in a hundred women's skirts, that let the unwashed copper of their overworked thighs come rippling to the eye. One of them, his cousin, widowed when her husband was crushed to death beneath a falling tree, had the smile of her unkillable ecstatic nature made toothless at the age of twenty having sacrificed her ivory to the precious thin milk of her flattened, tired breasts, spent trying to feed the two still drinking while the older of three already buried by his father for lack of solid food had given his name to the next, named as he was after his grandfather, Gaspar Culan, the eldest.

Maybe because he was told by revolutionaries or thought it up himself or deduced it from the speech of teachers or the tourists, whose presence always implied a life beyond the village full of things Gaspar's people didn't have.

Maybe because he saw it all and had not yet heard the stories, the teaching stories, the old stories, the secret stories, the Big Stories. Maybe he knew too much at too early an age, his body too small to grieve the extraordinary amount of pain his early brilliance could perceive. Too bright and awake at an earlier age than most, he would've had to have heard the story before the rest.

But whatever it was, he refused the stories when the usual time came. By then, at the age of fifteen, when he should have been sitting in the initiation house separated from his family with his peers listening to the otherwise inaccessible poetry of the old people as they told for the first time the

Big Stories as part of his coming of age, during the ceremony of the "Great Remembrance," Gaspar Culan the younger couldn't be found by the initiating chiefs. The truth was that Gaspar Culan the younger was already cloistered across the lake in a monastery school, deep in the rigors of seminary training, well on his way to an ordination as the very first Native Mayan Catholic priest of Guatemala.

He looked more like his mother Ya Chunet, a beautiful middle-aged woman, famed for her wild, perfect embroideries that covered all the blouses of her women and the short tribal pants of all the men in her husband's clan, minus Gaspar Culan the younger, who in a confusing combination of a monkish vow of poverty and revolutionary Marxist doctrine, refused to wear the short, elegant, royally embroidered pants held up with a long sash of a barbaric ornateness, even shunning the eternal red and black handwoven shirt, the tribal *cotón*.

His father, Gaspar Culan the older, had a head of banded black-and-white bristles that looked just like an anteater's back. Gaspar Culan the younger, now universally nicknamed "Padre" throughout the village, didn't have anteater hair, but had his mother's coarse black hair, stiff like a colt's tail, which he refused to cover with the requisite fedora or even poor man's straw tut, going poorer still as a bareheaded revolutionary, combing his hair parted on the side in choirboy style in deference to the priests and church officials at the monastery.

Though poor and struggling from the distant and foggy point of view of outside cultures, the Tzutujil people, no matter how raggedy, considered themselves royalty; every child a princess, or a prince, the women even refusing to braid their hair for fear of appearing to be serfs or peasants to the neighboring Mayan tribes and Ladino peasants, who were. They saw the rest of the world as "incomplete" people doing the best they could, considering they were not Atitecos. And yet there were many families, like the Culans, who were not patched and poor, who dressed and walked as queens and leaders, magnificently rigged like sailing ships who tacked up and down the natural paths of huts and compounds firing complex and flowering salutations to everyone they passed. Their movements through the village were a comfort to the people, as the sun must be to the sky.

But Padre had been planning his revolution before he could spit and whistle. By the age of twenty he'd already spent over five voluntary years outside the village except small furloughs to visit. In the seminary he'd found secret alliances, some religious, others Marxist, who shared most if not all of his sentiments and gave him the details he'd been missing to corroborate the need for a revolution, as well as how to go about it.

Padre's revolution, however, was going to be all his own. He knew that the "liberation" could never happen if the people were not united. This meant they had to stop being queens and kings, they had to speak a common tongue, they had to depend on the same economy; in short, they would have to stop being Tzutujil. A lot of things would have to stop.

So Gaspar Culan the younger, known as Padre, in his efforts to walk his thoughts wore a generic gray slacks, a plaid shirt, a gray windbreaker, no hat and a homely pair of store-bought sandals.

Though he didn't love the earth, the animals, the weather, his language, or the culture of his people, Padre most certainly loved his people. He loved his people more than he loved the seminary's God.

What some men want in the name of greed and fear, that we call power, in no way compares to what others will do for who and what they love, and for him to obtain what he wanted for the people he loved, Padre needed power.

Though Padre didn't want to be powerful, to be big, to boss the world, he needed power to liberate his people and in his twenty-year plan he'd always known the easiest road to power beyond the village where the non-Indians lived with all their machines, comforts, doctors and money was through the church. In Guatemala, political power involved a government position that was either a cosmetic, powerless pandering to the whims of bigger countries or a high placement in the military, mindless and violent to its own, but even those sad possibilities were unreachable for a single Mayan man in those days.

Padre would first become a priest, then finagle a hometown parish from the bishop, which he had already been assured.

His village of Santiago Atitlan would be fixed, repaired, taken out of the drowning muck of old customs, taboos and primitivism and the cycle of non-productive ceremonialism where the people spent all their food and money dancing drunk in ecstasy to feed a non-existent storm-like profusion of imagined deities, both new and ancient, mixed and hybridized with outmoded and uncanonized sixteenth-century Iberian Catholic images of saints.

Though situated on Lake Atitlan, which the villagers called the Umbilicus of the Fruit of Soil, or Mother for short, Padre would put in a potable water system; he would set up factories, get people dependent on money, ban the speaking of Tzutujil, set up a technical-vocational school to run and maintain machinery. He would stop the women from weaving, make everybody wear machine-made clothing, wire electricity into all the new wood and tin houses that he would've already arranged to be built in sanitary rows. There would be toilets, fresh drinking water, showers, plenty of food and everybody would be united by worshiping one God, the only God, with none of the absurd pomp, silver, vestments and procedures of the ancient Catholics. There would remain nothing from anybody's "odious past." Once his own village was pacified he was sure they would join him as he took on the country.

Yet in the face of all that, now at the age of twenty-two, one millimeter away from his secret goal as an ordained priest and primary step in his hidden revolution, Gaspar Culan the younger was in trouble.

He'd never once breathed a word about his revolution outside his little circle of cohorts, never to the priests or Catholic bureaucrats, and most certainly no one in the village suspected a revolution from him, though many were openly brewing them; we never expected one from Padre.

The village just thought he was a new oddball version of his extraordinary ancestors about whom so many tales were told. That Padre would be a Padre was just fine, nobody cared that he couldn't abide the village. They just thought, "Of course! He's going to be special, like a Ladino, a white person; his life will get easier; it's good."

So that wasn't the problem. Nor did it rest solely on the fact that for the last year Padre had fallen in love with Ya Chata. She loved him unabashedly, as much as he loved the people. Eighteen years old, strong and beautiful of face, her hands matched the boy's mother's for weaving and embroidery and except for a few mean-hearted people who are always with us, wherever she went, she was liked.

Since no one mentioned it to the priests, they hadn't known that Ya Chata was carrying their child in her proud womb, due by the moon to be born a month after his ordination.

Yet, interestingly enough, these things in and of themselves had not caused Padre any obstacle to the priesthood. What dropped a mouse into the stew was when the bishop got wind of how his prized candidate had been seen worshiping idols.

Padre and Ya Chata had made the village news not for the usual reasons or for any scandal, but because they had been seen, accompanied by Padre's anteater-haired father and his mother of the able hands, making the rounds in what was known as a "making a house" ceremony. Bowing low to enter the dark vegetation-covered sacred houses, the abode of the many deities of the world's soul, the four of them made the four-part ceremony in the traditional blessing of a new mother to bring her a good birth and to consolidate the marriage of Padre to Ya Chata, as it was a pregnancy that made them mates for real.

By visiting all these deities in four different sacred houses, a metaphorical house of blessing was made for the new expectant couple, each blessing in front of these deities consisting of a wall in their marriage house.

The young mother did not share Padre's revolution or any of his anathema for the old Gods or the blessings of old Catholic saints. Padre believed his people were spiritual people, he just thought their spirituality to have been misguided, and therefore went along with Ya Chata to keep the family peace and comfort his new wife who would not have felt blessed otherwise. Even so, at one point he scoffed at the Gods, going so far as to even call Holy Boy "the Horned One," referring of course to the Christian devil.

And because this was all news and good news to the people, it jumped from meal to meal, from one cooking fire to the next, chirped on down the long line of chattering women washing at the lake and on and on to the next village, until, in a somewhat altered form, the gossip reached the ears of the seminary bureaucrats and acolytes who in their zeal, envy and hopes of being petted reported to their hierarchy of Oklahoma farmers-turned-priests that Gaspar Culan was an apostate, an idol-worshiping lecher with children.

For the bishop, Padre was a prize student, his not-so-secret weapon in a religious war to achieve what his order's foremost mission had failed at, which now in direct competition with a recent plague of Evangelist missionaries and Mormon pastors was the complete elimination of any vestiges of paganism and image worship among the villagers, including the ornate parish cults of Catholic saints still going strong after more than four centuries.

For forty years his predecessors were consistently foiled by the persuasive and charming nature of the Tzutujil and their old ecstatic rituals, which had in several instances even seduced the priests and nuns assigned to the village into leaving the church and marrying each other. The bishop had reasoned that if Gaspar Culan the younger, the son of respected shamans and idol-worshiping traditionalists, could be made into the town's Catholic priest, then it would follow that the traditionalist's back could be broken and the entire generation younger than Padre would lay down their idols and come in with their hands raised to the Christ of his order.

It therefore hit the bishop hard when he discovered that this perfect student, this almost ordained answer to his prayers, was now in danger of being disqualified from the priesthood. The bishop didn't believe Padre worshipped idols and would not have cared if he did; he just wanted to win his war. At the seminary there were meetings, prayers, more meetings; adrenaline ran, unopened books were opened, people were called in, outsiders were pushed away, and more adrenaline ran. Finally, in hopes of absolving and reinstating Padre while avoiding a scandal, the bishop, in a subtle effort to mollify certain envious lower echelon church officials who wanted the bishop's little Indian demolished, disbarred and disgraced, succeeded in launching the idea of a combination trial, ecclesiastical review council, college dissertation and ordination examination, which after sailing the vast bland ocean of church bureaucracy landed safely and was unanimously endorsed.

Padre was notified at his wife's house, where he now lived, as they waited with the midwives for his first child's birth. A runner came from Father Stanley Rother, the present Catholic priest of Santiago Atitlan, another wheat farmer from Oklahoma, that he was to appear in person on the nineteenth of November accompanied by Father Stanley and an advocate of his choice: one, to defend his actions of the previous month, i.e. idol-worshiping; two, to denounce his illicit marriage; three, to convince the clergy to retain his nomination; therefore, to present a dissertation that would defend the spiritual nature of the Tzutujil and how this present spiritual belief was a misguided faith which he would show how he, if he was ordained, could redirect toward the loving, almighty God through his son the Lord Jesus Christ, etc. and so on. If he could pass the scrutiny of the council and all several hundred acolytes at the seminary, then he could still be ordained. It would be an inquisition whose outcome had everybody's hidden revolutions, hopes and agendas hanging by a meandering spider's silk of incomprehensible imposed foreign rules and customs. It would be a bizarre, third-rate inquisition, without the torture of the yokes, red-hot branding irons or the rack, but torture nonetheless, when one considered that the greater part of this inquisition would be carried out by the church bureaucrats in a nerve-curdling type of Oklahoma-accented Spanish, so bad it made your teeth ache.

But the worst of all the absurdities of Padre's situation was that he had chosen me, Martín Prechtel, to be his advocate.

This was a strange idea, the enormity of which was that he and his family wanted me to be his witness; to defend him against the accusations of a church that hated me more than it hated him, so he could continue with the same church; to convince these white priests that the Padre was not an apostate, when everybody knew that I was and was proud of it.

In the beginning these priests had ridiculed my existence in Santiago Atitlan, making a lot of jokes at my expense in their incredulousness that I was actually able to see the Divine and feed the Divine and even though I was from the outside eventually function, for better or worse, like all the rest as an integral part of the village.

With a couple of exceptions the priests and seminary officials were Americans from the United States and though this was the Mayan highlands of the Republic of Guatemala, they had somehow enjoined the notion that being a loyal citizen of the U.S. was one and the same as having been baptized a Christian and in this case a confirmed Catholic. Enough that I came from New Mexico, making me suspect to begin with, but that coupled with the fact that though I was an American, I chose of my own free will not to live there, but in the dust, travail and wild ceremonialism of Mayan Guatemala, far removed even from the tourists, hippies and entrepreneurs and unassociated with any mission or institution, plus the truth that I was not a Christian, made me a pagan and therefore un-American.

On top of this pile was the unpardonable horror that I had a wife from the village and together we had children, married not by the state or any church, but by old Mayan custom, which was binding by law in that country and recognized by village consensus. This didn't stop the priests from sending their lay officials and recent converts to call at our hut every week to give us the word and threaten us about the hell toward which we were heading.

I not only supported, but actively served as an official in an ancient spiritual organization that was dedicated to the daily "feeding" of a multiplicity of complex deities, through collective daily rituals, which had for centuries operated under the guise of a well-established pre-American Catholic institution.

These "new" enlightened American Catholics had been chafing to destroy this spiritual system for decades and erroneously thought that because they were outsiders from what they presumed was a powerful, "more advanced" culture, that this would cause the priests to garner a greater level of attention and respect from the natives to whom they were bringing light and physical comfort. By the same conceited logic, they assumed because I too was blond and from the great U.S., my active marching in the very hierarchies they had worked so assiduously to destroy was an embarrassment to the "truth" and a bad example to "their" Indians, giving them mixed signals and total permission to backslide into their well-established spiritual ignorance, thus keeping them poor, and apostate as well.

The very deities I fed, maintained, saw, understood and ritualized were the very divinities Padre was now accused of worshiping! How was I to help him out of what I was more deeply accused?

I hated everything I'd assumed Padre stood for and Padre hated my position as well, but we were friends, for each of us recognized how much the other loved the village, albeit in different ways.

To the old villagers, absurdity and irony were the footprints of the life-giving Divine, full proof that it was around somewhere. It was a mistake to change that or fix the confusion their presence implied, for it was the continual implementation of "solutions" that gave birth to the next litter of problems demanding solutions.

The Tzutujil fed the Divine. They didn't remedy its nature, because its insane amble was the life we were blessed to live out.

On account of this understanding, the people of the village saw the contradictions between Padre and myself as a kind of perfection, sent and set up synchronistically by the Divine, to protect and keep alive the rare and precarious sanctuary it had in the village in those times.

I was from the U.S.; he was from Home. He supported Americanism, Marxist revolutionary thought, American one-God religion; I supported traditionalist, polytheistic, nature religion and hometown Mayan ways. I was taller (not tall), light colored; he was dark, shorter. He dressed like a white man; I like a giant Tzutujil. He spoke always in European Spanish, and I in Mayan, and on and on.

These ironies made the village agree, unanimously endorsing us like sports figures, like little warrior twins with opposing natures, sent by the people to ward off the dishonor of Padre losing his priesthood. The rights and wrongs were irrelevant; Padre was their child and I had proven my abilities to wrestle the outsiders on their behalf many times before, looking like them, speaking some of their languages.

If Padre was the secret weapon of the bishop against the old Gods, I was the village's secret weapon against village dishonor, and the church was Padre's secret weapon against the unjust world whose left and right feet were irony and contradiction.

But for all these reasons and more, and conforming to true Mayan procedure, Gaspar Culan the elder and his wife Ya Chunet, the parents of Gaspar Culan the younger, known everywhere as Padre, had informed the village of my acceptance to the advocacy of their son long before I'd even known I was a candidate. By the time I was actually courted by their multiple visits, gifts and well-placed barrages of antique phrases intended to stir and touch the heart, the public assumption of my acceptance carried an obligation of such worth and nobility to the task, that in the name of this rare opportunity to make my own vengeful charge against the demons of such outside ignorance and still be useful and desired by a town in whose arms I'd found a home, I accepted the absurd challenge, and this is how I came to possess the telling of the "Big Story" of The Toe Bone and the Tooth.

two

AN ANTEATER, TWO
STICKS AND A MAN
WHO NEVER ATE

Every dawn the whole world shivered, held its breath and hoped for
day. After dusk every night when the great darkness fell it was not a
given, never a known thing, that the Sun, our Father, would return,
that he could positively survive the western horizon where the crocodiles of
oblivion gnashed their razor ivories or, escaping them, that he would come
through alive, new and ready after being reassembled in the dark bowls of
the unseen to be born again into day. What was known was that when he
did come he came wounded and struggling.

Every morning after the long, cold night when the small change of light
began, every little bird, every raptor, buzzard, cotinga, raven, motmot, day

bird, night bird, duck, crane, egret, grebe, hummingbird; every bat, squirrel, mouse, mole, lizard, tepiscuintle, monkey, raccoon, coati, peccary, tapir, tiny deer; every wild cat, ocelot, cougar, jaguar and otter; every furry being; every scaled fish, reptile and snake; every ant, cricket, bee, wasp, dragonfly; every tree, lichen, orchid, vine, grass; every flowering stump and dying thing, and even the wind held his breath. It was in that dimness that the Dawn-rising-Tzutujil, the Mayan people of the volcanoes, held out their arms toward the sunless sky, some with broken shards of red clay pots hot with the night embers where an ecstatic aroma smoldered called the "Sun's feast." The people caressed the struggling belly of dawn with words as delicious as the incense they offered, calling to the infant Sun with the same murmuring encouragement they spoke to their own birthing mothers and babies.

Even when the red sliver of the day's new head crowned the cervix of night's ashy womb, everything still shivered and the wind held off, the people prayed.

But as that great life-giving fiery bowl they called Father cleared the mountain's horizon, the World burst and fluttered into life, and like a mother deer licked her fawn of Dawn to his feet with a tongue of morning breezes, bird's songs, and the rustles, thuds and tinkles of a smoky village going to the fields.

Though never certain Dawn would come again, it was unspoken and assumed as fact by all the living that once in the sky the Sun would again leave, devoured by the dark, drunk deep back into the belly of the Unseen.

The stories we told in our huts at night, and we only told them in the dark, and a certain kind of dream we dreamt were known to help the Sun and his stellar relatives move through the ground towards day. Some birds prayed all night, twittering and chirping, hooting and moaning in a fretful way to keep the Sun from dying. Even the stones, which are just petrified flame anyway, told a fiery tale for the Sun so final and exact that only the Sun could hear it, which in his night-time journey kept the flame alive in his head.

And because night was upon us, Gaspar Culan the elder moved up and over the volcano of the Grandmother, below the impenetrable forest precipice behind Xecsis rising out of that moonless basaltic ravine like the evening star, who himself was just then climbing the purple of the eastern sky from where he watched his older brother jump into the dark jaws of the unknown.

With his short, bristly, anteater-hair, Gaspar was a most courteous man, handsome and able. His ears stuck out and his nose was good. His hands and shoulder blades were callused like all the working men but at sixty he still had all his teeth and unlike most could yet bend his knees, squat on the ground, jump up and move like a child.

For weeks on end he'd come to visit us. Every couple of days in the evening his entire family, minus Padre of course, would fill their large log canoe with flowers of every sort, some dragging in the water, along with fruits from the faraway coast and thick white slabs of brilliant ocean salt.

Boarding carefully between the cargo, his every child with a paddle in hand would stand and row from their side to our side of the bay through the calm, violet waters of the sunset.

After hitting our shore, they'd pile out and beach the cedar canoe with their mother and gifts still riding inside. Competing with the water birds for sound, they chattered and giggled up the shoreline trail past the terraced gardens of chilies, tomatoes, chipilin and pixnic. Ceremonially attired, they looked as lavish as the flowers they shouldered and as bright as the salt they balanced on their heads.

The little boys with new hats and fancy tinseled sashes cradled bundles of calla lilies longer than they were tall and the smaller girls brought nardos and enormous ruby colored cardamom buds. Shiny haired and thickly wrapped in queen-like skirts and shawls, their huipiles covered in embroidered birds, Gaspar Culan's teenage daughters swayed beneath new baskets heavy with yellow jocotes.

Buried in this sparkling mass of their twittering children, flowers, fruit and salt, Gaspar Culan and Ya Chunet were washed like a parade float right to the shore of our village compound. There at the threshold Gaspar called out with an ancient etiquette, asking if they would be welcome, calling our knot of humble huts a palace.

What then happened for the last time, as had happened for two months over and over, was the delight of the in-laws at receiving such honorable attention beyond the normal comings and goings of family and friends or the sometimes constant flow of old officials sent from the village hierarchy, who came loaded with ceremonial dilemmas with which they would have me wrestle and pretend to solve.

Our entire neighborhood came running to the compound walls, stood on their toes and craned over those jumbles of basaltic boulders to admire, envy and supervise the unloading of the gifts, reporting in normal exaggeration or contempt, depending on their village affiliation, to those behind who couldn't see, their murmuring lost in the clamor and friendly uproar of our people rushing about to fetch reed mats, things to drink, cups, little stools and whatever it took to settle the noble entourage in sitting and kneeling rows inside our largest sleeping hut of thatch and stone.

After devouring an hour and more with the necessary back and forth of village news, like the location of the newest landslide, or the erratic behavior of some person who'd been seen blundering through the village streets at night transformed into a cow, or the occurrence of firewood on Ma Petzai's mountain land, caused by a windstorm that tore down only the trees on his side of the ravine, or the incomprehensible price of tomatoes, the amount of fish in the lake and so forth, the subject of the banter would generally come to rest on Padre and how nice it was that I was going to save him. It was usually then that all these living relatives of Padre would rise and kiss my ring finger to compromise me further, not to mention that all my married-in-relatives and my quarter of the village had indentured me by the gratitude with which they slurped down all the fruit, divided up the flowers, "cracked" and distributed all the holy salt, leaving not a crumb of it in dispute to return or say "I can't," which in the village mind was considered a contract and ensured my total compliance in the cause of Padre's absolution.

Toward the end of the last family visit, late and in the dark, when all the little children lay asleep in the arms of those that were older, Gaspar Culan opened the conversation to another level. With what was left of the fire glowing a little off the right side of his face, Gaspar leaned over and whispered in a small voice meant only for myself to hear, "My father spoke to me last night and his heart is full of honey now that you've agreed to help my son, to 'carry his road.'

"In payment and appreciation the Swordfighter wants me to teach you the 'Story,' to tell it to you, to give the 'Story' to you as a gift for you to tell as your own, just as I have for these last years."

The fire ceased to pop and flicker, the wind went dead, the distant sounds of tired children quieted, growling street dogs stood and listened, even the Earth held Her breath, as did the people. It wasn't long, but it was thorough, and when the silence finally lifted the sounds of life all rushed back in.

Gaspar Culan the youngest was known as Padre. Though Padre's Grandfather was the original Gaspar Culan, of the three generations of Gaspar Culans only the middle one was ever called Gaspar Culan, for to all the peoples of the Mother Lake and beyond, spreading below us throughout the coastal plains and ocean villages, this original Gaspar Culan had been known as and was still remembered as "the Swordfighter."

Though dead for close to five years, the Swordfighter often came in dreams to speak with his son. He was such a powerful and legendary man that even now whenever his name was mentioned the World would go silent out of respect and mostly out of fear. All the people knew that when alive the old shaman could magically hear what anyone thought and could retaliate in kind to those who mocked him. Now relieved of his body the village was even more cautious, as his spirit, if summoned by name, could be anywhere inside anything.

Therefore, because of the dream and Swordfighter's desires, his son, Gaspar Culan, came this night alone without flowers, canoes or family, carrying his greatest gift and possession invisibly tucked neatly inside his prodigious memory.

That night no one bothered us, there were no neighbors, no in-laws, no jealous spies from other clans and districts, for everyone was sleeping or pretended to sleep, in order to give wide berth and respect to the gift, to the telling of the Story, to avoid hearing illicitly and uninvited what belonged only to the Culan family and eventually to myself.

The Story was a famous teaching tale that everyone initiated had heard many, many times. It was holy, very long and beloved of all the people. What made the version of the Story that "Swordfighter" owned so valuable was that it had been taught and awarded to him physically and personally by the very Gods who were the subjects of the Story, the Deities of the Mountain who'd been there when it happened.

The Story had been owned first by the Gods, then by Swordfighter, then for the last fifty years by his son Gaspar Culan. Padre had never heard it, and even refused to listen. Because he rejected anything ancient or ancestral he denounced the Story as childish, damaging, pagan and ignorant, brandishing in its stead, of course, a Christian Bible, which he declared to be the only story.

I'd heard the Story a thousand times as told during initiations by old folks, chiefs and officials, but neither I nor they had ever been witness to the telling of Swordfighter's treasured version. Beside which, though I'd heard many sacred stories, I'd never owned one.

Swordfighter had three great powers, or magical abilities bestowed on him by nature and supernatural beings. The Tzutujil called these powers "secrets."

Everyone, by the time they were forty years old, had to have at least one very small "secret power," a special knack or magical understanding or they could never cause the survival of their families, fields, animals or themselves in such a precarious world.

The occurrence of someone like Swordfighter who had "three grand secret powers" was very rare. That was the territory of shamans, heroes and supernatural humans from another time.

The most magnificent of his three powers was the Story, because it came directly from the Gods, and when retold it was claimed that it could renew life; it was a holy thing that made life good again far beyond the teller.

His second secret had to do with why he'd been dubbed the Swordfighter. Contrary to what many later thought, Swordfighter never fought with swords. He didn't even own one and had never handled a sword. What he did do was fight swords. Swordfighter fought against swords. This second power was centered on a set of unnaturally hard wooden sticks that looked like the ordinary walking sticks used by merchants when carrying heavy loads on their backs as they trekked the long distances between villages. But these particular sticks obeyed Swordfighter like two hunting dogs, or watchdogs, or sheep dogs, such that when he whistled or hummed in a certain way they would of their own accord, through the air or wielded in his hands, strike his desired target and against which all steel crumbled.

The third secret had been given to him by a certain wild animal and, though not so grand as it was strange, it became quite useful to him. This consisted of Swordfighter being able to squeeze into any small crack or hole and remain there hidden without eating or drinking for weeks if need be. The people were insistent on this, his third ability, on account of the fact that no one had ever seen him eat and in the desperate curiosity that villagers have for other people's business, often interrogated Gaspar Culan's mother, Swordfighter's wife, about it over the years, whenever they chanced to meet. She corroborated the fact that although she'd cooked for her family every day all her fifty married years, she'd never once seen him eat a crumb.

In the latter quarter of the nineteenth century, before he'd been called the Swordfighter, this original Gaspar Culan, at the age of eighteen, had been married to another woman, a pretty young girl who most certainly saw him eat a great deal.

For years the mountains that lay between Atitlan and the green rolling coastal jungle and the churning Pacific Ocean had been the steady and lucrative home to various bands of roving thieves, who on a regular basis interrupted the arduous journeys of the Ajbiyajal, or village walking-merchants, to levy tolls and bribes on their way to and from Atitlan and the villages with whom they traditionally traded.

Part of being a merchant in those days was knowing how to skirt the highwaymen or carry enough extra goods to appease them. This went on for over two centuries, becoming a tradition in itself.

Toward the end of the nineteenth century the situation changed and more serious gangs of bandits prowled the roads and ridges of the southern mountains who were not content to levy tolls, but sometimes robbed entire cargoes, often wounding or killing the merchants.

The original Gaspar Culan had been one of these proud merchant walkers, a carrier of chocolate and salt from the coastal plains and the ocean's edge, called by the Tzutujil the Female Earth. Respected like a hero among his peers, he sometimes traveled as much as twenty hours a day with over a hundred pounds on his back, his cheeks filled with powdered tobacco and lime, pushing his way past his hunger, walking and sweating in a trance to arrive miraculously sooner than any of his colleagues, thereby obtaining the best bartered prices for the reed mats, dried freshwater fish, smoked chilies and so forth that he'd brought from his native home to the trade.

Most of the walking merchants ran along the regular passes, ridges and roads. Gaspar Culan the Original, on the other hand, traveled on the much older salt and cacao trade routes and trails, which though well-established were much longer, harder to find and easier to lose and took him along some treacherous razor-thin ridges with five-hundred foot drops and through massive rushing rivers, all necessary and successful measures used in his family for centuries against the old-style thieves who'd been too lazy to go so deep into the unknown wilds. Swordfighter had inherited his trading skill and knowledge of the precious Mayan trails from his father, but his rhythm of movement, his incredible stamina and animal-like alertness were all his own. In the end, however, all of this was not enough and even he fell prey to a band of pirates who left him with nothing but his pants.

Initially the richer Tzutujil merchants had a few pack animals, but now even these donkeys, mules and horses had all been stolen, killed or eaten by the bandits. Yet even this was not enough to stop the original Gaspar Culan who by poking through unknown, forbidden lands so dense that even the ancients had never ventured, found increasingly untried and convoluted alternative routes through the wilds toward QuQoi Quej or Samayac. Though blessed with a year of healthy crossings and lucky return trips, he was caught again and this time lost all his cargo and very nearly his life to the heartless thieves who beat him senseless.

Soon, no one would venture away from the normal village farming areas into the surrounding woods. The merchants gave up trading and fell back on growing cotton, corn, avocados, beans and pumpkins and gathering edible field weeds, while others fished and some did both.

All was well for a while until for lack of income the bandits began plundering the village itself armed with cutlasses and the occasional flintlock, carrying off the precious harvest, raping the girls and thrashing any villagers who resisted.

Mayans in colonial Guatemala had not been allowed to bear arms. But, even after independence from Europe, Indians were forbidden to own any kind of weapon and were left to the mercy of predatory opportunists of every description.

Then the following year not a drop of rain moistened the earth and a drought ensued that lasted several years, stunting and leveling the crops, raising a choking dust, lowering the water in the lake and killing most of the fish.

More thieves arrived and they began fighting each other for the territory, hacking to bits any villagers who resisted or who'd been discovered giving their last kernel of corn to the opposing gang. While some of the more horrendous of the pirates took up residence in the village, other normally hardworking villagers out of desperation took to pillaging as well to feed their families. Still others led their families to the surrounding wilds hoping to hunt but most had to settle for eating rodents and insects to survive. Those that remained had to be content with digging, drying and grinding into flour the roots of the tule water reeds, which are known as the skirt of the Mother Waters.

Though already smashed and ruined, their world horribly violated, the people for the most part survived by following their instincts and legendary ingenuity until even that gave out to a merciless famine that swelled their bellies, raging through the land taking the lives and sanity of thousands of Mayans who now died from hunger and typhus as well as bandits.

It was then that the original Gaspar Culan secretly carried his beautiful starving wife and three-month-old baby to a hidden area, way out in the wilderness, that was known only to the "chocolate walkers" like himself. Held by all the Indians as off limits to humans, it was taboo to even cross, because this natural jungle belonged to the Gods of the Mountains; it was the kingdom of the Lords of the Center of the Earth.

Nobody ever went there out of respect to those deities who lived inside the mountain and earth itself, whose very beings were what pushed life into the plants, water into the sky, fruit into the flowers, and who when they wanted to be seen appeared to humans as animals. The few villagers who had accidentally ventured there and survived told tales of their companions who never returned at all, mysteriously disappearing from their midst without a trail or a clue.

That land was rich, always wet, mysterious, deeply forested, full of interminable steep ravines and continually covered in a thick fog both day and night. It was here he'd taken his little family. It was here as well, too weakened by famine and the fatigue of their impossibly hard journey toward food, away from the thieves, that both his child and wife withered and finally perished in his arms against all his efforts to maintain them.

The young man survived only by the tenacious inhuman vitality of his body, for his heart had no desire, nor his mind any reason to continue living.

He rambled in a rage, drifting and wandering aimlessly for days on end, drowning in grief, whimpering and bellowing at the maze of vegetal walls, until he as well finally weakened, slipped and fell from a moss-slickened guanacaste trunk, tumbling head over heels down a vertical wall of orchid-covered granite so deep and seamless that not even an ant could have found his way out.

A spiked and gnarled bush caught him, cut him, and bounced him down a hundred feet more, pinning him between a boulder and another trunk where he dangled unconscious above another fifty-foot drop over the rocky canyon floor like a stunned frog in a crane's beak.

Everything was broken; his ribs, his head, his joints snapped and undone. Yet he didn't die. His heart kept beating. He'd loved his wife and his child and now there was no sweetheart, no food, no village, no baby, no sunlight; there was nothing left and still he didn't die. Because he felt grief he didn't die. His sadness needed him alive to be felt.

His heart caught in that rushing dream of rage and sorrow, Gaspar Culan the Original, not yet the Swordfighter, lasted longer than any other human would have, then after several more days teetering unconscious high upon that point his eyelids lifted just a hair's breadth. Powerless to eat or die, he tried to roll and free himself, which caused the earth that held the stump to release him to the air and down he crashed, like a deer shot off a cliff, falling fast the remaining distance, dying on impact at the bottom of that narrow misty ravine deep inside the off-limits sacred kingdom of the Mountain Deities.

What happened after that or how it came to be no one could truly say. It might have been a year or maybe it was a week, but when he looked down at his feet they were slim and long and full of well-kept fur. He saw and felt the same upon his arms, his belly and his chest. His hands, where his fingers used to bend, were tipped with shiny black claws a lot like those growing from his feet but they could never match the massive curve and powerful raking rasp his front paws could deliver.

His face was a curving bristly cone with fine little long-lashed eyes set along each side. His nose took up half his body, which finishing the curve of his head narrowed down to a little black rubber button. The rest of him felt comfortable and healed, very capable and entirely covered with an impenetrable carpet of silk and bristles the color of burnt earth and gold.

Rolled snug inside the hollowed root of a cieba stump, his long thick tail covering his nose, Swordfighter found that he was now a little *tjoy snic*, a *tamandua*. Gaspar Culan had died and turned into an anteater.

He was hungry all the time now and was always humming, even sometimes when he slept. Slow, determined and deliberate, the bristly, thick-skinned creature moved at the approximate speed that rocks took to think, spending years raiding bee hives for their inebriating honey high up in the jungle trees.

There was nothing he couldn't climb and no hole could keep him out, he could dig and slash and think, humming all the time. Where his dense little body couldn't go his long scary tongue would, entering like a snake to haul out the bug that hid there. Swordfighter the anteater could split a termite-filled tree stump like a wishbone, snapping up all the little pale beasts with lightning flicks of his bristly rat-tail tongue.

Honey was his life, his goal, his art; honey was his heaven, his great achievement and the inspirational source for his better singing, because when he got to a hive, he'd really hum.

Sitting on his haunches, he'd begin to rock back and forth waving his fearsome front paws in the air in prayer and expectation, then moving forward in a coy kind of waddle like he wasn't really going, humming and commenting all the while about everything he'd passed over, he'd squint his little greedy eyes, slash the hive and push the nozzle of his muzzle into the dripping shell. Grabbing, tearing like a bear, his unstoppable rubber-tipped needle nose pumped out the sweet black ooze oblivious to the boiling onslaught of the furious bees. His tiny ears back and shut, his hide too tough, his fur too thick for the suicidal insects to pierce, he'd clamp himself tighter to the hive, sucking until he got so full and drunk on the wild honey that he'd go stiff with joy, release his grip falling numb and ecstatic fifty feet to the ground where he lay laughing in his slow anteater way.

All sticky, smiling, eyes glazed and belly up he'd nap for hours and sometimes days, at which point he'd right himself and stagger off in a wicked mood, grumbling like a Cockney in high staccato complaint, in search of bark grubs to work off the honey hangover.

And in this way Gaspar Culan the Original lived on for years as an ecstatic, honey-sucking antbear who very rarely lowered himself to consume hard, ordinary ants. He had so much contempt for ants that he actually stuck his tongue out at them, eating them only if he was starved.

The little golden honey-puncher roamed the very same wild ravine where he, his wife and his child had died, and right there he was killed once more when a large ocelot, taking advantage of the anteater's comatose condition after a long fall from his last honey binge, crunched his head and dragged him closer to her voracious half-grown kits who left nothing but his bones.

Though still belly up when he awoke, this time his fur was gone and his grief was less. He was inside the mountain now, in a cavern perhaps, softly lit and from where at least a thousand softly-colored eyes stared faceless from beyond the gloom. Barely conscious, probably alive, Gaspar Culan could smell the perfume of marigolds, beeswax, tree resins, corozo palm flowers, wild tobacco smoke and fermenting cacao. Whilst listening unafraid to a million natural voices of beasts and plants around him, the comforting smell of animal fur and milk drifted in on a breeze of vanilla, fetid orchid and the mahogany of tiny wild avocados.

He awoke suckling at the hairy breast of a giant howler monkey, whose powerful hands played with his nose.

"Is it really you?" She spoke somehow and he somehow understood. "We assumed you and yours had rotted away long ago."

Gaspar sat up in the mother beast's lap blinking in the murky old cave air, an archaic air, the original breath of the earth from before humans had been invented. A ponderously large woman came rolling and floating over to peer down at him, scrutinizing what seemed to her to be a little man. She had no wrinkles but she was old, and not getting any older she was smooth, scary, overwhelmingly sensuous and proud.

But for a stripe of deer-colored hair off to the right of center, her hair was as white as the moon and dragged on the ground. Her eyes were the eyes of deer; no whites, only pools of deep brown and crystalline black. Like a lizard she moved her head in some impossible ways to shift her gaze instead of her eyeballs, which were fixed.

Like the sound of a clear river, her deep and melodic voice caused Swordfighter to weep, remembering that sound had sung once from his dead wife's throat, a voice he'd loved which spoke no more.

"Look Father, Husband, he's got her nose," she rang out. "It's our grandson come to visit."

Looking up Gaspar saw another giant rushing over, detaching himself from the matrix of deafening chirps, moans, creaks and a thundering windy sound that rose up all around.

His more rugged and weathered face bent down and scrutinized Gaspar. When with his enormous long fingers, this husband of the beautiful giantess lifted Gaspar up in the air like a puppy for all the cave to see, the myriad beings of that palatial cavern made themselves apparent.

The top of that cavern was a kind of deeply colored sky up where, sitting like stars, a million beings flashed and flickered, dangling in the roots of the next world with a feeling of strong friendship between them.

Stretched out flat and beautiful for miles and miles, the cave floor was filled with the original holy forms of every animal, every plant, every flower, moss, cricket, weather, water, tree, bird and wind, and each of these millions knelt at that point, wept and began to sing each according to his kind, a different but powerful tune, the magic of which caused Gaspar, who dangled yet in the hands of the old giant, to grow back into the size and shape of a human male.

When the song died down and that world came to its feet Gaspar's appearance was much the same as it had been long before when he still lived in the village, but he would never lose the sooty bristle of thick anteater hair that now grew upon his head.

Though only coming up to the shoulder of the giant couple, they hugged him and pulled him along as they rolled into a slow deliberate dance into which the whole cave world fell, creating a swelling wave of ecstatic majesty as far as his eyes could see. As a boy Gaspar had seen this dance in the village when two or three ancient folk used it to dance the holy bundles, but here the world for miles surged and tossed like a sea, dancing slow in some strange grief, for some unexplained joy.

For some unknown reason every being in this world was gladdened by his presence and wept to see him. As each life form danced by they all touched him tenderly and called him grandson. For sometime this remained a mystery to him, but there was no doubt that he was dancing with the God of the Mountain and his wife Old Grandmother Growth, the sovereigns of the off-limits kingdom where he'd already died twice.

Gaspar lived inside that mountain for no one knows how long, for time there was a bubble and not a flow. What became his home inside that womb of mountain earth would be the source of all his secrets and his powers. When the Mountain Gods, who always called him grandson, let the story he told about the bandits, the killing, the famine, the death of his wife and little child, sink into their wild archaic understanding, a roar of compassion and tribal outrage thundered in a deafening echo, whose rumble undulated throughout the palatial cavern and its boundless chambers.

These particular Gods, the sovereigns of the wild mountains and untouched ravines, truly hated steel. They hated the steel of plows and axes, the steel of saws and machetes, the steel of hooks, nails, rifles and swords. They hated the steel of horseshoes and wagon tires, and would come to hate anything that steel could make, cut, carve or contain. When it came to metal, gold was good enough and silver they could abide, copper was a favorite and about lead they would negotiate, but to the Gods steel was the tooth in the jaws of a consuming monster called comfort to which humans were addicted. Steel had a soul that was a natural coward and demanded blood and it was the earth it cut. Because the Gods saw the problems of their grandson as having come from steel and for some other reasons, not all of them clear, Gaspar was to them an ally now. After several meetings of all the Gods and Spirits of the Mountain, Gaspar was shown to a hall where young extravagantly attired Rain Gods sat waiting for the day when they would armor up in hail and windstorms, hoping to rush forth to wound the annual troops of dryness, whose clear blood was rain, and whom they fought to pierce with their thundering arrows, lightning spears and jade axes.

It was here that Gaspar Culan the Original began the training he would use to fight the metal of the thieves. It had been decided that he would be taught how to fight swords directly by the Rain Gods to fill their times of indolence on account of the drought. In the most extravagant way they would show Gaspar how to employ two ironwood sticks the length of his arms stretched out. Made to struggle against iron, these branches of a tree now long extinct came running like two loyal dogs to a certain whistle and could be ordered to fight, spinning, diving, gnashing and cudgeling an adversary on their own when a magical song was sung.

Gaspar had to practice constantly, learning to fight; spinning the sticks faster than the beating of a hummingbird's wings. A multitude of rituals, songs, cooking of foods and magic procedures, not the least of which involved a dance, were part of the stick-fighting regimen. When a year had passed Gaspar could shatter any sword, pistol, ax or plow with his humble sticks and mysterious dance.

The life he lived there after his years as an anteater were to be his best. He had a lover there as well, to whom much later he would forever pray. Like most of the details of what was shown to him inside the mountain he divulged little to his people later on, probably because the Gods had made him swear to keep it secret, like they usually do.

Toward the end of that happy life he lived inside the hill, he asked again the giant Grandmother why it was that she always called him "Grandson" and would weep about the shape of his nose. He'd have to wait to hear the Story, she told him, the story whose annual retelling made the Earth itself jump back to life. By way of the story Gaspar Culan the Original, the Swordfighter, would come to understand why he was their grandson. This would be his last task: for him to learn the Story well.

The Story had taken place right there in that sacred off-limits land and these Gods themselves were the very same Deities as those heard in the Story.

Grandmother Growth and her husband the God of the Mountain would give the precious story to their grandson, the Swordfighter, as their third and most powerful gift before he was sent back to fight the thieves and their steel. He had to learn to tell it himself and for this he was told the Story and forced to repeat it thousands of times over and again until his ability to speak the speech of the Gods became second nature and he could make the Gods themselves weep with their own tale.

The day came just before the spring for the annual retelling and all the Gods were called. Because the Sun Father is captured in the earth for five days and almost dies wrestling death with "delicious words," it is the telling of the Story that aids his release again into the skies, bringing the world back to life, bringing back the green and the water. For this the winds were sent to summon every God of this and other worlds. As had been done in every year all the Gods, the animals, the landscapes, the plants and every Holy being alive and dead were brought inside the mountain to listen. The Rain Gods sat in front of the infinite and majestic gathering, their fine gold bells tinkling around their knees.

The Gods of other Mountains came in as jaguars of every color, Water Goddesses as ducks and frogs, and when they arrived they all vied to sit by their mother, Grandmother Growth. When the entirety of prayers had been made, the rituals set and the feast of smells properly laid, to be later consumed, the God of the Mountain and his Giant wife asked Gaspár to begin what was normally their own job.

Then, from the Gods and for the Gods, Gaspar Culan the Original, called Swordfighter, who was once an anteater, now told the Story of The Toe Bone and the Tooth.

THE TOE BONE
AND THE TOOTH

The winds were still, the Sun waited, the world waited. Swordfighter began the tale like everyone always did. "What happened here could've been a long time ago or not, or maybe longer than that or later, but whenever it happened it always happens like this again and again. Whenever it was that it happened, this is how it happened:

"There, in our village, this child lived who was alone, an orphan. He'd been starving since the beginning; his leg bones were crooked from starvation, his belly water-swollen with worms and malnutrition. Belonging to no known family or clan, nobody would share their hard-fought-for food or time to feed the dying boy.

"The people were tough, hard-hearted and knew only how to esteem what would bring them more food, honor and village standing and since this little baby was obviously of no known bloodline, a thrownaway child, no one would claim him for fear of the loss of social altitude that might occur by his adoption. The poorer folk wouldn't spare the sparse protein for which they struggled.

"If it hadn't been for another outcast, an old white-haired blind woman called Ya Sar, the little crooked legged creature would have melted into the unforgiving cindery ground of our village.

"Blind, discarded by the people as well, this lady barely stayed alive herself, and did so only by following the sounds of the snarling street dogs, quarreling with them over the husks and refuse the villagers tossed in their direction. Though covered with crusty sores that looked like salt, Ya Sar miraculously and inexplicably had a small reservoir of milk in her ancient breasts where the garbage of our village streets was converted into suste-nance for the little ragged orphan boy whom she fed, carrying him around as she felt and bumbled her way through the unpitying village byways.

"With her determined maternal affection the Raggedy Boy grew into an undersized toddler, who because he could see and was very quick, could feed his adopted mother much better than she could on her own. By the time he was eight he could actually beat the vultures, ravens and dogs at trash piles, grabbing the horrible tidbits before they could or scaring them off with a show of growling teeth equal to their own.

"Soon the old woman stayed at home in an abandoned hut at the edge of the lake where no other villagers would dare to place their houses or compounds for fear of certain underwater spirits who were said to hate the human race and who came to ground to drag them to a drowning death.

"Raggedy Boy brought her food and the two were each other's only friends in the world. Having never known anything else, Raggedy was fairly happy, for as he grew the little bit he did from the little they procured from what the rest of the world didn't want, he was able to get increasingly more food as well as clothes pieced together from the dirty wiping rags thrown away by the people.

"Things were getting better and better, it seemed to him.

"Made frail with age, Ya Sar rarely ventured forth onto the village roads, unable as she was to withstand or dodge the rocks and sticks the villagers chucked at the two of them on sight.

"Because Raggedy did all their gleaning and gathering he wandered about every day, heedless of the contempt and disgust people heaped on him and his adopted mother. He negotiated the projectiles and screaming abuse like a hunter in the forest routinely skirts bands of angry stick-throwing spider monkeys. To Raggedy the villagers' hatred was a natural phenomenon and like his companions, the village dogs, it was an accepted part of life's landscape.

"Every five or six days at dawn a great whooping holler could be heard echoing off the volcanic foothills at the narrow faults above the mud, between the Armadillo Mountain and the edge of the lapping turquoise lake we call Mother Waters.

"These bubbling yells caused the village women to rise from their cooking fires, to jump from their kneeling mats to their feet. After grabbing sharp knives, their smaller hand-woven towels and courting shawls of beautiful colors, forced by the narrow confines of their red wraparound skirts, they trotted the distance to the village edge.

"There they thronged, crowding up to a line of hunters, young men recently returned with dead peccaries and jungle deer across their broad, tired shoulders.

"The wild mountains provided the village with its only meat, most of its fiber, all of its greens and every material for shelter and tools. The wilds gave the people their life.

"Young men were always leaving the village to haul back firewood and the fruit of the wild, but to go on the hunt, which was for meat only, one had to understand a great deal to actually come home with food.

"Whenever the boys returned from their day's task, they were required by unspoken village ordinance and habit to wait after signaling for the women to arrive who, like mad coyotes, vultures, ravens and dogs, set to slicing and dividing the meat, thanking the boys in song and blessings, returning to their homes chirping, happy about the bounty and relieved to have sustenance for at least a few days more.

"The young hunters, however, were left only with the hides and tines, it being taboo for a "meat maker," as they were called, to partake of the animal he had slain. Like the deer they killed, the boys were almost vegetarians. It was only when a girl admirer or a relative cooked some of another hunter's meat and sent the broth to his house as a courting gift that the hunters would eat meat.

"Teenage girls got to see the boys they loved in the meat distribution and the boys were made to feel as heroes; the girls' mothers holding their hands, singing their thanks, the young girls waddling away with the meat wrapped in their jewel-colored cloth, balanced on their heads, sneaking a wet gaze back at the boys they loved.

"That Raggedy survived to the age when boys began to accompany their uncles or older brothers on the hunt or sojourns deep into the mountains was nothing short of a miracle.

"Albeit crooked, smelly, ragged and untutored, when Raggedy reached the age of thirteen he had no father, uncles, no brother, no friends or anyone to teach him, and was therefore left sadly to watch from afar the well-attended send-off and heroic return of the rest of the village sons who disregarded and hated him. But by that age he had begun to desire love, he wanted people to like him, and he wanted girls to see him as a hero and desire him. Raggedy Boy was now a teenager.

"He came to the age where he understood that it was they who provided the good food, the scraps for which he fought dogs and that because these young men brought on their proud, well-fed bodies the freshly killed bodies of beautiful wild deer, these young men were tolerated, longed-for and loved, admired and well received.

"No one kicked them, held their noses when they passed or pushed them away for their ability to bring food to the village. The young men had families and sweethearts and because of the food they eventually had wives and children; children who had fathers and mothers to care about them and teach them how to hunt and find and cook food.

"In Raggedy's estimation the only reason he was starving and unloved was because he didn't bring food. If he had meat to give, a gift everyone wanted, then they would want him as well for bringing it. And following that line of consideration, Raggedy studied closely the comings and goings of the hunters, taking in what he could each time they left and returned, daring each time to come closer and closer until finally one day he actually accosted one of the groups, hoping they would take him along to the hills with the other younger boys.

But they shooed him off every time he approached. Every day he tried with a different group until, beleaguered by his requests to go along, to learn to be a hunter, one middle-aged man with ropes criss-crossing his chest, bows and blades protruding from the netted pack on his back, his water gourd tied to its side, spun around and actually spoke to Raggedy in a more reasoning tone.

"'You can't come with us because you know nothing. We would spend all our time teaching you and we'd starve to death for our efforts, besides which you'd scare away all the animals.'

"Another man yelled back as they walked under their loads, striding away from the hard-hearted village: 'You come from nowhere, no one knows who you are or who is your father, you have no people or village standing, the village would despise us for helping what couldn't help us, so go back to your place, to the trash piles, we'll throw something extra for you next time.'

"A third man pushed Raggedy away grumbling, 'You don't have any weapons, no bow, no arrows, no knives, no ropes, no tumpline, no nothing; your father, your relatives have to teach you about these, and you have none, so how can you hunt with us, what would we get out of it, you have no one to send us meat for our efforts. So go home, leave us be, go fight the dogs and vultures. That's your job, that's what you do.'

"And that's how it was with the nicest of the men and much worse with the rest. Undeterred in his ashpile existence, Raggedy was determined to be a hunter, to be a hero, to be loved, to be needed, to be admired by the flashing-eyed beauties who would want the dead animals he'd kill for them.

"And taking the admonishments of the hunters as advice, he sought out old people to teach him about making bows and arrows, ropes and packs, but everywhere he was driven out as usual with the village dogs yelping and nipping at his bottom.

"Every road he took and attempt he made met with mocking failure and defeat. It was then, sitting alone on a rock off the edge of the lake, waiting for some hunters to creep out of the forest a mile away that Raggedy determined to make his own bow and arrows and set out alone on the hunt.

"He could do it! After all, wasn't a bow just a piece of bent wood tied up with a string and arrows just sticks with feathers and hard things tied at opposite ends, and hadn't he seen the dead deer hanging heavy over the hunters' shoulders, their glazed, slitted eyes and pink, dangling tongues hanging out of a big dry black snout? It couldn't be as hard as beating off buzzards and feral dogs from a rotten avocado.

"Knowing nothing but the village and lake edge close in and there-abouts, the Raggedy Boy, who would be a hunter, combed the rocks and spongy shoreline for a stick to form a bow until at some point the curliest, meanest-looking piece of waterlogged root came bobbing on a gentle group of waves. With visions of weapons in his head, the weapons that would fix it all, Raggedy dragged the crooked branch to the shore and, shouldering it, ran over the rocks to Ya Sar's little hovel, his bandy legs pounding his dusty bare feet over the rock-studded earth of that hard-hearted village.

"Plopping down panting by the poor old starving woman, Raggedy blurted out in between his breaths, 'Look, mama, I'm going to make a hunting bow.'

"With that her sightless eyes did roll and when the urchin had graciously shoved the wet wood into her mouse-like hands she almost laughed for pity, but her love for the little fool made her inspect with her paws the dreamer's fond discovery.

"Touching it from end to end, it was so convoluted and twisted that one might need a map to find one's way from one end to the next.

"Unconvinced as she was of his need to have weapons, she was nonetheless inspired to see his desire so avidly mounted on his hopeful naiveté that she decided not to dissuade him from his adventure. Though the stick itself was hopeless, Raggedy was not, and that in turn made her hopeful, giving her a feeling of usefulness and freedom beyond her sightless frailty and death-bound body. Feeling about carefully she removed thirteen of the long earth-dragging white hairs from her old suffering head.

"Then taking a couple of strands at a time, Ya Sar rolled them on her naked, wrinkled thighs, cording them into string, until in the end what she made was a very strong and resilient cord whose two ends she fastened onto the opposite tips of the crazy, crooked, would-be bow.

"Plucking the outstretched-hair bowstring it gave out one beautiful note as if from a harp and handing the wild crooked affair to a beaming Raggedy she said, 'Now you have your bow. Have you thought about making the arrows?'

"He had thought a little about them, but very little, because he'd spent his nights and days dreaming and figuring how to make a bow. Anyway, bows were the main thing. He'd seen arrows and there wasn't much to them as far as he was concerned. Just sticks with no moving parts, sharp on one end, feathered on the other.

"With the fire lit in his starving heart by his initial success with the making of the bow, Raggedy burst out of the hut like a swallow out of a cave, shaking with exuberance, and ran to gather sticks.

"But upon his return his old friend Ya Sar felt that what he'd gathered was an assortment of strange twigs, grasses, some reeds and another crooked branch.

"'Son, go to the back of the hut and inside the cornstalk wall pull out my old *kiem*, my old weaving loom; it's bundled there from my last attempt to weave before my eyes were lost.'

"Raggedy rummaged about where she'd suggested and soon returned with an ancient smoke-encrusted tangle of threads and sticks. Feeling about, Ya Sar removed the thin shed stick that she had so carefully put in long, long ago, now releasing all the old thread arrangement, hopelessly jumbling her unfinished weaving. The beautiful use-polished shaft of the weaving loom was very arrow-like. 'Take this now, little boy, and put an arrowhead on one end and feather the other end and carve a notch at the feathered end. Then you'll have an arrow.'

"Jumping up and down, he could hardly wait. Cradling his bow and weaving stick he bolted over again to the shore to pick up feathers from the grebes and egrets who fished and floated among the reeds. But when he got there only one feather could he conjure; not to be detoured from his joy of the possible viability of his weapon, a weapon whose ability to slay the animals would bring him village standing, a sweetheart and food, this Crooked Bow Boy tied one feather with a discarded loom string to the upper shaft just as he'd remembered the arrows of the village hunters.

"After tying on a sharp stone to the opposite end of the weaving stick, with another stone he rubbed a nock into the feathered butt of the shaft.

"Elated and anxious to shoot his bow, he didn't return to see the old lady, but went 'hunting' along the shore to see if his magnificent weaponry actually functioned.

"It was then that a yellow dog well-known to him as competition for the village refuse padded his way out from behind a black basaltic boulder, scavenging the shoreline as usual.

"Raggedy, surmising that this must be much like a deer hunt, decided to shoot the dog with his new arrow. He set the stick where it should belong, nocked the string and pulling back as far as he could let loose the arrow which, to Crooked Bow Child's delight, careened straight into the starving dog's rib cage.

"But about two feet from the unsuspecting mutt the arrow did a round-house turn, looped over upside-down and sped right back at the Raggedy Boy, whizzing a millimeter off his right ear.

"When the arrow had turned, the dog had looked and was now smiling himself to death for the funniness of Raggedy's absurd bow and returning arrow.

"What no one had told the boy was how three or four feathers set just right can rudder an arrow's shaft quite straight, and two set opposite work alright, whereas one feather brings the arrow back home to the shooter and this is just what Raggedy possessed.

"Not being one to give up on account of such trifles, Raggedy thought it out, and when the result of all his hard thinking was put into practice, he nearly killed everything he shot at with hilarity, never once even grazing the target.

"Raggedy Boy would stalk a bird, a cricket, a squirrel, dog or a vulture, then, with their position firm in his head, he'd turn around with his back to the prey and like a madman shoot his arrow in the opposite direction, dropping to his knees as he did so to avoid the returning arrow which then whizzed back over his kneeling body on to the original target in hopes of killing it. But every village scavenger he shot at was so stunned and tickled by his energetic and persistent backwards hunting method that none did flee, but rather stood there and laughed, preferring to risk a wounding to losing the amazement of the moment.

"And though no one was ever hit, Raggedy was never deterred. Day after day he practiced stalking, turning, shooting and ducking, retrieving his arrow until one day he felt that he was now ready to really hunt. He surmised that the central explanation for the failure of his arrow to connect lay not in his crooked curly bow or the one-feathered arrow but in the fact that he did not have the right sort of things to shoot at. Hunters didn't shoot cornhusks and dogs, they hunted peccaries, deer, tepisuintles and monkeys, and so would he.

"Old Ya Sar was against his leaving. 'The wild world of the mountains where the natural animals live is not the same as the village; there are big cats that could eat you and snakes that could bite or strangle you and all sorts of poisonous spiky plants that have no love of humans. Don't go, son, it's too dangerous.'

"So deafening was the rush of his desire to become a hero, so loud the song of possibility that he too might be able to feed her and himself, the village and be accepted, so loud was the tidal wave of his untutored daydreams that he was unable to hear the small voice of the old woman's concerns and in the middle of the poor white-haired creature's harangue Raggedy Boy shot out the fallen doorway of the tumbled hut, never looking back, yelling in his crackling teenage voice, *Xtin nula*. 'I'll return.'

"And away he trotted with his extravagantly gnarled bow with the old blind woman's hair as a bow string and his one feathered arrow made from her sacrificed weaving bundle. The boy had hoped for a hunter's send-off but the village was the same as ever.

"Sticking close to the curve of the lake's shoreline Raggedy Boy wandered toward the place where he'd seen the hunters disappear into the thick forest, at the base of the Three Boys Volcano up and away from the water and the village.

"Knowing that hunters tracked the animals whose meat they brought, Raggedy kept his eyes to the mud and before he'd even cleared the village shoreline he came across a stretch of shorebirds' tracks, each on top of the other going everywhere, and picking out the big, funny, flat prints of a duck he followed them excitedly straight to the water where on a rock sat a great old frog.

"'He's a lot like a deer, he is,' he thought to himself. 'He's got four legs and a nose, two eyes and a mouth. He's some special kind of deer. I'll shoot him.' And setting his one-feathered arrow to the old woman's hair, he aimed, turned and shot away from the big frog, whose eyes got very big when the boy dropped to his belly as the arrow flew over his head, very nearly whacking the old amphibian.

"Turning to see if he'd killed his 'deer,' all he saw was his arrow floating close by and the frog pulsing his throat and belly, his mouth curled in a silent frog laugh. The funniness of that crazy boy's hunting method inspired such a depth and quality of laughter in the frog that it would take generations of frogs to laugh it all out, and that's one of the prime activities of frogs ever since; trying to pay the laugh debt every time they remember that day.

"But that frog knew as well that the boy wanted to kill him and he jumped into the lake water, sinking and disappearing.

"Furious at his miss and at being laughed at, the little hunter pulled his sopping arrow from the drink and stared deep into the water's surface at the exact point where the green beast had entered.

"All the hunter saw was his own rippling face and he took to questioning it as to who he was and if he knew what had become of the only wild animal he'd come across that day.

"But the person in the water spoke the same words he did, and moved at the exact same moment.

"'Stop doing that and answer my question. Hey, I said stop iiiiiit.'

"And in his frustration to get the face to listen he slapped it to shut it up and the face broke into a thousand pieces of ripples and light.

"Mystified, he wandered farther from 'home,' the dogs, the trash and his blind old friend.

"Away from the village the smell was different and a certain tension left the air, the world had another tune and everything was new to the boy.

"At some point he noticed the tracks of what would be a rabbit marked in the generous soft ground at the shady edge of the thicket beneath the forest, and knowing nothing, having no one to show him how, Raggedy Boy began to track the rabbit in reverse, assuming that the two front prints made by the rabbit's hind legs were actually the two toes on the leg of a gigantic deer.

"Finally, then, he entered the forest tracking backwards, and much to the astonished chagrin of a little *umul,* or rabbit, the little hunter actually came upon the beast, unaware of what everyone knows: that rabbits always run in elliptical circles and figure-eights, returning and criss-crossing their own comings and goings, which gives the slip to certain predators, but not all the young fools of the world who always track backwards for a while.

"The rabbit was so amazed that the boy had actually found him and so fascinated by the strange appearance of his crazy curly bow and one-feathered arrow that he stood unbreathing and still while his yellow eye, like a gumweed flower in a nest of fur, never blinked, waiting to see what this strange boy might do, which is why rabbits do this to this day.

"But the boy couldn't actually see the beast, looking as he was for a gigantic deer, so when he'd finally focused on the fluffy rabbit frozen there he didn't understand at once that it was he who had made the trail.

"Realizing then that this was a real deer and this one was even furry, he suppressed his overwhelming urge to catch and cuddle the little animal and backed up, set his one-feathered arrow to the string, squinted hard, turned in an instant, shot in the opposite direction and dropped to his belly as the arrow whizzed over his head harmlessly past the rabbit.

"The rabbit couldn't take it anymore and his lips curled up in quiet rabbit laughter so violent that it split his lip and to this day all rabbits assist the frogs in a vain attempt to laugh out all the tickle that their insides feel to remember the Raggedy Boy's bizarre method of hunting.

"The rabbit was a rabbit and he ultimately disappeared into the leaves and thicket under the big trees of the evening forest. Retrieving his arrow, the boy crashed through the dense thicket keeping his infuriated gaze on the white tail of the fleeing rabbit.

"Catching glimpses then losing sight of him, then scaring him up again, the boy spiraled farther and deeper, twisting himself into the jungle tangle in pursuit of this furry 'deer' until darkness swallowed the sun and no track, deer or direction was discernible in the thick blackness of the forest night.

"Lost, alone and hungry, Raggedy Boy had wandered into a world he'd never seen and of which he had no knowledge: the world of nature, a land with no humans.

"Unable to see in the dark and figuring that he'd already learned how to track, Raggedy Boy would, upon the return of the Sun Father in the morning, find his own footprints and follow them back to the lake. He would track himself just as if he were a deer, backwards to the unforgiving village whose attention he so desired, now that he found himself lost, with no food and at the point where a scavenged, half-rotten meal shared with dogs sounded wonderful. Tears came to the eyes of the Hunting Boy as he remembered his beloved blind friend whose hair he carried as a bowstring on his hopelessly crooked bow.

"The taut hair string made a sound as he plopped down, raked and itchy from the thorny under-thicket of the pitch-dark forest floor.

"Continuing to pluck a note from the bow like a one-string harp, he kept a droning rhythm humming by striking his hopeless bow with his pitiful arrow, creating a comforting sound that pierced the terror of the wild, lonely night; the old lady's hair singing back to him in this faraway place.

"At first he took to humming along with the surging pling and pong of the bow and arrow, but at some point he took to singing and wailing about what had happened in the day. Melodies formed and then a main melody was found with a returning chorus between which he sang verses:

"'Looking for the eyes of the one who could see me
'I came drifting into the dark.
'My mother's hair sings.

'Oh me: The eater of food,
'the drinker of water. My face breaks into stars.

'Oh me: an eater of food,
'the drinker of water. I look for home, I search for home,
'Tracking the deer, I search for home.

'Oh I, the great eater of food,
'and drinker of water, where are my dogs and vultures now?

'Oh we humans, the eaters of food,
'the drinkers of water. Where is she
'whose eyes I want, tracking her food for days?

'Oh we the eaters of food,
'the drinkers of water. Oh we the thirsty trackers of food.
'With nothing over my shoulders, whose eyes would wait for me?

'Oh we the eaters of food,
'the drinkers of water. Drifting into the dark, my mother's hair sings.
'Shooting arrows made of song, my bow and I track in the dark.

'Oh we the eaters of food,
'the drinkers of water.'

"His funny voice saturated the night as the stars filled up the sky, a sky Raggedy Boy couldn't see, as it moved toward dawn on his song, for the dense forest canopy overhead.

"With the plaintive drone of his banging bow, the boy, strangely older than before, sang to forget his starving belly, sang to forget his thirst, sang to drone out the mews and groans of all that would eat him in the night. He sang to what he searched for though not altogether clear, but to she whose eyes would want him, she whose desired gaze had pulled him into this naïve road, this lonely time. For all that, he sang throughout this first time alone inside the dark until the night began to redden into dawn.

"And after rising from his song, like the Sun was at that moment rising from the earth, he searched for his own footprint in the murky forest light of dawn, hoping to follow his own tracks away from this lost place back into a more familiar starvation in the hard village.

"But he panicked when no tracks were found, for in the dense leaf litter of the forest and inexperienced as he was, he found no sign of his having come to lead him back to his familiar home.

"He tried to reason, keeping himself more steady, but he'd almost lost himself in a frantic alarm when he heard a small snap and a rustling among the leaves. Looking up, he saw her. What was this that he saw, they say, was it a road? Did he find some food, or was it the village close by after all? No, no, no. Then it must have been some wonder that stopped him from the worry, took him from the scared frenzy of his desire to go back to the horrible place of the village.

"It was a deer that stood before him. Not the kind that you only glimpse and then they bounce off shy or scared, but a fine and overly large doe with a big, wet, black nose and whiteless eyes so brown and deep that you longed to fall in and drown.

"It was a perfect deer with her left front leg lifted and bent, never fleeing, sometimes flicking her ear and always looking at the boy without a bit of fright, but with the strange confidence of those who have lived a lot and fear very little to be robbed of possession or life.

"Our Raggedy Crooked Bow Boy could only stare. He was so stunned by a devastating awareness of the magnificence of the living beast that stood before him staring back at him that he not only forgot that this was what he had set himself to slay, to bring the body in for its meat so he would be received as an honorable, respected youth, a marriageable man and loved, that he not only forgot to shoot his ridiculous arrows with his crooked bow but after each of them had gazed without moving for an hour, he was so mesmerized by the beauty of this first big being besides a human he'd ever seen that he began to sing to the deer, hitting the bowstring lightly with his arrow, quietly chanting in a lyrical and haunting curling voice, the previous night's melody with new words:

"'Who are you who comes all furred with eyes like the one I ache for?

'Crazy me: the eater of food,
'the drinker of liquids. Who are you there who stands so clear, well-made and ready?'

"The deer stared and stood, never putting her right front foot to the ground, in a deep gaze of animal amazement.

"When the singing fell off, the deer lowered her head and in a lavade, twisted back upon her flanks, then straightening, walked gracefully, directly behind where she'd been holding, in what seemed to be slowed motion. Silently, except for the almost inaudible click of her hoofs, the beautiful deer disappeared into the thicket.

"Up until now his feet unmoving like the roots of an old tree well-established in that earthly humus of his fascinated enchantment over the appearance of the beast, Raggedy Boy, not wanting to lose her, or part from her, found a way to move them. Listening for the sound of her delicate feet, he, carefully as the deer herself, pushed quietly into the same brushy exit.

"Around and through, over and twisting below, he was drawn in, his heart pounding in hopes of seeing her again. The boy trailed forward for the first time, tracking the real footprints of the Lady Deer. All thoughts of food, water and going back had drowned in the Deer's eyes, and the desire to see them pulled him yet deeper into the forest.

"Just when he was certain he'd lost her altogether he rounded what came out to be a small grove of straight-growing wild anona trees, with a clearing in the middle where the tracks of the deer disappeared.

"And where those cleft hoof-marks left off, a different creature stood, much taller and more magnificent. Her eyes were still the eyes of that same deer, but these were cased in a furless sea of copper doe skin softer than eagle down, and she was human.

"It was a girl who stood there, a young lady; she was tall, taller than any person he'd ever seen. Like the deer before she gazed at him unendingly with clear black pools generous and amazed. Neither spoke but each stood mutually entranced by the presence of the other.

"Her skirt was filled with every hue of turquoise and there were hollows in it like the eddies of rivers under which long-tailed serpentine water spirits swirled and swam. Her skirt, scintillating in the dawn, filled with scales of liquid jade. Even blue-winged ducks and other water birds could be seen rising from the covering of her hips and knees. Above that, on her *huipil*, living animals were embroidered; jaguars chased peccaries through the cloth, deer and curassow birds grazed above the luscious hills of her young wobbling breasts.

"What could Raggedy say or do? Dead with hunger and thirst, the crazy hunter could only fall in love, himself captured by what he'd hunted, and fall in love he did.

"Older yet in the most mysterious maturation of time, Raggedy, seventeen years old now, did the only thing he could do, faced with what he loved as she stared expectantly, eager and pained, filled with some other-worldly type of surprise: Raggedy began to sing.

"'*On the road of frogs and rabbits, tracking, the hunter is captured.*

'*Oh, once the eater of food,*
'*drinker of liquid. On the road to home, to slay for her eyes, a Raggedy Boy is slain by her water pool gaze.*

'*Oh, we poor eaters of food,*
'*drinkers of liquid. Oh, from her hips the sounds of water birds rise, from her knees turtles dream in the sun.*

'*Oh, I the poor eater of food,*
'*foolish drinker of liquid. In her eyes I fall drowning, clubbed to death by the fisherman of beauty, I become the food for love.*

'*Oh, the eaters and drinkers of liquid and food.*'

"And on and on, he rang his bow with his arrow and sang for who knows how long, but when that time ended and the song fell off, the tall girl straightened and swayed a bit toward him, her whiteless eyes fixed on his whole being and parting her lips a bit. He saw that her teeth were like moons rising behind sunset clouds.

"'What are you, boy?' she said, in a tone like a bubbling creek.

"For the first time in his whole life someone was talking to him, interested in him. With one phrase, all things were changed.

"'I am Raggedy Boy from the Umbilicus village.'

"'You are a *vinaaq*, a human, a twenty, a named being?'

"'Yes, I am human.'

"'Oh, I've been watching you from the eyes of dead deer on the backs of insolent hunters, from the eyes of laughing frogs, from the yellow eyes of over-confident rabbits. I've been in love with you for years and now you come singing to me with what others have used to slay. I love you. I want you. Let us marry, what do you say, Singing Boy?'

"Earthquakes, goose-bumps, lightning and a thrilled panting rose in the Singing Boy and would have spun him so hard as to kill him but the ache of his love for her kept him braced while he realized that here were the eyes, the one he'd wanted all along. She was not from the village, but greater than anyone could have ever been. Others had used their efficient weapons to kill and eat beings like this girl who was a deer, but the boy had turned his weapons into songs by which she'd found him. Remembering the hard-hearted village where kicks in the ribs were what he'd grown up on, he mumbled a sort of timid 'yes,' as he'd never really known how to talk to anyone other than Ya Sar and before he could say it better, she, the Water-Skirted Beauty, began again.

"'We can go live with my parents over ...'

"'You have parents, actual parents?' Singing Boy interrupted, speaking clearly now.

"'Of course I do, yes and you'll meet them, and I don't care what they say, I love you and I'll watch over you forever.'

"'You have a family? I have no family; you mean I could have family with you? Not only do I love you, but you have a family that could be my family as well?'

"Weeping and happy, they spoke and chattered, embraced and kissed until finally the Water-Skirted Beauty proclaimed, 'You are starving, we

should go to my house and introduce you to my family. There is plenty of food for you there.'

"She was a Goddess; she covered more ground in an hour than Singing Boy could run in a year and though at first the poor boy rolled ecstatically down the hills and ran up the next singing all along, he soon tired and they had to rest every hour. To the girl's great wonder she could not with her great magical abilities do much to speed the boy's entrance to her world of the great, green, rocky wild.

"Deeper and farther, denser and thicker, the land grew more hilly as they traveled, but every footstep took them deeper into the other's heart and farther away from the horrible human village where the boy had fought dogs to eat garbage.

"The journey to the other world took a long time, but the couple felt the toil and strain of the trek as a bitter spice in the recipe of their love, bringing out the more expanded flavor of what was already more important to them than the trials of life's obstacles in the route of looking for a home together.

"Then climbing mysteriously out from an indistinguishable hole set in the underbrush at the base of a rocky cliff under that old anteater's home, they came to the girl's village.

"Like all villages the dogs were on alert and came sending up a ferocious signal. The dogs of this village, however, were not canines but oversized jaguars of every color with angry tails as thick as your ankle, whipping and curling over their backs, while snarling grimaces and a coughing roar emanated from their thick-furrowed heads.

"A couple of them running up to the Singing Boy would have snapped his skull like a rotten pumpkin between their huge ivory tusks if the girl hadn't scolded them, after which they rolled over for her to scratch their white belly fur beneath their wildly spotted flanks. The screams of several two-headed, grimacing, flare-eyed eagles on the roof combs of the palatially proportioned huts of the other world brought the occupants running up barefooted as they do in all villages when something strange comes around.

"What Singing Boy assumed were thatched huts like those in his hated home village were upon closer scrutiny a rolling gathering of large grass-covered hills with layers of stratified red and black volcanic stone at their bases which opened on one side with doorways made by the trunks of great old trees in whose crowns of bared branches birds and monkeys chattered and sang and now complained.

"At first sight it looked as if thousands of animals crowded around them, spreading out under the hilly knoll for miles, but after blinking a couple of times he saw that they had faces and looked like people and among them fighting toward the forefront were several figures larger than the rest of the clamoring crowd, to whom they immediately yielded space. After pulling back into an enormous horseshoe there emerged into the clearing a fierce tall woman with a leafy face and coarse white hair with a dark strip in the middle that trailed on the ground, upon whose tail behind her to the left a cat-muscled man with a headcloth woven from red dyed milkweed fluff swaggered up and stood.

"These were Grandmother Growth and the God of the Mountain, the parents of the Water-Skirted Beauty.

"Grandmother Growth stopped short of their daughter and with the husband in tow they both sat on the prone backs of two crouched jaguars using their spotted, willing backs for benches, rising and falling with the deep excited breaths of the cats.

"'What's this you brought home with you, Honey?' the cloud-haired Grandmother of all plant Growth mewed through her irritation and jealousy, which caused her to grit her carved and terraced teeth.

"'Isn't he beautiful, mother?' Water-Skirted Beauty replied.

"'If I didn't know you better I could swear that what you've got there is a, what do you call it...' the Mountain God fumbled, when his wife stepped in.

"'That's a Human Being. I swear to it. I've seen them tearing up our hills before.'

"'But look how strange and wonderful he is, he can't even kill with his bow, he makes songs and sings to me. I want to keep him. That would be fine, wouldn't it?'

"'Keep him? What, are you crazy? Did you eat something strange; what's bitten your bottom, young lady?

"'You know full well that he must be destroyed. You can't keep humans around, they kill everything, they think they own the place after a while; they do nothing but eat, consume, burn, kill, enslave the soil, the animals, your brothers and sisters, and mostly they forget us, we who feed them and give them life through our very flesh and existence, giving us nothing in return.'

"'How could you deny this one, though; he doesn't kill, the humans hate him as well, he's been thrown away by them too.'

"'Oh, that's just because he's small. You know when they are that age they're all cute, cuddly and clumsy but as soon as they grow up they'll bite you. Did we bring you up to play with such terrible things?'

"'But mother, I love him. I'm going to marry him.'

"The big Gods jumped to their feet, the jaguars sat up and the world held its breath.

"'Love? Love?! What do you know about that? You can't marry a human, that's unnatural and suicidal. You cannot keep him, much less marry him!'

"'I will because I'm a Goddess and I have my right according to the Old Word and you'll treat him as your son-in-law, because that's how it is with us. You know it and so do I.

"'He will be my husband and no matter how small or strange, he'll stay in my mountain, in my house temple, and we'll live here in the Flowering Mountain together.'

"They were aghast, but silenced by the hate and the noose in which the bewildering truth of her words held them, for though they were Gods, they still owed allegiance to something bigger than themselves, the force of a bigger picture of the Nature of Deified Things that was put into motion in another layer of existence, another world, another layer of time where all things were constantly created through sound and called the Old Words. Like the Sun, the Mountain and Growth Gods had not wanted anything to do with the creation of humans, but the lazy old race of Rain Gods had pestered the previous Sun so relentlessly for a million years to create a new being to feed them that the Sun had finally given in.

"But every God had come to regret having put their power into this being and now the Daughter of the Mountain and Growth had come home with one of these pitiful, self-centered, larval creatures and wanted him for a husband. It was disgusting, unthinkable, filthy, maddening and scary, but in the interest of the bigger picture which the daughter had invoked, the old couple had to give in, but they only did so after making her swear to the time-honored conditions of marriage, in which the Singing Boy would have to work alongside his father-in-law, succeeding in any tasks put to him, ful-filling the same responsibilities as if he'd been one of the young Animal God suitors of their world. This was not what she wanted but for the moment this was as close as the Water-Skirted Beauty would get to giving her beloved Singing Boy a place where they could both be together, which is all either of them was hoping for anyway.

"Singing Boy, in the meantime, was only delighted to have so many peo-ple, beings, Gods no less, so interested in him. The palaver and debate with all its hidden understandings, complexities and hatred, like all the struggle he'd been through to finally find her, only added to the boy's delight. When had anyone thought him important enough to fight over?

"Finally Singing Boy was allowed to enter the palatial hut of his beloved Water-Skirted Beauty where she made a food and drink specifically for him that to him tasted like she looked. He was at home, in a house, eating real food, with a normal grumpy family, surrounded by a village whose individuals shared all their triumphant affection for the girl, once her parents had wandered away muttering with their brothers and sisters to a hut off to the edge of their world, their jaguars and pumas at their heels and their eagles flying with them above their heads.

"The natural world, every grain, fur, feather and chip of it, loved the girl and saw her love for the Singing Boy as a thing to congratulate, while Grandmother Growth and the Lord of the Mountain went off with their relatives who would console them but ended up themselves drinking lightning water, becoming increasingly drunker and drunker.

"Yelling out things they meant or didn't mean, the world suffered immensely from floods and earthquakes as a result, because of course the words of the Gods make things happen. It was during this time, away from their compound, in the mountain hut of Whirlwind Hail, as they were recovering from their hangover headaches that the Lord of the Mountain and his wife decided how to kill the Singing Boy. By putting him through the time-honored custom of having the son-in-law work for his father-in-law they hoped to eradicate him from the world and in time their mysteriously deranged daughter would come to her senses as the boy became a distant memory after a thousand years or so.

"After a couple of days spent 'fixing their faces' for the task, making themselves appear friendly and as if they had finally accepted the boy's presence, the parent Gods called in the daughter and her human lover to eat breakfast with them in the kitchen adjacent to their palatial hut, which was a well-furnished mountain.

"To Raggedy, to the Singer, this was an arrival to heaven, to be invited to sit at the fireside and eat in regal company with a real family without being chased away, derided or beaten with sticks and stones.

"The boy spoke and spouted, calling them mother and father, while the old powerful Deities did all they could to keep from vomiting; gritting their teeth and holding their tongues in a very powerful charade, appearing to listen, care and respond. The girl however, in her great wisdom, cooked and kept her dignity fully suspicious of her parents' sudden good behavior.

"Toward the end as they were digesting their meal, sitting back on their mats made of clouds and stools of live animals, the old Grandmother suggested:

"'*La´*,' it killed her to call him son-in-law, *Nu jii*, you know you and your wiiiife have agreed to the old custom. By this I refer to the fact that if you want to be truly together forever with our daughter, you must work for Father here, the Lord of the Mountain, as he goes about his daily activities.'

"Singing Boy couldn't believe that finally he would be allowed to accompany a man to his job in the hills, much less the God of the Hills himself.

"'Yes, son, today I want you to help me up on the mountain. If you can do this one chore with me then our girl may have you as her husband. You must first pass the test. What do you say, boy?'

"Who could say what Singing Boy thought and what he felt, but when he finally pulled out something solid from the rubble of his joy at being asked he spoke like the life-loving idiot that he was, 'It would be an honor, Grandfather, to serve you in honor of your daughter, however and whatever she honors!'

"Rolling her eyeballs at the boy's implacable gullibility and inspired hope, the old Goddess spoke, 'Honey, tell him what work you two have to do today.'

"'Well, first I have to burn the side of a far off mountain, which is about ten square miles of huge old dead standing trees, so the grass can grow. I'll go to each corner and set lightning fires, then blow strong wind in from every corner until it all burns to ash, and it will get so hot it will burn the rock.'

"'And what will be my work, father?' Singing Boy inquired, ecstatically entranced by all this, feeling that he actually had a father to bring him to work.

"'What we need you to do is stand in the middle of the forest so I know where the corners are and stay there until the fire is out. This is your challenge. If you can do just this small chore then I'll give you my daughter.'

"Knowing that this meant her sweetheart's annihilation, the Water-Skirted Beauty neither protested nor endorsed the plan, fully aware as well that to argue only meant a replay of the days before and a more intricate plan for her lover's demise. Keeping steady and flinching not a width of a flea's hair, each woman stared away from the other, each searching from the corners of her determined eyes for some sign of having damaged the other, one by her actions, the other by her lack of reaction. So well-trained was each one by the other that neither of them showed anything.

"The old man, oblivious to that silent ten-second battle, went on to describe to the foolish love-drunk boy the tools he would need for the day. Right then and there he began loading up the boy, criss-crossing his chest with heavy ropes, shoving stone axes and hoes into his uncalloused hands and string bags full of this and that, all the tools Raggedy had seen grown men haul out and back to the village ever since he could see, but which up to now he had never been allowed to touch or comprehend.

"Like a daydream come alive, Singing Boy thought nothing of the danger, in love as he was, and in love with the idea of his possible acceptance as a useful man, a man with men, a boy with a father, a man with a sweetheart whose eyes were the deer that he'd followed out of his starving life to find a real home. And here it was, all of it.

"'I don't care about the danger, I'll do anything for what and the woman I love,' he sang and yelled like a tree frog drunk on desire. And with that the Gods knew this human fool's eradication was now only a matter of details.

"Like back in the old village of people, the Father God, Lord of the Mountain, walked in front of his son-in-law as they headed out and away from the village of the Gods, toward their work into the forests and mountains. The Mountain God, impatient to get the killing over with, of course, said nothing to the boy, who lagged farther and farther behind the old God, the strain of the charade bending the God's power and arrogance the wrong direction. Why didn't they just kill him like humans killed flies, easy, no thought to it whatsoever? Just because of the bigger law, the Old Words, that bigger thing even the Gods had to obey. It had been discussed at the Gods' drunken meeting where all the powers of the Earth and beyond had met to give their consolation and make decisions. The Gods would not simply kill the human because then the whole universe would collapse in on itself, each piece compromised by the deliberate action of a natural force. That was what humans did that made the Gods desire them gone. The purposeful manipulation of the surroundings for their own comfort and success was a human thing whose vision of human success was so small, momentary and disregarding of the beauty of the whole Big Picture beyond them, beyond now, beyond before and after, that the Gods became almost human in their frustration.

"If the Gods killed the human then that would be a human activity based on forgetfulness, an amnesia, the very one they feared would bring all the Beauty to an unthinkable, finite nothingness. Humans created and endorsed nothingness, forcing the Gods to constantly fill the void that human amnesia maintained by filling it with new life, renewed possibility, plant and animal growth and more; things that humans took for granted and upon which their very existence depended.

"No, the boy, if he were to die, must die on his own in the line of natural circumstance. The Gods all obeyed Chance and Chaos as their most ancient parents and all the Deities' natures were at risk if they used anything unnatural to cause anything to happen. The Gods or Goddesses of all things each had to function according to their given nature and if the human died during the normal operation of the Great Whole then the universe would remain whole. This didn't stop Grandmother Growth from bluntly stating to the council of deities that it was her 'nature to have the Boy dead.' But she was drunk and like most village mother-in-laws put in similar circumstances, said exactly what she meant, although the next morning when the storms had cleared she knew she would conform to the old rule: the boy could die but only in the line of normal operations of the Earth. Because all of these ruminations ran through the old God's head, he transferred his anger to his stride, trudging too fast up and off away from the boy, of whom he was oblivious until his hated son-in-law was a full half a mile behind him.

"Singing Boy struggled with his load of tools, sweating but triumphant in this new status as a full-fledged man accompanying a God to his work. Strangely older now, the one-time Raggedy Boy looked better and happier, mindless of the impossibility of the task set before him, but rather elated by the moment and the love he felt for the old man's daughter, a situation once totally off limits to him.

"Like his angry father-in-law groveling up the hill far in front, he too was lost in a trance of consideration when he heard a softly-whispered airy sound like that made by a deer tail wagging.

" *'La´.'*

" *'La´,'* it said.

Turning his head to the left to peek from the steep open trail to the deep woods from where the sound emanated, he saw the beautiful deer he'd followed to the girl walking parallel to him beneath the tree.

"'*La´*, boy.'

"'*La´*, boy,' the deer repeated.

"And he was magically pulled off the trail into the forest to stand in front of the beast that immediately turned out to be his sweetheart, the Water-Skirted Beauty.

"'Quickly now, listen to me, my beloved; my father aims to destroy you so we can't be together so ...'

"The boy interrupted, feeling insulted, 'No, your father is a good man, I'm going to meet the challenge he rightly sets to me to earn the straightforward right to be with you, his daughter. It's the custom.'

"'No, boy, my sweetheart, you'll be incinerated into mountain ash like a gnat in a volcano. But listen, please, put this in your string bag,' she said, pulling a great vine called *raxcaam* from her luxurious hair that made up her *xq´ap*.

"'Don't let my father see you with this, but when the flames roll in on you from every side and nothing but fire is visible above and around, dig a deep hole in the ground, crawl inside, then wrap yourself from head to foot with this vine I give you, like a giant cocoon. Bury yourself in the ground by pulling a great rock and earth over you.

"'When the heat increases in the earth the vines will sizzle, you must breathe the vapor of my head-dress, it is this Holy steam which could save you from being burnt to nothing.

"'Then, if you survive, wait until the ground is cool enough to tread and move out of your hole, leave the bindings behind and come down the mountain safely to my waiting arms. Now go before he finds us.'

"Then, becoming a deer again, she bounded off.

"Sobered and somewhat more awake, he re-entered the trail and pushed to catch up to her father. Because everything he thought and felt was so confusing and going different directions, what would cause him and his love to survive was hard to keep clear and he forced himself to remember, rehearsing over and over the secret instructions of his intelligent beloved.

"As promised, the old God had Singing Boy clear and gather a great pile of brush in the middle of a very dry forest. Then, after he made the boy stand in the middle of the brushy mound, the God of the Mountain, father of the Singing Boy's sweetheart, let loose four types of wind from every direction toward the brush mound from miles out.

"Four lightnings, like an old deer's rack, sizzled and slapped the ground in an ear-splitting whomp, instantly permeating the air with a sickening odor of ozone that practically suffocated Singing Boy.

"The blaze that rose lashed the sky and every tree for miles, raging toward the boy, simultaneously racing in from every corner, raising such heat that birds melted in mid-flight a quarter mile off.

"Having already dug the hole under a giant basaltic stone and his incineration immanent, Singing Boy muttered his sweetheart's instructions aloud to himself, while pulling her blue-flowered vine from its hiding place in his handmade string bag. Rolling it around him he found that it miraculously extended to reach all of him except his little finger on his left hand which he used to wind the last bit of the vine, then falling into the hole earth slid over him, covering him like a planted seed.

"He lay there buried in the mountain earth forever and more, bound in the woman's vine, awaiting the great heat which came, and then increased each time to a point where he was sure he would burst and suffocate. Though the fire raged faster and hotter it cooked the vine until it steamed and sizzled, keeping him moist and cooking underground, where he inhaled deeply the vapors, sucking in their life-giving steam, resigned to die for this was too impossible to survive.

"For hours he drew in and sucked life from the cooling vine around him until the heat began to subside. Two days went by, after that then a third, and knowing he would die otherwise the Singing Boy began feebly digging like a mole out from under the stone, which was still too hot to touch.

"When he reached the surface of the earth, the fire ash of the ground nearly choked him for good, but clearing that, he filled his amazed lungs with the delicious clear air of a fine morning sky.

"Barely able to stand, but older now, maybe twenty years old and looking as humans do at twenty anywhere, he forced himself to stand and stumbled down the mountain toward the village of the Gods.

"And before he could collapse at the front door of the hut of the Mountain God and Grandmother Growth he yelled as much as he could, 'I've finished my work, father, mother.'

"Hearing the squeak of a human voice, they ran and stopped, astounded at the sight of the live boy, now more a man, who survived what no one could. Mumbling, 'How could he do it; who is this boy?' under their breath to each other, they feigned friendly behavior to him and, acting as if everything was natural, they addressed him, 'Welcome home, son, I knew all along what a good worker you would make.'

"But before they could drag that boy into their cooking hut the Water-Skirted Beauty came running up and grabbing his left hand saw he was missing a little finger, which having been left unprotected had burnt off. Kissing each other all over, they held each other and wept from the happiness and the grief of it all, eventually tottering together into their hut where she washed him, fed him and put him to sleep.

"It took days for him to revive and when he did the couple looked even happier and more mature than they'd ever been. This only further energized the jealousy and clannish hatred of the girl's parents who met and mumbled, hissing and plotting a new 'natural' way to get him gone.

"Once again a little older, only a little less naïve, more in love and stronger, Singing Boy was called one pre-dawn day to eat with his in-laws again.

"The Water-Skirted Beauty and he arrived and all was a-bustle, with a grand cooking going on where foods were being prepared that Raggedy Boy had only smelt from afar. He'd always felt that that kind of smell meant people together, happy with their families, no hardship and full bellies.

"Today he ate as a man in their midst but like the last time, the moment arrived when the old man spoke. 'You know it's traditional here to accomplish several tasks for your future father-in-law and today I'm short-handed once again. If you can do this one task then I'll give you my daughter in marriage.'

"Less enthusiastic but still a good willing boy, the Singing Boy replied, 'That last task was a cooker, but I pulled it off, didn't I? I was thinking I was finished with tasks as you promised.'

"'You know, work with men is dangerous. Don't you want to work with men or would you rather be a tottering child, looked after at home?'

"'Oh yes, I want to work and will do what I must to be with my wife.'

"The parent Gods held their breath and tried not to grit their teeth. A split half second of a split second passed where even the fire didn't move.

"'What's our work for today, father?'

"'There is a mountain that needs trimming, up from where the fire burned. Half the mountain must erode and collapse making room for a new gentle slope where trees can come and grow in the next couple of centuries. I want you to stand at the base of that mountain so when I shake the earth I know exactly where to aim the landslide.'

"'Sounds like I could handle that,' and sucking air the boy stood, adjusting his sash, standing proud, like a death-doomed, moronic cadet going to his duty. 'Which tools do we need, father?'

"Like the time before, the old man loaded him up with all the men's tools, the ropes, hoes, machetes, water gourds, string bags, a pair of *xoy xjap* sandals, a *mangax* and an ax and off they trudged, back up the mountain.

"Once again the old man out-walked the boy, getting way ahead of him, lost in thoughts about the mess he'd begun and rehearsing what he'd planned with the wife, old Grandmother Growth: how to arrange it so a billion tons of rock, earth, sand and stumps should bury and grind him into oblivion.

"The Singing Boy, like the time before, remembering with even greater tenderness and wonder the love he'd had with the old man's daughter after he'd returned from certain death in the first task, considered now how to accomplish this second one, caught up in the charade as much as the adults, having completely forgotten that the Water-Skirted Beauty had been the only reason he'd been magically extricated from mortal danger.

"But lost in all this he once again heard his wife's deer voice calling him into the cover of the adjacent woods.

"'*La´.*'

"'*La´.*'

"And seeing her, he followed her into the thicket long enough for her to transform into her tall, suede-skinned woman form. Removing her rippling, water-scaled, wraparound skirt, she spoke.

"'My father aims to kill you by letting the cliffs collapse on your frail human bones. Hide my skirt in your string bag, then do what my father asks and when you feel the earth to take up a trembling, wavy motion, remove my skirt and wear it over your head, shoulders, back and legs like a shawl, then kneel and call out my name.

"'Every rock, tree, and grain of earth loves me and seeing you covered in my clothing will refuse to harm you. You will be buried in a mountain of scree and dust but a space big enough to breathe will remain and nothing will strike you in the avalanche. You will have to dig your way out after all has settled. Calling my name, remember me to the earth and because they'll recognize my skirt the rocks shall shift and give way as you proceed, making an exit for you to the fresh air. Then come home down the mountain well and healthy back into my waiting arms. Now go, hurry, or my father will find us out.'

"Singing Boy watched her turn back into a waggy-tailed doe, bouncing off into the woods, leaving him alone. The old man was yelling and coming back to get him by now, but the boy scrambled back up to the old God tying up his sash making like he'd been taking a pee along the trail.

"The old man fell for the ruse and up they went to the 'work.'

"Arriving at the base of a mountain so tall the morning sun was blocked, or maybe the Sun Father didn't want to see what he could neither stop nor endorse, the Mountain God told the boy his job was to stand right up against that cliff and he, his father-in-law, would surmount the ridge in the valley opposite and sight the line of the landslide. When he felt the earth begin to quake he was to get out of there and they'd go home 'together.' It was a trap of course, because the landslide was to be an instantaneous deadfall of boulders and earth at least a mile square and no human could have escaped the crushing and grinding press of that kind of tonnage.

"But when the moment came and the earth began to rumble and the dust to cloud the air, Singing Boy wrapped himself tight in his sweetheart's water-skirt and yelling out her name, which was a secret, but one that all matter knew, miraculously not one pebble or clump of cindery earth struck him or dared trespass the circumference of ten feet on either side above or around him, and when all the earth's splitting, cracking, grinding, thundering and quaking had quit and the place had settled the boy was still quite intact and sat shaking inside the earthy womb covered in the placental skirt of water of the lady who saved his life.

"After a day in the utter darkness of that magically-made hall and when he'd regained enough composure, the digging began. As promised, each rock moved out of the way as he dug giving him a narrow tunnel through which he dragged his belly, pulling himself inch by inch to the surface of an unrecognizable landscape, to an earth rearranged by Divine beings in search of his demise.

"The air rushed into his lungs with the same lack of reserve that the deep ache within the rest of him longed to lie in the arms of the Water-

Skirted Beauty and like a dusty halfwit he wandered and stumbled out of the scree mounds down the forests and trails back to the village of the Mountain Deities.

"The Beauty ran to catch him holding him as he yelled like the men he'd seen as a boy returning from their everyday struggles to earn a living, '*in penaq anen, exkola aii?*' 'I have come home. Is there anyone here to see it?'

"The old couple ran out of their palatial mountain hut, interrupted in their satisfaction over his assumed death, eyes wide, angry, amazed and unsure as to what to say.

"'Who is this guy?' the old Mountain God who'd returned without the boy the day previous said to his wild-haired wife.

"'He can't have accomplished this on his own, I know what's going on here,' she mumbled to her mate.

"Then in a loud imperious sound of fake royal welcome, 'Oh, son-in-law, you are truly a great worker, welcome home.'

"The boy was now much broader of shoulder, deeper of heart, less about dreams and more about gratitude to be alive, but most of all he was now in his early twenties.

"He rested and was doctored by his magical wife but again and again the father-in-law, the God of the Mountain, put him to tasks beyond his knowledge, magical ability or physical capacity. Every time he grew in stature and craftiness and passed the task only by the secret intervention of his wife. She had all the power of both her parents but combined with the loving heart of the earth.

"Eventually it became evident to her brilliant though hard-hearted, jealous mother that the daughter was with child. The Water-Skirted Beauty had a big, smooth, coppered belly in which for the first time in the world the child of a human man and a goddess was growing.

"To Grandmother Growth, whose powers were what made deer have fawns and plants fruit, this was an abomination and a threat to her territory, over which she reigned supreme and alone. She had known fully that the only way the boy could have survived into the man he'd become was through the divine intervention of her magical daughter. Without her he would have been less than a dust speck ages ago.

"Now, in a fireball fit of rage, Grandmother Growth's power to make things flourish turned to an obsession with killing not only the boy and not only their child; but she resolved that the daughter must be killed as well.

"The mother wanted her daughter dead, her daughter's happiness gone from her view, her love of the stink of weak, forgetful humans, the creations of the rain ancestors, gone, done, destroyed.

"Grandmother Growth was big, knowledgeable and the most inordinately able Deity of all. She knew that the Old '*Beyal*,' the natural rules of which Chaos and Chance were parents, stated as they did even in human villages, that when a child was born who had parents from adversarial blood then that finished the feud, making the adversaries blood relatives. Being relatives with humans through her daughter's half-human child would mean that the Gods of the Mountain and the humans would have to see each other, find ways to respond to each other and become close.

"This was unthinkable, impossible, undesirable, insane and why would powerful, beautiful, nature-bound, excellent beings want to be on a peer level with filthy, fragile amnesiacs like these humans which even Singing Boy had to dodge to survive.

"This course the Gods would never sanction: to simply kill the boy, the young Goddess and the creature in her belly. White-haired Grandmother Growth would try to *bojchij*, to cotton-mouth her husband, convincing him to go along with her murderous plan. She would poison them all at breakfast. She would make a beautiful breakfast of all the things the girl loved to eat and all those foods the boy was enamored of after his early life of deprivation. The food would kill them. That's when poisonous plants began on Earth.

"The old man was not totally comprehending of why the daughter needed killing, but he feared the divine rage of the wife who could not be successfully countered in a final face-off and in the end gave in to the plan.

"Tomorrow morning she would make death food and wake them to eat. That would end it all. The parents would have their way with no thought to what might happen to the universe for the unnatural human-like character of such deliberate action against all that they were.

"But they did it anyway; such was the all-encompassing fury and jealousy of that girl's mother.

"And while the couple plotted throughout the night in the off-limits inner sanctum of their temple mountain, their daughter, asleep beside her beloved husband in her own smaller, happier mountain, awoke with a start, feeling the sick ache of her parents' plan in her joints.

"Listening to the earth, every plant, chip, insect, dust and wind betrayed what was being planned against the happy couple, whispering as only she, the girl, could hear.

"A powerful being herself, now made more able and insistent by having defended her human against this relentless divine hatred, she was yet more endowed with her natural power because of the child in her belly, making her a mother instead of a child.

"As a child she was horrified and crushed by the reality of her mother's intention to murder them all, but as a mother herself she now took on a way of being dedicated only to the survival of her child and her husband.

"Rousing the Singing Hunter, who was still recovering from a near drowning in a flood as part of one of the murderous tasks set upon him and was slow to open his eyes, she spoke in a whisper.

"'Husband, *La'*, my parents' plan to kill us at breakfast, we must elope, we must flee to your village, love.'

"'That's not possible, *Ya Xtan*, your parents would never do such a thing to you or their grandchild. What makes you think such a thing?'

"'The ground and all creation tell me. We must flee; if we make it to your village and can have my baby in your village, having crossed the line from this world of Gods to the world of humans, if what rides my womb is safe in your people's world then we are all safe, for in no way will the rest of the Gods allow them to kill what would then be blood relations to them all.'

"'We can't go there. For one thing, I have no idea how to get back there. It's not even a village; it's a horrible place of heartless people. I've no relatives, friends or anyone who cared anything for me except old Ya Sar and by now I'm sure she's passed away long since.'

"'No matter what you think, I'm not asking you a question. Whether or not you want to go back where you came from or know how to get there is beside the point. I know where your village is and though it's a long way to go because I'm with child, you still move slower than the rest of us. What does matter is for us to protect what we both love: our child's life and the love we have for each other. What I'm saying is that you and I are going right now to your old village of humans, because as bad as it might be it is the only way we as a family might survive; even then, getting there in one piece is very unlikely given the fact that my mother is so powerful and long-seeing.'

"The young Goddess having made her command known, the young

man relented and began to prepare to leave in the darkness. At her direction he prepared their sleeping mats, ropes and blankets with the proper lumps and curves to create the illusion that a man and a pregnant Goddess slept together beneath the covers so that her mother would think they were still sleeping in the morning, which might give them a little more time undiscovered to rush a little farther ahead on the trail home to safety in Singing Boy's village.

"He went about all that with a great deal of ingenuity, hiding two opossums where their heads would rest, so as to have the sound of their breathing and tiny snores to convince anyone that people were actually sleeping. While he was occupied with the opossums and blankets, the Water-Skirted Beauty, one hand filled with white deer fat and the other hand cupped, filled with ground chili seeds, stole unseen into another hidden place where only the Mountain God himself was allowed to enter.

"Once inside she didn't dally or let the memories of how her father had held her here as a toddler in his lap deter her from her mission. It was here he'd shown her all his secret *q´ijibal*, magical God tools, like the concave fire mirror made of some ancient volcanic glass and pyrite which he'd held up to her to show how he could see any minute or great thing anywhere at any distance in his kingdom of the mountains.

"It was here that he kept his backwards *puub*, or blowgun, which instead of shooting hard-baked clay pellets at the eyes of birds like the humans did, worked in reverse. After pointing it at a desired object or being, by sucking in through the long tube the old Mountain God's powerful, windy lungs could pull whatever he wanted right into his reach.

"Quickly, without reminiscing, the Water-Skirted Beauty bellied through her father's study, removed the volcanic mirror lens and smeared it thoroughly on all sides with deer fat, the kind that comes from the kidneys.

"With one hand replacing the mirror the other reached over the doorway to pull down the long tube of his sucking gun, which she loaded and packed with the powder of the very hottest *quejic´*, or deer chilies, all the while praying for momentary invisibility.

"The boy was finished with his props by the time she returned and it was then carrying only very little food that the pregnant Goddess and the beautiful young man headed up and over the ridge they'd come in on in the beginning.

"The Water-Skirted Beauty was only a few days away from giving birth, her belly wonderfully swollen with their kicking child and though she moved more ponderously than normal across the familiar ground of her people's domain, she was still as graceful as a mother deer and it was all that her human husband could do to struggle behind her over the uneven ground that slowed them.

"Confused at having to flee the only place that had ever actually welcomed him, albeit in a lethal sort of fashion, Singing Boy was also pained to see how his beloved wife had to carry herself and their unborn child away from her homeland, the land of the spirits, all because she'd loved a human.

"'Let me carry you on my shoulders,' he called from behind as he negotiated a boulder over which she glided, panting a bit herself.

"'No, let's go, keep going, we must get to your village soon because this child must be born there and I can feel him coming soon.'

"They trudged and trudged, hardly ever resting, hoping to escape pursuit.

"When Grandmother Growth had finished preparing the beautiful and fine-smelling poisoned breakfast, she hoped that the eternal hunger of the human would make the delicious smells of her concoction irresistible and pull the boy and his lover straight to the cooking hut where both parents waited nervously.

"But by mid-morning when nothing was heard to stir up in the girl's hut mountain, Grandmother Growth took to calling out in the voice of mothers rousing the compound to eat.

"'Little jaguar whisker, Mrs. Young Lady, the food is tiring of waiting for your eating. Come down, come over, breakfast is waiting.'

"And after a while when that didn't make anything happen she called again, then again and again.

"Frustrated at the fact, she mounted the deep-worn boulder waterfall of steps heading to her daughter's hut and peeking inside heard the breathing of the opossums and saw the lumps and returned to her hut. By midday she went to rouse them for good and when she pulled off the covers, at the fierce sight of her, the blinking opossums rolled over stiff, playing dead, as if to say, 'You can't kill us more, we're already dead,' which is why they've been doing that ever since.

"The old woman's face could have melted the sky and a scream of wild, tunneling rage tore through that world with such a shrill rasping squeal that wild honey in the tree trunks was petrified into amber on the spot and stones crumbled to talc.

"Running up, the God of the Mountain couldn't hide the tiny smattering of relief he felt when he realized the pair had escaped, not because he was nice, but because he didn't have much taste for killing his own children.

"Grandmother Growth spat, hissed, rumbled and nearly strangled her husband, demanding that he pursue them immediately, commanding him to track them, just like human hunters did to the Mountain God's animal children.

"But the old man said, 'There is no need, I can easily pull them here.' And coursing up to his inner sanctum, he took out the obsidian mirror, took it out into the day and found that he couldn't perceive a thing, so thoroughly greased it was. But wiping it made the smear more complete, such is the nature of deer's fat. With no time to lose and with the wife's wild peccary tusks grinding behind him everywhere he went, he ran and took down his backwards blowgun and started sucking-in in all directions, but the fierce heat of the finely-ground deer chilies all but killed him. Choking, wheezing and hacking, whooping and searching for enough breath to breathe, he cursed his daughter whom he knew was the culprit, for not even his wife knew of his tricks.

"The old woman kicked the husband in the ribs repeatedly, admonishing him in his incapacitated position to jump to it, to trail the couple and kill them instantly before they could arrive at the boy's human village.

"And taking the blows until he could rise and remove himself to the hunt, his shame at how she beat him combined with his hatred of his daughter's multiple betrayals gave him the impetus to truly want the couple destroyed.

"Turning into a jaguar, he easily picked up the trail and followed it hard and swift down away from the mountain heights of his ancient domain.

"Knowing the slowness of the boy, he'd hoped to overtake them swiftly, but after running a full day for a distance that astonished him, he finally lost the trail at the base of a dead tree full of woodpecker holes and pitch, which leaned tenuously over a small rocky ledge out of which a spring, clear but reluctant, barely seeped out.

"The jaguar ran up the sides of the ravine and back, looked up the trunk, ran into the spring muddying the waters and, frustrated, turned back into the God of the Mountain, in which form he interrogated the tree.

"'Have you seen my daughter go by here?' making no allusion to his murderous mission. The tree, however, remained mute and turning to the spring he repeated his questions. The spring had a lot to say and in a voice much like his own mother spoke, 'Do you mean that beautiful girl? The one we all love so much? The one with the slow-brained human husband, the one whose belly is swollen and lovely, filled with the child of ... '

"'Yes, yes, that one, have you seen them?'

"'Actually, they came through here a long while back and they went up that ridge of the ravine, along the ridge toward the Sun and disappeared from my view down the opposite slope.'

"Without so much as a thank you or a farewell the old Mountain God sprang from boulder to boulder up the side of the ravine following the spring's instructions, but by nightfall had failed to find any sign of them whatsoever and though he feared it, he returned home to receive his licking from old Grandmother Growth.

"Just as he expected she was pacing, muttering and grinding her peccary tusks when he arrived and after debriefing the poor old God she threw him up against the tree.

"'You split-open, rotten avocado, vagina-brained dove louse like what buzzards refuse to eat, you think. You didn't lose them at all, it's just that you are stupid. The tree, old fool, was the boy and the spring you muddied was her and the two fish that played in the spring are our unwanted grandchildren. How could you be such an imbecile? AHHHHHHHHHH!' roared the old Growth Goddess, more enraged than ever before.

"And before she could say another word, the Mountain God picked up his lightning weapon and ran back to the tree and spring which had mysteriously dried and he blasted and blasted and blasted away until the whole landscape was razed, scorched, twisted, melted and made uninhabitable.

"Feeling he'd killed them, twinges of remorse were just beginning to creep into his thick-skinned heart as he trudged into his palatial hut again, weary from the strangeness of that day.

"'You are the stupidest God in the universe, I swear, don't you understand who you are up against? This girl of yours has both of our powers combined. By the time you arrived back at the tree and spring they had long flown who knows where, but for sure headed to that terrible human village to give birth to that half-breed mess in her womb. It's just the boy who slows her. She's got big powers, don't underestimate her. It's her love for that boy that keeps her vulnerable. Without him and what's in her belly, which is half him, we wouldn't have a chance, but then we wouldn't want her dead either.

"'They must be destroyed; you've got to do it. This time, don't be fooled.'

"Once again the old jaguar ran toward their trail and finding it ran an astonishing distance until the tracks and scent disappeared into a cave full of big red bats and lined with crystals.

"'Have you seen my daughter, her tracks lead into here,' he inquired of the *zotz*.

"'You mean that beautiful girl, the one we all love so much? The one with the slow-witted human by whom her swollen belly awaits the birth of their child ... '

"'Yes, yes, yes, that's her. Where is she?'

"'You just missed them. They camped here when the mushrooms in the grass were just sprouting and now they're fully opened, so they've gone up the ridge there to the top, turned left and went down the other side...'

"And just as he was turning back into a hunting jaguar the old Mountain God, feeling the lumps on his ribs from the drumming his powerful wife had laid over him, turned without a thought and blasted the cave, the bats and the crystals with lightning until only cinder and molten rock glowed as it cooled.

"Satisfied he'd done the job this time, he returned more confidently, hoping to finally rest from all these nefarious proceedings and get back to the normal life of a deity.

"'What, what, do you never learn, you banana-headed, nut-less, cold-spermed, sparkless idiot?' the old woman barked at him before he could cross the threshold into this own house. 'What have you got against the Dogs of the Lords of Death, the bats?

"'The grass was your beloved son-in-law, the balsa tree your daughter and the shelf mushroom on its base the children in her belly for whom we shall be disgraced.'

"And again before she could stop him he ran back to the spot, crazed with frustration and shame. When he arrived neither grass, balsa nor mushrooms were to be seen.

"By using her powers to transform who she was and what she loved into different forms, as all daughters do when pushed by their parents, his daughter succeeded in outwitting her father for days on end.

"And this went on and on, the daughter each time transforming into what all of us today know to be what is female and turning the boy into the male parts of the universe. She went defining the world as it is today, but every time as these things were sacrificed Grandmother Growth realized that the whole natural world was more sympathetic with their daughter and totally willing to risk extinction for her, because of which the natural world was now endangered by the zealous and powerful hate of her frustrated husband. If his blunders continued they would have no kingdom or living things left to regulate.

"Therefore the white-haired Goddess of Growth decided that she would have to kill her daughter, the boy and her grandchildren herself.

Her eyes turned piercing and yellow, and jutting out her fierce jaw, she stretched her magnificent and coppery neck out until bones were heard to creak and crackle as she sprouted bronze-colored feathers so strong they could be tied into knots without kinking and then rebound undamaged back into their original shape, and with her fluffy bandy-legged waddle, Grandmother Growth bounced about a bit then leaped effortlessly, flapping up into the windy morning to the crest of her mountain hut, perching, screaming there, having now transformed herself into a gigantic, oversized harpy eagle with claws bigger than a giant anteaters and a beak so strong it could snap the neck of a tapir as if it were a cricket.

"Moving off and away, closer to the humans and increasingly more pregnant, the Water-Skirted Beauty, the wife of the Singing Hunter, fully felt and knew that her mother had grown impatient with her father's fumbling attempts to kill them.

"She stopped still and listened. 'My mother is coming,' she told her husband as she searched the skies with her whiteless brown-pool eyes.

"'I will not be able to outwit that woman. So I will have to battle her and even at that I shall only have three chances at beating her off. If by some miracle I succeed at that then on the fourth she shall kill me if we are not yet at your village, for that is the rule.'

"'Let's travel quickly,' the Singing Boy said, 'we must be getting close to that human town of mine by now.'

"'That is true, but with each step toward the world of humans time becomes a heavy thing to carry and my pregnancy comes to the day of birth increasingly faster, not to mention that with my mother harrying us we shall be doubly impeded.

"'I'll help you more, I'll carry you, you can't fight, you must rest, you are my love. I will fight instead.'

"'You would be killed instantly by her, I tell you. We must keep moving and I'll fight when she comes. If I succeed we shall keep traveling in hopes that we can arrive in time for me to have our child in your village. If that happens we are safe; if not, all is lost. Let's get going.'

"But before they'd gone far the surveillance of the harpy eagle had noticed them scrambling through the last valley toward the lake village. The girl knew her mother better than the mother knew her and the Beauty knew that her mother intended to land, turn herself back into a

Goddess and dispatch them all in a flash. But before the harpy could maneuver for a landing her daughter had already become a laughing falcon with black stripes through her eyes, a white head and a blood-curdling cackling laugh for a call. Rising fast on her blade-thin wings the falcon was so small compared to the eagle that if caught she'd be mangled and eaten on contact.

"But the falcon rose high and the two began an aerial battle, which the boy watched anxiously from the ground.

"Like a snowstorm, feathers fell from the sky, the falcon outmaneuvering the furious harpy, who for all its enormous flying power and strength could not cut such sharp turns and was repeatedly screaming hatred at the daughter, who screamed then in hawk talk right back. They succeeded in taking small pieces out of each other, the one zooming, the other smashing, the one cruising and folding her wings in a death dive, the other locking her talons onto her mother's until they would have crashed into the earth, but each of them releasing the other an inch from the fatal ground, swinging back up into the high skies above the ravines to battle and scream again and again until the eagle, seeing it was no use as long as she was too big to grab her hated daughter, returned exhausted to the mountain kingdom, her chest heaving and panting, and perched once again on the apex of her palatial mountain hut there in the off-limits kingdom of the Mountain Gods.

"The laughing falcon landed by her sweetheart, panting as well, exhausted, but turning herself back into a Goddess. They pushed frantically down the canyon toward Singing Boy's old village. Her belly had dropped and the child's birth became evident within the day as they got quite close to the village of safety.

"No sooner had hope risen in their hearts than the old Grandmother reappeared in the sky as a laughing falcon. To be certain not to allow the old woman to come to ground and kill them in her form as a Goddess, the Water-Skirted Beauty turned herself into a sparrow hawk, a kestrel who, because she was smaller yet but well-taloned and fierce as well could not be outmaneuvered by her mother in any way.

"An even harsher battle ensued in the overhead skies which came close to ending it all when the sharp black talons of the laughing falcon grasped at the belly of the fast-flying, striped-tailed kestrel, missing by the thickness of a flea's thought, the falcon clutching only tail feathers.

"Mother and daughter battled harder than hard, screaming all the while in shrill hateful shrieks that caused the world to shudder and fear. Feathers again dropped like snow but as the larger falcon could not gain a kill she retreated when her strength waned to regroup for a third attack.

"The kestrel mother dropped to her husband's side and turned back into a full, panting, Water-Skirted Beauty, who between sucking breaths spoke, '*La*', let's move fast for there is only one last battle left in me and after that the Old Mother will destroy us if we haven't arrived at your old village. One toe over the line will save us, husband. Let's go.' The young husband helped as he could but her belly kept dropping lower and lower as if any moment she would go into the labor of childbirth.

"Like tired ground-moving clouds they moved up and away from her rightful domain and entire life arriving at the very place they'd first come to know one another.

"Just then, as they came to the last steep drop before they could climb the last ridge above the lake, upon whose edge some miles further down the boy's village was planted, a loud scream could be heard overhead.

"Her mother had returned as a harpy eagle again, but when the daughter jumped into the battle as a laughing falcon the old woman turned into a falcon as well. By then, however, the swift, wind-riding daughter had become a kestrel, which then caused her mother to also become a noisy chittering kestrel, so now the daughter, in her last change permitted by the rules of the Gods, transformed into the fastest, smallest of all the fiercest birds. She became an iridescent hummingbird.

"The mother, who was also allowed only three changes, remained as a furious kestrel and took out after her shiny bee-sized daughter, sure to destroy her once and for all.

"The hummingbird didn't stay to fight and maneuver but headed down the opposite side of the ridge away from the lake, leaving the cool mountain air for a bank of muggy fog that rose off the coastal jungle.

"The kestrel, with her wings folded, raced faster than the speed of hate on the tail of the little metal-bird, the fleeing jewel, both of them slipping at deadly speed down a sluice of wind toward what both could hear as the roar of the Ocean as it pounded the shores of the Holy Earth.

"The young girl could hear the waves speaking a long ways off, growing louder by the second as she sped out of the fog to the open, glittering immensity of that angry salt Ocean.

"'*Ctjo yali, ctjo yaxtan.*'

"The Ocean spoke, every crashing breaker was a sentence into the girl's amazed ears, 'Quick, into my crashing arms, daughter-in-law, fly into my foaming arms, little girl. Into my salty arms, little mother of my grandchildren, into my watery arms, beloved of my son.'

"The Grandmother Ocean was as angry at Grandmother Growth as Grandmother Growth was at her daughter on account of the fact that Singing Boy, the Raggedy Boy, was her true son taken from her at birth in a harsh circumstance from before.

"But the girl was pursued; a split second more and she'd be all death and feathers, and with nothing left but her courage and the offer of the unknown Goddess of the Ocean, the beautiful hummingbird raced even faster with folded wings like a pin driven by a thumb and shot straight into the tallest wave beneath its foaming crest, entering at the speed of thought but leaving the opposite wall of the wave at a slightly slower speed, still airborne, a fate not shared by her larger raptor mother, who, right on her tail with talons out and wings extended, slid smack into the wave as it crashed over her deadly abusive head. She didn't drown or lose her way, but was stranded for quite a while as she floated glaring in rage, totally soaked, until she could climb exhausted to the shore and dry herself back into the Grandmother Growth.

"The hummingbird knew nothing of all this, for upon exiting the wave the hummingbird sweetheart flew a big loop and headed back to the mountain ridge where her weeping husband waited, frightened that she'd been destroyed.

"How long she sat panting or if she ever stopped before the birth began, no one can tell, but begin it did. Unwrapping her magical skirt she had her husband spread it well over the small new leafy twigs of the conifer trees, over which she lay propped up against the old Jaguar Tree, which can still be seen to this day.

"It was then the storms began, the water broke; the earth's rivers flooded, rains poured and lashed the world. Amidst thunder and the returning rain of mid-spring the Water-Skirted Beauty, wife of a simple man, struggled, breathed hard, pushed, rested and succeeded in giving birth to not one, but two little babies.

"One was ivory colored and the other amber colored; one was a girl and the other a tiny boy. Each of them shone so brightly in the dark nest of fog their mother had thrown around the family to hide them from the next coming of their angry grandmother, that their extraordinary beauty would have been unmistakable to anyone, much less their happy weeping father. Together, however, it would be understood that these translucent children with bright, jeweled eyes were not only Divine, but were destined to become the core reason humans would become people.

"The babies were held on their mother's breast waiting for all the juices to enter from their mother through the vine of the umbilicals.

"These babies were Najbey Jal, the first corn, the bright jeweled corn ancestors of all the corn that came thereafter.

"Corn had never existed before them. These half-human, half-Goddess children were the first of their kind and they shone just as all new corn does today when it first arrives in the village from the wilds where it is grown.

"And just like those corns of today these babies would have to be taken by the husband of the daughter of the Wild Mountain and Grandmother Growth to the village of humans.

"The Water-Skirted Beauty taught her beloved husband how to tie off the little umbilicus at their bellies, but then, when that was done, the new mother, the young Goddess, was still waiting to deliver what we call their souls, the placenta afterbirth. 'Husband, you must take these children of ours to safety in your old village, leaving me here. When you find women to care for our little babies, return here without delay with the men of your village and carry me to safety as well.'

"'But what if your mother comes while I'm gone?'

"'Then at least the corn twins, the little girl and the little boy, the sign of our having loved, will survive.

"'If you get there quickly then my mother will be bound by law not to kill me because the humans and I will be kin through the children, and she'll be kin as well.'

"'I'll carry you now and the children. We're only some five miles away. Come on,' and he leaned over to lift her, but she weighed as much as the earth itself and he wept, cursing his human weakness, frustrated as to what to do, so close were they to home and yet what could be done?

"'I can't move until the afterbirth is delivered and I have had a rest, otherwise I shall die that way instead, so run because if my mother catches us all our running, all my wisdom, all my battling, all your tasks and the challenges you have met, all our love will be lost to her hate, for surely she will kill all four of us without thinking. Go. Go. Go now quickly.'

"And caught between his frustrations, his love of one and then the other and lost to it all, he resolved to obey, understanding that he could make it back to fetch her. So, with a vision of living together forever, he picked up the beautiful corn babies and clutching them to his breast he kissed his magnificent wife, asking her forgiveness for all he'd caused her and for it all having come to leaving her alone in the bush in the fog in such an unbearable way.

"'Go' beloved husband, quickly, save the babies, but I tell you, please do not forget me. Don't forget me.'

"'How could I forget you, you are delirious, how could I ever forget you, Goddess, the one who gave me life, risked her own for me and the mother of our children, the people's corn? Of course I will never forget you.'

"'When you cross that boundary line between the village of people and the village of the spirits, that frontier between the human and the Divine, it will be very hard for you to remember me, your Divine wife from the land of the Gods. Look at your children and you will remember. Come and get me. Don't forget me, La´.' And loosening her warm coppery hand, she asked him to pull her skirt out from beneath her, which he did. At her demand he handed her the magic skirt which had saved his life and which now was full of all the fluids of birthing. Cutting and tearing the skirt with her teeth like a fox, she made small squares of the entire cloth.

"She then, with an incantation, breathed on the patches and threw them as far as she could and given her tenuous supine position and the exhaustion she experienced for all her struggles she did very well, for each piece landed at the base of the opposite hill. Where each landed, a hut formed, each a hut from Raggedy Boy's old village. Miraculously, within less than a half-mile the boy's lakeside village had appeared, even the surrounding volcanoes, everything brought well within his reach now.

"'This is the last thing I can do for you, so go, take the babies, don't forget, return and bring me home to your village with the men.'

"Assured now of his success as the village was so much closer, the relieved Singing Hunter rushed toward the village, arriving there quickly but quite out of breath.

"Though it was changed somewhat from how he remembered it, he recognized most of it and it wasn't long before people began to gather in great crowds to see what shiny unknown things he held bundled in his arms.

"The people of this skirt-village helped him find women with milk in their breasts, children of their own, who took his babies and began to nurse the hungry corn, the jewel-like babies of the wild mountain. And it wasn't long before some of the people recognized him and asked him how he'd come to survive out there in the dangerous wilds so long having gone there as a child, and how he'd come to be such a fine, handsome, able man, who was obviously a hero of some new sort who returned with the great gift of cultivated corn instead of the flesh of deer upon which up until now they had been singularly reliant, and in search of which he'd originally sallied forth.

"And when they asked him how he'd come by such Divine gifts as the white and yellow corn babies he almost remembered, but he was so thoroughly inoculated with human concerns that drink the shine and eat the flesh of the Divine which is the earth itself, and so quickly beguiled by the people's affection and his new-found acceptance in this place where he once fought dogs and vultures for scraps of rotten things that he was overwhelmed by normal human amnesia and like a dreamer who can't remember his dream of having breakfast with a God, the Singing Hunter couldn't recall what had actually happened to him and completely forgot the Water-Skirted Beauty, the mother of their children, who waited in vain for him to return to bring her home.

"He completely forgot. Like all of us do every day; he forgot her.

"The Singing Hunter, once called Raggedy Boy, grew in notoriety. As his beautiful children grew so grew his fame until he was universally called The Father of Our Food and looked up to in all matters of import. The Father of Our Food not only gained the home and respect he so longed for as a child but all the young women brought him food, wove him clothing and walked differently when he was in their presence. Some even accosted him flashing their eyes hoping someday to join with him or marry.

"Courteously handsome and manly in every way, he became such the model and ideal of what a man should be that all young men now looked to him as Raggedy had once looked to the young hunters returning with slain deer.

"For a year something nagged him but he could never grasp it. He spoke well in public and even then, as in private, all his conversations ended with, 'There was something more I wanted to tell you, but I can't recall it just now. When I think of it, I'll let you know.'

"He refused all the girls' advances every time they tried to corner him, making excuses about some vital responsibility he'd forgotten, then ostensibly running off to perform it.

"Though all his original desires would have been fulfilled, his reluctance to accept fame and comfort baffled the villagers, who eventually assumed his behavior was due to his saintly more-than-human abilities. He grew inexplicably more sorrowful by the day until he rarely went anywhere, forgetting to eat and living in a state of morose hopelessness until it looked as if he might die. Then one night he had a dream.

"In this dream he dreamt of Her, his beautiful Goddess, his beloved, the mother of his corn children. She caressed him and kissed him and they were so happy to see each other. The dream was real and it went on and on forever, it seemed, until sweating, full of fever, his eyes popped open in the pitch, black night and he remembered, remembered it all.

"He remembered how she'd been left all alone, incapacitated, to await his return before the angry mother Goddess found and killed her. He remembered how the beautiful girl had told him he would forget and how he had done exactly that.

"It all returned to him, crushing him like the landslide she'd saved him from, remembering how she'd risked the whole world of Gods and her own existence in the Spirit world to save him and their children and how he'd made big speeches and made up stories about how he'd rescued the little corn babies, as if he'd done it all himself, how he was a big hero, a human without the help of the spirit and while now he remembered in an instant of intolerable heart-biting grief, self-hate, rage and absolute sorrow he began scratching himself, yelling uncontrollably as loudly as a hero's voice can yell, crying out through the night:

"'*Ay Nutie*, my little mother.

"'*Ay Nutie*,

"'*Ay Nutie* ....

"'No, no, nooooooooooooooooooooo,'

until the entire village was awakened. Terrified and shaking in the dark, cold water rose out of his pores and ran off him like a hurricane rainstorm.

"A ragged, wrinkly, hunched over, ancient man and his equally patched and bent wife hobbled in on wear-worn iron-wood canes forcing their ways to the man's quaking side. Outside they'd left tracks in the village dust like land-bound crabs looking for the lake.

"They held him and listened and held him and listened until he began explaining in a confused babble what he'd seen and known and what had happened in those lost years in the other world after he'd gone searching for life.

"The old couple were in no way amazed or surprised but muttered to each other under the boy's tears and talk, 'It happens this way every year, doesn't it, honey?'

"'Yes, every year, it's always the same, isn't it, my little boy?'

"'Yes.'

"'Yes.'

"All of a sudden, in the middle of it all, while hundreds of villagers massed around his hut, the young man, Raggedy Boy, the Singing Hunter, the Father of Our Food jumped to his unstable feet and ran naked as best he could, fast and crazed into the dark whilst yelling Her name out at the sky, heading for the cliffs and canyons where he'd seen her last.

"Like a wild man, a sprinter, like a scared swallow, like a reckless jaguar chasing a deer, like a deer chased by a jaguar, the young man who remembered flew heedless of the pits, holes, boulders, stumps, thorns and trees in the dark, arriving cut and bruised at the spot where his beloved had lain, given birth to their children and thrown his village up against the wall opposite where it stands today.

"The old man and woman knew a quicker route to get back there and were already converging on the spot when the boy arrived, which would have surprised him had he not been blinded by the rawness of the grief and terror left underneath the skin of his forgetfulness, having now painfully molted off the truth.

"In the dimness of the pre-dawn he hunted the place like a mother cat searching for her drowned kittens, desperately pacing the ground, clawing up the leaf litter. Looking for any signs he called her name in piteous cries, a name to which no one could respond. Then the Sun Father crowned the horizon and in the clarity of the day the boy found a little something for his frenzied search.

"Blown and polished by the wind, washed pale by the rains, embedded there where his beloved wife had lain, the young man found one perfect canine tooth and one toe bone from her right foot, from the littlest toe at the tip.

"And knowing that that tooth had once smiled at him, having sat in the jaw of a Goddess over which words of love and words that saved his life had once ridden on her holy breath from a chest whose form was lost, gone into the earth, that man who forgot, that grief-crazed hero spent tears in a weeping that flowed longer than we have ways to measure. He'd forgotten and she was long gone, her bones scattered who knew where, her breath mixed into the winds. She was lost, rotted away and his heart was destroyed.

"With that precious tooth clutched into the mighty grip of his right hand and the toe bone from her suede-like foot, which had carried her across the wild mountain earth and guided him home twice, tightly closed in his left hand, he pounded the earth in hopeless anger, yelling and weeping: 'No, no, no, no, no, no, no, no, no, no, no, no, no, no, no, no...,' until he'd wept out all the water from his eyes, all the water from his body and cried out all the water of the world because the world that loved her wept through his eyes. Though the spot where his children had been born, where she'd been left and where he wept and pounded grew wet and soggy with grief, the world for having spent all its water on the same sorrow, dried up and a drought ensued that almost did the world in.

"Praying for the bliss of forgetfulness to cloak him in its numbness, the Singing Hunter, the Weeping Forgetter, would've killed himself but for the old couple who, almost drowning in their wrinkles for age and experience, held the boy rocking until he collapsed, muttering all the while and after, 'It's like this every year, ain't it, honey?'

"'Yes. Always the same every year, my little bird.'

"'Too bad it never works out; every year the same.'

"'If anyone could've done it, it would have been this fellow right here, don't you think? He really liked her and he's very determined.'

"'It's impossible. Besides, it's like this every year. No one ever succeeds in reassembling the Water Goddess and bringing her back to life. How could this boy do it?'

"'He doesn't need another source of sadness, another grief, another chance to lose her again. No matter what they say, he'll never be able to see her face again. Besides, it's like this every year, isn't it, honey?'

"'Yes, like this every year, little bird.'

"And on they rasped and mumbled until the young man, his head buried in his chest who until now barely listened, sat up shaking in the teary mud. 'Put her back together again? What do you mean, the same every year? Bring her back to life? See her face again? What do they say? Who says that and what are you talking about? No one has ever loved her before I have, she was mine, only mine.'

"Looking in different directions, their monkey-like blue-glazed eyes meeting in quick glances every couple of moments, the old couple tried to fend off the interrogation with ignorant stares, causing the boy to vent his desperation toward them instead of trying to kill himself.

"With nothing to live for, losing all his honor and any sense of good and bad, he grappled both the old man and the old woman by their wrist-sized, turtle-like necks and very nearly strangled them when he threw both of them up against his chest whilst continuing his demand for them to explain their reckless talk about his beloved for whom he wept and wanted to die.

"'True, true, you're right of course,' the old fellow croaked, moving his words expertly past the boy's massive howler-monkey grip which he now released to reward them for their undivided attention.

"Trying not to patronize the grief-crazed hero, the old woman attempted to explain. 'Of course, you probably know more about all of this than we do. What are we thinking by speaking such banana-brained non-sense?' she said, slapping her old husband with the back of her hand. 'We're just a couple of old opossums almost dead from drowning in our wrinkles, who chatter like birds drunk on fermented cherries, what do we know about anything? It's just a rumor, you know, that since this happens every year, that the Goddess is broken into pieces, that the right person could reassemble her if all her bones were gathered up, every single one. Then by arranging them in their original order and singing the songs, the right songs, they say ... but who knows? No one has ever succeeded in gathering up all the scattered bones.'

"'What happens if all the bones are gathered?' the boy blurted out impatiently.

"'By singing the ancient songs, the big songs, the 'jump up and live again songs,' the vine-rising, the tree-rising, magical word songs over the arranged and complete bones of your lost beloved, then they say she'd jump back to life, back together again, just like she was before you forgot her into pieces, before she was dismembered by your forgetting.'

"'That's what they say?'

"'Yup, yup, *hiach*. That's what they say, but of course that's impossible.'

"'Why, because of the songs? Who knows these songs?'

"'No, not because of the songs, we know all those songs by heart. That is no problem. What is so difficult is gathering up all the bones.

"'Considering what must be done to make the beloved Goddess of Water's face come back to life, the old man and I have always been of the opinion that this trick is impossible. No man has ever been strong enough or determined enough to go around gathering up her bones from where they've been dragged and scattered across the face of the Earth.'

"'I can do this, I must do it. I'm strong enough and if I die trying what's the difference? Wouldn't I be better off dead than alive without she whose death I've caused with my forgetfulness?'

"'That's very nice and brave the way you're thinking, boy, but you would have to find every tooth, every rib, all the tiny wrist bones, ankle bones, toe bones, finger bones, the skull, her vertebras, ulnas, tibias, every large and every small bone, so we, the old lady and I, could lay them out in order on the very ground where she was lost, the ground where your children were born. We would put the bones end to end in a skeleton and singing over them, call them to be refleshed and jump back to life. No. This is too difficult, child. Let it all go, her memory will fade again. You will learn to carry your sorrow, let's go home.'

"'I've got the strength, I've got what it takes, just tell me where these bones are and how to find them and I'll begin now.'

"With the assistance of the more hopeful young man, the old couple crawled up their canes on to their feet. Standing upright and waving before him the old lady spoke.

"'Every living thing has one bone of this magnificent woman, your beloved. Maybe this is hard to comprehend, but the bones of the Goddess whose face you so desperately desire to see alive again and for whom you claim to be willing to do anything to make that happen are scattered throughout the world and have become the most precious, life-giving relics, the personal possessions of each kind of tree, every plant. Others are with each kind of animal. The fish have many, the birds, the insects too. Every type of being has one hidden in some unknown place.

"'Since her scattering, all the Earth who loved her so when alive has scattered itself into private worship of her pieces, each piece giving every species, each plant, every speck of a being the life it now has and cherishes.

Why should they now want to give it up to you even if you claim to be able to bring her back? How will all the myriad beings believe you and how do you know you can do it? What you must learn if you are to even come close to achieving this challenge is how to court every living being on its own terms.

"'The boundary mouse would have its ceremony, food and procedure, the grebe a different way but just as intricate, the butterfly and then the ceiba tree. Before you even approach any of the things that lives, to ask it to hand over its piece of what you love, you must first be able to speak an eloquence that conveys your sincerity, as well as feed with words the soul of whom you approach. Every being would have one thing in common with you and that would be your grief and feeling of loss, your *biis* will bind you to the world's myriad things. But the diversity of all those beings makes it such that in order to approach them each must have its own particular gift, prayer and feast. Only then perhaps those beings you petition will acquiesce and give you their prize, the bone of she whom they covet. For them to trust you, you must make yourself trustworthy and in so doing make what you all so terribly miss, become what binds you. For in each of her bones the power of every plant and animal resides. The combined sum of all these powers form a complete world when they come together. Just as the sum of all her bones can bring her back to life. She must be re-membered, sung and spoken into view. If you are missing so much as a crumb of her she will not go back together.'

"A silence hung in the morning, the sun burned dull throughout the day.

"'So you see, to do this thing that you claim to have the strength and determination to fulfill, requires several years of study of the ritual approach to all the myriad things, to learn how to make and present the offerings that each being requires to exchange for the bone you are petitioning. Only after such learning could any such attempt be made. Even then the likelihood of finding your sweetheart is very distant indeed.'

"Every being on Earth has always wanted to see her re-membered back together in her original powerful form, but lacking that they would prefer to have a chunk of her, although this has been what has always kept her in a dispersed form as the myriad of things.

"Dropping dust on his head, the despondent boy now moaned, 'Where would I possibly find someone to teach me all these things? I know of no such person.'

"'Well, if you ask nicely we might agree to teach you, what do you say, old man?' But the old man had wandered off and was trying to dig up a huge forest root.

"'Old man!'

"'What?' the old guy shouted, looking in the wrong direction as only one of his ears could actually hear, the other ear reserved for another world. 'What's that you say?'

"'The boy wants us to teach him all the intricacies of giving gifts and rituals and approaching the trees and animals for the bones. What do you say, do you want to?'

"'It happens like this every year, doesn't it, honey? Sure, why not? It happens like this every year.'

"Though he'd cried out all the tears that were on the Earth and his body was set and willing to melt into the mud he'd made there with his weeping, the young man let the muddle-brained words of the old folks crack the hard husk of rage and self-hatred that had him still in seed, from which the first green blades of hope sprouted toward the warm possibility of seeing once again his deer-eyed, suede-necked, river-eyed Goddess. The reason for his life now became the memory of what had been and trying to reassemble what he now remembered propelled him into a feverish motion of learning and alertness much beyond anything seen before.

"He sought to establish what had been, never thinking that things could change, or that Chance and Chaos are the parents of the permanence our short lives misinterpret as Now. But all that aside, what this man moved toward was only made possible by the longing he had for what had been dismembered by his forgetting and in his effort to re-member Her, he learned things he never would have tried much less been able or aware.

"Every language of every thing, animal, plant and weather came through his lips. Every holy motion of his hands as he spoke raised the value of his prayer, oration and petition. Instead of learning the normal thievery of humans who mined the earth, enslaving plants and toppling trees, and pulling animals to their houses, Raggedy Boy learned neither to force what he wanted from the earth nor to accept only what was presented to him by lazy fate. There is no short way to say what he was doing, but in short what he did was learn to court the particular things of the world, both the hidden and the large. He fed their peculiarities with a uniqueness delicious unto each one, remembering each of them one by one to keep them whole, unlike the one he'd forgot. In this way he hoped to exchange what he gave to each particular thing and being in the world for a particular piece of what he had lost by forgetting Her. In this way he hoped to remember each particular piece of her into a remembered whole.

"Through a diligence powered by this grief and love, the young man learned how to praise, learned how to speak life-giving words whose depth in themselves were jewels enough, and to add to that he was taught to use his thumbs, his magnificent opposable thumbs. For between his thumbs and four strong fingers ornate gifts and ritual presents, each according to the desire of the being he would later address with the corresponding delicious breath of his well-worded throat, were formed.

"Because she whose presence makes life worth living was gone, time didn't exist for life to ride along on, so how long it took the grief-stricken boy in love to learn all the languages of all the things and beings around him cannot be measured or even known. Whether it was that immeasurable space of time or those unused muscles this learning caused him to use, no one can say, but by the time he emerged well-versed and able, with the infinite rituals of all things, the young man was more textured, much stronger, a little slower and had a distinct resemblance to a true adult.

"When the old couple were sure he'd learned how to court and could carry what he knew, they released the impatient poet-shaman-craftsman to the world where he promptly launched his campaign to gather every little piece of his beloved.

"The first animals who allowed him to approach were those very ones about whom he worried the most. These were the animals who liked to eat bones, those that fed on memories and because of this, this young prayer-maker went first to see the *kix wuuch'*, the thorn opossum or porcupine, then the *xq´e´ chóy*, the boundary mouse, then *nimchóy*, the wood rat, then the *kuk*, squirrel, then *bayh*, the gopher, the shrews, the voles, the moles, the possum, the monkeys, the kinkajous, the jaguars, the ocelots, the margay, the cougars, the jaguarundi, the cacomistle, the alligator, the fox, the crested magpie, the yellow bird, the eagles, the hawks, the motmot, the quetzal, the cotinga, the kingfisher, the curassow, the hummingbirds, the ant bears, the anteaters, the ants, sloths, butterflies, moths, the mushrooms, the cedar trees, the ocuy trees, the poplar trees, the ciebas, the fire flower, the jaguar tree, the bat tree, the oak trees, the balsa tree, the wild avocado, the jocote, the cacao, the *choreque*, the *clantun*, the *Tzantzuy*, the spruce, the pine, the amate, every tree, the lake reeds, until he had given all his eloquence, ritual, gifts and feasts to every single living being in the world, exchanging his poetry and the product of his hands for each bone of his beloved that each of them had kept secret and tidy.

"Taking no chances, the young man placed every gathered bone, both large and small, into a finely-woven net bag that he carried on his back, the burden strap running wide and sturdy over his hopeful, sweating forehead.

"And when he had gathered up what he considered to be the complete skeleton of his beloved, the boy, bent under the weight of all the bits and bones of her heavy memory squeaking and creaking on his back, trudged back to his teachers, the old man and the old woman.

"The able young man hoped to find the old folks present and immediately disposed to helping him arrange all the bones he'd gathered and bring his sweetheart back to life with the magic songs that only they seemed to know.

"However, upon his arrival at the spot where he'd left the Deer Eyed Girl years before, he found the old couple grunting and puffing, straining on their haunches opposite each other, struggling in vain to uproot a gigantic, turnip-like tuber of an enormous weed.

"Though he'd learned some graciousness and courtesy through all he'd done and been through, the young man having arrived tired and sweating and so delirious from years of hope was as impatient as a milk-stranded calf separated from his mother, so when the old couple continued their campaign for what seemed like a lesser cause, despite his standing there in obvious victory, having gathered up what the old folks had said couldn't be done, the boy blurted out in desperation: 'Please, *Tie´ n Ta´*, leave off with the root already. I've gathered all the bones of my beloved, can you put them together as you promised, can you bring her back to life?'

"The old couple gave the root one more concerted tug which ended in failure, each falling head over heels out on to the powdery drought-bitten earth. Righting themselves, catching their breath, the old people thumped out the dust, mumbling half to the root, 'It's like this every year, isn't it?'

"Then whispering thoughts and holy words they lifted the bone sack off the boy's back. After dumping the contents, which clinked to the ground in the most perfunctory way, the two wrinkled creatures bent and stumbled about dragging the big leg bone over here, cradling the tiny little wrist bones over there, planting a vertebrae here and a shoulder blade there. The dry basin of the girl's cranium was filled with the jaw, where stood her fine teeth that once spoke and ate.

"In a terrible moment when they'd almost finished, and the remains were lined up in a tumbled, fleshless abbreviation of the original girl that the boy had been waiting to embrace, she suddenly seemed so immense and remote.

"The painful sight of his forgetfulness blew through him like a bitter wind and the boy wept upon the bones, which he could only reflesh then in his heart with tormented memories of sweeter times.

"But the old people bit their lips and recounted the bones several times, yelling out to the boy, oblivious to his plight, 'It's not complete. There are still two bones missing: one left canine tooth and the smallest toe bone from the left foot. I thought you said you had them all and that you'd visited every living thing? What happened?'

"'This is not possible, I did not lose any of the bones and I went to every living thing. Except for Coyote, who said he hadn't taken any bones, every being gave me what they'd kept,' the bewildered boy replied.

"'You went to Coyote's place but he didn't give you anything?'

"'Yes, he said he didn't have any bones.'

"'No bones? That's ridiculous. Coyote has the other toe bone and the other tooth as well.

"'When you started out to gather up the bones you and Coyote were even, both of you with a toe bone in one fist and a tooth in the other, but none of the beings on Earth trusted Coyote enough to let him have the Deer Eyed Goddess. In his famous laziness, Coyote decided to let you go through the years of hard learning and do all the work of collecting all the pieces knowing that the world would give the bones to you. But now that you have all the bones, save his two, Coyote will try to get the gathered bones for himself. He'll try to reassemble your Goddess with the crazy songs he knows and put her back together for himself.'

"Spinning on a tail he didn't have, with goose bumps up his spine, the young man spat his words like a clench-jawed wild cat, 'Her memory is mine alone. We'll see about who gets what. Only I was her sweetheart. Together we did what we did. The gathering of her bones is my accomplishment alone.' Outraged, angry, jealous and trusting no one with what was left of his beloved Goddess, he buried the bones where no one could find them. He stomped off with a warrior's grudge to find gifts of the greatest worth and enchanting words to charm Coyote for what he lacked.

"And the old people said, 'They always say that, don't they? It's the same way every year, isn't it, honey?' and they went back to pulling on the root.

"For the last two bones the man made a furious study, learning how to make his face go in ways it didn't feel, turning his hatred into patience, hoping to seduce the rascal Coyote with the shimmer of his gifts and the empty praise of his words.

"Where his grief and longing had before driven him to the diligence of courting each and every being, with Coyote it became a war of wits driven by his jealous will and outrage.

"Forgetful in a new way still, unable to distinguish between his will and his original longing, the man only thought, 'If I do this right I will cause Coyote to hand over those lost precious bones of Her whose face I long to see.'

"When all the speeches had been practiced and the gifts perfectly prepared, the man trudged, bent under their immensity, into the territory of *Ajau Utiu*, Lord Coyote. It took him a while to get there as overloaded with gifts as he was, but when he came before the old dog this second time, Coyote was leaning back from the feast table picking his teeth, grunting, full bellied and burping with a grin.

"As he would before any God or regal thing, the young man dropped his load and fell instantly to his knees, clearing his throat in hopes of speaking first, but Coyote tyrannized the air before the boy could even squeak.

"'Well, well, well, if it isn't Mister Forgetful, the holy amnesiac, my little brother the nauseating hero come to fetch the last bits of what he wasn't man enough to keep alive the first time. As if I couldn't smell the hatred that bites hard with dull teeth on that tiny, naïve muscle you call a heart.'

"If the young man wanted Lord Coyote dead before, he wanted him burnt and blown to ashes now, but he knew what Coyote wanted most, like every scavenger, was to steal the hunter's kill, to drive the young man away from what both of them were after so as to steal everything for himself. For that Coyote needed the boy to lose, to be demoralized, to be distracted, to make him spin into confusion, to make unplanned reactions instead of thinking clearly so as to reveal in his rage the location of the bones the boy had prudently hidden and maybe even fall for any deal Lord Coyote might be peddling.

"But the young man kept his stirrups. Focusing on his mission, abandoning his pride for his longing, he replied in the most dignified and genteel regard, hoping in turn to mollify the crafty dog into giving him the two tiny missing bones.

"'Yesterday and the day before when I saw you, Lord Coyote, I thought the Sun had fallen from the sky and was wandering the Earth, but I was mistaken, it was really your shining face lighting up the world in ...'

"'Shut up, you forgetful imbecilic moron! Who do you think you're dealing with here? Do I look like another one of your stinking wood rats? Do you think I'm like a stupid goddamn fish? Can you really believe I care an ant's fart for all that mellifluous crap you spout, much less all your lousy meaningless gifts?

"'Little brother, let me tell you. You have absolutely nothing that I could want except that pitiful sack of bones you've spent your life groveling and cajoling all the world's fools to get. Don't you know who I am? I am your older brother. We are brothers, fool, brothers; we are brothers. Brothers. I mean we have the same mother, the same father. What do you mean by sloshing in here with all that trash on your back and holy bullshit gushing from your miserable throat? Don't you know who I am?'

"Utterly lost and dumbfounded, having never encountered such a creature, much less one that claimed to be his brother, the boy knelt in the tense silence, then announced in a tone designed to feign a confident familiarity while hiding the fear and sorrow of his startled hopes which now hung by the spider silk of his response:

"'Well, you are Lord Coyote ...'

"'Lord Coyote, Lord Coyote, Coyote, Coyote, Coyote, is that it? Listen you ignorant forgetful jerk, remember this at least, I am Coyote the Lord of Unforeseen Events, Coyote the Lord of Chance, the Lord of things that aren't supposed to happen, Coyote the Lord of Sudden Changes, the Lord of missed targets, the churner of the earth. I am the anomaly of every rule. I am Coyote, the Lord of Chaos.

"'When we were born, both of us abandoned, left to die on the ashpile of the world, no one would touch either of us. You were pitied; I was feared and avoided. You were born to forget, you the beautiful, holy amnesiac, the singer, the courter, the praiser, the lover, the lost boy. I, on the other hand, came into this world unable to forget. I am the memory of the Earth; I remember everything, chaos is my only relief.

"'I so long to forget, or like you struggle to find again what I must have already discovered, to slowly remember, reassemble some reoccurring lost, deeply nostalgic thing. If you gave me all the bones of the Goddess, the sweetheart whose parts you seek, then I, Coyote, Lord of Chaos, could bring her back to life with my never-forgetting power, I could very easily re-member her back into her flowering magnificence again and I, Lord of Chaos, could sink into her body and forget finally. In her arms I would be able to lose myself, forget and live in the relief of her overwhelming beauty that causes humans to lose sight and memory of the whole churning tumul-tuous mess whose every infinite, irritating detail, in my present state, I can never, ever forget.

"'If, little brother, you give her up to me I will promise that never again will chaos or unforeseen disaster ever plague the world.

"'If you hand over the bones, for eternity humans will be able to plan, no chaos will exist, no untowardness, no unforeseen things to mess up the world. Chaos will cease. The world's fate is in your hands, you have the power to eliminate chaos forever, only you.'

"Keeping his nerve, hiding the hurt in his chest, the boy spoke calmly as himself, in his own voice now, with his own thoughts, in a straightforward fashion, 'No, Lord Coyote, I only want the toe bone and the tooth of my beloved, nothing else. What do I have or what could make you give her toe bone and tooth to me?'

"'I want all her bones, the bones of her who could make me forget like you do, to posses the beauty you threw away by forgetting. You don't deserve her anyway. If you don't give me the bones, I'll kill you.'

"And telling the truth the boy yelled back, 'I'd rather die than live with-out her anyway, so kill me or give me her tooth and toe bone.'

As amazed as the boy was confused, Coyote whipped the air with his tail, which he then bit into, circled, then sang awhile, pondering.

"'Then there are only three possibilities, little brother.

"'First, you keep your incomplete bones and I remain with her sweet toe bone and tooth. Both of us can then long for her forever, never possessing her and the world goes on as it has with a little chaos, a lot of beauty and mostly forgetfulness.

"'Second possibility, you give me the bones. I bring her to life as my woman and the world is freed from all chaos.

"'The third deal, little brother, is that I give you the two bones you seem to have lost to me and then chaos will irrevocably be an eternal presence in the world on account of you.

"'That's it: you make the decision for every living being and all humanity forever. Take the bones, have your sweetheart and condemn the world to chaos forever or save the world.

"'Which will it be? You decide now.'

"Coyote laid the ivory-colored toe bone and the clear pearl of her eye-tooth on a dark rock in front of the tormented young man.

"Confused, impatient and confronted with so much news and eternal responsibility, the boy remembered the affectionate voice that once purled over that tooth of his lost sweetheart and he chose.

"He didn't choose to protect us or his children from chaos, but traded the welfare of the future to maybe see his beloved's face again, figuring in his calculating mind that if she could come alive again, she who was so powerful could rearrange all of this, renegotiate chaos and make things better in the world.

"So, with a care known only to those who have lost what they have loved and stood to regain it, the boy picked up the toe bone and the tooth, condemning us to the chaos we know life to contain.

"Running to the ledge beneath the tree under which he buried his dead sweetheart's bones, he dug them up and added the last two bones to her squeaking, creaking bones. With them clanking on his back, his own heart drumming in his chest, the young man toted this final and complete unassembled skeleton to the old man and the old woman who were still hard at the futile game of trying to pull up that huge unyielding root.

"Cursing and grunting, straining more adamantly than ever before, the old woman groaned, 'This thing is stuck in here harder than last year. What do you think, old man?'

"And the old man yelling at the root replied, 'How come you're in there so hard, you crazy, lusty old root?'

"Pacing up and around the old couple, the complete bones of his

beloved on his back, the boy watched his patience break the line of his politeness and in an exasperated tone, driven by his hope-lightened grief to see his sweetheart again, blurted out, 'Old Grandmother, Old Grandfather, here I come with the complete gathered bones of my beloved, every one of them. Maybe we could see if you could bring her back to life? Please?'

"The old timers looked up at him from where they squatted, beleaguering the gigantic old tuber. 'Could you please help us pull this root out?' they replied.

"'Forget the damned root please and let's put my wife, my Goddess, the mother of my children, my beloved who I forgot and now remember, back together. Let's re-member her out of her dismembered state, pleeeeeease,' the boy commanded and pleaded.

"Panting and sweating, sitting on their haunches just as still as threatened rabbits, they stared back at the desperate boy a bit, then both of the old people replied at the same moment, 'You've got all the bones, you say?'

"'Yes, old-time mother and father.'

"Knowing what that meant for the world, the old couple stared at the ground for a while in silence. The two dusty old people pulled each other up right onto their tottering knees and when they'd balanced themselves they begun talking to the expectant boy. 'You know, child, we are very old and because we are old, like you we are always forgetting things, overlooking certain details.'

"The boy knew that it is always a bad sign when old folks start out by saying such things.

"'We seem to have unintentionally neglected to tell you that even though you might have all the bones of your Goddess, of your beloved, in order to bring her back to life, in order to put her back together again, we need to have her heart. Without her heart we can't do it. Lucky enough your beloved's heart is still around. But I bet you can't guess who has it.'

"The young man, embarrassed by his decisions and chagrined by the naïve assumption that his challenges were over, blurted, 'Ah, Coyote has it, right? Why didn't you tell me before? I'll get it right now.'

"But the old lady grabbed the boy as he turned to leave and the old man spoke:

"'The heart of she who you miss so much and want to bring back to life and whose heart we need in order to do such as that is being held by the Lords of Death and Disease in the Underworld. We're sorry we forgot to tell you; you probably want to give up now.

"'Even if you wanted to and could make it to their Palace, it is unlikely that you could take anything there other than your life that they would exchange for her heart. Death is like that. Who would bring her heart back here for us to bring her alive, if you have been eaten by death? Who but you? Nobody makes it out of the Underworld in one piece. Nobody.

"'Anyway, it is now only her heart you lack. There are no bits left forgotten and if there was a way and her heart could be retrieved with all the bones we could in all probability bring that beautiful girl back to life. But you would need her heart and the Underworld has it.'

"Though no longer deterred by the probability of danger and accepting the fact that he would most likely fail, the young man knew as well that he couldn't live without her, without her heart, without her face; that her memory would kill him as sure as his forgetting had killed her and therefore this death in the Underworld trying to retrieve her heart would be little compared to living without trying, and on these terms of understanding the young man resolved to enter the Underworld.

"And like every time previous he asked the old man and the old woman what gifts, offerings, words and ritual understanding he should gather and learn in order to hedge his chances with the powerful Lords and Ladies of Death and Disease in the Underworld.

"'Speak to them as Kings and Queens, as royalty. Address them beautifully, slowly, sincerely and seriously. Any signs of faltering, self-doubt, weakness or insincerity on your part, they will see it and you'll be eaten as their offering; you will become their feast.

"'Take the finest tail feathers that shine from rare birds, trinkets of jade, amber, opals, gold and fat, for Death loves fat. Bring them tobacco, bring them resins that smell, bring them cacao...' the tally went on and on. The young man took great care to commit them all to his memory, which because of all his years of training to retrieve the bones, he was able to do.

"'Above all,' the old woman ended, 'you must receive a magnificent gift of uniqueness from every living being in the entire Earth. To every place you gave a gift to get a bone, you had better return and explain your intention of talking Death out of your beloved's heart. Beg for help from all the diverse beings of the world.'

"And so, the man who would see his dead wife again went to gather, carve, cut, sift, cast, braid, grow, dig, sweat, trade and beg for offerings for the Underworld, while practicing delicious and enchanting words for his journey to beguile Holy Death and Disease.

"Nothing in the world held back, every being of the Earth from every place that once held one of her bones now gave up to him their most beautiful fruit and finest parts of themselves as gifts to help the boy retrieve the heart of she whose pieces had caused them to thrive and flower to begin with. Everyone except Coyote, of course, because he didn't even ask him, recollecting that Lord Coyote's finest gift of Chaos had already been bestowed.

"The man grew accustomed to bearing the bones of his beloved with him on his back everywhere he went. All the years of sorrow, effort and learning he'd spent wandering the Earth to finally gather each bone into one single place, plus Coyote's promise of chaos, made it so the man would trust no one but himself to care for her fragments and kept them on his back to keep them close.

"When he'd finally joined together what he needed to descend into the Underworld the old man and old woman could hear him coming from miles away before he showed, like a caravan of mules with new saddles, loaded as he was with the enormous cargo of both her bones and Death's offerings grinding and squeaking so loud on his straining back that no human voice could be heard above it as he moved.

"When that day came for him to descend into the other world toward a certain death, in his attempt to bring back to life what he'd killed by forgetting, the man found that the old couple had made some progress in their unrelenting campaign to hoist that gigantic root out from the earth.

"Yet, despite their continued sweating, digging, grunting, cursing and pulling, they had only succeeded in loosening it a bit, the root refusing to come all the way out.

"And looking toward the man, as always, they implored, 'Son, could you please help us get this stubborn root out of the ground?'

"'In truth, old Grandmother, old Grandfather, I've come looking for you today to show me the entrance to the Underworld and the road towards the Lords of Death as we had agreed.'

"'That's good,' seemingly unconcerned, the old people replied, 'but could you please help us old folks pull out this blessed root?'

"The man laughed at the irony of his dependence on two senile lunatics, unnaturally focused on eating this monstrous root, while he was probably on his last day of life. Because of that irony and because he'd probably never see these two crazy wrinkled creatures again, who had been the only ones who'd really cared about him, and had never abandoned him during all his hardships, the man grabbed one of the tough exposed stems of the root and decided to help.

"In unison the three of them tugged and grunted on the jungle root until it tumbled out on the ground like a huge sweet potato the size and general shape of a human.

"It took all three of them to hold it up by its leaves off the ground. Long rootlets dangled off of it. Attached to them like nodes or berries entire constellations of stars twinkled, hanging there like galaxies off the root.

"So entranced was he by this root of stars that the old man had to grab the man's head and point his nose into the root's old hole, saying, 'Look into the hole, son,' as he did so.

"Lying on his belly, while sticking his head inside the great hole, the man peered into what he saw was another world, a world in which he was in the sky. The roots of all the trees and plants dangling down into that dark world all held stars in them as well. What looked like firm earth to us where we walk and live was the topside of the sky to the world below.

"'This root's hole is the doorway to the Underworld into which you say you are ready to descend.

"'Do what you can in that hard place, son, to retrieve the heart of she who has given you life and for whom you live. Do your best.

"'In that Underworld all directions lead to the Lords of Death, so no matter which way you descend you'll end up at their bench.

"'Just keep trotting until you get there. The sky will darken and the stars will disappear. Just keep moving. Then the road will cease to be solid and there will be no up nor down, no left nor right, no forward or backwards, only you and not you, just keep moving. All sound will cease. You will hear nothing and will also be unable to make any sound. Just keep moving, more and more until you begin to smell something. Then you'll see some dull glow in the dark, these are their cigars, meaning you've arrived at the feet of the Lords and Ladies of Death. Though they are only sparks and smells to you, address them beautifully as you've been taught and if they find your speech to their taste, they'll show themselves and their world to you.

"'Try to trade your most delicious speech and beautiful gifts for the heart of your beloved. The Big Deaths are magnificent, noble and go by the rules. But their children, the Little Deaths, though not as powerful, are many and hungry and are a law unto themselves. They are the ones you must watch out for. They'll take you down bite by bite.

"'If, as unlikely as it is, Death does return the heart to you, you must leave the gifts, turn and move away from Death toward this little hole which, after you've passed again through the land of silence and darkness, will appear as the morning star in the sky of that place and toward which you must move. The old woman and I will wait right here for you, remembering you, ready to pull you out of there like this root and back into our world if you somehow make it home to this blessed hole.'

"With the young man kneeling, loaded up and ready to descend into the door of the Underworld sky the old couple prayed over him and blessed him.

"They lowered him feet first into the hole where the star root once grew and just as his head was about to disappear something grabbed his top knot and powerfully jerked him back up out of the ground a bit, just enough to free his arms. Strutting and panting, out of nowhere it was Lord Coyote come to detain him a moment.

"'I am glad I caught up with you,' Coyote spoke. 'Why didn't you come to my place when you were gathering offerings to descend into the Underworld? Why did you avoid me, little brother?

"'I've been waiting a long time to give you these,' and handing the man four shiny knuckle bones, shiny from continued use, Coyote, Lord of chaos, chance and unforeseen events, sang out his message through his fancy inlaid teeth.

"'A bone from each paw of the long-dead Wind Jaguar; when tossed together on the ground they are gambling dice. The Lords of Death obey only one power greater than themselves and that is Chance. Because the Lords and Ladies of Death and Disease are addicted to gambling, people, animals, moments, plants and things die when and how they do, not by plan but by chance, at their moment appointed by the dice roll.

"'If the Lords of Death defeat you and all your ritual attempts at exchanging your gifts and prayers for the Water Goddess's heart, then before they can move on you, tempt them with a gambling game using these dice. They cannot refuse. They are crazy for gambling.

"'For stakes, play only for the heart, against your gifts and your life. Throw one time only, throw hard and throw true.

"'It's unlikely that you will win, but if you do, leave the Deaths with the gifts to keep them busy and hurry home with the heart.

"'Never, ever, ever, ever look behind you as you move away from Death. No matter what taps you on the shoulder, calls your name or gnashes its teeth while moving towards you from behind, you mustn't turn around or look back, for then you shall lose the heart and yourself and never return to us again. You would remain in the Underworld, forever consumed by Death or eternally moving toward it.'

"The man thanked the Lord of Chaos and tucked the four narrow, ancient yellow bones into his belly sash.

"Then the three of them, with Coyote helping, let Raggedy Boy into the root hole, down into the Underworld past its roof of roots and stars on to a journey toward Death to retrieve the heart of his dismembered sweetheart, the Goddess of Earth's Water.

"What was strange was that it didn't strike him as strange that he was walking down the inside of the Underworld sky; that it seemed not only natural but familiar as well.

"When he hit the road on what would be the earth of the Underworld, he did think it a bit odd that there were spacious flocks of birds whose twitterings and cries rose and fell as their swirling flight swelled and scattered.

"As he trudged on with the bones of his beloved creaking on his back, eventually the place dimmed and soon there were no roads or trails.

"It was not until the creaking stopped and the birds' voices disappeared that the darkness reached a density of sap where there was no up or down, no forward and no behind. He moved hard and fast but he couldn't see any part of himself, so he felt like he flew at the speed of light backwards, though he kept his limbs moving in the direction his concentration tried to tell him was forward.

"He yelled with all his strength but there was no sound of air rushing into his lungs and not a peep coming out of the force of his yell. He yelled and screamed, always moving, as terror began to creep over him.

"All was darkness, all was silence as he trudged on with nothing solid underfoot, not sure if he was actually moving in the Underworld or if he was already dead.

"Almost mad and lost in this prison of nothingness, he remembered his loneliness and terror during his first night lost in the forest and how he sang his way till dawn. Remembering the song he'd made at the first moment he met her whose heart now brought him to this place, he started to sing.

"Searching for his heartbeat to have a cadence against which to sing and unable to find it, he remembered it and began to remember singing the song.

"Though no sound issued from his lips or thundered in his chest, the song he sang he imagined inside his own heartbeat and his imagination could hear it, though silence swallowed all else.

By way of the singing inside himself, his mind was able to be carried on the tune straight toward where the rest of him was headed.

"It was this song for his beloved that kept him alive and moving toward her heart and the Lords of Death who live deep in the Underworld, without losing himself in its perfect oblivion.

"No one could say how many centuries took place or how many years, weeks or months went by in this same tiresome way of anxious walking in place through an immeasurable oblivion to the rhythm of his silent song before he began to smell the rank, skunk-like, odiferous smoke of Death's tobacco and feel the over-heavy bones of his beloved once again creaking loudly on his callused back, but when he did, it wasn't long before in the still thickness of that dark world he could just make out an erratic field of dull yellow stars or maybe sparkling embers stretched out forever in the dark, away from him, in front of his face.

"Supposing them to be the *Q'aq'al*, or fire souls of Death, the long, smoking cigars of Death, the man stopped and stood to address them as the royal beings we know them to be, but in the instant that his movement ceased, the lights disappeared and he had to walk a long, long time again through utter darkness until the smell of Death's dull lights did reappear. This time he kept walking, speaking past the loud creaking of all the heavy gifts and bones loaded upon his back, past his panting, past the song cut deep into the rhythm of his walk. Past all this he addressed the immense ocean of smoke and starry embers rising out for miles before his forward movement.

"It was only then they let themselves be seen, but so startled was he by the immensity of this village of Eternity, whose handsome, ornately dressed Gods and Goddesses of Death stood not two feet in front of him with bands of tiny carved bells of gold tied beneath their knees and above their graceful elbows, whose company stretched out forever away from him in an endless entourage of murky wonder, that the man forgot to move. Again, darkness and silence in its pitchy fog of utter nothing oozed in around the man and again it was a long time of exhaustive walking until the Ladies and Lords of Death reappeared upon the issue of his loud prayers over the din of his shouldered load.

"While maintaining his stride and beautiful harangue though somehow not moving forward he arrived at the part of his address to the wild and noble gathering before him, where he called them, 'You, the never-withering-flowering trunk of all that lives, you the jade tooth of the great feast, you the makers of humus wherein sprouts the face of Day, you the undreamt dream of abundance too big to carry, I come at your feet and at your arms, at your roots and your branches...'

"At this point the whole Underworld began to quake and roar with waves of deafening cheers rolling back across the gathered village of eternity, back forever, disappearing beyond what he could ever hear. Death and sickness, feeling fed and feasted somehow by his words, told the man as such that since his words had now been heard by the present Lords, ancestors of the ancestors of Death and Sickness, whose origination point had now been addressed, that now because of that the man could stop his incessant walking because he'd finally arrived where he was headed.

"Though clear-faced and pleasant and covered in polished jade, glowing gold and the best *pot, uk, pas* and *qu´*, these Lords and Ladies of Death were parents to some very ugly, tough-looking, howling children called 'Little Deaths', who were unruly, hungry, sharp-toothed creatures who kept leaping past the stretched-out lines of Big Deaths to eat the young man, his gifts and the bones of his beloved.

"Raggedy Man tried to beat them off, but it was their parents who finally quelled them, pulling them back like dogs by their copper collars.

"'Is it true what we've heard that you, the child of Thunder and Ocean, little brother of Coyote, the chooser of Chaos, have come here to find the Heart of the Mother Waters, the Goddess of all living things? Is it true then that you, the Ashpile Boy, the Crooked Bow Boy, The Singing Boy, the Father of Corn, comes here seeking the Heart of your beloved, whom you forgot for having become a hero to the humans, thereby abandoning what you loved, causing her to be scattered and dismembered? Is it true that you, after having gathered all her delicious bones, have come here to talk us into giving you her heart so you can reassemble with her bones what you couldn't do with your memory? What does your heart say?'

"'*Ctzij ni bi xix*, it is a true thing you say, Lords and Ladies of this world, true that I've come at your roots and your branches in hopes to sprout at your feet and flower in your arms, you ...' and speaking both deliciously and well for what may have been a long time, he tried to make Death drunk on his traditional speech and when it seemed to have done so the man began speaking his heart.

The Toe Bone and the Tooth

"He ended in the best Mayan way, by coming to his point not until the very end of his eloquent petition:

"'You, Lords and Ladies, I've come to trade you for the heart of my beloved, the Goddess of Water, whom I indeed forgot and now want to remember back to life. Here are the shimmering feathers of rare birds made into capes, boxes and headpieces, polished jade, golden bells, resined face paints, body rollers, chocolate, fat of every animal and plant, flowers, incense resin, liquors of five kinds, female tobacco, male tobacco. Every living being has sent a piece of themselves to you, Death, with the promise of rituals and food for all of you, yearly, forever.'

"Death and Sickness liked to huddle, and huddle they did, drawing into an infinite knot away from the man where after a lot of listening and waving of arms, they unfurled again into Death's endless troop.

"The oldest of those aristocrats up in front blurted out, 'Why don't we take all the bones and we can put her back together? You leave all your gifts here with us and we'll let you go back to your beloved Earth with your life. There's never been such a good deal, if you ask us. What do you say, friend?'

"'That's very nice of you to make such a generous offer, but the truth is I would rather die than live without my beloved, so I think the best deal for all of us is for you to take my original offer. Plus, if you give me back her heart I'm sure if we can bring her back to life on the Earth, she will think of something more wonderful than any of us can imagine to send you Lords and Ladies.'

"'We understand your situation and though we are not normally accustomed to making deals with the living, because now we have her heart we have become strangely ornate and imaginative. So, why don't we take all the bones of your beloved off your back and you let us put her back together? After all, we have her heart. You give us all the gifts, which we will agree to like, and then you can live together here with your beloved as one of us. What do you say, friend?'

"'That would be pretty good, I suppose,' the man replied, trying not to anger them, 'but then wouldn't we both actually be dead, living in the land of the Dead? I want to live in the world of the living with my beloved.'

"At that the Deaths huddled up again and when they'd finished their palaver, one of the old Lady Deaths spoke:

The Story

"'Well, good, then,' the Deaths seemed to agree, 'if you'd rather die than live without her, then we can arrange that, plus we could eat her delicious bones for our feast, eat you, your offerings and be done with the whole mess and everyone's happy. After all, this is our world and we do what we please. Here we have no obligation to parlay with you.'

"And in that instant, several of the sharp-teethed offspring of Death broke the line and leapt onto the man with hundreds more in pursuit. But before they could sink any of their gnashing tusks into his flesh, the man had spun around, having withdrawn Coyote's gift of the four jaguar-finger bone dice out of the folds in his sash and holding them aloft, yelled, 'You mean to say you eat before you gamble, you decide before you roll the dice?'

"At hearing what the man had bellowed over the din of Death's hungry children, the world of Death withdrew and stood drooling and shivering in their steps, waiting to hear more about what none of them could resist.

"'I'll roll my jaguar knuckles, my four dice, for the heart. A game of chance I have. Are any willing? I challenge you, Ladies and Lords of Death, to gamble for the heart. What do you say?'

"They more or less forgot about killing him. Big grins took over their faces as the entire Underworld drifted into a collective delirium of feverish anticipation that once again resulted in a massive and writhing huddle, where all the jade did click and the bells jingled as they shook.

"After emerging from their excited throng, the head Lady and Lord of Death inquired of the man on behalf of the Underworld, 'What are the stakes, Boy?'

"'I'll play only for my beloved's heart. I will roll the dice one time only. Out of five possible outcomes only one represents the heart. One up is a tail, two up is a hind paw, three up is a front paw, four up is the head; if any of these I roll, you kill me, take the gifts, take the bones of my beloved and that's the end of the game. If, however, in my one and only roll I throw four down, this represents a five and means I've rolled the heart, and if this happens I will leave you with the world's gifts and you will then allow me to leave with the heart, the bones and my life to find my way back to the Earth. Either way, you keep the gifts.'

They jumped back into a huddle and when their representatives emerged, the Deaths sighed and spoke, 'It seems that the odds are slanted more toward you, but we'll agree to your terms.'

"The Underworld roared in excitement as the Lords of Death, trembling, spread out a great old worn jaguar gambling skin in front of them.

"Like any gambling villager the man knelt and prayed aloud to *Ixoq Juo*, the Goddess of Five, the patroness of all gambling.

"'That's cheating,' yelled some of the Little Deaths, but the adults just ignored them.

"Breathing on the bones in his folded hands, the man spun around, rising to a standing position and dropped all four bones off his shoulder, letting them roll down his left arm, over his palm, to tumble onto the jaguar skin one at a time.

"One down, two down, three down, and four ...

"Down. Four down, representing five or the heart. The boy had won.

"The Lords of Death couldn't believe it. Raggedy Boy had won against the Underworld with the gifts from the Lord of Chaos.

"'Two out of three, two out of three,' screamed a mob of Little Deaths, but the Lords and Ladies kept their agreement and when the man asked for the heart of his beloved, two dwarf-like Death women from another time came tottering forward from deep within the crowd with the Goddess's heart wrapped and neatly knotted inside a red cloth.

"He made his farewell speech, keeping it short but well spoken. Removing the gifts from his back, thus considerably lightening his load, the man kissed and breathed on the heart of his beloved and placed it inside his *joron cotón*, next to his own heart.

"With the rest of her bones loaded on his back, squeaking as ever but now in a more hopeful way, the man commenced walking straight out of the Underworld, toward life and the living Earth.

"As soon as he'd lost the sound of Death and the stench of its tobacco, the man began to race toward home, knowing full well that the Lords of Disease, Death and Decay obey nothing but chance and chance could change their minds about killing him and come running in pursuit.

"Clutching his beloved's heart over his own heart, he ran and ran, again singing his way through the Underworld until he'd cleared that immense barrier of emptiness and darkness, racing toward the entrance of the Underworld where he hoped the old couple would be ready and waiting to pull him up and out of Death's land by way of the old star root hole.

"He could see the hole already, it was like the morning star in the sky upon whose road he was almost running up, when he heard screams and the determined thumping of something coming upon him from behind.

"Having been forewarned, he dared not look back and he didn't look down, but kept climbing the Underworld sky. But these were the children of Deaths, the Little Deaths, who came clawing after him to rip his calves and thighs, hoping to pull him down, kill him and devour him.

"Soon they'd have killed him for certain, for so many of the little demons had their talons in him and were hanging on his back that he could hardly move, with more arriving by the second, but still he didn't look down, he didn't look back and kept climbing toward the little light.

"In the desperate thinking that desperate moments sometimes produce and always demand, the man, in order to save the heart and himself, grabbed a rib of his beloved out of the net and without looking back tossed it over his head, behind him aways, and in that instant all the Little Deaths left him for the moment it took them to jump onto the bone, fighting like voracious dogs and snarling over it until one succeeded to run away with it back into the Underworld.

"This gave the man a little time to continue running toward the hole, but soon Little Deaths were on him again, even more than ever. Every time they came they took a little chunk out of the poor man and to keep moving he was forced to keep throwing her bones over his shoulder in increasing amounts, getting just barely ahead of them each time.

"But he didn't look down and he didn't look back, he just continued running and pushing furiously toward that door of the Underworld, throwing bone after bone, his load getting lighter and lighter as he neared the world of the living, but there was less and less of him left to carry the lighter load for all the pieces bit out of him by the swarms of Little Deaths.

"He could see the hole close now, barely able to move, but with the heart still clutched to his chest he heard the yelling of the old couple frantically urging him to hurry up and extend an arm so they could grab him.

"Down from the hole in Death's sky out of the living world's Earth ten hands descended grabbing the half dead man up and out of that place onto the solid ground of the day and light world of this beautiful Earth, just as the last Little Deaths were coming to pull him finally back into the Underworld.

"The man was finished; the grief of losing all her bones again had been too deep for him. The cuts of Little Deaths had been too many and too vital. He had wanted to die anyway, knowing full well that he would now never see his beloved again.

"The old man and the old woman wept upon him for some hours. 'Well, it's like this every year, isn't it, honey?'

"'Yes, it's the same every year.'

"But the sound of another weeping raised a deeper wail, for looking up, Grandmother Growth and the God of the Mountain stood there with them, weeping in remorse because now they realized that because of their clannish prejudice they had not only pushed their Holy Daughter into a world where she was invisible and broken into pieces, but now the father of their grandchildren, whose undying love and willingness in his heroic attempt to bring their daughter back had failed, lay perished on the earth before them.

"In this very place where the poor lifeless man now lay, the same place where he'd descended and returned from the Underworld, this very place where he'd found her toe bone and her tooth and pounded the earth to dust in self-disgust and wept out all the water of the Earth was the same place where his children of corn had come into life, born from their lost mother.

"It was there, after a long while, after the Goddess of Growth and the God of the Mountain, the old man and the old woman were pretty much spent in grief, that Lord Coyote was seen sitting quietly, opening his dead brother's tightly clenched fists.

"In the left hand was one of the lost woman's teeth and a little toe bone and in the right he'd clutched another toe bone and a tooth. From the man's *joron coton*, his shirt, he removed her beautifully-wrapped heart. In the man's sash he found the four jaguar knucklebones, which Lord Coyote tucked into his own.

"'Grandmother Growth, Father of the Mountain, Old Man, Old Woman,' Coyote sang out in a dignified tone, 'What would happen if the five of us tried to bring her back with just four of her bones and your daughter's heart? What would happen if all five of us tried to bring back alive this poor man with what death has left him?'

"There in this very place upon that holy Earth they laid the poor boy and next to him they arranged the four bones of the girl around her heart, after which the old couple, the two Gods and the Lord of Chaos wept upon them both. Grandmother Growth took off her wild serpent skirt like the one her daughter tore to save her children and spread it over what was left of their daughter and her man.

"The world wept and whimpered in the ground while two Gods and two old humans sang the ancient life-giving songs and Coyote did unknown things, spoke words that no one understood and remembered any detail the others might forget.

"After some two hundred songs something began to move under the skirt, but they kept singing and doing the magical things that each knew how to do, hoping in their teary eyes that what was moving would continue to form and swell from the combined efforts of Gods and humans, whose grief and affection for a common thing under the direction of chaos and Coyote's old animal magic could make something come alive.

"Working together in their separate ways, they kept it up until all the songs had been sung.

"It was then after a little patient waiting that a sound like a single migrating crane sighed from under the cloth, followed by the snortling grunt of a peccary swearing.

"Not daring to guess to whom or what those voices might belong, the five of them stood silently gazing in the most steadfast way at the large human-looking forms fidgeting about underneath the skirt of Grandmother Growth.

"The old woman said, 'It happens like this every year, doesn't it, my man?'

"'Yes, year after year, that's the way it always happens, my little girl.'

"Surely, but very slowly, like the rising of a fog or the coming of dawn, the turning of a season or the gradual sprouting of corn, the old man and the old woman pulled the skirt of Grandmother Growth up and away from the earth to reveal what had happened underneath.

"What was there, sitting up and chatting to the other, was an ordinary woman of great beauty, not a Goddess, but a beautiful ordinary human woman who had to eat, who dreamt, who had changing, outlandish opinions, loved life, loved her children, failed a lot, made mistakes, felt guilty, argued, lied on occasion, knew pain and longing and lived her life. Though an ordinary woman, she definitely smiled like a Goddess because she had two of the Goddess' teeth. She could move a little like a Goddess because her feet had two toe bones from the Divine Woman. And she had the wild, unfathomable heart of the Divine Girl, but just like the man who now sat beside her, the rest of her was much smaller and frailer, capable of fear and cowardice, destined to die, and above all didn't remember everything about how she came to be.

"The man who sat beside her, once the orphaned child of Thunder and the Ocean Goddess, Raggedy Boy, the shunned resident of ashpiles and the hero of the Underworld, was now an ordinary man who could no longer remember much of what he'd been, for so much had been eaten off his back and scarred by the Underworld that now he was a regular man who, as he looked around at the Flowering Earth who is the Goddess Dismembered, he could almost remember what he'd lost, but instead he saw only what he loved in the eyes of this ordinary woman.

"And from these two holy amnesiacs, my people are descended.

"But Coyote could never forget."

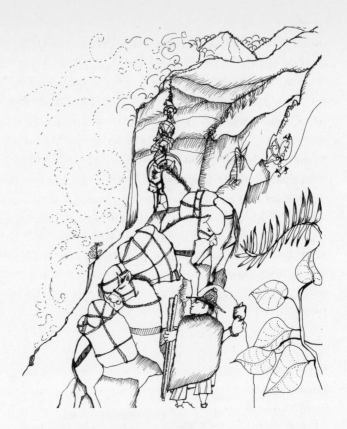

A MAGICAL
IN-BETWEEN AGE

ll the world and every God wept when Swordfighter left off the tale.

The Story had been the story of the God of the Mountain and Grandmother Growth and it had been their own daughter who'd been taken to the humans, lost and lost again.

Because all the humans in Swordfighter's village were descended from their daughter and that man and because one never knows how the puppies in a litter will turn out, Swordfighter had been born with their long-dead daughter's nose and had the look of that crazy, longing orphan boy from a previous millennium. For this reason all the long-living Gods of all the natural world felt that Swordfighter was a living human visit from a piece of the beloved Divine Girl and the orphan.

The daughter now lived on in everything distributed but came together only as gathered water and the telling of the story made that water flow, made the world weep, made the Divine weep and it was this grief, the annual weeping of the Gods, that somehow kept their lost holy canyon world alive, kept the thickets green and the rivers rushing and the fog lowering to hide the animals that climbed, dug, ran, bounced, grazed, hunted and dreamt.

Swordfighter could never remember how long he wept with the Gods, or how much longer he spent with them inside their mountain place, but he woke up slowly one morning outside of it having his ears cleaned by some tiny jungle fish, as he, the Swordfighter, lay floating face up in a murky, mud-filled pond with only his forehead, eyes and lips protruding from the puddle.

At the bottom of a canyon, steaming and filled with vine-covered spaghetti-rooted *pataxte* trees, it had been the strange undulations of the frogs' puff-throated din translated underwater which, while he slept, he could still understand as the speech of one of his Rain God stick masters in the hill, that now roused him from his sleep into his new life.

Though the puddle was shallow, brackish and warm, in front of him, from the magical line where the vertical cliff wall of layered stone, knee-like roots of trees and *calawala* leaves loomed out of the pond, a reflection radiated toward the Swordfighter, who looked like a mud creature when he sat up in its midst, still holding the two smooth rippled ironwood sticks for which he would be known among the humans.

He never told anyone what happened after that, how long he wandered in the forest, or if he did at all, or if he was lost or knew where he was right away, but much later when he did finally enter the village again, he entered from the south on the *xejuyu´* trail driving an immensely long string of golden-nosed, chestnut-colored pack mules, loaded up with trade boxes, packs and nets full of rare blue bottles, silver money, salt, bound live iguanas, chairs, hand-carved chests, cinnamon, chocolate, bundles of machetes, grinding stones, dried peccary meat, yellow die bark, indigo, a ton of dried corn, an unreadable book and two small bottles of rosewater.

Most important of all was the fact that when he returned to the village the rains resumed and within a year the crops began to trickle in and within a couple of years the villagers were full bellied again, as full bellied as they'd ever get anyway.

With the return of the water, the bandits had disappeared as well.

Bad enough when starving and much worse when they are fat, villages are places where wonder and resentment often breed, giving birth to large litters of gossip, from which strange accounts of every color and possible perversity are carefully raised beneath lifted eyebrows and fed in mealtime side-mouthed whispers until, too fat to stay inside, they leave leaping and creeping like mice from hut to hut, mating and birthing again, the great-grandchildren of the slander finally meeting each other coming around opposite ends of the town, so diversely evolved beyond their humble prehistoric origination as to be mutually unrecognizable as having descended from the same ancestors, but who in turn are adopted by the rumor-mongers who divide and feud violently about which of them should be considered truth.

In this time of renewed abundance, rumor had it as truth that the Swordfighter had actually become a bandit himself during his long absence, which, of course, explained to the less courageous, the cruel and the envious how he came by so much wealth; especially since a certain amount of what came on the backs of his mules were things certain villagers claimed their relatives had traded for in the past, relatives who could no longer corroborate this since they had died at the hands of the bandits one of which Swordfighter was now whisperingly accused of being.

This envy-born opinion ran rampant throughout the town until several scattered coastal Tzutujil merchants from Cunen began straggling up through the now bandit-free trails, camping in the courtyards of acquaintances on the way to higher mountains in search of cattle to bring to the coast to butcher and sell the meat for profit.

On the coast the story ran that a wild jungle man jumping from trees and boulders had driven the bandits from the trails and hills, shattering their machetes, their swords and muskets with a couple of regular merchants' walking sticks. He didn't always kill the bandits, but for the few he did, he dispatched them with his sticks, confiscating in every case all their goods which he then loaded onto their stolen pack animals and hid no one knew where.

To the coastal folk, the Mayans of the heated piedmont zone, this man was none other than the Swordfighter, who was now forced to tell his story, which soon everybody knew but only his family had the right to tell, and whose grandson didn't want to hear.

Many of the people had seen his sticks; some of us had even held them. He was a hero to us all and like Chiviliu, Francisco Sojuel and a few others, he was the last occurrence of a magical breed that had always returned in times of need.

A strange magical in-between age began with the disappearance of the bandits throughout which the Swordfighter lived peacefully in the town. He lived a long time and when he died, the modern age began. He was buried with his sticks and still had his bristly anteater hair and no one living had ever seen him eat.

ON THE ASHPILE

Towards the lake of our Mother Waters, a mile or so around and away from the cinder-tempered clay of Nishti´ in which we buried Swordfighter, perched the present permutation of the Tzutujil Village of Santiago Atitlan, whose dense maze of meandering, hut-studded, tree-lined basaltic walls, walkways and the moody crowds of chattering people that filled them, became for me what the village of the Daughter of the Mountain God and Grandmother Growth had been for Raggedy Boy.

If you dug into that village floor between Panaj and Xechivoy, beneath the layer of exposed volcanic cinder that held up the cut-stone base, which in turn held up the cornstalk upper walls, smoky beams and thatch of what would someday become my hut, after only a hand's width of depth you would come upon a layer of potsherds, old animal bones and thick white ash.

This had once been the northern refuse pile of the now invisible "Deer Village" upon which Raggedy Boy, centuries and millennia before, had fought off the adroit and ragged, multicolored, starving street dogs for scraps of food, of a kind that the villagers still eat, to feed himself and his old adopted mother, blind Ya Sar.

It was the tangible memory in this original layer of ashes and stories that formed the cultural humus in which the village of Santiago Atitlan of the 1970s was rooted, and upon whose mythological vine the people's everyday life flowered like a dusty living hand that would, in my very early twenties, finally hold my heart.

On this exact spot, where my little family had its home overlooking the Mother Lake, whose stony shore ran just below this ancient ridge of ashes, there once stood in those fragrant days a large and famous *amate*, or paper tree. Figuring in many stories as the place where magical individuals throughout the cycles of Mayan time were washed ashore as babies in gourds, or found loudly wailing in the mud, everyone of the town of thirty-thousand was aware of where this fabled paper tree stood, growing out from under a thick, flat, polished boulder that lay mostly in the water but a little bit on land.

From our huts upon the ridge we used to watch the young men of the village roll their one-legged friend, Mazuuts, or Cloudman, from that same flat rock to watch him swim off like an otter.

Once out a-ways he'd always scream back in ecstasy with vicious taunts to the rest of us two-legged fools who jumped, wept and cheered to see the miracle of his graceful power, his ability and the enormous distance he could go once unfettered in that liquid turquoise, whereas on land his whole existence was gravity's call and a hardship on his shoulders.

The boulder from where they launched their friend the Cloudman was known by all to be the very stone where the frog had sat trying not to die from laughing when Raggedy Boy tried to kill him for a deer with his crooked bow and backwards-shooting arrows, and from where the boy had kneeled to argue with his own insolent face reflected in that same holy water, the same rock that Cloudman, like the frog, now moistened in his wake.

From that ashpile ridge, looking back across the crowded town away from the shoreline in the bright shadows of certain sunny afternoons, you could see that the village was a hungry place, whose many rows of inverted clay cooking tubs, topping off the thatched huts that poked through the surrounding flowering trees, under which were hidden as well large jeweled piles of newly husked corn, winnowed beans, dogs, turkeys, chickens, barebottomed little kids, chittering birds, back-strap looms, some idle, others being thumped and thundered into the people's clothing, smoky cooking fires, men returning with loads of carefully split and tied firewood on their backs, were really a broad and crowded field of reptilian bumps on the back of a gigantic flowering alligator who made the earth quake when she shifted in the night, but who mostly basked for years on end at the base of two cutoff mossy stumps of the volcanoes the people called Pral and Ctit, which loomed immediately behind the town.

The hidden springs that fed the lake from those volcanic mountains must have run with water made of Time. Somewhere inside those forestcovered hills, Time of every-past-age-combined had frozen into one ice, which was melted by the heat of nature's constant Now and trickled into the muddy water of everyday human village time causing a flood of deified possibility, who was the Lake herself and at whose edge the village alligator dozed with her stomach rumbling.

The dwindling traditionalists could feel and wondered, as they made their usual rituals that fed the earth around, what sacrifice this kind of giant hunger would eventually demand. That's how it felt, like something was waiting to happen.

It was here in this same village, just five inches of time beneath this bumpy hide of huts and people trying to feed their children, where Raggedy Boy had been beaten, pushed away and starved, and from where he finally drifted off in search of life, a home and a young woman's heart, that centuries later, as a young man, I would come in stumbling, lost from my own exile from another hard place, hoping to find a home in that ashy cliff at the edge of that pool of possibility that the world called Atitlan and the people who lived there called *Rumuxux Ruchiuleu*, the Bellybutton of the Face of Earth.

I hadn't come here simply fleeing an enemy or some series of troubled losses and I didn't come to study shamanism or crack the code of Mayan calanderics or their priestly religion. As a young man I'd come here called or maybe even sent, but most definitely pulled into Atitlan like a stubborn struggling fish, by the will of some otherworld thing that wanted me here; some kind of being who desired me as much as I was in pursuit of what I thought was Her, which turned out to be the Divine Female whose heartbreak I saw in every animal, plant, person, rock and thing. Drawn toward her bosom, toward the Umbilicus of the Earth, I was looking for a home for all my longing, to be suckled by the very touch of her watery heart where the heat of all my grief-wrapped desire could steam freely away, protected by her cooling embrace which mercifully kept me from drowning in my own fire.

As early as I can remember I'd always felt like Raggedy Boy; like a baby whose ancestry was possibly majestic, but from a wilder time, from an older earth no longer seen and unremembered, who just appeared one day tossed up from that forgotten ground out on an ashpile. A person from a place nobody alive had ever seen or even knew that it was a place to be from, a place that I myself could only sometimes barely recollect upon waking from certain dreams.

This is not to say that the land I grew up in or that all the people of all the cultures I was raised in didn't like me or treated me with contempt. For unlike Raggedy Boy I was brought up in Northern New Mexico at the end of an era where most older Native people or old-time Spanish speaking citizens never actually considered themselves as U.S. citizens, much less as members of the homogenized culture they called Americano or Melican.

Because of my mother's job as a teacher on an otherwise closed-to-outsiders reservation I was graciously allowed to grow up on the land of a certain integral Pueblo Indian village whose desert hills, grassy flats, piney canyons and streams were permeated by constant ritual reminders that every natural thing on and in the Earth was awake, alive and listening and whose people manifested gifts to all of that in cyclic, magical events whose antique, self-renewing mystery, albeit secret to avoid defilement, was not a rarity, but the common experience of everyone living close enough to the earth-born vitality of that ancient New Mexican culture.

Though unlike Raggedy Boy I also had a family: a mother, a father and a younger brother with whom to wrestle and sometimes be a friend, it had been as if they were a mildly bohemian, American family complete within themselves, all of them born in January, thinking the same thoughts, going similar directions, inside of which I'd somehow ended up.

I always felt like an ash-covered foundling raised by well meaning peasant parents, or more like an interesting but terrified exchange student from five-thousand years before who was generously fed, clothed and sometimes listened to, who learned to speak their English and not to swear too much, but whose translations of his own thoughts over dinner were never quite understood.

My parent-sponsors worried a lot about my foreign heart being too wide-open, afraid my strange lack of greed and heroic unconcern for self-preservation would make it impossible for a creature like me to survive in the synthetic world of the America of the 1950s and 60s, which they thought was widespread, real and here to stay.

Despite the fact that there were plenty of animals in my life, wild animals as well as horses, dogs, cats, turtles, horned toads, spiders, birds and crickets, calves and mother cows to rope, brand or milk; as well as warm sand to grow corn, melons and chili along the undammed Rio Grande and miles of high desert hills in which to walk, ride and dream under the endless blue, holy sky, and though I had many books and some conversations, was clothed and my belly usually full, I was nonetheless sentenced at birth to be alone and set apart by what my parents and other people must have sensed, as loyal dogs do in the presence of a wolf, the quiet and wild otherness of my given nature.

In my youth the things I thought, that I slowly found I shouldn't share and what my quiet, animal-like soul felt and understood, left me stranded for human company in a kind of spiritual isolation, alone on a cultural ash-pile where, as I grew into a teenage boy, to keep my endangered soul alive, I learned to fight and scramble for the crumbs and tiny seeds of visionary knowledge, scientific, spiritual and otherwise, of a kind that might corroborate my lonely understandings; seeds and crumbs that were usually left discarded or growing unsuspected in the cracks at the edges of a supposed modern reality where they survived overlooked and disregarded by the extreme wave of consumer culture that had begun its routine ingestion of the intactness of the Earth and season-oriented people in whose midst my family was ensconced.

Unable and unwilling to climb down from the inebriated height of military victory to assume the unexciting everydayness of peace, instead of taking the time to grieve their losses and slowly grow accustomed to a non-war way of moving, after the second world war America decided it would "attack" all the country's problems.

Riding on the euphoric shock of what the country saw as the victory of technology over the world's "evil" during World War Two, the country embraced a new type of machine-dependant civilization whose effective organization was developed during the war and was now applied to "civilian" peace-time population, an application in a new war to bring the "benefits" of America to the so-called outlying areas.

After the second world war and with increasing frequency ever after, Northern New Mexico became a place where a particular version of this application came with its supporting economy, to rehearse its policies and experiments for the Third and Fourth Worlds without having to leave the political boundaries of the U.S.

Well away from the controversial messes it had already made elsewhere in the country and would here foreseeably install, it advertised itself as an economic boost for our state which it claimed was unemployed because people ranched, farmed and worked for themselves, under-populated because there was still 80 percent open public land upon which they ranched and farmed, uneducated because New Mexicans spoke many languages besides English, and poverty stricken because every family had an outhouse, a milk cow and didn't owe the bank.

Once this clumsy, post-war new machine culture was in place a new so-called science-based education system was established throughout, ostensibly designed to train local individuals for the good jobs the machine people said they were offering, which would bring them cash, give them credit to get them installed with lots of mass-produced stuff into the American dream and thereby raise their standard of living. But whose standard was it? In the end it all disguised a kind of internal colonization.

Ironically, in what had already become an established tradition in Northern New Mexico before my time, there was the parallel immigration of other outside peoples who were opposed to all of that, dissidents who were trying to escape the same cultural ravages rent upon their people in other parts of the country.

But no matter what, regardless of their thinking or on which side of it they stood, all of these new-comers came out of what we used to call the "gray sky" area of the world.

These gray sky people were not only white people, they were the descendants of many races and ethnicities who'd lived so many years or generations in an unexuberant world of functional brick buildings, smoke stacks, tasteless cold sandwiches, bad gray air, flat, practical language, steel and concrete, monocultural literalism; generations of women stuck inside unhappy, dark houses with their Hoovers and scrub brushes, an addiction to post-war science which they were positively certain would provide material cures for all the problems of their heavy hearts, which they didn't view as some valid form of sorrow or generationally inherited depression for their own cultural losses of language, land, clothing, food and way of going, but as a purely mechanical problem like a burned-out clutch or broken pump that could be fixed or surgically removed like a malfunctioning tank at the front, and having lived under this for so many years as to think such a life was normal.

It's easy to imagine the exhilarating relief and hopefulness the newly-wed, post-war children of the gray sky people must have felt when they first saw the juniper-scented, clear blue skies of the snowy desert winters, the clean mountain streams and laughter of Northern New Mexico with what must have seemed to them as plenty of room for their suburban bubble of post-war expectation to spread and sink its wells.

In they poured, parents and married children alike, bringing their gray skies and depression with them. Instead of trying something new, they re-established the same brick-building way of life, with what was then a new and heartless assembly line, militarily derived technologies bringing mass production and creating cash to buy what nobody here knew they should want. For this, advertising was brought in and grade school policies inaugurated that mercilessly shamed the local way of life: their adobe houses, their mud barns, their rituals, their three cows, their little flocks of sheep, their goat cheese, their songs, their languages, their clothing, their food, their smoky fires, their methods of healing, their spiritual understandings, their religions, their slow, extended family way of doing things, until an entire generation of kids had grown up with a kind of self-hatred and cultural shame planted deep inside their bones, who, as adults, in order to cover up their origins, their color and their languages, adopted the lifestyle that the gray sky people were peddling and with whom they had to get a job to get sufficient cash for them to sustain and be respected by these people who only respected money.

Coming from families with many diverse backgrounds, those of Spanish-speaking ancestry had been in New Mexico for 350 years, some of whom were descended from Sephardic Jews, who'd left Spain in the sixteenth century to elude the fires, dismemberment and forced conversions of the Inquisition. But no matter whether children of Basques, Andaluzis, Mozarabics, Gallegos, Catalonians or beautiful admixtures thereof, or with Native Otomi, Tepehuanes or Tiguex, all of the Raza farmed the river valleys, grazed their animals in the mountains living in beautiful little clannish towns sometimes close by and sometimes apart from the Native American population who had been here since the rocks stopped moving on their own and who continue living in nineteen culturally intact villages and five other tribal districts with over seven distinct unrelated languages between them. If any of these Spanish-speaking or Native American people wanted the gray sky people's jobs, they had first to graduate in their secondary schools to get them.

This meant learning to speak, think and walk like a gray sky person, while taking on their prejudices, buying and wearing their clothing and abandoning your own except on feast days; giving up weaving, drying fruit, covering yourself with silver jewelry, bells, buttons; getting a haircut which for certain Indians was traumatic, especially the girls. You would have to learn to shake hands energetically while looking away saying things you didn't mean while grinning and agreeing to sell your farmland that you were told you wouldn't need any more to suburban developers and your sacred things to collectors. It meant tearing down your beautiful, snug, mud ancestral homes painted with goat cheese and colored earths and paid for, to freeze, sneeze, roast and sink into bank debts in the gray people's carpeted houses, while the gray sky people's wealthy segment built ugly adobe mansions that conformed to building laws they had installed that no native New Mexican could afford and now no longer wanted.

That's when New Mexico became impoverished. Instead of jobs, honor, work and cash, they simply found out that they were poor and were going to stay there. Up until the gray sky people imported poverty, New Mexicans maybe didn't have a lot of stuff but they knew themselves to be proud, ornery, able and rich because the land itself made them so and because of the rituals that each of their cultures kept alive, ensuring that the holy earth was fertile and giving. This was what New Mexico's people had cherished and maintained. But now all this was trivialized and overlooked, eroded by the children of the smoke-stack civilization who declared it all unprofitable, impractical, unmodern and even backwards, while some of them sold what their presence was destroying to tourists as being quaint reminders of bygone days.

The gray sky people were not all unfriendly, but only a few were ever friendly to what we loved.

For all of this, the magic of the diverse peoples of Northern New Mexico fled into secret places, into hidden ways where even today some still survives, but only as a thing concealed, held in a trust for the initiated, no longer as the happy, common thing we'd known it once to be.

This hard situation, brought on by the mechanical civilization from the land of gray skies and the subsequent self-destruction it brought about in its newly made adherents who sacrificed their origins to subscribe to it, comprised for me what for Raggedy Boy had been the village that shunned him. As aware of the situation as I was at such an early age, in my smallness I felt powerless to do anything about it. My own subtleties and magical nature were as invisible to the machine people as the original culture and land that was being gridded out, thrown away, trampled and disgraced.

Though there was a lot of sadness in me, it was not only because the people in charge couldn't see me, but more for their unrelenting inability to see what I was seeing: the delicious complication and deep magnificent detail of the unfathomable mind of the teeming holy earth.

Like some little person who one day finding a single thick bristle off the crested neck of a wild bear, I could probably summon the bear with the hair and maybe have her come, but if she didn't come, by looking at the bristle I would see the bear in the hair, then become a bear, pull up a stone, eat some ants, chase a dog then disappear into the ponderosas, or then without a bear to see or be, I could sleep with the hair bristle clutched in my little fist and, dreaming, feel the bear close and hum as I suckled in her coarse fleece and longer nose-tickling belly fur.

I was always able to find a huge awareness and complex warmth in the smallest things. But if I ever tried to show anything like my bristle to the world, to the gray sky people or their friends, I only ran into people who could not see my bristle for all the bristles on bear skin rugs they trod upon outstretched upon their floors, who could chase and kill bears but never really know anything about them, while other people were uninterested and didn't care about animals at all, much less the one that ran inside of me or my single little hair, both of which would evaporate in the white-hot literalist heat of the molten-steel thinking that their numb, unhappy culture was pouring for our future.

In one of those miraculous examples of the durability of the youthful human heart, where what I loved kept me secretly alive like old Ya Sar, I never felt quite like an alien in this great land from which I sprouted, because what would have been killed inside of me, disregarded, made invisible or mocked by the invading mediocrity of post-war American culture was actually indigenous to the place.

Even though my body and some of my life was forced by the gray sky people's law and their followers' convention, to attend their schools, shop in their stores, struggle in their workplaces where not a few of their own children felt lost and thrown away, the rest of me, like Raggedy Boy, was kept away from complete spiritual starvation by the bits of intactness, vision and durable beauty I was allowed to glean on the ashpile of New Mexico's discounted and discarded cultures by an old woman who cared for my indigenous nature, who was herself the wild and generous unpeopled land.

Sometimes like a wind, and sometimes like a boy on foot and sometimes on the back of a half-broke reservation horse, I scurried around her crests of dry, glittering, potholed tufa cliffs or in her alluvial arroyos, rolling in her dusts of many colors. Coming carefully upon her special untouched places, I offered white cornmeal into shallow puddles of hidden frog-filled water, knowing the secret of the line where the vertical pillars of chlorite met the pool was where this sacred woman lived during times of rain; she who gave us all her verdant body as the flowering desert that you could smell already in her snowy winter's wetness that buried tall trees in the surrounding mountains whose run-off in the spring made all of it to happen.

Tossing wildly aromatic juniper branches loaded with dusty purple berries into the growing twig-loaded wave of mineral foam that pushed ahead of the flash floods that dangerously careened out of her tributary wilds, I carried out childhood divinations by watching how they rode the thundering water beyond my sight. And then, putting my footprints into the newly smooth talc-fine dust beside the tracks of kangaroo mice, I'd search the sculpture of the cut-bank ledges reconfigured by the violent water of the day before, to find a petrified camel tooth, enamel from a mastodon tusk, crystal-filled miohippos cannon bones and once a dinosaur toe.

Every season throughout my youth I wandered and searched the upper reaches of thousands of unpeopled arroyos which every year in their lower reaches received that sudden raging water that killed many wild animals, cattle and people, but also brought life to all by watering the world and our hand-tilled fields.

My personal secret arroyo in these wilds, on the other hand, disobeyed the rules of tributary floods, for after crashing and cutting for so many curly miles, it gurgled like a gigantic sink drain right back into the unseen, into the holy earth, disappearing in a swirl of bubbles through a bed of red jasper, quartz, flint agate and polished garnet gravel so thoroughly gone that the sad arroyo whose job it should have been to take the precious water farther down its course into the bigger rivers stayed dry, depressed and unemployed.

Every antler of deer and elk shed and altered by the chewing of ground squirrels, wood rats and porcupines; every solid red or yellow-banded desert hummock covered in solid sheets of mica or topped with slabs of selenite, logs of bending spar or hills comprised of massive piles of perfectly round sandstone pellets the size and shape of marbles, every animal I found laying dead that she chewed back into her earth with the weathering teeth of her changing seasons, ground between molars made of wind, coyotes, sand, ravens, snow and mud until the entire carcass of the vanished beast had transformed in its entirety into deep-rooted, high desert grasses that grew exactly in the shape of the animal itself as it lay in its final sleep; all of these events were love letters from Old Lady Earth to my lonely boyhood soul and though I'm not sure how much I gave to her, it was she who let me hold her, without whose embrace my soul would have surely died.

But when my middle teenage years blew in on me like a cold aching wind, those same ravines where I'd chased the wind on horseback, those open landscapes which had been the childhood woman of my life now became places I would be alone, longing with a pitiable serious face for a warm, human sweetheart, someone smaller and more opinionated than the land, who would be just for me alone, whom I could hold and touch and be touched by, whom I would understand and be understood by, to sing and be sung to, someone who could see the mystery of the land the way I did.

But like Raggedy Boy when he sat watching from a distance all the young hunters returning from the forest with the sustenance of dead deer hoisted on their backs and the way the village girls all admired them for the food they brought but not for who they were, I watched the human world around me in the schools that were pushed upon us and I too saw what the obvious girls were watching and with no one older who could know the particulars of my heart and help me to see more clearly, I saw only what I was missing instead of what I had.

What I saw there that made all the girls flutter were fine, broad-shouldered boys who never mentioned nature or anything I loved, who wore class rings and used throwaway cups, had close cropped hair, some kind of sports ability, bad music, cigarettes, cash and cars, and the endorsement and high regard of the adult male teachers who were nostalgic, pot-bellied, elder versions of themselves.

These boys had the admiration of girls too grand and distant for my shy dignity to dare to even look upon. They had cosmetics and exotic smells, magazine clothes and seductive walks, and some of them kissed the boys and others slept with some of the greater heroes, young men and women who, oblivious to anyone remotely like myself, were in their heyday just before being dropped, alive, straight into the boiling stew of the gray sky people's homogenizing work force.

Disregarding the dullness they were heading for, afloat their sports and girls era, and not understanding that they were being groomed for sacrifice in the wars in which their country was embroiled, I saw only how high they were riding there above me, mistaking, as they must have done as well, all the attention they were receiving for love, the love I longed to find.

It was then that the gray sky people's mediocrity and mechanical approach began to colonize a small shore on the edges of my heart and for a short time I naïvely tried to be like everybody else, thinking it would bring to me the attention of the men and the love of all the girls it seemed to bring to everybody else.

I tried to talk their talk and walk their walk and watch their television and pretend to care about the shows. I tried to like cheese puffs and eat fast food, wear tennis shoes and cut my hair, listen to their tunes and sing their songs while telling everybody who would listen in the English slang of the day how I planned to become a chemist, or a real estate salesman or a wrestler or some such drivel, until no matter what I tried or how much sweating shyness I sacrificed there was something in and around me that would be there my entire life that most every human sensed was not from their species, district, social class or tribe. Barring those social worker types who pitied me and wanted to socialize me and fix my quiet natural emanation, to most of the gray sky people and their converts the presence of my gawky teenage majesty brought to their surfaces an archaic knee-jerk reaction from a deeply buried fear of what it unconsciously remembered as an ancestral hatred of the free, unfettered nomad, whose quiet dignity and natural bearing had been seen in those distant times as untaxable, barbaric, arrogant, dangerous and untamed, which, manifested in the terms of my school years, meant that I wasn't mainstream factory material. Therefore the girls, whose instincts were always sharp, must have known they would be wasting their wonderful hairdos, hard-earned makeup and well-studied sexy walks on me, a half-breed boy whom they could sense would never end up as a plumber, a scientist, a lawyer, bank teller or a coach and therefore not a model gray sky woman's providing husband.

Like Raggedy Boy who got lost out in the unfamiliar jungle looking for a way to be loved, seen and be part of the world, it was here in the overwhelming synthetic complexity of the modern human terrain where I got lost tracking my desire backwards right back to my lonely place, backing into the thorny impenetrable thicket of incomprehensible social entanglement where I remained surrounded by what I couldn't touch, still invisible and spiritually isolated.

There were other young people, mostly Indian boys, who felt thrown away as well, though usually for reasons more insidious and sometimes different from my own. We'd band together anyway out of common loss and exile outside the gray sky people's gates we were told we had to enter but weren't really allowed inside, and to feel more like we were something we sometimes got a pickup truck and cruised around getting drunk, going fast, singing songs and just being glad to be together.

This went on for some of us for longer than it could be sustained and half our friends ended up killed by alcohol or spending their lives in the penitentiary. The rest of us divided into those who married village girls and lived the lives of traditionalists and those that found ways to survive inside the gray sky people's work place in Albuquerque or even bigger cities far away.

And then there was me, who was not allowed to continue in the village of my upbringing and yet had no desire to be a part of the gray sky people's plan either, like the Ashpile Boy after he failed to convince the hunters to let him be one of them in order to get the weapons he needed to kill a deer, to find the admiration of the girls. After a year or so of my own predictable failure at trying to be a part of what hated my soul, I, too, like Raggedy Boy, began to make things with my hands, until I became what some might call a self-taught artist.

With no resources to hire someone to teach me about music or painting, where my teenage desire was now directed, and the glaring absence of anyone who thought art might be something worthy enough to seriously pursue, for in these times it was not known to bring in any money, I refined my early joy-filled ability of making things into making paintings which I made on pillowcases stretched over apple crates using sifted colored earth, sized with eggs and homemade goat cheese like we'd used to paint the old-time inner walls of the adobe houses in the Pueblo. I was frantically driven and using what was lying around, I soon developed my own ingenious style of painting the face of the woman I was looking for, over and over again.

But she didn't come. In sheer fits of loneliness there was nothing left to do but sing. I sang to myself; I sang to my weeping, my grief, my story; I sang about the beauty, about the possibility, about the impossibility; I sang to the animals, about the horses, the plants, myself, and myself again and more about myself, myself, my life and me until I actually got good at it, accompanied by a homemade three-string guitar, a kind of *guimbris, tovshar,* or banjo that I feverishly constructed with what I found lying around.

Like a wild, desire-crazed prairie chicken, I was actually trying to court, spreading my tail and puffing my chest in all the beauty of my painted colors while singing and stomping out my songs in hopes somehow a girl or goddess might hear my uniqueness on the tune and if she were magically the right one, know me by what I created with my voice and hand and maybe even want me as well.

My songs and painting I didn't do only out of sorrow, romantic rage or in hopes of being seen, but from an equal force of inner obligation my indigenous nature demanded that would always want to make beauty, like every other natural thing did by just being itself.

By the tail end of my teenage years, when I finally owned store-bought guitars and oil paints in tubes, I was in a very hard way orphaned by my cause-fighting school-superintendent mother's untimely death at the age of forty-two.

I was determined after that to use my art to "hunt" for a living, to find a way to sustain myself, find love and position, all of which I idealistically imagined could not be but the thickness of a bear's hair away, and in so doing found myself as ill-prepared and naïve in that pursuit as a shunned, starving boy with a crooked bow and grass arrows.

Crooked Bow Boy didn't bring in any more meat with his supposed weapons than I did money in those days with my art, but both of us would fall in love with what we hunted when it found us, for the beautiful sounds we made when our failures had us sincerely singing instead of chasing or seducing, calling out instead of shooting, had us finding love only when the road back to the familiar was completely lost.

Sometimes it doesn't help to know what it is you're really hunting, or what love is supposed to look like, because the beauty that the hunter becomes and creates through his willingness to fail in pursuit of what he or she deeply longs for, but doesn't yet understand, can cause that uncomprehended thing we hunt to show its Divine face, instead of missing that opportunity by chasing the string of lesser forms our insatiable and impatient greed insists must each be the very one.

If we have not been taught that it takes years of patient struggling with our own unrequited hunger and that the generosity of the Holy, especially in Nature, shows up mostly, if not only, when we've tried and failed, then there are a lot of frogs and rabbits who are inexpertly shot at along the way, and some are taken and consumed to fill that hollow longing; each of them, like a string of bad marriages, our impatience keeps telling us must be the one.

Having no adults who could teach me about that and no way to learn it in my youth, before I'd wrestled my hunger enough or learned to turn my failures into beauty for such a Holy thing, not just a deer or a beautiful woman, but that thing who would pull me into my mountain village home of Atitlan, I had already married and chased away the first frog I'd come upon, continuing after that to track backwards like the life-searching fool I'd always been, continuing my quest to find a welcome and a home in the eyes of every girl I met. In that I wounded more of them than I caught and lost every one of those, until I finally lost myself in a great waterless, tropical Mexican forest literally dying of thirst and hunger, only just beginning to realize that what I was actually hunting was my own soul; a spirit bride for my heart, a small piece of the Divine Female whose infinite parts resided diversely spread out in all the animals, trees, plants, mossy roots and bugs in whose jungle arms I was dying.

Having not yet heard any story like The Toe Bone and the Tooth, I had no way to know that the first female who could love me wasn't even human and the magnificent flesh and blood, human girl she would send me who would have her heart, her toe bones and her teeth and with whom we would be in love would not yet be born into this world for another six years and who I would not meet for another thirty.

A long time before all of that and a short time before I would have headed south, I lived on La Cuchilla above the Arroyo Hondo on the canyon ridge opposite where the stream ran past the ruins of Turley Mill just beyond Des Montes, north of Taos, New Mexico. It was December and my mother had been dead for seven months, I was twenty-one years old and alone, for my frog wife had run away with a schoolteacher who owned a ranch.

It had finally begun to snow and like any boy from the reservation, I decided to hunt deer at dawn out on the clean, fresh powder of the wild, fir-covered mountains up behind my house where I painted, wept and sang.

TRACKING BACKWARDS INTO THE EYES OF MORNING STAR

I f people could eat what the Tzutujil Maya said the Gods ate, who are kept up and moving by feasting on delicious smells, then that clear winter morning should have stayed my hunger as if forever. For hidden in the cloud army of the incoming weather that rode the northeastern breeze, there must have been the Snow God's chef who filled the warmer pre-storm air, which in that still dawn came very lightly coursing across the powder-covered frozen ground, with a deliciousness that caused the same nostalgic tugging in me that it aroused in mountain cats, eagles and minks; the irresistible obligation to hunt beautifully, irregardless of result through the otherwise smooth, untroubled snow; tracking easily by sight and smell the trail of wild browsing animals like rabbits, elk, deer or others who owned the high tree-covered mountains.

After wrapping up my father's childhood plinking gun inside an old blue and yellow striped wool blanket whose nap had been burned away by use long before I was born, I saddled Morning Star, mounted and headed down into the canyon before the sun could light the rim opposite, hoping to ford the stream and push up one of the mountain ridges in the easy light of that violet dawn.

Morning Star was not my mare, but my landlord's who could never ride her. A solid red horse with hooves as black as water buffalo horn and a tiny star between her eyes, she was almost heavy boned but graceful and very fast. A small red mustang, not fourteen hands, upon whom my one-hundred and thirty pounds fit so well that we could glide and climb at youth's desire's unholy speed, bending and tacking around and over rocks and under thickets like a cross between a swallow and a cheetah.

But this morning we went slow, so as not to scare the world or what we hunted. When we'd quietly shed the final human habitation, a little ranch down in the canyon, we waded into the *rito*, the little river, whose water was so clear that some miles below in a warmer valley an entire village still drank directly from the stream.

When we'd reached its middle, I hesitated, not wanting to right away crush the brand new untrampled snow and lacy ice that hemmed the skirting of the opposite bank and we stood in the center of the river a little while to admire it.

But because of that we didn't beat the sun and when its light of breeze and glittering powder hit us where we stood, in the bubbling center of the jewel-bottomed brook, I could see myself reflected on its surface, but mysteriously my shadow lay two feet beneath it in the water, running on the stream bed bottom off a little to the left.

The sun was such that I also saw a trout who held there rippling, looking up between my shadow and the surface, hovering right inside the reflection of my head.

Fascinated, we stood and I stared, somehow trying to hold the moment like an object I could possess, thinking about the unlikelihood of it ever having happened and how the sun was moving and it would soon all disappear when out of the water of what had been the reflection of my head, the fish jumped and turned me into something wholly changed, for what had been my head was now all concentric ripples.

Like a valley of time that opened up forever, those few seconds of ripples were full of smells and thoughts, when I noticed that the trout hadn't fled but continued to stare back at me while still residing in my now slightly recuperated head.

At that point for some strange instant I thought to think like some of my friends in my early youth to shoot the fish and take it home for breakfast and call it all a hunt. I was immediately embarrassed that such a thing had even occurred to me when in the millisecond that big thoughts ride, I realized if I'd actually done it I'd have been shooting at my own head. The animal inside it continued to float, unafraid, just above my shadow.

Then the sun got higher and the whole thing lifted and still stunned we sloshed on to the icy opposite shore that marked the edge of what was human to where the world of trees and wild animals took up and where I should begin to hunt.

But wrapped in thought I drew my horse on up the ridge, considering that something jumped and flipped and lived inside me, outside me, looking back, and that all wild things must then be our real souls, running and living and looking back and that by killing them we could feed our hungry families whom we loved, but our souls would then be known only in their deaths, or maybe they lived on jumping into another beast, but in any case we would continue longing.

All these things came thundering through me pretty loud I think, and considering we were in the mountains I forgot what I'd truly known that had been taught to me since forever, what the old Pueblo men had always said was to leave your human quandaries at the house, because in hunting, the animals can hear the loud grinding of your human brain, which for them is like a blaring siren. And even then if an animal pities you and lets you kill it despite the noises of your thoughts, the animals become whatever you were thinking when they die and they are these thoughts that you will be eating and feeding to your family in the meat.

So to hunt it was best not to think at all, to stay awake and see what ran in front of you, but if you had to think, make sure it was a happy thing. By happy thought was meant the thoughts of the animals themselves, who were happy in their rugged heaven-like land, across the river up the mountain and into the skies.

All my hunting knowledge had been overridden by how a good-sized trout for New Mexico had jumped out of my head when a mule deer doe jumped up to our left on the parallel ridge from which we were separated by a sheer abyss. I shot too late and over her back only to watch her rise up the hill and then disappear under the piñon trees who dropped their accumulated snow in dusty puffs that chronicled the doe's otherwise invisible flight into the higher ponderosas and deeper snow.

Where the ridges met I began to hunt in earnest, for I easily caught her trail and let it pull us up the mountain.

Large breezeless clumps of snowflakes like eagle down molted out of the sky's chest, falling so slowly that they almost hung there without moving, seeming to fear joining their relatives already gathered some ten inches on the ground.

In all the thoughts that once again rustled in me, none of them was about how the blue sky and its sun had gone and as I tracked excitedly behind the lady deer, I rode higher into deeper snows, into a place I'd never been, straight toward the beginnings of the biggest, coldest snowstorm of that half of the century.

The temperature never stopped dropping and for the last two hours of unsuccessful hunting I finally wandered back trying to find my way back down until I'd lost both the deer and myself, sliding into what ended up as four feet of snow with only a thin blanket to warm me, no matches, nothing to burn, no water, no food. I didn't even have a knife to cut and kill my horse to climb inside like old men told us they did when things like this happened.

The snow was horizontal and howling, blowing in every direction. It must have been zero degrees Fahrenheit by now and dropping. With only swirling vertigo in this white-out there was no up or down, no south or north, on this snow-covered vertical slope of stone on which Morning Star had slipped but stayed steady, shaking, unable to go where I was demanding.

Feeling the need to urinate, my wet, frozen blanket still wrapped around me, I dismounted, laying my gun across the saddle. Stumbling after clearing a space, I stood as best I could, unzipped my jeans and peed into the snow.

The wind was so bitter that the urine froze as it hit and I couldn't close my hands enough to zip up again.

My little bird was close to freezing off. I stuck my hands under the saddle blanket in hopes that the mare's heat would thaw them. Finally after pulling out my partially thawed right hand, Morning Star shifted and I grabbed the rifle by the side-plate to keep it from dropping and found myself frozen to the gun.

My piss frozen, my pants dropped, my genitals hanging out, below zero, lost and freezing, headed toward death, one hand under a saddle whose horse was stuck in a snow bank and with my other hand thoroughly frozen to a rifle, it was a situation as comical as it was deadly.

I surely would have perished if Morning Star hadn't turned to look at me. She didn't look to me asking for help, nor did she look at me in disgust as if to call me stupid. She didn't look at me in pity. Like a carnelian dropped in a bowl of cream, her back was entirely covered in snow. She turned her head to look at me and peered through her ice-clumped forelock with an eye in whose sweetness and depth I saw again myself reflected, but this time inside the eye of the Divine in whose arms I'd been hoping to be suckled. When I understood that my face was inside the eye, devoured by its seeing, to feed the beauty of what had allowed me to live long enough to be so foolish, make mistakes and die in its pursuit, I forgot, for a second only, how truly close to death both of us really were. But in that instant, surrendered to the beauty, I lost my panic, the gun came loose, and my left hand was thawed enough to pull up and buckle my trousers which were now full up with snow.

Brushing off the saddle I climbed up into it, turned Morning Star, put my hands in my armpits and feet hard in the stirrups and urged that brave, sweet-eyed mare with no reins, signals or direction to go wherever she would take me for to die was to die, and if she got me home, so be it.

After over six hours of pushing, sliding, rolling, barely breathing in the sub-zero chafing snowy air, hoping to miss any barbed wire fences hidden in the deep snow, I finally recognized the canyon where the snow was not as deep and realized how far up we'd come out up on it.

Frozen to the bone and in an exhausted state that would no doubt be pneumonia by the next day, Morning Star had dragged us home in the diffused light of the snowy moon at around three o'clock in the morning.

Though there was no one there to welcome us, worry or make us warm again, when we arrived I got a fire going in the old adobe fireplace and though I don't remember how, cooked an enormous pot of watery oatmeal, went outside and shared it with the mare. Neither of us could eat much, but it warmed us up a bit. Too weak and tired to unsaddle that pool-eyed horse who'd saved my life, I went inside and on a sheepskin in front of the fire of sabino and encino I curled up like a wounded fox. Morning Star stood among the peach trees in the moonlit snow looking in at me through the sagging, rippled glass of the frosted windows and looking out at her I drifted off into a dream:

The moors were composed of piles of polished cobbles shaped like huge lentils, from an inch to four inches in diameter of every type of stone; some were opals, others turquoise, serpentine, jasper or jade while the bigger ones were of alabaster, feldspar, granite, gabbro, slate, gneiss and polished schist, but there were also rocks of every type, some translucent and others opaque, of every nuance, color and sparkle.

The earth clacked and tinkled as we humans rambled over these rocky lenses, through the ground-hugging mist of that horizonless land, gathering up groups of people as we went.

As we proceeded through that seemingly endless expanse, I began to notice that these convex discs of polished stone were in reality the gemlike eyes of giant trout. The entire earth was made of eyes on top of stony eyes, translucent, seeing and friendly. No matter where we wanderers put our feet the Earth was always looking back at us from eyes of every age of Earth's accumulated time, polished into fish-eyed jewels by the strain of constant seeing.

I was a friar, eighteen years old, with big jug-handle ears, who wore a light gray, hand-woven, heavy-hooded woolen monk's frock that hung down to my unshod, pale, uncallused feet.

There was no telling where I had come from, but dropping down out of my own minor tributary trail I'd come walking into a major stream of surging hordes of migrating people who were for the most part barefooted women with babies on their hips and little girls and boys trotting at their sides. All the ladies wore head scarves of beautiful colors or other ingenious adaptations of what had been in the past until now, in every age, touted as modern dress styles, adapted gracefully to the seeming refugee existence of all the tribes and villages that poured in to join us along our route. Though I was utterly unaware of what was going to happen or why this crowd was forming I slowly discovered that this was the entire human world flooding in from every side like a tidal wave of people strolling, whose fervent and common intention was to converge as one walking village upon a town that lay ahead to witness some event both wild and grand.

It was a vast thing that was to happen, a cyclic, holy occurrence that had always taken place but in intervals of such great distance apart that no one alive had ever seen exactly what would happen.

Those hundreds of miles of millions of adults and little kids were centered on a beautiful lady who knew all about what they were hoping would happen and it was she alone who had the complete ability and knowledge to make it come about.

After days of endless walking over the fish-eyed covered earth the trails began to widen and the crowd reconfigured until without knowing how, I now seemed to be positioned in that ocean of pilgrims right behind the beautiful woman who was leading from the middle.

The crowd ahead had approached the shore of what would be the edge of all solid land in the world and it was here that I noticed, from his speaking in her ear, then how he ran up ahead to reach the water before the people touched it, that the beautiful lady had a tall man there for an assistant.

I couldn't tell if they were sweethearts, for although they'd strutted barefooted side by side for days, they did so without speaking, but when they did speak it was toward a single purpose, and as accustomed to one another as two wings on a bird that, though opposed, flap together in time to propel some unseen center that existed between them, which their mutual experience, this migrating world, was hoping they could bring about.

Instantly I disliked this man, not for his self-righteous and superior attitude that the entire world tolerated just for his alleged capacities or for his Gandhi-like cotton loincloth, shawl and simple turban, or his wispy trust-fund, youthful, white-man, hippie beard, yellow eyes and tallness; I hated him more fully at every step we took because I had fallen crazily in love with the beautiful woman and he was too close to her in a way my youth could never be.

Jealousy being what it was for a jug-eared friar youth, I had no way to wrestle my heart or make myself known to her, much less survive the inevitable rejection if I even tried, or worse still, know what to do if she should accept my friendship.

Luckily enough she never noticed me at all, oblivious to anything but her movement toward her mission.

After a few more days of walking along the shore we entered a point of ground against the sea where the world came to an end and where sat a sordid unhappy town of timbers, white clapboard houses, unpaved streets and suspicious people. Out to the sea stretched an almost endless pier of hand-hewn timbers toward where the sun might have risen, that merged in color and distance with the substance of both the water and the sky, for all three had a diffused, dawn-like light that at some distance made them run together.

Unwilling to appear as unknowing as I really was to the beautiful lady, my youthful pride refused to let me inquire what was going to happen next, but by listening around the shoreline camps, standing in my friar robes looking mighty official and feigning a great involvement in the preparations I came at least to discover, that some being gone for eight-hundred years was going to come up from beneath the ocean, whose appearance would give life to everything it gazed upon in the world; not salvation, enlightenment or happiness, but life enough to survive and keep all things growing until it returned again in another eight-hundred years.

Looking out to sea with the pier running out perpendicular from the shore and the gathered company, whatever was going to come would do so to the left of the pier out in the water. Whatever it was that would come could only arrive at a certain pinpoint in time in this exact place and only if beckoned by certain songs and ritual movements that only the tall, wispy-bearded know-it-all and the beautiful woman seemed to know.

Excited and expectant the entire diverse and murmuring world waited on the shores, camping as one gigantic village whose common longing gave them peace. They didn't even rebel when a fat sergeant with a mustache, a badge, a pistol, wearing khakis, and with six henchmen from the angry town behind, announced that a permit would be necessary, that had to be solicited from the town's bureaucracy, without which no event of this sort could happen in which case everyone would be forced to disperse back where they started.

According to the people, without the blessing and return of this being that all waited for, the earth and world of people would disintegrate.

It was harder still when they discovered as they tried to get a permit that the town had voted unanimously against giving permission to any such scary nonsense as this and we would be denied no matter what.

I was so entirely enamored now of the beautiful lady, of her eyes, her capabilities, assertedness, how she moved, her coral-red see-through sari which showed even more what she looked like and her vast knowledge of all things, and to such a degree as young men so easily can, I became possessive not only of her but also of her causes. I turned into a great clannish, tribal fool so outraged that I would have defended her side of things even if they had been despicable.

But no one paid me a bit of mind, when in my puffed up romantic fervor I, the eighteen-year-old friar, tried to take on the sergeant single-handed, especially not the sergeant or the lady.

That's when I noticed how her eyes had looked into the sergeant's in some ancient secret recognition which was shared by this fat fifty-year-old man, where, unspoken, they had a conversation of gazes in which they both found me to be superfluous and an irritation.

Having seen all this and not been the least bit perturbed, her tall, bearded assistant, knowing his personal opinion was in no ways as important as what needed to be done to bring tomorrow's blessings, went off somewhere to do exactly that.

Once night had fallen and sitting afar watching the lady's camp, feeling all was lost, I noticed in the darkness once all the world was sleeping that the dark-haired lady rose up unnoticed and in total silence walked gracefully alone into the town.

Following her at a distance, I watched her enter a cantina that had only a counter and serving a single type of drink. I stole up to the doorway and peeking in unobserved, I saw her drinking with the sergeant and removing her clothing to reveal her sumptuous beauty and allowing the sergeant and all his men to fondle her.

Sickened to the heart, heartbroken, disappointed, furious and shocked, I fled up to the cliffs overlooking the water and the camping world where I wept and pounded the fish-eyed pebble earth.

By the morning all was fixed, everything running according to the plan, for I guess she got the permit. As disgusted, hurt and judgmental as I was, I remained to see what might happen.

The sun was already mounting, sending a bright flash toward us across the sea when the tall, wispy-bearded know-it-all in a bright red loincloth, cape and turban glided out 150 yards on the pier. The beautiful lady stayed dancing on the shore, making movements with her beguiling hands twisting in the air. Crowding at the sea, holding its breath, the entire world waited, when the woman waded out into the water and along with her assistant tossed long lines of offerings into the water where the sun's reflection made a road on the sea while both of them called out and sang.

A subsonic, earth-trembling rumble was heard beneath the water, accompanied by a roar in the wind. Some of the small children began to flee but returned when out of the ocean a six-foot layered nipple of turned brass or solid gold pushed out of the ocean surface making rings of continuous waves.

The woman coaxed and the man sang even harder, never letting off throughout, and through the unrelenting efforts of the two, this little mysterious hill of gold that *rode upon the water continued to rise until it was seen to be the topknot on a gorgeous, amazing head made of every polished metal. Some seven stories tall and just as many wide, it was the precious head of an enormous, friendly being who was powerful beyond our understanding but totally dependant on the water out of which he could poke only because of the subtleties in the singing of the man and woman and the magic of their dances.*

His eyes were neither in the front nor in the back but formed a layer running completely around, as did his nose and mouth, but he did his listening with two huge pointed, jeweled ears that stretched up the entire sides of his head like glittering filigreed wings. He rose and rose and rose out of the brine causing waves to crash upon the shore that nearly washed us all away, until he stood so tall that the depth of the sea came only up to his ankles.

He was beautiful, sparkling as he too danced from side to side, so long that the open sky itself was lost from sight, but the scintillation of his body lit up the earth, the people, the ground and the air he shadowed against the sun with a moving array of prismed light of every color except white, with whose substance and ocean spray the world was restarted, renewed and fed.

He too was in love with the beautiful woman and it was their dance together that blessed the world though they were never able to touch except through the matter of the salty water in which they both stood, the one tiny and red, the other huge and sparkling. As long as the beautiful woman danced, the God danced.

Right then, however, all things were changed. There was no more of this God, no more pier, no more wispy, bearded, know-it-all assistant.

Though still a friar in my hooded smock, I seemed to look a little better now and was up several stories in one of the wooden houses in the town.

The beautiful lady was dressed in black woolens from her head to her toes, like an Irish or Spanish matron in mourning, with a black shawl over her shoulders and she rocked incessantly at the rear of the room in a large old rocking chair, weeping inconsolably to herself while distantly staring into her thoughts.

Just one other person was with us in that room, an old, powerful man I'd never seen before, all dressed in black as well, but more like the stereotype of an American television gunslinger with a black felt hat and a leather holster and a great big revolver resting inside.

Through slit-like windows only five inches high that ran along at eye level the entire fifteen feet of the room, the old man and I could peek down into the street opposite our room where a mob of angry townsfolk stood shrieking threats at us while taking turns trying to shoot us through the slit with a great variety of guns. The most enraged citizen and the one who coaxed the rest of them into the concentrated attacks was none other than the sergeant from the cantina whose name, strangely enough, was Martín, who now wore only a tank top, and was barefooted with slacks.

Though they kept shooting and shooting and yelling a lot, the woman, oblivious to both our assailants and ourselves, was never hit by any bullets for she rocked herself just right without looking or calculating in such a way that the bullets flew on either side, always whizzing harmlessly past her, but only just.

I was angry as I could be about it, but my old friend in black was in charge and told me under no circumstances to shoot back. But I was so outraged by the stupidity and unnecessary waste of such a hopeless situation I felt determined I should retaliate at least to protect the mourning woman. Therefore, since he alone among us was armed, I chided the old man for not doing so himself.

With bullets whining all around us, the old fellow, not one little bit unnerved, patiently responded to me as if we were on a quiet street corner some summer afternoon, casually shooting the breeze. "I have only one big blue bullet and if I shoot it at that crowd, every person in the entire world outside of us would be annihilated. That's not what we are here to do." He showed me the big, blue bullet, which looked like a bear phallus, and then he put it back.

"Your job is to snatch those incoming bullets right out of the air with a hinged, cast-iron cornbread pan and turn those pesky bullets into beautiful corn."

Retrieving one set of molds from a pile that lay there in the corner, the dapper old fellow demonstrated how to instinctively catch the bullets after they'd been shot in our direction.

Holding the bottom pan flat with his left hand and the top one open over it in the right, he pointed it toward our attackers. In less than an instant after they were shot at us, the old man snapped the cornbread pans down and open again with a clank, just as the hot bullet hit the top pan. When he'd opened the pan, a long jeweled ear of blue corn speckled with a few translucent amber kernels fell out of it onto the floor.

Then, nodding and smiling he handed the pan to me, having no doubts that I could catch bullets right away and with no rehearsal I commenced to snap the cornbread molds over speeding bullets, catching them like flies and tossing the beautiful ears of corn over my shoulder.

Though I got so proficient at it that it became a kind of joy to me, it seemed only to frustrate our adversaries who instead of cooling down ran for more ammunition and more people with bigger guns.

The rear of the room had filled with so many bullets turned into food that a mound of jeweled corn rose almost to the ceiling and surrounded the rocking of the beautiful woman until all you could see was her head rocking back and forth out of the pile.

Soon the bullets came faster and faster and sometimes several at a time but still I caught most all of them, becoming better and better at it.

But they increased without rest until they reached ten to fifteen a second and in my long wool tunic I was sweating, clanging bullets and releasing corn at a rate that became a literal blur.

For once in my life I had learned how to do something that mattered, that fit me and filled me with a feeling of camaraderie and friendship with this handsome, gifted, ancient man.

The unrelenting profusion with which the bullets began streaming in on us became so dense that soon I would be unable to keep up with them. My failure to do so would most certainly cause the beautiful woman, myself and my old teacher to be riddled to death in the fusillade which would follow.

At this point, as I tried to hold on, the old man casually headed toward the side door on the right side of the front of the room, speaking as he walked, "My job has always been to die and since now you have your job, they are just going to find more and more to shoot at you and bigger things to throw at you, when what they really want, which will put it all to rest, is my death."

With all the bullets whizzing in and no break in their implacable barrage in which I could move from my post to stop him, my old friend stepped outside and was cut down in an instant. The same instant the shooting stopped I was shaken awake by the violent tremors of my inevitable pneumonia.

That old man's first appearance in my dreams marked the beginning of my friendship with the first person who would truly like me and know the kind of person that I was, instead of just what I did, or what I could produce. Another couple of years would pass before we could actually shake hands in the waking state. He would show up regularly eleven times in that first week of pneumonia-ridden delirium and sleep, and again for years until his chiding, camaraderie, pushing, pulling, teaching, laughing, nudging, tripping and spiritual navigation in the dreams steered me through the waking life I would live for the next years as I lived out my version of the Toe Bone and the Tooth and that until then all his traditional people had lived out as well, but in a more massive and deliberate collective initiation, monitored by a large division of old Mayans whose ancestors had been doing such things for millennia.

This old man was from Santiago Atitlan and was as much an anomaly to his village as I was in my land, but his village treasured his differences while I was shunned in mine. Named Nicolás Chiviliu at birth, I just called him *Tá*, or father, as he called me *Lá*, or son. Though I was blond and born far away, we were the old and young generation of throwbacks from other times and layers of existence, in which a humble dynasty of people in spiritual service to the remembrance of the Dismembered Goddess was continued from century to century.

Old Chiv served the beautiful lady I searched for, the same lady who I found in moments, in life-saving horse's eyes, the swaying walk of a distant girl or trout in watery streams, who called me through Chiviliu to Atitlan to take over where he left off.

Forever, throughout my life that old man would appear, after having lived and died, continuing to reappear in my dreams, along with the Divine woman, in whose service and spiritual remembrance we were both happily indentured.

But in that hard sickly afternoon after awaking shaking from that first of eleven dreams I knew nothing of any of this as yet. I had no idea that Atitlan even existed much less that it was a place I could go, should go or would go. I hadn't yet even considered leaving the country.

At that point I would have had a difficult time remembering what country I was in to begin with for my head was spinning and my soul in some scary, fever-driven chill and the involuntary thrill of that half-dying place made me shake in a weakness so strong I couldn't even sit up or speak.

But I did remember that I was still on the floor by a fireplace whose coals were dead and out in a house eight miles from the blinking light, north of Taos. Outside the windy horses of the blizzard's army still carried the storm upon us, hurling snow so hard that it had formed eight-inch high piles of powder through otherwise unnoticeable hair-line cracks in the low-cased windows of the 1920s adobe, through which I could barely glimpse how high the blowing snow had been heaped in drifts that almost covered up the horse.

Between the frosted window and the line of piled snow I caught my last glimpse of Morning Star's red steaming face, who was shaking just as hard as I.

The sun had left and an anxious cold purple was creeping in, but I was as yet unsure if I'd awoken on the same day I'd drifted off, until Doña Clotilda, my landlord's wife, came stomping and thumping into the house muttering to herself in good Taoseño Spanish, "Mira el locote, que malcriado, que va, que no peinsa en uno. ¿Que? Ni siqueria le ha dado ha sostener al pobrecito animal, ni echar un chonco de sabino en el jobon, valga me Diosito Santo hasta su chanate su hizo peirda por 'charse hielo."

Having noticed, as country Doñas do, that the mare was still saddled and unfed and that the chimney was smokeless and knowing that the bone-cracking cold could have crept in the rented house and frozen up all the water pipes enough to burst them, Clotilda came rattling around to check, but only in the kitchen, the only room with plumbing, two rooms away from where I lay speechless, half dead, shivering on the floor, where there was no water to worry about and therefore it was unlikely she would look.

But blessings being what blessings are, Clotilda strayed from her usual nosey route and mysteriously found me anyway and seeing my situation and comprehending in a flash, left and returned with Abelino her molybdenum miner husband and the true owner of the mare.

He built a roaring fire and then both of them disappeared until Abelino returned, quietly ranting all the way, through the deep snow and purple dark with our famous neighbor Doña Crecencia, his dead mother's sister who with her bear fat, *Aciete Volcanico, ruda, moradillas, osha, oregano de la sierra, immortal* and *matzranzo*, went to work heating grease, rubbing me, heating me with towels, making infusions and forcing me to drink, throw up, drink some more, wrapping me in blankets until I slept some more to bring me back from death.

Though I don't remember waking or all of what took place during her struggle to make me live, old Crecencia stayed there for the four days it took to get me out of danger. During that time the weather grew so cold that all my chickens died and fell frozen on their sides, deer and trees died, frozen to their cores and some coyotes froze to death eyes open, sitting up.

For those four days, I dreamt, again and again, waking up to eat and drink Doña Crecencia's medicines, then slept to dream again, then wake once again as she heated me with warm river stones, more bear fat and burning towels, to sleep again to dream, particular dreams sometimes continuations of the others, whose every hair-splitting detail I would remember forever:

In the same place where the God had shown but on the opposite side of the point, the world had become a long, flat and gentle beach in a sandy cove lined with jungle thicket, lianas and a canopy of trees.

There were no people anywhere and by now the town had disappeared.

The air was warm and I was young and wept into the tide which was the color of Burmese jade, but as I wept the tide pulled out and away from me in a single, rapid, sucking, retreating foamy wave.

Stretching out like miles of tidal pools revealed beneath by the exit of the tide, I could see several hundred little knots of gathered people chattering and fully dressed in distinct ceremonial attire and everyday clothing from a myriad of tribes and villages and places I'd never heard of before. These people were all working together on a grand underwater project on the bottom of the sea, but every group and village did so separately, each according to its way.

When the tide would go out they would set about gathering more materials in the forest and on the shoreline, carrying and dragging different things to their watery spots before the tide came in and covered them all up again.

It was just this they'd all commenced when a lunch break was signaled and the people all turned into birds of every kind. Some turned into drab and nervous little shorebirds poking their long beaks into the sand to snatch a crustacean or a little mollusk for their lunch, while others became large cranes, swans, wild geese and ducks who flew away on the symphony of the determined cries and flapping wings of water birds, to lunch some place where the eating was more to their style. Several hundred people became brilliantly colored birds, warblers and tanagers, a few contingas, a trogon and a dove scattering throughout the world in search of seeds and insects.

Because it was understood that all the bird-people would return from their long lunch by the time the tide was ready to rush back in as fast as it had receded, my curiosity overrode my shyness and native respect for the propriety of other people's sacred places, relics and rituals, which I never touched or inspected without an invitation, and I wandered through the large horizontal planks of highly polished serpentine and agate embedded in the sea bottom, in a pattern only a soaring bird could comprehend, in a massive mosaic stretching for hundreds of miles.

As I was looking out across it, a tall, well-built old man smoking a little straight-stemmed pipe emerged out of the water and lumbered in from the tide, coming straight for me and examining from his angle the gigantic inlay that I couldn't comprehend.

When he got to me he trumpeted out a "Ha hai" that blared like a cross between an elephant and a squawking macaw. "You finally made it down, that's very good, son, I'm so happy to see you. Let's get to work."

Dressed a great deal like a Greek Orthodox priest but without the cap and beardless, his cassock was black with gold edging and on his feet were boots of silk embroidered buckskin, that as he walked away from me back towards the incoming water, hoping I would follow, left the tracks of a wild crane behind him in the sand.

Looking back and noting that I wasn't in his tow, he turned and beckoned for me to trail him back into the water. But I was afraid to walk into and underneath the water where the old man had already disappeared.

Though very sad this welcoming old guy was gone, I was wondering how he expected me to breathe underwater when he came out again, returning with me to the beach a little above the present tide and where we sat together in the wet sand between some of the great planks of polished stone smoking and talking about just anything.

So absorbed by the fact that I now had a friend, my sadness was beguiled into such a fascinated interest in the old man's account of his underwater work that I failed somehow to notice as it was happening that we were both soon covered in the water of the returning tide, breathing quite easily under the salt sea just as if it were air.

With an intact male dignity commonly found only in certain tribes, the old man invited me to rise up to my feet and walk with him through the happy and struggling underwater people laying down their lustrous planks of carnelian, opal, turquoise and polished agate which were of as much as thirty feet in length, a foot thick and as wide as a person is long.

Ceasing now to be birds as they returned in droves from their lunches, the minute they hit the water they were people again, straining mightily under the sea with the planks, some of which must have weighed ten or eleven tons, and who amazed me with the immediate grace and ease of their cooperative determination and well-learned abilities which caused the huge crushing stones to glide in slow motion right to where they wanted them positioned on the sea floor, in a plan whose overview they seemed to all understand.

Starting off with a brick of jade that weighed a mere fifty pounds, the old man taught me to do the same.

He showed me how to be aware and then move every single part of me which we both knew was a certain type of bird whose song and sound when made just right caused the stone to move a little on its own and more easily in my arms.

It took a lot of patience to get my body to respond to its nature in just the right way in order to lay the jade in increasing sizes and weights into the forms that the old man was making. But little by little, working side by side, the two of us together like a brick layer and his assistant, I was finally able to shuffle new blocks to him in a way that was actually a help to him so that together we laid out a tight jade mosaic at the bottom of the sea, stretching out for miles in all directions.

When we ran low on jade we were forced to once again leave the water, turn into the birds we were and sift through the sand of the beach with our beaks, swallowing tiny pebbles of jade into our crops.

Once back in the ocean, when we spoke planks of jade slipped out from our mouths and once again as people we resumed our enormous art. As my skills intensified, the old man pushed me harder, increasing the pace over time until I was working as fast and well as he. It was only then that he commenced an explanation of why all of us here underwater worked so fervently to create this jeweled floor.

"At one time, a deity lived beneath the sea floor, with a grand beautiful woman who was the spirit of the water. When something jealous outside the water blew her into as many pieces as there were pieces of all things in the world, then the sea-bottom God fled in his misery away from all the water to live in grief up in the sky.

"So now we reassemble her constantly as a great, flat, sea-bottom jeweled mask as a gift to the sky who is the only one big enough to see what the entire face of his reassembled sweetheart actually looks like. The Holy Sky peers through the lens of the sea's warm tide and perceiving the mask becomes happy again. His happiness is where everything lives according to its nature. His happiness brings the world back alive.

"We are feeding the sky."

And after that for years on end the both of us continued to gracefully coax jade planks into the reassembled face of the woman of the water, to continue feeding the sky.

We breathed salt water, lived sometimes as birds and worked hard at the bottom of the sea when I noticed there were a lot of women helping us and a whole enclave of nuns arguing a-ways down the line. . .

Smelling Crecencia's *osha* root and bear's fat that had chased my fever through my skin, when I awoke I was breathing hard and dripping in sweat from my soaked hair to the soles of my cramping feet, my clothing as wet and salty as if I'd fallen into the sea.

The room was still dark, it was maybe a little before the next day's dawn, which I vaguely recollect was when my neighbors came and added to the cure. That's how it was for me, coming in and going out, from one dream to the next, until eleven dreams and four days later I could finally sit up and slowly eat. Then ten days after that I would rise and walk around a little bit, while outside a strange, almost balmy weather turned the daytime world into a knee-deep soup of icy mud and the nighttime earth into frozen chocolate ruts.

Though beyond a doubt Doña Crecencia had saved my life, we never became good friends, but a little later when I'd brought her all the money and gifts I could in payment, she said that after such an illness, such a dreaming wildness so close to all the saints and death, that since I'd been cured by them, I would now have the ability and spiritual permission to heal other people, animals and myself with the same plants she used to bring me around. This would turn out to be the case, but not for many years beyond that January afternoon.

All the time that I lay almost dying, dreaming, sweating and struggling and before I could get up and move around enough to see her, Morning Star had suffered as well and finally passed away.

She hadn't died from any sickness, pneumonia or from the stress of anything we'd been through, but from an accidental bullet that had pierced her brave kidneys from the barrel of a loaded revolver in the hip holster of Manfred, the spoiled twenty-year-old grandson of the same man who'd called Crecencia in the snowstorm, who'd saved my life and the grandson of the same man, Abelino my landlord, who'd owned the poor little red horse.

Instead of being proud that an orphaned wild filly, unwittingly caught in a herd of cows belonging to a cousin who was bringing them down for the autumn, had grown into an unbroken mare that his family barely knew they owned and could never seem to ride, and was then transformed into a heroine on my ill-planned hunt by saving me from myself, this grandson felt a loss of face.

Less than one year younger than myself, the twenty-year-old boy couldn't comprehend that my foolishness was not a form of laudable bravado and hadn't made me grand, or that the loyal horse had brought me home despite my own stupidity. He would never comprehend the reason why Morning Star and I could course the Earth together was exactly because I knew I didn't own her and that the two of us knew we were both the property of nature's enormous churning heart, and I more animal than man, our friendship was based on her having given permission to be ridden for the natural joy that two swallows feel in each other's company as they wheel and bank at breakneck speed in utter ecstasy.

Like the 2,500 years of myopic, human-centered thinking that had always been snapping at my heart, Manfred was going to take back Morning Star for himself to show me that he was the real "owner" and for that he figured he'd have to dominate that sweet-eyed mare himself.

With black leather head to foot and a loaded pistol at his waist with no hammer on an empty chamber, he mounted her. Goading her with chrome-plated spurs as long as his arrogance, he prepared to buck a little, but she was from the wild and jumped forward, crow-hopped like an elk three times to the right, then spun to the left and without a single buck and unable to drop him off she smashed against his truck then dropped herself like an anvil from the sky, flopping down onto solid ground on one side like wild horses do, so hard she caused Manfred's femur to snap clear across and his elbow to crash down on the hammer of his gun which released a charge, sending a bullet sliding clear through the saddle skirtings into the horse, passing to the right of her spine, creeping into the wild goings-on of the inside of a horse whose minds are wind and souls are made of heart-break.

While I was asleep, full of fever, shaking inside a world of dreams, Morning Star, that deep-eyed heroine, took a long time to die.

We are told that we shouldn't hate, but when what you love is killed, the grief of all that most easily lives as hate. And so I hated that boy and I knew he hated me as well for my being brought back alive by what caused him to always limp, by what for me had been a friend and what he could only get close to in her killing. Manfred himself was killed in a car crash two years later, driving the same truck into which Morning Star had smashed him before she died herself.

In some kind of way everybody knew, though no one but Crecencia said it, that the mare's death was a terrible gift of sacrifice to some old force that had been chasing me since birth, without which it would have eaten me instead. This would not be the last instance some being named Morning Star would die to keep me living.

Not too much after, while still fairly weak, I packed up the little I could carry, borrowed five hundred dollars and crossed the American border south into Mexico.

My earlier crossing of that winter stream where I'd seen a trout jump out of my head had been a spiritual border, after which I wandered for years on and off roads towards places and doing things I'd already seen in dreams, lost in the aching search for the look that I'd seen last in that mare's eye when I asked her to take me home; eyes that kept me from staying in a place where I would have surely frozen.

On friendly little buses, dump trucks, lorries, trains and my own feet, I zig-zagged for months through Chihuahua, Jalisco, Michoacan, Queretaro, Guerrero, Oaxaca, Tabasco and Chiapas and finally to Guatemala, carrying my dreams and longings like rare seeds that sprouted and leafed out into growing understandings that had me traveling toward the place that would be my home, where my nature could be trained into something useful, into a man, a member of the Tzutujil Mayan of Santiago Atitlan, in the Umbilicus of the Earth. There with my good friend and zany father, the old man Chiviliu, and several hundred other old Mayan men and women, like a friar I became another of their wool-blanket-wearing order, dedicated to remembering back to life. She who had been dismembered and thereby do what we could to keep Holy Nature dancing.

But none of this could have happened for me, if back there in the States, as she continually did, the Holy Female hadn't looked my way and brought me home, only to die a hard death, sacrificed to what chased me. But this time, at least, she'd not been forgotten.

LOS OJOS DEL ZAJORIN:
STANDING IN THE
MIDDLE OF THE FIRE

P adre and I had agreed the month before that he would fetch me out
of my hut in my in-law's family compound on the morning of the
date set by the seminary prelates in which I was to defend this
Grandson of the Swordfighter. After sitting holed up in his parents' big
thatched house for more than a week now preparing his written presentation, on the appointed day, we were to walk up the hill through the village
together to the wooden rectory built on the ruins of the sixteenth-century
earthquake-tumbled colonnaded stone priory of the still upright Spanish
colonial church of Santiago Atitlan.

It was here we were to join with the town's parish priest Stanley Rother, or Padre Francisco as this Oklahoman coached his Indian parishioners to address him, who had agreed to drive the three of us over the rough and rutted dirt track at the southeast side of the lake between Mosbaal Jolom and XeCoxom to the not-much-better pavement below Toliman up the rising road over the eastern lake above Palpój, past Psaccab, to Godinez back west up and down the verdant tufa crags above Santa Catarina down to Panajachel and back up the mountain on the north side of the lake above San Jorge to the seminary just shy of Sololá, positioned immediately opposite, five-hundred feet above and only nine miles across the lake from Santiago Atitlan.

Here all the Catholic officials, novice priests, monks and acolytes would be waiting for Padre's hearing.

But of course we lived in the village and when Padre came early as planned that February morning to escort me to our ride, I wasn't in my hut, nor had I been home for three-and-a-half days.

But of course because we lived in a village he found me anyway by asking around and everybody knowing everybody else's habits and knowing I was a functioning prayer maker and *Ajcun*, Padre found me easily in a sacred house directing the finish of one of those non-Christian rituals, praying at the foot of Holy Boy, the very deity Padre was accused in the Seminary of having worshipped.

Kneeling in the blazing heat of a narrow waxy corridor between four hundred handmade candles which burned on either side, I was busy spreading a fog of bilious smoldering *pom*, or copal, the "food of the Gods," whose intoxicating smoke carried my very best esoteric Tzutujil oratory language in a flowery praise to feed the sleeping deity, which was ending with an amending plea to be graced with the ability to defend my unbelieving Christian friend, the grandchild of Holy Boy's old friend the Swordfighter.

Of all the many complex deities and powerful understandings hidden in bundles and other forms away from the uninitiated, outsiders and others whose minds couldn't comprehend, housed in the string of public and private sacred houses spread out through the village, Holy Boy was the most visible and easiest of the Native Gods to find.

Because of this he was also the recipient of a hundred mocking epithets and slanderous, trivializing names, given him not only by insecure

Christians in particular, both Indian and otherwise, Catholics and Protestants alike, but by tour guides who, for the benefit of their curious hordes of onlooking non-Indian monotheist and atheist tourists, mercilessly belittled how he looked and dressed and the nature of his worship which to many of these travelers appeared to be childish rituals of an unevolved people, all of which they deduced from the tiny fraction of kneeling, praying, smoke, candles, alcohol and dance they were permitted to witness during their half an hour away from the tourist boats.

Hated for centuries by all assigned foreign clergy out of resentment of the incorrigible love the people showed him, Holy Boy was also the one deity whose obvious and famous presence defended all the other Gods by digesting all the negativity heaped upon him, drawing all the fire away from certain more delicate deities, less visible but just as grand.

Chiviliu always comforted my indignation over the treatment and accusations Holy Boy accepted, telling me to only begin worrying if the outside world should ever see past his dress and all the obvious things about him they didn't like and that they judged him for, from their own cultural limitations, to discover the enormity of his real meaning and function or the numbers and words of which he was made.

One of the most prominently used derisive nicknames for Holy Boy employed by sneering clergy in the past and originally during the time of the Spanish Inquisition was "El Gran Judio," or the Grand Jew.

But the Tzutujil people, being what they were, absorbed this term with great affection as well and soon the Big Jew became a great friend of the village.

I loved as well this deity "El Gran Judio" as much as I loved all the rest, but because of Chiv, who was a favorite of Holy Boy, I served the deity, the Grand Jew, in greater deference for many years.

Ironically, though, at the moment that Padre entered through the reed-covered doorway into the smoky temple house, I had only just returned at two in the morning after a three-day meeting with a group of rabbis who'd become friends of mine in Guatemala City, a hundred miles away.

It was for a few of them I prayed at the very, very end of my ritual. After expressing gratitude for my safe return from the capital and petitioning the God for help in defense of Padre, I prayed for a couple of the old Jewish teachers who had secretly given me candles to pray, on behalf of their families, with the "Grand Jew."

These rabbis, from all over the Americas, I'd come to know in life's natural roundabout fashion through the Israeli Embassy, but with which they were not involved.

Menasham Havel was the assigned ambassador from the state of Israel to the Republic of Guatemala and besides being a shrewd and very powerful servant of his government in the non-Mayan world of Central American politics, Menasham and his wife Dolly were above all else great lovers of every kind of art.

During the most beautiful part of the dry season and through some of the drier parts of the wet, Dolly forced Menasham, accompanied by his entire bodyguard, to lead some weekend picnic tours to visit the country in what seemed to me like those outings once practiced by the Victorian British Raj.

These outings became so popular that after a while all their acquaintances, ambassadors assigned to Guatemala from all over the world and their families started tagging along.

These ambassadors, like the aristocracy of old, felt they were at great risk from various guerrilla groups, both left and right and even unaffiliated bandits who might abduct them or their children in hopes that the country they represented would post the demanded ransom.

Besides the Americans and very few others, almost every other embassy in Guatemala City was guarded by the local secret military police representatives required by the Guatemalan Government, who stood assigned at the embassy doors in bad suits with gold teeth, a lot of pomade, no training and automatic pistols, who if they looked to all the world as indistinguishable from right-wing hit men from clandestine paramilitary organizations, it was because they were one and the same, but although they could not on their own have prevented a concerted kidnapping or drive-by anyway, the ambassadors were nonetheless as afraid of these guards as they were of their supposed kidnappers.

For this reason none of the lesser guarded diplomats from Belgium, Uruguay, Finland or Spain or a hundred others dared to venture out with these guards alone. This made the most enticing attribute of Dolly Havel's jaunts to the "country" in search of art for her galleries that were housed in old, thick-walled crusader castles in Tel Aviv and Jerusalem, the highly trained, courteous, thoroughly armed, grenade-bearing, tear-gas toting, machine-gun bristling Israeli security guard of as many as fifty-six soldiers, but usually half that number, with which Menasham went escorted everywhere.

Because it was required of even the Israelis, when any of the ambassadors traveled, that the local gold-toothed fellows in polyester had to come along, the Israeli guards spent a certain amount of energy keeping an eye on these lone local guards that traveled with their groups as suspected kidnappers.

It wasn't long before the picnics grew to such a size that Dolly had to form a waiting list, but still, when they sallied forth, they looked like an invasion force as they caravanned across the highlands in their long line of limousines, armed Landrovers fluttering flags and soldiers ready on the roofs.

Some of the hamlets they visited were more than doubled in population by such a visit, especially since most mountain Mayans would have grabbed their babies and little kids and fled into the bush out of sheer terror at not knowing what kind of trauma to expect from such a highly armed, unannounced division of tall pale people.

But after a while, when the most tourist-callused Mayan merchants figured out what enormous sales of weavings, carvings and so forth they could pull in from these invaders, the news ran throughout the land, and the people began to look forward to Dolly's armed and cheerful picnics.

Their first visit to Santiago Atitlan was unannounced as well and embarrassingly orchestrated to seem like some serendipitous search for me, for which they'd driven to the north side of the lake to some rich ally's chalet and obtained an oversized motorized boat to come across.

When that tub came steaming into the pier at Chinimya with all their guns pointing out thick across the bow and after docking when the gang plank went clanging down, this picnic looked like a landing party of some conquering force which of course was Dolly, who like an Israeli Margaret Thatcher marched boldly down between her royal guard onto our basaltic cobbled ground in her nylons, curled hair, red leather purse and big rose Liberty print dress, pointing and offering firm commands to her husband's soldiers and the ambassadorial picnickers alike.

Terrified for all the unexpected guns, strange perfumes, tall people, wild languages of all the diplomats in holiday attire and funny-colored hair, of the few villagers who would let them come close enough to speak only the dwarf MaXuan Duy, who'd pulled me from the mud during my initiation, would talk to them, although he claimed to have never before heard of me, figuring from the looks of them that they'd all been sent to kidnap me.

Dolly marched up the facing hill into the village, right up to the teeming open market while her long entourage, out of breath, struggled up the hill quite a bit behind with Menasham and his guards. Not a person to be discouraged or deterred, she captured a couple of teenage boys and commanded them to show her where we lived, which she carried out in such an inspired, royal way and in such a thickly accented Israeli Spanish that these young village Mayan speakers could barely understand, but after due deliberation they decided that this bossy woman must have been my mother and Menasham my quiet father, so they could hardly refuse and brought the picnic army right to my door.

Two beautiful rosy-cheeked little twin daughters of one of my terrified initiates had been sent running fast to our compound from the neighborhood of the boats the instant the village gave Dolly Havel the runaround to warn us that some strange *mosi* were in the village looking for me by name, but because the little children had waited so politely and delivered the message so shyly and so cutely, we thought they must have seen another couple of jealous Norman tourists coming to tell me off about how my presence in the village was a disgrace, and to whom our women folk always figured how to sell them something anyway.

Thus, though warned, we were unprepared for the unexpected violence of their entrance into our compound around whose little plaza we were all half dressed, relaxed and bantering, each involved in some light chore, combing each other's hair and winnowing beans, while the sisters-in-law all wove on their back strap looms, when giving us a fright, the guards with no warning jumped in with their machine guns posed, securing the place, after which Dolly appeared in her print dress, nylons and shiny shoes, sort of yodeling hello as she strode into our midst, towing Menasham after her, wearing one of his good, everpresent suits, with more diplomatic clones of themselves piling in thickly behind them all the time.

Like wild startled animals, proud jaguars, eagles and brightly colored birds caught in a tree, who were powerful enough in their own ecology, but now surrounded by hunters with a strong and intrusive gaze, we had to know our limits.

Though their presence was offensive, voyeuristic and obscene, every one of us knew hospitality came first. It would only be our hospitality, if anything, that would cool their white-hot, molten-steel hatred of our smallness and what they saw as dirt into something more solid, less intimidating, hardening them back into their natural cold, unbending state.

Vacating any stump or stool, tiny chair, chest, upturned basin and after anything else that could be contrived as a sitting place up off the ground, toward which we knew they would not go, had been hauled out of the huts and into the open little plaza where we stood, we asked the emissaries to please sit and take a rest. The invaders for the most part refused, some even fleeing to the road, but the few that acquiesced had their wives spray our makeshift chairs thoroughly with Lysol before any of them would sit, cans of which every woman in the troop, save Dolly, held clutched like weapons, white knuckled, in their hands, having produced them from their purses. Luckily the proud women of our compound in those days didn't know the significance of what they were seeing.

The invaders were probably afraid our primal earth-oriented lives might be contagious or that they would catch some rumored sickness that village poverty mostly causes anyway, or maybe they feared that they might contract poverty itself which they thought they saw and were appalled by in my compound, which was actually very clean, quite well provendered, healthy and, in the village, considered very rich.

What these embassy cloistered diplomats wanted was the look I'd sought for my entire life that was in all my paintings, the look of She who in one form or the next was looking back at them now in the compound, from whom they wouldn't even take a seat in the bosom of the people who knew Her best.

After introductions had gone all around and we realized by whom we were surrounded, Dolly explained that in her continued effort to keep her galleries filled, the Israeli ambassador's wife was here to buy some paintings.

She'd seen my picture on the front of a Guatemala City women's magazine featuring an article on my life that described what I ate and whom I was married to and covered an exhibition of my paintings ironically sponsored by the Ministry of Fine Art from a cabinet in the Government who years later would advocate my deportation or removal.

Under the picture of myself the caption ran, *"Los Ojos del Zajorin,"* which had actually been the title of the exhibition taken from one of the paintings whose picture was on the inside with my misplaced name running beneath. For years people meeting me for the first time outside the village would think "Ojos del Zajorin" was my given name and shake my hand addressing me as such, "It is a great pleasure to meet you, Mr. Zajorin." Ojos del Zajorin was good Guatemalan Spanish meaning simply the "Eyes of the Shaman or Calendar Priest."

Inside the village, besides the retired hierarchy who kibitzed and heckled behind me in all my painting bouts in my village studio on the ashy ridge overlooking the hidden cove of Xechivoy, nobody knew me as a painter, but my recent rise in popularity as an artist in Guatemala City funded my life in the lakeside village and made it so I could pursue as well my healing art and help the old folks keep the world alive in their expansive rituals.

Whatever cash I earned by putting bits of color on a stretched cloth, then hauling them to the capital to sell, I brought back to the village and spent it all inside, which made me feel a little like Swordfighter returning home with laden mules.

But now this new style of selling art in bulk in our own hut at gunpoint was something new for me, and mighty mystifying for the village, who could never figure out what people could value so much in a painting unless it was infused, like an icon, with the magic of something holy that gave us life and could therefore be ritually fed and prayed to, which was accurate for me, and unconsciously accurate for the buyers, who were trying to buy what in their lives had been forgotten, to keep them on their walls as trophies.

When all the bargaining was done Menasham and Dolly shook all our hands around, for they alone of all their group had not feared our poverty. Then they ordered half their efficient guard to sling their machine guns on their backs and, gently cradling some thirty paintings, had them march single file like coolies and gun bearers, carrying the bagged quarry of the royal shooting safari back to their little ship, into which they all filed waving and blowing kisses to the ten-thousand gathered mystified villagers who weren't waving because they missed them but out of gratitude that no one had been arrested, shot or kidnapped, figuring somehow they'd settled for taking the paintings instead of me. When the boat with all its tall people with a lot of guns, who disinfected our chairs, wouldn't eat our food, didn't speak our language, who left us with money, finally disappeared from sight, there was a second when the village didn't breathe, after which a huge simultaneous sigh was heard throughout and I was mobbed for details as the entire town drifted back to their homes and cooking fires there to mythologize this visit into the story.

This armed art-buying picnic, as invasive and comical as it had been, signified the beginning of a continued business relationship with many ambassadors that often bordered on true friendship, who would influence the art world far from our village in my favor causing travelers of many sorts, most of them unarmed, to come and buy paintings in such an amount that for several years I found it unnecessary to ever leave the village.

This in turn made it possible for me to accept bigger spiritual responsibilities and positions that required one to be either cloistered or always in the town.

During that time, without my prior knowledge or permission, Dolly had engineered that I should win the competition as Guatemala's premier artist and be honored by both the Israeli and Guatemalan Governments in a cultural exchange in which a well-known Israeli painter and a Guatemalan painter should each visit, have an art exhibition and paint some paintings in residence in the other's country.

Though I wasn't by law even a Guatemalan citizen, to the Indians of those days who didn't think of themselves as Guatemalans either, but as citizens of their villages and languages, my presence in Tzutujil country by that point was no longer questioned, and to some outsiders it must have seemed as if I'd always been there. Many non-Indian Guatemalans on the other hand, who had long ago lost their tribal affiliations, became very tribal about being Guatemalans and the jealous protests they levied against my choice as Guatemala's artistic ambassador to Israel were loud enough for even us to hear all the way into our mountain village, where the butchers told us about it, having read it in the newspapers that the cattle walkers brought in bundles to wrap the meat.

Israelis never back down and my work was sent to Tel Aviv anyway. Though I was unable to travel to Israel because of spiritual duties in the village, the offer was always open.

But because of this, an American couple visiting relatives in Tel Aviv the following summer saw my painting in Dolly's crusader castle gallery and again in Jerusalem. Then a few months later, the same couple, Itsak Winer, or Izzy, a retired sewing-machine mogul and his wife Vera came to see Vera's brother, Salo Harshov, an Eighteenth Calle shoe sales mogul in Guatemala city, and visited the Israeli consulate in Guatemala City to find out where I lived out in the mountains.

At the onset of Izzy Winer's retirement and much to his disgust, Vera had taken to the idea to open an art gallery in California. Like Dolly, but in a more suburban set, without the picnics, big cars and guns, she forced Izzy, who hated all of it, to take her to all the places in all the countries that she wanted to visit, and to bankroll all her purchases of paintings and other art which in Guatemala brought them to my hut.

On the afternoon of their unannounced arrival I was just returning from seeing off the mail boat, after loading it up with the dead body of the Norwegian ambassador to Guatemala, Frode Nilsson, who'd come earlier that morning in his normal friendly way with his generous wife, with no gunman, bodyguards or parades to buy a painting of a wild lightning-shooting rain deity for his home, which they did, but then the poor man died immediately after, right there in my hut.

Though elderly, he hadn't been so very old. He was a good man, not superficial or full of soap operas or intrigues, and all of us felt full of grief about his loss, especially for his widow.

But either those people are made of ice and granite or she was stunned, for his wife, though sad, remained unfrantic and undestroyed and didn't forget the painting when we loaded up her husband's body, holding it in her lap as she sat just above him on the mail boat's inner bench as it pulled off to the opposite shore nine miles away, to the waiting car to carry him back to the airport in Guatemala City on to Oslo and to his people's village somewhere in Norway.

Itzak Winer, on the other hand, coming in on the tail end of that, was a massive Jewish American with a big heart and a harder head, who didn't take no for an answer, even before there was anything about which to say "no."

He wore a big, flapping, badly-made, light blue polyester suit and shoes big enough for a full-grown housecat to crawl inside and sleep, which you had to watch out for as he rammed his equally persuasive belly into you, bumping you around in his efforts to get a deal for his little Vera. Knowing that Izzy still thought he was selling sewing machines, forgetting he was buying paintings and how that was all he'd ever known how to do, Vera, a tiny Polish Jewish lady, used him when making deals like an intimidating thundering tractor to crack the ground enough with pushiness and blatant suburban gauche for her to come in, after silencing the brute, to plant apparent seeds of kindness so as to seem the one who had all the class. The relief one felt at her silencing him was so welcomed by most people, that between the two of them deals were quickly done, after which though satisfied, the two of them would amble off with hurt looks as if they'd been somewhat cheated after doing us all such a favor.

Unfortunately for them, the Tzutujil were merchants by birth and probably selling things to Jews before the Jews knew they were Jewish, and the Pueblo Indian jewelry-sellers I grew up with were better at the game than anyone. So, married to the one and having been taught by the other, I watched Yalur wrestle around in equal fashion with Vera and Izzy, until they were weakened enough, that I could come in lowering my prices way down to just a little above half of double, making it so the four of us got along just fine.

We liked them because unlike most of the outsiders they had a lot of style and because they came with no Lysol and when invited, they politely sat down with us in our smoky earth-floored hut, didn't take our pictures, didn't try to buy our spiritual secrets or relics, actually drank our coffee, ate our food, laughed and joked and shot the breeze.

Several months later after Vera's first village foray, Vera's brother Salo Harshov, the shoe store mogul, whose son Nehemiah had gone off somewhere to study and returned home as a rabbi, and who as rabbis have to do, got together with other rabbis and learned individuals on a weekly basis to have discussions about other people's discussions about the midrash of other discussions or issues that concerned Guatemalan Jews, all Jews, etc. and so on, was doing some discussing of just that in one of these discussion groups when the conversation strayed from the modicum of some holy reference that all the learned had chewed up enough for the rest of them to swallow, when this new upstart rabbi, Nehemiah Harshov, Vera's nephew, asked the gathering of men why it was that Guatemala, of all nations in the world, had been the first, in 1949, to recognize Israel as a Jewish state, thereby causing lots of Eastern Europe's Ashkenazim to join the earlier migration of Sephardim in Central America, who didn't want the hassle of who owned the land in Palestine and so on.

One visiting Rabbi, Benjamin Shabes, a Sephardi from Mexico City who the Mejicanos called Benito Chavez, not very old but acting old, thought it might have been because, in his considered opinion, Guatemala was mostly a Mayan Nation, since over ninety percent of all the non-Indians were Indians by blood if not by culture and there were those who said that all the Mayan people were obviously the lost tribes who'd drifted off on one of the earlier Diasporas.

"Have you ever listened to the way these Indians speak and seen the things they do? You could swear you were listening to some sounds of ancient Hebrew and wouldn't you know some of it even sounds Yiddish."

Then Eli Malik, a Russian Jew of Khazar ancestry who'd been living in Argentina butted in, "What? What's new about that? Even the Spanish thought that way. Look here, in Guatemala to this day, Indians that give up their own language and take up speaking Spanish and European culture, who stop being Indians are still called Ladinos, which as you all know is the Spanish dialect spoken by Spanish Jews, the Sephardis.

"The Inquisition in Spain was set up just like you-know-who, or the other you-know-who and you-know-when, to find out who was Jewish, or even who had just a drop of Jewish blood to weed us completely out of their world.

"When these inquisitors came to Central America and Mexico they too were quite certain, because of their speech and customs, that the Mayans in particular must have been Jews.

"The only thing that saved the Indians from some of what the rest of us endured was the massive forced conversions to which they on the surface acquiesced, and because the civil authorities, who were often opposed to the church and who ironically held up the laws of the king which strangely protected all his possessions, which had the Indians classified as non-human along with the wildlife, on the bottom rung of their human ranking system that delineated the comparative value of people according to mixtures of race.

"So they weren't human, therefore they weren't Jews, so the Inquisition couldn't force them to confess with their molten lead.

"Maybe they are Jews, who could say? They've always been treated the same, they sound the same, maybe they are the same."

The issue was in no way exhausted and when it came time for the little council of rabbis and learned men to set their hungry teeth into the feast that their women folk had been together preparing off in the next room they unanimously agreed to search for a local expert with whom they would make a more in-depth discussion in another of their discussion groups about the possibility that all these millions of Mayans were actually Jews, if not Jewish.

Nehemiah Harshov's father Salo, whose sister Vera had been to our village and my house and who remembered seeing my picture in the newspaper with the caption "Ojos del Zajorin" and reading the accompanying article which referred to me as a practitioner of "ritos Cabalisticos mayances," or cabalistic Mayan rituals, thought for some reason that I was a Jew and should therefore be invited to the discussion as a Mayan-speaking expert to be examined by the rabbis and learned men to compare the details of Hebrew and Mayan customs to determine for themselves whether or not the Mayans were Jews.

Having agreed to this unanimously, they drafted a formal letter and posted it to general delivery to Santiago Atitlan.

Besides the non-Indian government bureaucracy and store owners in the town, it was rare for villagers to participate in any part of receiving or sending mail, for the most part, because only a fraction of the village population spoke Spanish and even fewer of them had been able to learn Spanish writing.

Therefore the official Government mail and telegraph fellow stationed in our town made any mail that came addressed to me into a major event, delivering it personally to the hut and waiting to see what it contained. This mailman and telegraph operator was convinced my name was Nicolas Petzai. No matter how much I pleaded or how often I explained, even writing my real name repeatedly for him, this mailman refused to deliver my mail unless it was addressed to Nicolas Petzai.

I had to fight him for my mail, sometimes resorting to sneaking into his little stone and timber office and writing Nicolas Petzai on my mail and then showing up when he was there to claim what he now knew was really mine.

In the end I had to write, telegraph or tell everyone to send my letters in care of Nicolas Petzai, of whom nobody ever heard tell besides the man who was in charge of all my mail.

This the rabbis did, and after a couple of letters back and forth we agreed by telegram from Nicolas Petzai to Nehemiah Harshov that I should, the following April, on a certain date pass by their meeting place in Zona Nueve in Guatemala City to join their discussion, by which time I would have been released for a couple of months from my recent spiritual responsibilities in the village and would need to go to the city anyhow to renew my visa, collect some monies owed me at the Israeli Embassy, buy some candles, *pom*, machetes and ax heads for the people in the village.

In the interim, the delicious river of beauty and strangeness that was our everyday village life of farming, fishing, reed mats, smoke, tortillas, friendship, funerals, painting, childrearing and ceremony surged on and we, like happy nesting ducks, floated in it fairly undisturbed.

The Israeli retinue, however, reappeared several more times, occasionally without the ambassador himself, with others in his place but always with the guards, during which time an unexpected phenomena began to brew: the bodyguards, both the Israelis and the Guatemalan fellows with gold teeth, began to take an active interest in my art and took out extensive, protracted loans against their future pay from the consulates to buy some of my smaller paintings.

Scary looking and over six feet tall, the local bodyguards towered over most of Guatemala's much shorter population, including myself. The greater number of these men were descendants of German immigrants who'd colonized the desert regions of central-eastern Guatemala in the middle 1800s, where on becoming cattle ranchers, they married local mestiza women of varying Indian, African and Spanish ancestry.

Over the years, a violent tribal frontier cowboy culture had developed around Zacapa and Zanarate from whose ranks had emanated the bulk of Guatemala's most feared military leaders, both right wing and left, including several presidents, all of whom brought their "cowboys" from their ranches down to guard their persons and who also formed the bulk of individuals making up the small warlord-type armies of the rich and powerful.

Born into poor families inextricably attached to rich ranching families, these hulking, tropical henchmen had been given guns at birth. These severe people, instead of baby blankets and tiny shoes, put new revolvers and spurs in the cradle during the family ritual of naming a baby boy and a fancy lace apron and silk hair ribbons if she were a girl.

As friendly and honorable in certain ways as these fellows could be, they'd kill you in a flash if ordered, for they'd grown up having never seen another male, except their ancestor's bosses, growing old; knowing then that they and everybody else had been only born to die and knowing nothing else, they could just as easily take you with them in any fracas that ensued.

Which is why it seemed so heartwarming, a little sad and disarmingly bizarre to myself and even their employers when these dangerous thugs with gold teeth, combed pomaded hair, callused killing hands and rented uzzis started holding sincere discussions with me about why they preferred my blue and violet paintings to those in fiery reds, greens or yellows, and for which they sacrificed their already meager pay, then sheltered the pictures in their big heavy arms all the way back to the tiny hovels in which they lived, deep inside the cardboard ghettos of the capital city, where they'd finally hang my painting up on a nail pushed into their leaky rain-streaked walls where now they felt they had at least one thing as classy as the boss.

Some of them even showed up with their wives at my art shows, proud to be there as private citizens who knew the artist personally, visiting and carrying on rather long conversations with the terrified gallery owners about the meaning, the feeling, the colors and the motives of the work.

One of these fellows, a major in the Guatemalan army's secret police and permanently assigned to the Israeli embassy as a bodyguard, was a Lebanese Arab born in Guatemala, named Ishmael Daud ben Galeb. He looked bad and was bad in the most stereotypical sense of bad, for he had a pockmarked face, crooked pencil moustache, Siete Cabras pomade, a gold ring, gold teeth, patent leather shoes, a polyester suit with a gun in his belt and had shot and killed people on several occasions. But he'd been to our house in service as Dolly's guard and was one of those many art-collecting guards who'd bought a painting.

On the day and a couple of hours before I'd arranged to be questioned by the rabbis, Yalur and I were expected at the Israeli embassy where Dolly was to pay us for previously delivered paintings I'd done especially for her notorious "cultural exchange" for which she was already in arrears, having sold them in her galleries a year previous.

We walked there from the bus and when we turned the last corner before we arrived, we turned and walked hurriedly away, terrified of all the national police, paramilitary troops, bodyguards, soldiers and the like that surrounded a million shiny cars and limousines that drove up squealing, clogging up the entire road to discharge their highly-guarded political figures and business folk who were rushed behind the embassy walls.

Before we could get more than a city block away I could hear the cylinder of a revolver being rolled behind us as we fled, its well-greased clicking like a little pulley on the docks, and soon it was accompanied by the hurried footsteps of city shoes, a raw irritating voice that called me by name, mixed with lewd and racist anti-Indian abuse.

And doing what someone like me should have never done, I lost my stirrups and turned indignantly to confront, unarmed, this pistol-brandishing bully, whom I instantly recognized as Ishmael Galeb, who then ran up laughing and hugged the both of us, starting right in about why he didn't like my red paintings either, and would I make a special one for his daughter in Coatepeque, making sure that it was blue.

He'd been posted by Dolly to look out for us and deliver us through the crowd, right into what unexpectedly turned out to be a highly guarded afternoon garden party, where every ambassador and opposing presidential candidate in town, as well as the incumbent regime, were to meet with certain foreign business folk under these controlled circumstances, as refereed by the Israelis on behalf of the obviously invisible U.S. to agree to something which I'm quite sure would have disgusted me, but over which I had no say and which we witnessed only by accident, hoping to quickly get our cash and leave. This didn't look very hopeful after Ishmael had delivered us to the much scarier Israeli security at the cloakroom and past the first check in the foyer, where after being searched for weapons, bombs and recording tools and x-raying my hat, a short, courteous Israeli lady with a white shirt, pink mini-skirt and over-the-shoulder gun escorted us into the party as if we were some wild dignitaries from a useful bush tribe, into Dolly's cocktail party welcome after which we were pushed again into one of the revolving knots of mixing people right next to the Guatemalan defense minister, and the sister of the president of Panama.

Because we'd come to the city I didn't have my usual Mayan clothing on, to avoid the usual non-Indian hatred that it inspired; Yalur, on the other hand, was dressed as the Mayan queen all Tzutujil women knew themselves to be, and it wasn't long before a jealous lady, the wife of one of the highly-guarded presidential candidates, who were eyeing each other suspiciously, with their brandies and champagne from their knots of only three bodyguards each, as requested by Menasham in the interest of fair play, came along and began making fun of the different-colored tinsel sparkling in Yalur's ornate hand-woven gown, claiming that the "Indians were screwing up the country by adulterating the 'national costume' by making such additions."

The truth was, of course, that this small but powerful echelon of non-Indian Guatemalan right-wing political families thought all Indians should remain as maids and gardeners and certainly not be admitted as equals in a party with the likes of them.

But Yalur, with whom I couldn't go anywhere even in the village without her throwing a berrinche or starting up a feud, was in no ways ready to acquiesce to this lady's unsolicited abuse and after only two minutes in the party interrupted the CIA guy, who half-heartedly ran an American insurance firm, and who was unexpectedly defending Yalur when she blurted out to her cocktail assailant in her Indianized Spanish, "Are you wearing any underwear?" To which the lady, setting her teeth, replied, "We know you Indians don't wear any underwear at all."

"We don't have to," Yalur spit back, her eyes glazing for a fight, dangerously beginning to cross, "because we keep our bottoms clean."

"You Indians are filthy and breed like dogs, humping their sisters in the street."

"At least we're Indians and proud of it, instead of smelly mongrels like you, whose mother can't tell which end to put the diaper on because when they speak it smells like shit." And that was the end of all the talking which escalated into screams as the both of them like rabid dogs dove into each other, biting and kicking and pulling out each other's hair, at which skill the white lady was definitely out of her league and at which Yalur came up the champion, having had so much more practice, as it was not an uncommon activity among angry young village women of child-bearing age.

It took five Israeli security and the CIA guy, all of whom lost a few buttons, to get the two brawlers separated, after which the tension in the garden was running pretty high.

I'd only come to pick up my money, which Yalur considered Dolly owed her, and leave, but at this point I would have gladly settled for the latter if we could just get out in one piece.

But Yalur was having none of it since we'd been insulted through no instigation of our own, and she insisted we be given what we were owed, especially for all the extra trouble they'd put us through. She wasn't budging. Like a fool, I reached for my cheap Guatemalan pack of Rubiós cigarettes to fetch one out of my inside coat pocket to smoke to ease my nerves, make an unseen prayer, swallow down my rage at both Yalur, who was oblivious to the danger she put us in, but of course more at the horrible woman who represented the politically endorsed ignorance and hatred against all indigenous people and their natural vigor. When as I did so, I very nearly died.

The bodyguard of the incumbent president and the guards of the opposing candidate, who each already had one hand on their guns, were worried and on edge about the other's group, since all of them had made assassination attempts on one another throughout the year. They interpreted the speed with which I was reaching for my cigarettes as a further act in the brawl against one of their own and, assuming I was going to produce a pistol and shoot someone, before my hand had left my coat I had over thirty guards with cocked guns drawn and pointed at my head.

Like Raggedy Boy faced with the trial of being annihilated by fire on every side, that part of me that was more deeply in love with the village, the earth, my children and the life I had yet to live, wrapped itself into the coiling vine of human-inspired possibility, and with my left hand I very slowly removed the entire package of cigarettes holding it above my head, trying not to shake, whilst yelling out, "Don't shoot, please, don't shoot. I surrender; each of you can have one. You don't need to point a gun at a fellow just to get a smoke. Does anyone have a light?"

Then the guns went back, everybody breathed and laughed and fifteen men tried to light my shaking cigarette.

In those days I was still a village boy with no idea of what this was we'd walked into.

The United States government could not legally give Guatemala any military aid because of the military's notorious human rights infringements. But big business people from the States and other countries, plus the U.S. State Department, wanted to keep Guatemala at war against the so-called Left to supposedly keep Cuban-style communism from creeping into Mexico and from there into the States. So instead of making things better for the people in the country, therefore alleviating the necessity for a revolution, they wanted to give them guns.

Israel therefore was recruited by the U.S. to maintain Guatemala's military by supplying arms and advisors and serving as the message carrier for all U.S. communication with the Guatemalan military. By making complex deals with arms makers and dealers from Belgium, Argentina, Italy and Uruguay, to name only a few, who vectored it all in through their embassies on behalf of the Israeli embassy with money shuffled through other businesses and governmental activities, the Americans were able to supply the Guatemalan military, paramilitary, and maybe clandestine hit squads with so much extra firepower, like missile-firing helicopters, flame throwers, mortars, guns and ammunition of fairly modern types as well as antipersonnel bombs, grenades, armored vehicles and all kinds of tear gas and mob guns, plus communications devices and training directly from Israel and other foreign militaries, that Guatemala's forcefully, illegally conscripted army swelled from 15,000 to 75,000 overnight.

The problem, of course, was finding enough people to shoot at with all these new gizmos, a great deal of which were consequently stolen by anti-government guerrillas who until then were grossly under-armed to properly run a war of insurgence against even the original small Guatemalan army and most of whom had been government-trained conscripts to begin with.

This garden party was one of many attempts by the Israelis to get communications going between all factions involved in official circles in hopes of convincing all the internecine pettiness that ran in the right wing to unify and make themselves look decent enough so the States could again communicate outright.

Almost every guest at that "party" was at the center of what would become the most concentrated, brutal onslaught against people of indigenous ancestry in the Western Hemisphere in the twentieth century. Three percent of the entire population would be eradicated in the next four years by the command of one of the men at the party and another 20 percent would be forced to leave or be internally displaced permanently in the next eight years by the policies decided by big business, the States and those politicians whose gunmen almost killed me for my tobacco. They would hunt my family and myself as well, but we knew nothing of that yet, and we were still not sure that day if we'd even survive the hatred of all these hideous people at the party eating small food on crackers and drinking strange liqueurs, who had no love of anything I loved, or recognition that it even existed.

We'd just come to pick up our cash so we could continue on and were unceremoniously shoved into this vicious party by Dolly, who now by some miraculous turn, which probably had to do with her people trying to get us out of there as well, asked us if we'd like to be paid what she owed us.

Yalur, who hadn't said more than nine muffled Atiteco curses to herself since her brawl, all of a sudden blurted out in good merchant Spanish, "Cash only please."

Dolly Havel owed me close to nine thousand quetzales, which had the same value as dollars in these times. This was about eighteen years' wages for a normal Guatemalan family, a lot of cash for us to be carrying around bandit-infested Guatemala City, especially where the buses docked, where all the thieves and pickpockets like to converge, in and around the terminal market.

Dolly wanted to give us a check, complaining that she didn't have that kind of cash in hand.

"Cash only please, in ones if you got them. You took too long to pay, we don't trust you anymore, people beat us up, point guns at us and we don't have a bank. Cash only please."

I would have taken a check and found a way to cash it, but Yalur was getting mad again and though I was mad at her for insisting on the impossible, thinking we should take what we could get and leave, after all I'd done all the work of painting them anyway, so I should get to say how we got paid, but forever Yalur felt she owned everything and everybody owed her something and if you argued, you'd be in another brawl, so I just sat there wondering where it would all end when Dolly, who had disappeared into the unknown inner sanctum of their home, after whispering a minute with Menasham who was busy with all the bosses, returned with a big box full of quetzales and counted out nine thousand.

Where she got them, how Yalur knew, I'll never fathom, but the worst of it all was the fact that Yalur just put them all into her shawl like a pile of corn husks and tied them into a tight little bundle and throwing the shawl over her shoulder, shook hands and said we were leaving, which we did.

When we finally got to Salo Harshov's house, toting in ones the equivalent of today's buying power of a couple of hundred thousand in cash, we were tired and scared but highly comforted by the friendly way the fifteen rabbis, six learned fellows, Nehemiah Harshov and his wife Miriam and the other women, none of whom we'd ever met before, graciously greeted us and welcomed us as honored visitors.

The ladies all had aprons tied on except Eli Malik's wife, Sharon, who was actually sitting doing all the kitchen bossing and making sure her Armenian and Georgian cooking was kept separate from the rest, but the smells were large, beautiful, dark and strangely comforting after all the ruckus at the embassy, the aromas rushing out toward us when the kitchen door opened as Yalur was ushered into the throng of women, while I was gently herded into a corner room with all the men.

Most of the men had yarmulkahs on their heads, each from his own tradition, save for two older, pale, very serious-looking bearded fellows with really good black hats and beautiful black coats who sat at the very back, a little off from the rest, rolling their eyeballs when they saw me, and whose chairs were at such an angle and close proximity to the large, low window as to suggest to me, who was seated at the head of the inner facing gathering, that if what proceeded didn't suit them they might just climb out the window to escape into the wealthy Zona Nueva neighborhood into the windy April world.

Nehemiah Harshov, wearing yarmulkah, tallis and tzitzit, introduced me to his gathering, with whom I shook hands going around returning to my seat and who afterwards sang out a short Hebrew prayer and the session began.

We spoke in Spanish because it was the language we all together had most in common, though Yacov Baruc spoke English, Yiddish, Hebrew, Spanish, Russian, Polish, German, Italian and Macedonian, and the Sephardic fellows from Argentina, Mexico, Guatemala and Morocco spoke Yiddish, Spanish, Hebrew and Arabic. The two fellows at the back spoke only Yiddish, Polish and Hebrew, and weren't speaking to the likes of me for whom Nehemiah translated and a few others as well.

Yacov Baruc, right away breaking the rules they'd just laid down, asked me the first question in English, just to show off.

"So we read that you are the favorite son of the Tzutujil Maya, how is it this son is so golden and not such a shwartzer, eh?"

Nehemiah explained in Yiddish all about my life as he knew it, my coming to Guatemala, my teacher Chiviliu, my marriage, my sacred duties, my painting and so on, going on and on for fifteen minutes in which I hadn't said a word, and with whom Yacov had already begun to argue until one of the old guys in the back shut both of them up with one word and some half-hearted hand waving.

Then Benito Chavez, Benjamin Shabes, the rabbi from Mexico City, tried to politely enquire of me about something for which somebody else began to respond, into which Nehemiah butted in, answering instead.

Then I said, standing, "You men go ahead and talk, I'll go eat."

Everybody laughed; Eli Levinsky grabbed me, sat me down and asked Nehemiah in Yiddish which he translated back to me, "How is it that you became a Zajorin?"

"Am I a Zajorin?"

"Didn't I hear somebody say that you are a Zajorin?"

"Some people say I'm a Zajorin. I don't call myself a Zajorin. Who called me a Zajorin?"

"You must be a Jew. Why do you keep answering everything with a question?"

"Do I?"

Except for two old fellows in the back who looked even more disgusted, everybody laughed and relaxed a little and after which I tried to disentangle the mix-up in the magazines and newspapers where earlier, at the beginning of my career as an artist, a serious-looking photo of myself had been mistakenly captioned with the title of one of my paintings: "Los Ojos del Zajorin," or the Eyes of the Zajorin. The subtext went on to explain that this "zajorin" was responsible for carrying out "ritos secretos cabalisticos," or secret Cabalist rituals. Though the general big city readership of 1970s Guatemala would understand this to mean "the eyes of the Indian shaman," shamans in charge of secret native ritual, to the many Jews and Arabs in the country this implied that the young man in the photo, me, Martín Prechtel, had the far-seeing eyes of the Zajorin, who was logically though mysteriously a devotee of the Cabbalah. In my attempts to clarify the situation I had only dug myself in deeper with the rabbis, for which I was now even more deeply interrogated.

I went on to explain how among all Mayan hill people that still resided for the most part in southwestern Guatemala, when they weren't speaking among themselves in one of their many Mayan languages of Quiché, Cakchiquel, Tzutujil, Pocomchí, Pocomám, Mam, Qekchi, Ixil, Chortí, or any of the twenty other distinct dialects, they communicated to the non-

Indian world in a beautiful Mayanized antique Spanish that had its roots in sixteenth-century Spain. In the various dialects of spoken Spanish used by the first European colonists, the word they employed to signify a Mayan shaman was zajorin, a tradition carried on to this day by Mayans, mestizos and big city Spanish speakers as well.

Originally, however, the word zajorin, zajorim, zahorin or zajori was used throughout Islamic and Sephardic Spain before 1492 and was descended directly from the old Hebrew root word "zahor," or "zajor," meaning literally "to remember." In those days for over four centuries Arabic was the preferred spoken and written language of all Sephardic Jews, Spanish Christians and Muslims. Zajorin is the "Andaluzi" Arabic form of the Hebrew word zahorim meaning "those who remember" and came to be applied to those individuals who were born with the Divine ability to innately know the Nature of the Holy, who had the ability to spiritually remember and see beyond present time to report the roots and historical reasons for the present. The zajorin was an ecstatic who could also "remember" the future beyond the present, who knew the Big Stories without having studied them.

Though not sanctioned by the official institutions of Imperial Islam, Rabbinical Judaism, or the Christian Church all living together in Andaluzi Spain, these singular men and women, the zajorin, were a continuance of something quite ancient that survived popularly among the regular people who summoned them to communicate with deceased loved ones, ancient prophets, ancestors and various spirits in springs, mountains, trees, animals and all nature.

After the cruel and unintelligent expulsion of Jews and Muslims from the forcibly synthesized political entity of Ferdinand and Isabella's Catholic Spain in 1492, use of the Arabic version of the word zajorin in Spanish continued, but was eventually demoted during the Inquisition period to signify a wizard or sorcerer and specifically an Arab or Jewish magician in league with the Devil.

Because Europeans thought all non-Christian, tribal peoples throughout the world to be heathens and all heathens to ultimately be Jews from the widely distributed tribes of Israel, the Spanish in particular used the word zajorin derisively to describe the multitude of locally respected, subtle divisions of shamans, diviners, doctors, teachers, tradition keepers and priests that they found among the thousands of groups of native peoples during their traumatic colonial rampage throughout Asia, Africa and what they would come to call the Americas.

On the other hand, for the Sephardic Jews and Arabs dispersed throughout the world, in the very same instant the Europeans were interrupting the rest of the world's cultures, the word zajorin continued to mean a person who magically didn't forget the deeper spiritual understandings. This caused the Jews, who fled to the so-called New World trying to initially escape the Inquisition, to respect the Mayan peoples' spiritual life more; for the use of their word zajorin as the great rememberers, ironically did more accurately describe the function of native spiritual memory keepers, some of whom are shamans.

That I, the "zajorin" in the photo, was involved in maintaining secret Cabalistic rites got the rabbis even more worked up.

The Cabbalah, or Cabala, was the great spiritual unified field theory of certain non-rabbinical Jews, mostly Spanish Jews, descended from Jewish Temple priests of old Palestine, which in turn was based on an even older understanding of the Divine as a Tree of Life, manifested by certain magical sounds, numerological relationships of matter and living things to each other and the nature of the invisible force behind them in which humans could participate as devotees through mystical combinations of Divine breath and the Hebrew alphabet.

The Cabala highly influenced Spanish Islam and Christianity, gestating in a marvelous complexity of language, magic and ecstasy, most of which has remained as secret understandings both orally transmitted and written, but which inspired many written manuals and commentaries in old Andalusia and continues to inspire to this day.

With all things Jewish and Saracen demonized and banished from sixteenth-century Spain, the Spanish clerics and invaders, while watching the *Aj Qij*, or Mayan calendar priests, read and divine from their almanacs of deified numbers, words and magical sounds, once again lumped it all into the category of Jewish heathenism and said the Mayans were practicing Cabalistic rites, an application of the word which, like zajorin, has survived in Guatemalan Spanish for close to five centuries until the present day.

Though after the horrible treatment of the Jews by Ferdinand and Isabella, these words Zajorin and Cabalista became accusative and mocking terms for things the Europeans refused to comprehend, their use ironically caused other folk to respect us more for our careers as *Aj Q'ij* and *Ajcuna'*, for whom the words Zajor and Cabala were still respected and whose ancestors had a common experience of being oppressed for their similar devotions to equally exuberant understandings of what was Holy.

The rabbis and I dove into questions about the details of all kinds of sacred things in which even Holy Boy, who'd been mocked as the Big Jew, actually was in many ways a Mayan version of the Cabala, who was a tree made of language whose fruit was sound, that flowered in cycles of deified time and whose construction, rituals, language and secrets could never be comprehended by those that would write them down, and so on and on. We reveled in the like until Eli Levinsky, who obviously had not been listening, inquired politely, "When you worship, how do you address your God?"

To which I replied, "There are a thousand names for what gives us life, but none of them are the word for God. We have no name for the Holy, we give gifts to the Holy, summon the Holy, feed the Holy and failing as beautifully as we can trying to feed the Holy, our magnificent and sincere blundering keeps the Holy living whose generosity and forgiveness is our life."

After all Nehemiah's translations had gone through, the two bearded fellows scooted their chairs up to the front and we began an earnest discussion that lasted for several hours in which we bantered back and forth about Mayan marriage customs, words for this and thoughts about that, until the time to pray and eat our feast at sunset had come, by which time we hadn't even come close to resolving the issue of the possibility of whether or not the Tzutujil were their lost Jewish relatives or not.

The table was laid out with every kind of Jewish food: Argentinean Jewish food, western Russian Jewish food, Polish Jewish food, Armenian Jewish food, all kinds of Jewish food laid out and cooked according to how they'd all been spread out and dispersed but not lost to each other and also in honor of my love of discovering people's diverse and particular approaches to preparing the deliciousness that was the blessing of being allowed to live.

The women bossed us around a lot, telling us where to sit, how to sit, what to eat and to make sure we ate some more and more and more, which we all did.

Since our business about the Mayans and the Jews was far from finished and our first meeting had been such a success in every way the women insisted it become a custom. Every year thereafter, sometimes even twice a year, we came together with a swelling and shifting roll call of learned folk, rabbis and cooking wives, until our people were dispersed as well. But for now, in Nehemiah Harshov's house there were no bodyguards, intrigues, shiny cars or guns; only food, friends and questions.

eight

LANDSLIDES, SHRINE PONDS, A WILD BOY AND GORGEOUS DAYS OF JASMINE-COVERED WALLS

Sitting in the front seat next to a Tzutujil store owner, Atun Reanda, the driver and the owner of the little yellow fleet truck loaded up with German weaving tinsel, blocks of indigo dye and a couple of bales of every color of silk and rayon embroidering floss for the village women's weaving of their blouses and the men's ornate short *scav* pants, I arrived back home in the village at two in the morning from my seventh visit with the rabbis. I headed straight for the sacred house where Holy Boy was housed, to make my offerings of thanks for a successful run and for looking after my family and our sustenance in my absence, and adding more offerings I'd picked up in the central market to those I'd already sent up, I also petitioned the Old Boy to see if he would grace me with his legendary cleverness for my intellectual battle with the priests, for Padre's freedom and our safe trip to and from that affair, ending with a prayer on behalf of the rabbis.

Though he found all sacred house rituals repulsive, he was still a village man and courteously waited while I finished up my prayers. Padre, who'd found me here at dawn, thought that I, like all the village shamans as far as he was concerned, was in some kind of theatrical fascination with the shaman's life, in which we acted out the shaman's role, hoping something good would come of what for him were empty and mechanically performed formulas. His rationalist mind, the only part of him that considered itself real, was both disgusted and bemused by what it couldn't see, while the old Indian part of him that could feel what was really here, for all his lack of initiation and never having heard or understood his grandfather's telling of the Story, was held prisoner by his acquired cynicism, which he interpreted as original thinking instead of a depressive trance of mediocre righteousness and flat equationary action.

Saying our formal goodbyes to all the smoky sacred house leaders who were proud to have the two of us in front of their Gods and Saints, Padre and I returned to my house to deliver up my bundles and distribute all the gifts I brought home for the extended family members and things my neighbors had asked me to buy for them. Before we went up to the church we had a bowl of chocolate each and a bowl of *pchín xcuya rquin ch´u*, little dried fish cooked in roasted tomato broth, accompanied by five slices of ember-roasted *buak´*, throughout which Yalur's father had a heated chat with Padre in which both of them sided together against some adversary none of the rest of us could see. Because Yalur's father was a tradition-hating "new" Catholic, he resented my prominent status among the traditionalists, but he loved Padre. Padre was his hope for the future.

By then Padre Francisco, as Father Stanley Rother coached his Tzutujil parishioners to call him, had come searching for us, creeping around the rocky paths and thoroughfares of the big Tzutujil village in his khaki-colored old-time English Landrover supplied to him by the parish, which had a little sheep and cross decals emblazoned on the doors, coming upon Padre and myself trudging up the incline a quarter of a mile from my family compound.

Father Stanley thought that by having himself addressed as Padre Francisco, or as he ended up being universally referred to in Tzutujil slang, *A Plaas,* he would be equated by the villagers not only with San Francisco, or St. Francis of Assisi, but more popularly with the great Mayan prophet, ritualist and government resister, Francisco Sojwel, who had continually appeared, disappeared and reincarnated, even sometimes reappearing in the form of different animals to disappear again, for centuries on end, without ever physically dying. His last generally agreed upon appearance had been in the latter half of the nineteenth century, only to be witnessed in 1903 walking alive back into the ocean to disappear beneath where his divine parents resided.

All the people, Christians and otherwise, knew about him but the traditionalists in particular had been waiting for him to return for the entire twentieth century.

Several old men and women had known him well, especially Chiviliu, whose very birth had come about on account of the spiritual power of that divine man.

By using a time-tested strategy of the church, employed for centuries worldwide when dealing with tribal people whose non-Christian faith is very strong, Father Stanley reckoned that if he adopted the name of this original hero of the people, who ironically had always been an enemy of all church and government institutions and a strong devotee of Holy Boy, then he felt the people of the village would become more conducive to Stanley's dream of getting the entire village baptized, confirmed and into mass, surrendered to the living grace and their possible entrance into the Catholic heaven as afforded by his order of the church towards whose seminary we were headed for a trial.

Padre and I had spoken many times in our huts about how he was going to aim his words, but Father Stanley, like the gray sky people in the New Mexico of my youth, never had much to say to me and on that ride he didn't break with that tradition.

But since I was conveniently left bouncing in the back on and off the jump seat at the side, Stanley took advantage of the hours that he and the grandson of Swordfighter had together in the front seat to go over what each of them thought and what they planned to present.

Their engaged dialogue and Catholic banter gave me time to drop into the deliciousness of an indigenous traveling trance, where, like the men I'd learned it from, I retold the story of The Toe Bone and the Tooth in my chest, throwing blessings from my heart out the window to all the places over which we drove, ground through and clattered by, where Raggedy had traveled as well, searching for Her bones, speaking elevated spirit speech to this tree at that place, or this bird at that cliff, or even the lake herself out there in the distance between three layers of cliffs, and there where he forgot her, where he left her and there where he went to hunt, then changing tales because the car didn't go where the land and walking did, to the cliffs of talc where three boys in another story tested their magic chocolate stirring sticks before fighting the metal monster of coffee, where you could see, as we passed it by, the marks they'd made against the stone way up high where the flowering *izotes*, curved out growing upwards, had their elephantine ear-like leaves climbing up their stalks to the grassy rim to where Iq Utiv Juyu took up: the mountains of the Black Coyote.

Right here behind that mound, Raggedy Boy had bargained for the last toe bone and tooth, choosing to allow eternal chaos for human existence so he might see her beloved face again.

Like all natives as they traveled in those days, traditionalists at least, I was utterly borne along, painlessly, inside the story itself, which I knew better than I knew my heart, for every inch of ground we crossed was named and claimed by a piece of the story which ran in image through the landscape of one's spiritual seeing like a deer made of memory, whose traveling was a kind of remembering that put the world together as it ran through the story, over the story, who was the story; whose trail and track once remembered enough to follow, left its footprints written somehow in the face of the one who was seeing the story in the land. This deep sparkle and intensity the story left in one's eyes was an indigenous thing, and that look is what some religions wanted scared out of our faces just as corporate farming had begun to plow it out of the land itself.

To the Tzutujil, the earth was made of sacred nouns, whose trees were active verbs, fertilized and held together by possessive pronouns of the shifting wind. When all the words were put together, the world became a herd of spoken stories who needed divine remembering and creative oral storytellers to keep these trees and winds from falling into manicured dogmatic ruts.

When they altered the indigenous names of the hills, rivers, trees, flowers, canyons, caves and plains, all of which the Tzutujil knew as words with meanings from one or many stories, these religions seemed to be ordering the land not to speak its native tongue or not to speak at all, implying that both the land and its people needed saving instead of being small eloquent parts of the land's native story.

By reassigning the places of our world with titles familiar to themselves, calling the "Cliffs of Black Coyote" the Mount of Calvary or turning the "Mountain of the Goddess' Sweeping" Sinai or the "Canyon of the People of the Bats" into the Road to Nazareth, they sought to replace our ancient oral God-stories with a single written, historical, human-centered tale imported from another suffering and anciently ravaged land, whose poor people had lost themselves when they discarded their real old stories at the frightened insistence of a small desperate group of their own relatives, who having become spiritually exhausted and enslaved became neurotically addicted to the uplifting convenience and re-establishing of self-esteem provided by an exclusive oneness that promised to transport them from the misery of their human-caused depression.

By forcing their single story of another people forced to flee their home and diversity upon our Earth, renaming all her places with names either too corny and short or with meanings too far away and mythologically buried, these so-called modern religions verbally dismembered our stories which effectively dismembered the Earth for their allowing it, it having been given to them as dead matter in their story for them to do with as they please.

Instead of seeing that the brightness and mischievous vigor in our eyes and the eager listening of our ears was holy and came from the land who was Our Lady, the Story remembered, in whose words of earth we could be born, walk, splash, fail, farm, dream, make love and die, merging into her living dust to become future nouns from which to regrow the trees through her retelling, these religions wanted all the brilliance in our faces tamed and to have come only from their single God.

But I was shaken from that trance into another when the stiff suspension of the British car, which had been reducing my already skinny bottom to a more meatless bony state, lurched to miss a boulder, tossed me rolling to the floor. Uprighting myself, I took to thinking how much love I bore my life, my friends and the Holy that I knew so well in the village and how that was always being tested like a spring sprout out too early in the frost; full of trials to keep its ornateness and smallness alive, consistently besieged as we were by human forces outside our village who wanted to control our lives for reasons we couldn't even want and how all of that was just as in the story Padre's father had given me and which the Swordfighter from beyond the grave had wanted me to have, to help Padre through the story he had to live instead of understanding, but which had caused me to begin to know how much my own life was a living version of the tale as well.

I thought of how our surprising visit to the Israeli embassy had nearly got me killed and a thousand other strange run-ins with politics and the like and how much I was like an over-eager jaguar kit saved by its mother who, pulling him by the loose skin around his neck, was kept alive by the secrets that the village gave and what the Story taught and how my family, even then, more than once avoided destruction by what I'd have to learn and relearn: about how to be small, how to remember under fire, how to breathe the steam your own soul's beauty emits as it is cooked in the hatred and heat of the dogmatic ancestral opinion of the father, letting the fire burn over your seed-like smallness in that steam to sprout slowly into a man who might be able to listen and then in action to carry the gift of the story that the land rolling by me at the moment contained for those who would learn her language.

And no sooner thought than done, Stanley braked to a sudden squealing stop. Blocking our way, running off the road and over the edge of a sheer *barranca* on the road a couple miles east of Godinez, the next cliff above Santa Catarina Polopo, a landslide of white tufa ash, volcanic scree and dislodged pines and oak trees lay tumbled two stories high across the little road as the eternal quaking of the highland mountain ground did its best to buck the pitted asphalt off his wounded back and heal the highways unwelcome cut.

As we were the first vehicle to arrive at the impossible wall of this landslide, Gaspar and I, without a word, both leapt from the truck after unsheathing our small traveling machetes from our gear and perfunctorily set to slashing down two full armloads of long leafy saplings which together we carried stiff-legged back down the steep grade of the narrow cliff-edge road to a dip behind a tight blind curve, before the rise on whose grade the avalanche of stone had fallen. Then, dumping them in the middle of the road, we left our waving sacrificed saplings as the universally accepted Central American version of the traffic flare to warn the less wieldy, overloaded, little inter-village school bus transports that up ahead was a situation for which they'd be better off turning around down here.

The Mountain Gods all hated the human invention of steel, out of which we made our hoes, axes, cars, tractors, airplanes, buses and weapons and with which we dismembered the earth and each other and though he was technically our blood kin now, he'd get mad off and on and try again to get revenge by killing or maiming any humans he'd come across by dropping landslides on their heads.

Though not as nervous as I was, looking up, about the humbling immensity of the unstable cliff face looming immediately above us as we trudged back to the landslide where Stanley sat still in his Landrover, or the three-hundred-foot vertical drop down over the other side of the road where the canopy layer of dense stands of mossy-trunked trees covered in blue candelaria flowers grew up in a massive curving unison desperately reaching out from the bottomless misty crevasse, both Padre and I shared a shudder, well aware that in places not so far from here, several Mayan villages had been buried alive or swept away, overnight, when smaller hills than this came undone and that once an unstable knob like this began to travel down, a great deal more was bound to follow.

To get to where we were bound was less than twenty miles away and driving over or around this size of rock fall was impossible. We'd all been delayed dozens of times before by landslides and knew that if enough people were backed up and sufficiently determined to get through from both sides of the avalanche, that if every person with either poles or bare-handed and sometimes even with shovels or hatfuls of dirt, people could, like jungle ants, often clear a tiny, treacherous path wide enough to dangerously allow one vehicle at a time to squeak around the rearranged hill.

This landslide however, was too big for that. Plants and trees would eventually take roots in the exposed earth and humans would slowly cut another road through it just like the one before, but a little farther out, until the nomadic tufa they laid it on decided to move again one day after the rains returned in some future year to loosen the new asphalt enough for the constant tremoring of the Guatemalan ground to crumble it and crash it down into the canyon a little farther toward the sea, where all the mountains of Guatemala were trying to get to anyway.

We had three choices, one of which was to head back, cross up to

Tecpan to the Pan-American highway, head west, turn off at Los Encuentros and come down to Solola' from the top, which would take us the remainder of the day and that route at that very moment had been blocked off by both Guatemalan army and certain rival groups of opposing guerrillas shaking down passengers for bribes and tolls and sometimes worse.

Another choice was to leave the car, hike over the pile of dust and stone to the other side and catch a ride in one of the inevitable trucks or buses returning back after finding the rock slide and go with them back where they came, which is where we wanted to be.

The third choice, which was the one I voted for, was for us to turn around and go home, but the Catholics were not to be deterred, not even by acts of God. Just when they'd decided to risk the guerrillas and the army, who should poke his big bald glistening head over the thirty-foot high newly-made powdery ridge, perilously crawling up and over its sliding crest, then standing, dangerously stumbling, then hopping after skiing the dust the remainder of the way right toward us, looking like a mouse stuck in a flour bin, his good, dark-gray, Basque wool sweater, his shiny shoes and polyester socks permeated in tufa dust, yelling out in his friendly lispy Spanish while waving his powder-spewing arms, beckoning for us to wait, but Padre Pacho Praxedes, the parish priest of Solola.

Pushing out the double doors of the back, dropping onto the road I ran up the hill a stretch where Pacho and I embraced, steadying one another from rolling down the grade before Stanley got the message he should set his brake. While rattling away simultaneously, as is only right with old friends, we were happy to meet here again after more than ten years, where as veterans of some younger times, bad decisions and adventures, and holding some distaste for the other's theology, we still both admired the other's courage and accepted the other's story. For my part, I owed him my life. All of this we expressed noisily and exuberantly on that hillside, much to the shame and silent disapproval of Father Stan, whose Oklahoma wheat farmer's upbringing taught him that such behavior among men was frivolous and demeaning and among priests, anticlerical.

But, taller than me and shorter than Stan, Pacho took no notice and shook the hand of Father Stan like the crank on a butter paddle until he saw Gaspar Culan, the son of Gaspar Culan, the grandson of Swordfighter, who hugged each other like orphaned brothers at the front.

Pacho had the good Spanish custom of consuming toasted, freshly baked *pan dulces* with coffee for an early breakfast, and when this morning the bakery had no bread because the truck that brought the ones he liked couldn't get through for another landslide further up, he telegraphed us. But knowing that the telegram would have to rattle and travel from post to post, town to town, some 490 miles of wire to make the round trip that was only thirteen miles by canoe, Padre Pachito Praxedes drove his church-provided Landrover with its own little sheep and cross emblazoned on the doors, to the landslide to pick us up, only to find there was another avalanche of stone between his landslide and this big one where he found us.

Pachito had brought one of his novice priests along who was waiting in his car a mile back, and once we'd climbed the three *derrumbes* this young man would return with Stanley's keys and drive his parish butt-breaker back to Atitlan, park it behind the church, catch the boat across the lake on the following morning, then ride the bus for seventy-five cents up to the seminary, which I'd been wondering from the start why we hadn't done ourselves.

Loaded down with their packs, papers, attachés and gear, and I with my string bag, machete and *paquan*, we followed Pacho, still babbling, who informed Stan and Padre about the bishop who was already at the seminary and certain problems they might encounter.

After crossing the second landslide and before the final one, a tall, very slim but forceful waterfall from a spring much higher up the mount cascaded into a placid roadside pool, misting and spattering enough upon the road for me to see its brilliant rainbow running over the entire track where the other three men, who'd gotten appreciably ahead of me, disappeared, chattering over the last steep incline, leaving me alone between the mist and the tufa slide. Walking back to the pool, I stood inside the rainbow camouflage of its cool spray, renewing my exhausted, overheated state, noticing as expected that the tiny pond was a little shrine, a church to She whose eyes I'd always sought, at whose bottom others had left their gifts of necklaces, earrings and money, to which I added my own offerings.

Maybe they didn't see it or didn't care, but their voices were either gone or deflected by the water's armor of rushing sound, inside of which what I spoke to Her was heard only by Her and I could not hear the voices of those that couldn't see Her. For this was the eye of the Daughter of the Mountains, the eye of Raggedy Boy's beloved wife, the first deep love of all men ever since. I prayed creatively and eloquently within the bounds of what village shamans know the water wants to hear, praying not for my good luck or success or desires but as a gift of thanks to Her for my being able to still see Her face, for Her willingness to show it and for pulling me this far into Her rainbow-guarded heart.

I drank from Her pool and put some of Her into my little bone-colored water gourd canteen with a wine cork for a plug, the one the old ladies in the village liked so much and the young men mocked, themselves preferring the new fad of ugly gray striped plastic jugs.

After bathing in Her blessing, much refreshed and happy to be alive, I walked out of the din of the waterfall's seclusion and proceeded up and over the last landslide, meeting the acculturated young Indian man, Pachito's assistant, coming back down, who recognized Her blessing in me that he was hoping to find in the place the rest of us were headed, who already sealed inside their steel car were howling and swearing about my tardy arrival in the way only Catholic priests can seem to manage.

Atanasio Pascual Praxedes Mendizabel was a half-Basque northern Spaniard whose father and only brother had been lost in the last Spanish Civil War when Franco and his team brought the Nazi air force to bomb the Pyrenees and, when his young mother was killed as well, dying of pure sorrow, Pachito, having just been made a priest, left his homeland. Like a lot of Basques and endangered Spaniards, he came to Guatemala to wait in a place of more relative peace until his heart could bear to return home to the source of all his heartbreak.

Though he did go back to visit his relatives twice in every decade since, he'd found a home in Guatemala for the stranded love his early losses demanded while serving his first assignation as the back-up priest for Solola. He had been forced to take over when his superior was mysteriously drowned in the lake after which Pachito retained undisputed sovereignty over his parish, not because the Bishops liked him or said so but on account of all the threats the Bishops received from the Indians whenever they tried to have him moved to some other district. His stern, no-nonsense Cakchiquel Maya parishioners, who loved the fact that Pacho visited every hut, transported old folks, drank their coffee and their liquor, made jokes, cared for the sick and fed the starving, had in typical Mayan fashion re-lengthened and turned around the already shortened form of his given name, transforming Pacho Praxedes into Padre Pachito Paredes, which everyone alive thought was his real name. Though he was a diehard Catholic and a mildly Marxist Christian and I an ecstatic pagan, Padre Pachito Paredes had never tried to save me, or make me into a Catholic, even as a young man a decade previous when I'd managed to become a more inspired idiot than he'd initially imagined me to be, when he did try to save my life and, later on, with his second try actually did in fact.

Toward the end of my early roaming years, just before I'd come across Pachito, I was stopped from any future wandering by my poverty. Like a wisp of floating wool caught in a drain filter, I landed like so many others on the north side of Lake Atitlan, opposite Santiago in what was then the beautiful Cakchiquel Mayan town of Panajachel, whose name meant the place of custard apples.

In those gorgeous days of jasmine-covered walls and bougainvillea-tangled eaves, I'd arrived, dropped off into the humid and flower-perfumed evening by another American named Stan, but this one in a Bronco, who continued on to Panama.

I'd had my first distant glimpse of the Lake in the dark, her stars running out in stripes like her hair from the shore. A recognition, the nostalgic feeling of being at home began then to creep in towards my noisy heart but would not make itself a full-time presence for quite awhile yet.

On that night, I dropped down into a corner of the fifty-cent pension to sleep the sleep of a two-year-old held in the arms of the sweet-smelling braided pith of two handmade tule mats.

Startled awake after dawn by a loud animal mewing that grew into yelps and screams until it rode up a strange melodious scale that ended in a nasal cow-like mooing, I pulled myself from the same position in which I'd hit the earth, my petrified neck semi-permanently twisted to the left.

I knew this sound that had murmured, blabbered and blustered right into my ears for its point-blank proximity on the other side of the paper-thin walls, which was now being scolded by someone just as loud, trying to hush it up.

Though the world outside had already bubbled up and boiled over into the day's daily work, it was not like Santiago would sound to me a year and a half later where an hour before dawn the village would be bathed in smoke and people packing to fully stride toward their fields, fish or firewood in the hills toting hoe and machete, the women trotting to the mills in the daily corn-grinding rush hour. This town in which I awoke had for some time, save for a few of the original Quiché refugees, who married a few of the local Cakchiquel Mayan farmers, who still retained small vertical plots of farmable land on the *laderas* of the deep canyon off the northern shore of the lake, succumbed to an economy of merchants. These original farming inhabitants had also already gone to their fields past the steel-grated store fronts all closed up until mid-morning except the Panaderia, the bakery, which spiced further the jasmine-scented lake air of the canyon-darkened dawn with the smell of burning oak and hot bread.

I'd been roving homelessly for almost a year, so why should I know this voice, this strange animal's sound? The author of the sound was like a fish I couldn't see and knew was there, knowing it was seeing me, but who refused to jump onto the hook of my cognition to be fished out of my memory's murky pool. I could not remember what I knew until the voice had been silent for a spell and I noticed with something of a start that there was the pupil of a yellow eyeball looking at me from a little oblong hole, the kind invariably torn into the walls of cheap pensions by peeping toms. When a voice that scolded in English seemed to have accompanied a scuffling gasp which rudely jerked the eyeball from the hole, I put my own head down to the aperture and peered into the adjacent room where I saw the only other person besides myself out of the four who'd been caught out in the wilds that same day, who'd survived the blizzard's blast of the year before.

While the courage and instinct of a sweet-eyed mare was what the people said had brought me back to safety, no one knew what had looked after this wild mewing boy. Frank was a robust, yellow-eyed, drooling kid two years younger than myself who the modern world called retarded. Wearing only a tee-shirt, a thin pair of pants and big tennis shoes, Frank had wandered off from behind his parents' mountain house up into even higher mountains than I had. With no food, no horse, no blanket, no fire, no hat, he'd climbed up into the same killing blizzard on the same day, which would freeze to death two hunters on the same mountain who were fairly well-equipped, under which if it hadn't been for Morning Star I should have succumbed as well.

After searching for two days, when they found the hunters frozen to death in their parkas, the rescue teams gave Frank up for dead.

But that afternoon this tall, strange, babbling boy came lumbering home, shaking his long-boned arms, dry as the day he'd disappeared, with no sign of frostbite, weakness, discomfort or unusual hunger, just as if he'd been out playing behind the house for an hour and had come in out of the cold.

I knew he was a part of nature, for his windy soul blew evenly through his wild uncaptured heart, and that he hadn't survived because the spirits were watching out for him, but because he was unafraid to die and was himself watching over them, who I knew he could see because he was half of one himself and it was written in his eyes.

Like most all of my companions on the Pueblo reservation who became excellent craftspeople of every indigenous type, I'd become a silversmith at an early age. In times when I was short of cash, which my pre-blizzard days, before and after the death of my mother and the disappearance of my wife most definitely were, I sold my jewelry to Frank's parents in a trading post that they owned. They were hard people and only bought from natives and people like myself when our lives were up against the wall and we had no other choice but to take the little that they offered. Nevertheless, unlike other trading posts or boutiques who wouldn't always buy, especially when you were down, you could count on the parents of the tall bellowing boy.

After Frank's miraculous survival and mysterious reappearance from the sparkling deep freeze of the wilds, his workaholic mother and alcoholic father sold off their store, packed up and disappeared with Frank, traveling south to find a home in another land faraway from the memory of their greed, which they'd used to keep themselves fully occupied and away from their wild and funny son. He was blessed of course, because the world assumed he was unblessed, for only those who seem unblessed can bless those who cannot see, and Frank blessed his parents who in this first instance of consciousness went to naïvely search for a Shangri-La where their son could be seen as blessed and not shunned as something damaged.

Like a giant yellow-headed blackbird, his whiteless, yellow eyeballs staring right through my face, he swung his powerful flailing arms around me as we hugged, almost crushing me as he laughed, recognizing each of us in the other the desire with which the flowering curse of nature's mercy had filled us, for having mutually survived the same degree of honest folly to live out with no hesitation our everyday lives which we both knew could so easily be taken from us. They must have had to keep on moving for I never saw any of them again.

There were at least three distinct and thick layers of outsiders piled up like tangled driftwood in a flood of searching people hoping for the perfect place where they wouldn't have to see people like themselves ever again, all of whom contributed to the unique character and bizarre un-Guatemalan nature of this once normal Mayan lake town called Panajachel.

When each of them first came streaming in on an incessant crowded torrent of Germans, Americans, Italians, Australians, French, Canadians, Columbians, Ecuadorians, Peruvians, Africans, Japanese, half-German Qekchi Mayans, expatriate, big city Ladinos, hippies of every length of hair and suburban background, Presbyterians, Adventists, Bahais, Mormons, Evangelists, Persians, Danes, Finns, Swedes, Spaniards, Guanacos, Catrachos, Ticos, Nicas, Swiss, Poles, Russians, New Zealanders, Scots, hillbillies, fortune tellers, drug dealers, intellectuals, musicians, witches, Californians, bus drivers, bakers and pickpockets, they were so entirely beguiled by the unexpected smells and disarming natural beauty of the place that they were unable to recognize that they were in a colony swarming with people exactly like themselves who each felt that here they could finally live in peace, just as they'd always dreamed, surrounded by flowers, even yearly temperatures, laying on the dark sand beaches of the most beautiful lake in the world without having to learn a new language or change anything about themselves, who with a modest income from the sale of their apartments could afford to live for years in big windowed chalets with grassy lawns, little gardens and avocado trees, whose rent included Indian gardeners, Indian maids and cooks. Whereas before they'd had to drive angry through gray snow and traffic to impersonal offices to punch keys for someone they didn't like in Indianapolis or Amsterdam, they could now live from party to party like aristocrats pretending they were actually living in Guatemala instead of a suburb of their fantasies.

Another layer of people had come there as well with their little families, bought land and tried to live off the interest of their trust funds, but with nothing much to do, unwilling to merge into the quagmire of the self-interested outsiders trying to "find themselves" and unable to find a way to live integrally in the disparity of class and caste, formed a ghetto of bitter expatriates who themselves ended up as landlords for other expatriates, living off the rent.

Landslides, Shrine Ponds, a Wild Boy and Gorgeous Days of Jasmine-Covered Walls

The Cakchiquel Mayans of Panajachel, the northern cousins of the more southerly Tzutujil, had originally lived between the base of the molar-like edges of the sheer pine and oak-studded canyon walls and its river, into which for millennia the basaltic pillared rim had loosed house-sized cubical boulders, sometimes crashing through their huts and little farms that used to run along the river to the little cindery delta where the stream crept into the lake.

By the time I'd arrived, those two miles from where the canyon straightened to the shoreline of the lake, which the tourists called a beach, had been appropriated by every means imaginable, most of them legal, none of them kind, by the most powerful layer of outside people, who had pushed away and all but buried what remained of the indigenous population of this majestic place, filling the river and lakeshore strip with white-washed colonial palaces they called their resort homes, which included sprawling lawns, narco-gardens, big boats, docks, guard dogs, servant quarters, grounds keepers, cooks, maids, servants, high walls and iron gates.

As an elitist neighborhood of the heirs to international big business and well-known political figures, most of whom came from Europe and the United States, there were several powerful Guatemalan oligarchs who owned places there as well, but nobody with Indian blood.

After several of the Indian families displaced by this unchallengeable invasion, who were now landless, unemployed and fragmented, allowed themselves to be converted into various American Protestant missionizing religions, they turned away from their hard indigenous lives as canoe fishermen, small-time traders and shoreline vegetable gardeners to become whole families of Mayan middlemen and women who lived off a percentage fee they charged the families of other Indians recruited from faraway villages with different languages and clothing styles to serve as maids, gardeners, cooks, guardians and general service people for the rich and not-so-rich chalet owners who now lived on their former land.

After a while, these new Indians brought in by the original Indians, who were just as shrewd, began bringing their own relatives along who'd gather up all their worn-out clothing, tools and the like, to sell to tourists and the chalet renters on the side, in what became such a popular and lucrative trade, that by the 1970s the town was basically one big, enormous marketplace filled with hopeful tourists and tourist-hustling Mayan merchants wandering all the streets.

It was then that the Peace Corps gave one new resident Quiché family a treadle sewing machine and the idea to cut up and re-dye these traditional types of clothing, most of which were simply worn-out and not antique and only sold moderately well to the tourists. By sewing them into patchwork versions of boutique style jackets, shirts, skirts, bags and so on, the tourists could actually wear them in the illusion they had on their backs "traditional" Mayan, tribal outfits, giving birth for the next thirty years to the famous Guatemalan clothing fad.

Almost mining the highland mountain villages for discarded traditional clothing for which they traded new dyed weaving thread to the women to weave new outfits, Christian Indian entrepreneurs began arriving in Panajachel with literally tons and tons of clothes which they cut up in chop shops, in what became within ten years a half mile or more of gridded rows of tin-roofed shacks, selling stalls, more formal looking stores and sewing factories to supply the export businesses and the desires of passing tourists which left at least a few of these Mayan families fairly well off by the standards of the time.

Some of the resident lawn and garden variety of straw-hat-wearing rich people took exception to the enormous swelling hordes of milling tourists, hippies and business-hustling Mayans, who disturbed their illusion of a life unhindered by the rigors of having to actually see and negotiate with the locals and paid the local police large bribes to randomly harass and run off as many of these "undesirables" as they could.

The successful Indian merchants on the other hand, mostly a blend of Cakchiquel, Ixil and Quiché peoples, were not to be outdone and unwilling to lose their businesses, willingly in turn paid off the police as well who then agreed not to bother them at all and to warn them just before the "purges" that the rich folk paid them for would begin, so the merchants could warn their precious clientele.

Besides the double pay-offs they received from the two warring sides of the issue, the three enterprising policemen of the little town, in order to carry out the earning of their wages from the rich folk, shook down any tourist they could catch in their nocturnal round-ups, giving the three of them a pretty good living, far above the meager amount that blue-uniformed national policemen were officially paid. Every policeman in Guatemala wanted to be stationed in that village.

It was an easy job; they simply visited the merchants the day before a purge, going booth to booth letting them know, collecting up their protection pay, then once or twice a week the three of them would go around herding anybody with long hair who looked like they could pay, or anyone pointed out to them by one of the rich house-owners, then, driving them like goats, they would crowd their unlucky captives into the tiny police headquarters where one by one they reviewed their visas and documents, finding something wrong with every one which could be straightened out with fifty quetzales, after which they were put on the 9 PM bus to anywhere but there.

Because there were so many people coming and going and the police only operated at night, most tourists never even noticed until they were in their trap. Those who later tried complaining to higher authorities found it did no good, for some of the policemen's illicit employers were well-connected with those who politically ran the country, and the police supervisors who did not were located sixty miles to the east in the capital, between the seventh and eighth avenue in a castle-like fortress which was where all the torturing for the country was carried out, all of which was much scarier than paying the fifty dollars.

Despite all its perils and stupidities, the town remained a marvel covered in flowering vines, trees with blossoms as big as your head, where the smells, the beauty, romantic abandon and possibility that tinged the lakeshore air put a nose ring in the stubborn bull of my gypsy hunt for deep eyes, love and home until I too was dragged into the sickly sweetness of its quagmire, no less beguiled than any other traveling fool.

STEALING
BENEFACIO'S ROSES

Like Raggedy Boy singing alone lost in the woods, in the beginnings
of my days in Panajachel I sang and played my guitar alone on the
beach, but to feed myself I was soon enough giving concerts in rich
people's garden homes, which is where I saw Hipolita Cavek cleaning up
after a soirée one afternoon.

Still a child of sixteen with skin like the belly of a golden seal, she was a
Cakchiquel Mayan girl in service as a maid who was carrying on with the son
of her employer, a pale-skinned, wispy-bearded, slacks-wearing twenty-two
year-old from a family who owned several trans-oceanic shipping companies.

I was a half-breed guitarist with no shoes, madly in love with the possibility of being in love, hunting my own soul in the deep brownness of her Indian nature, a homeless romantic boy who thought she should be mine and that I was better for her.

During my concerts for his parents I sang my songs to her, to get her away from him for me, shooting, so to speak, my backwards arrows as I'd done so many times before, hitting in this case only myself, which meant this time that I was fired from my guitar job.

As anyone might've guessed this in no way stopped me. When I discovered where Hipolita lived, it turned out that she had seven little sisters and a baby brother, a mother and no father, who were all very much nicer than she would ever be.

Though welcomed whenever I visited her beautiful family, who were as poor as anyone alive, I was too shy to express my feelings when Hipolita disappeared every night to be with the white man, returning stoned on pot and staggering straight for bed.

At that time I was living in a tiny slatted dirt-floored hut on the east side of the river in a coffee grove surrounded at a distance by its Cakchiquel owner's family compound of huts that lay between a gathering of boulders.

To get home every evening, just before the place where I had to wade the cold stream, on the high point of the trail, in a little piece of the uncut original forest sat a cottage of white-washed stone and clay Spanish roof tiles, behind a walled garden filled with brilliant and enormous roses.

Though in every respect the cottage seemed to have been built according to Quiché Mayan aesthetics, there was something about the eaves that came from southern Spain. The six-foot high walls of the garden, on the other hand, were totally Central American, for a foot taller than the average Guatemalan, they were topped off with a gruesome row of razor-edged broken bottle glass set firmly in the plaster.

Inside the walls, two large dogs, like Rotweillers but different, would throw themselves like angry jungle peccaries, crashing into the closed wrought-iron gate, gurgling, gnashing, snapping their jaws and barking whenever I passed in the mornings into town on the little hard-packed trail. But on my return in the afternoons they were usually sound asleep.

Even so, passing by those roses was no casual event, for with dogs or without them, one had to stand and smell them; there have never been other roses like these roses whose aroma brought up every emotion I'd ever had all at once.

After weeks of feeling hurt and useless, small and stupid about Hipolita and my failure at getting her attention, a small notion grew daily in my aching heart until it had assumed the complexity of a concerted plan with the quality of a commando raid, the crux of which was that after having plotted out its sequence, I vowed to steal some of these roses for Hipolita.

This seemed to solve so many of my problems. After all I could not give her what the wispy-bearded rich boy could, since I was a waif and washed up economically, nor would any kind of monetary gift express the immensity of my love for her, which of course, was not for her but for something I did really love that she would never be. But how was I to know about such complexities?

I would show her, without the expenditure of even one centavo, through my courage and rash ability, I would show her how much danger to myself I was willing to risk to steal so much beauty and fragility as a rose to gain her heart or even just her sympathy, for now I didn't even have her pity.

Reckoning as I traveled by the roses daily and after making a couple of half-hearted exploratory feints, I determined that one afternoon when the dogs were sound asleep, if I ran fast enough, then jumped against the fire flower or tzejtel tree that grew crooked at the wall's closest corner, that if I got up enough speed I could foreseeably roll sideways over the wall, then grabbing the inner edge of the plaster by the tip of my fingers, stop my momentum enough to drop down into the little courtyard silently enough to keep the dogs from waking, pick three unopened roses by their stems, then quickly moving a sturdy-looking carved wooden chair that was always in the garden close to the wall, climb swiftly upon its backrest, most likely with the vicious dogs snapping at my heels, and dive quickly back over the wall with the roses tucked under my chest, like a high jumper, rolling back onto the hard ground outside in hopes at least one of the magical roses would survive the crash. It was a good plan, I thought, with enough room for failure and the likelihood of getting maimed to raise the value of my efforts if I survived, which seemed the only way for an unmoneyed boy in love to get a decent present.

On the afternoon I'd planned to jump the wall and snatch the forbidden roses from the garden of broken glass; as I approached it I could hear the voices of at least two women and a man in a loud, heated discussion, so I just kept walking by unnoticed, save for the dogs, who for all the ruckus must have been awake and set up a barking and a snarling that calmed down once I'd exited their beat.

Not having found work in two weeks, I was eating only once a day and getting pretty weak. When the following afternoon approached I'd grown quite ill with fever, diarrhea and vomiting and wondered if I'd have the strength to carry out my schemes, knowing in my love-sick heart that if I got any worse I would never steal the roses and the moment would have passed, besides which Hipolita was getting more and more involved with that wealthy, wispy-bearded hippie, so I decided it was now or never and that evening headed toward the garden.

The two big dogs were asleep, curled up under the eaves. The sun was almost down. I approached the garden wall in a hunter's walk somewhere between an informal stroll and a stalk, then carefully peered into the forbidden garden through the grate to ensure everything was right.

With my fever throbbing and ringing in my ears, I pushed up against the tree, placed my hands on either side of the razor glass and, holding my breath and with only a little thumping of my right knee against the inside surface of the garden wall, I dropped successfully but dizzy to the bouncy sedge grass of the courtyard floor.

The big-headed dogs were even bigger face to face but were still snoring with a volcanic rumble and tubercular wheeze as I quickly snapped the first rose, then another and then a fully opened one, after which I tip-toed toward the chair, which wouldn't budge because it was carved from a massive wooden tree stump still rooted in the ground, and in the millisecond it took my desperate brain to rotate two thousand alternate plans, the dogs woke up and came a-running and a-snapping like a two-headed dragon and whatever plan I'd come up with disappeared with their charge and almost flying I leapt without a thought with one foot on the ground, another up to the stump and sprung up with all my might, twisting in the air so as not to cut my stomach open on the glass, whose blades I pretty much cleared as I came crashing onto what had seemed like a hard mud path but which now felt like granite.

Though I broke again a single rib a grade school teacher had smashed with a two-by-four for my not speaking the required English on the reservation, I sat up in the twilight and in the din the dogs set up I discarded the idea of catching my breath and ran anyway the two miles to Hipolita's house with the adrenaline coursing in my veins, knowing well when it should vanish I would collapse, aware of how sick I was and crazy to have done this.

But when I crossed it in my wobbly trot I could see by the streetlights of the main road that the only rose which had survived the fall was ironically the one that was open, whose smell had kept me going. In some kind of triumph a little reanimated now, I wheeled to the right, like a lame Olympic runner with a torch whose light only lovers could see, arriving at the house of Hipolita's mother, Doña Chona, where I broke in on their family dinner in which eight girls, the mother and baby boy were seated on the ground around the oil barrel lid *comal* still full of reheating tortillas over the fire and drifting past them all I handed my single stolen rose to Hipolita.

As I fell to my knees from right where I'd stood, gasping for breath, fainting from the fever in which the adrenaline crash now left me reeling and shaking for its lack, Hipolita's mother put her baby in its little hammock and gently took the rose from her ungrateful daughter's hand, who had been holding it upside down like a dead mouse by the tail while bad-mouthing my ragged and uninvited appearance.

Putting the rose carefully balanced in a blue enamel coffee cup that another of her little daughters had filled with water from a clay *tinája* of river water, the mother put the rose up on her little altar in front of the pictures of San Simon, Maria Concepcion and Nuestro Señor de Esquipulas, then hoisted me up and off the floor with the help of all her valiant little daughters, minus Hipolita, who had already gone to meet her man, and somehow pulled me into the corner behind the cornstalk partition onto one of their little beds of tule mats where I spent the entire night unconscious in the fever's shaking grip.

When I awoke, Doña Chona had fixed me up a remedy of *yuquillo, yerba buena* and *pericon* that was basically a paste, a gallon of which she forced me to gulp throughout the day, which by the next morning had put me almost right.

She invited me to eat breakfast then with her on the ground by the fire in her old clay tiled warehouse.

"You know my oldest daughter is a brute. She needs someone to kick her rear, but since her father's death there's no one she'll listen to. You are an even bigger fool than she has you for if you care even a bedbug for her fickle gaze."

I let the sweet healing Indian coffee, one third of which was pan-toasted corn, another third toasted coffee husks and the remainder actual coffee beans which had been roasted on her fire then ground by hand on her stone *metate*, trickle into my still untrusting esophagus. I could not do more than mildly agree with her, for every breath cost me the memory of my early rib beatings and how unimpressed Hipolita had been. Doña Chona was three hundred times more beautiful than her daughter, having been cooked down by life into what she really was, a tired type of pretty, full of pride, survival and grief, vital and able and more substantial in her soul than anyone I'd ever known before.

Her baby boy, Benefacio, started fussing and she fetched him from his net and giving him a chocolate and copper breast swollen with milk, asked me, "¿Reycito de donde traias esta rosa bella que regaló usted a mi hija ingrata y bruta?" "Little king, from where did you bring that beautiful rose of which you made a gift to my ungrateful brutish daughter?"

When I described the whereabouts and how I'd come by the now fully opened flower, whose singular perfume, like no other rose I'd ever smelled, even cutting through the thick smoke of smoldering corn cobs that Doña Chona in her poverty was obliged to use for fuel instead of the much preferred and expensive firewood, she bit her elegant lips and wept quietly, staring at her child, but did not explain, whispering instead, "Mi hija es una bruta, mas inutil ... mas babosa..." and then began to speak in Cakchiquel to little Benefacio who was looking up, laughing and kicking his strong chubby legs moistened by his mother's tears.

The two rosebuds that had been sacrificed during my fall were still lying in the path as I crossed in front of the fortressed rose garden on my way to retrieve my guitar and pack up my few belongings to resume my rambling far away from here.

Just as I had gotten past the fire flower tree I'd used to jump into the courtyard, I could already hear and smell the little river mixed with the afternoon odor of the roses as I rounded the pathway down the hill, when a voice yelled out behind me half in greeting and half in pretended anger, "¿Vos, Señor Patajo, a donde vas tu con tanta prisa?" "You, Mr. Feet and Eyes, to where are you going in such a hurry?"

I continued on my way, but turned a bit to look behind to see if that voice were directed at me and saw that approaching me somewhat rapidly was an elderly barefoot man wearing an old Quiché straw hat accompanied by the same two dogs that had chased me from the garden, only now their tails were wagging and they looked up at him.

"¿Por favor, vos, despasciate un poco, se corta mucho la vida andando como tu, pero porque cortor tanto la dicha lo que el Divino te ha dado largo?" "Slow down a little please, one's life is shortened at the speed you travel, but why cut the happiness so short that the Divine has intended to be long?"

By then I'd stopped and turned to face the old man, who was almost on me now and who appeared to me to be a Ladino wearing homemade hand-woven pants and white cotton button-up shirt and whose well-trimmed mustache followed his crooked handsome smile.

Grabbing my left arm, the old fellow continued to talk as he practically dragged me back to the rose garden and forced me into the courtyard where I'd risked my life then sat me with an emphatic graciousness on the immobile chair carved from the stump from which only a couple of days before I'd leapt to escape the jaws of these now very friendly dogs.

"¿Tranquilisate papito. Descanse un rato con nosotros reycito. Sentate aqui por favor en su mero trono?" "Make yourself tranquil, little father. Rest a little while with us, little king. Please sit here on your real throne."

Then smiling wide and showing all his big yellow teeth, none of which were broken or missing, he asked me point blank, "¿No sos el mismo fulano de tal que se brinco esa mi moralla pa´ taquacharse tres rositas, que por poco se lo samparon pa´ mis chuchos?" "Are you not the same mister such and so who leapt my big old wall to opossum off three little roses, who was almost eaten by my pooches?"

"Ah, it's true. It's very true. I confess I am the brute that stole your roses."

This mysterious man disappeared laughing into the house, his two dogs right behind him. Wagging both their bottoms and thick heads, they were still on his heels when he re-emerged from the darkness of the cottage bearing two small glasses of cool, mild, homemade wine, made from *nantzes*, a sweet yellow jungle cherry that the Mayans call *tajpal*.

As we drank this healing wine he resumed his friendly interrogation, "I want you to enlighten me," he said, "about various things: firstly, why didn't you simply ask me for the roses in the first place instead of doing all this damage to yourself?"

Amazed, I tried to smile at my heroic foray into yet another foolishness, "I never suspected," I told my fascinated questioner, "that any person in this neighborhood, having such a formal house with such a formidable wall, terrifying guard dogs and broken glass would be the least bit conducive to giving away such beautiful roses."

"But, my friend," he replied immediately, "the whole town and even people from other towns, Indians and Ladinos alike, everybody comes here to get roses. They have never asked, they just open the gates, come in, pick what they need and leave. The Indians always give me some good avocados or mangos or a sack of corn when they see me in the plaza, but everyone just comes right in and gets them.

"My name is Gustavo Rodas, I'm from Chichicastenango; these are my dogs Sonya and Mamon." Mamon meant the nipple on a baby bottle. "Do you think the glass on my garden wall is to keep people from stealing roses? Nobody can steal what is freely given. Anyway, another man named Benefacio planted the roses and ever since, the more people take, the more they grow; I can't keep them down.

"No, you see, I'm Gustavos Rodas and I go barefoot," holding up his callused feet to show me, "because I hate to see animals killed, eaten or made to suffer. I don't eat the flesh of any animal and I don't use their leather, even for shoes. I don't use plastics because it comes from petroleum, which comes from ancient animals as well. Using gasoline or diesel to me is the same as wearing leather, using plastic or eating meat. I don't ride horses, drive mules or pack donkeys either because I hate to see them suffer. I have *caballerias* of lands, thousands of *cuerdas* everywhere which I loan out to all the Indians and Ladinos everywhere, who send me little bits of what they grow or make and that's how I live.

"No, I'm Gustavo Rodas and because I'm Gustavo Rodas I love all the people, even those from the Big City and other countries, but I don't like at all what they do to animals by the lives they live and of course those people hate me for not allowing any of those rich *babosos* to build on the land that crowns the holy water of the river that my family owns, who are themselves descendants from Quiché kings, not Tecun the general, but from the kings themselves from G´umarcah.

"No, I'm Gustavo Rodas and the rich people, though none of these *morosos* are as rich as I am, have paid off even my children to betray their father and these things that I believe, who now only want me to sell off all my land to these horrible developers and rich folk who are killing this canyon and the entire lakeshore, illegally, for you know only villagers can own the communal holdings and nobody can legally own within two hundred feet of any shoreline, but they find ways around it.

"No, I'm Gustavo Rodas and the rich people here have fingered me to the police, who they have paid off to harass me into selling and giving in, and to whom I refuse to counterpay to keep them off, the police who are supposedly here to protect us from thieves are thieves in the employ of thieves.

"No, the green bottles and broken glass and Sonya and Mamon are only there around my house to keep the cowardly paid-off police from entering my little garden while I'm away, because the police persist on trying to transplant marijuana bushes so they can come by with the Gaurdia de Hacienda and haul me off to seven years in prison, so they can confiscate my holdings and auction off my land.

"No, now you know, I'm Gustavo Rodas and that these dogs only bite people who come over the walls. The entire world comes through the gates and gets all the roses they might need. Now answer me this next thing, my friend, there are only two reasons for a man to risk his health to jump a wall bristling with razor glass and rushing in front of angry powerful dogs just to steal three roses he could've gotten by walking through the gate. The first one is a woman and the second one is a girl. Which one is she? "

"Don Gustavo, vos me tienes totalmente asombrado..."

"Don Gustavo, you have me utterly astounded, how did you know? I stole your roses as a gift to a girl named Hipolita Cavek who ..."

After waving his forearms around in the air while I spoke, his left hand rose up pointing to the sky while with his right he gently backhanded my left shoulder and interrupted my response. "You don't mean Doña Chona Tecun Cavek's stuck-up oldest daughter?"

Then slapping his skinny old thighs repeated,

"Ay, Dios mio.

"Ay, la pobre.

"Ay, el pobre.

"Malaya Dios los pobracitos.

"Ay, Dios mio."

Then he sighed and went silent for a while, while I sat quietly thinking I'd said something wrong. Don Gustavo looked off tenderly into the distance, his eyes misting up with the memory of some old hurt not so different from Doña Chona earlier in the morning.

In the purple light of the balmy, mosquito-driven twilight that was filling with the not-so-distant mournful chortlings of the parpuac owls, I stood and took Don Gustavo's hand to shake it, "It's time for me to go, Don Gustavo, night has come and I don't have a flashlight, without which I'll never find my *chozita* among the boulders in the dark."

Like a determined egret holding down a frog, Don Gustavo, mildly insulted, quickly stood and pushed me back into my trunk holding me there with both hands, one on either shoulder.

"No, son, you sit and listen. When I'm finished with my charla, I'll accompany my new friend, with my little lamp, to his little *choza* among the boulders inside his landlord's *cafetal*.

"Benefacio Cavek was a very fine man, a Quiché man, like my mother's people from the very same land up by Sacualpa. Benefacio was Hipolita's father and husband to Concepcion Tecun, Doña Chona, whom you know.

"Benefacio loved Doña Chona almost as much as she loved him and the two of them owned a large compound of beautiful little Cakchiquel thatched houses, or *chozas* as you call them, inherited from her father, that had lined the river from here to the lake for centuries, even before the Spaniards, where now all those people have their chalets and lawns. When Benefacio refused to sell the surrounding land on which he and Chona had their avocado orchard, cornfields, *pitaya* garden, plus the compound where they lived, those who had bought up every piece of land surrounding them through a straw man, promised the police a large pay-off if by their own methods they could convince Benefacio and his family to sell their beautiful little land that now sat in the middle of one of their resort-house building plans.

"In those days Benefacio worked for me a couple times a week, planting and harvesting my garden as his father had worked for my mother's father and it was Benefacio's grandfather who brought these roses to my grandparents' land in Quiché, and Benefacio himself who'd planted these very rosebushes that you see here and whose buds you thought to steal to give to Hipolita Cavek, his daughter.

"Benefacio maintained these roses of his father and always took some for his wife, who would put one in her hair and another in front of her Santos, crumbling the remainder into petals over their *Cabuil Abaj*, the family spiritual beings on Chona's altar, as offerings.

"Because their extended family had succumbed to the threats of the police and accepted the lawn people's money, thereby selling off all the farmland of the family, Benefacio, with eight daughters, was hard put to earn a living. Though still refusing to sell their ancestral home site, they were sorely tempted at that point when the same people offered them 35,000 quetzales to accept, which is when Benefacio and Doña Chona came to me explaining what had happened and how they would finally be unable to resist now for having no source of income. I gave them 40,000 quetzales not to sell what had always been theirs and a little of my own land here up the canyon to farm.

"I am sure you know how the gossip ball rolls and it rolled right to the police, who ambushed Benefacio and beat him bloody to get him to give them the cash I'd given them, which it was rumored he'd hidden somewhere in the ground. This country is bad to Indians and they will do anything to them to get the things they want, but nonetheless with all that Don Benefacio, God bless him, still wouldn't tell them anything.

"Still under pressure to get these Indians off the land, three policemen caught Ya Chona returning from the corn mill and raped her, dropping her half-dead in the courtyard.

"Three days later the entire compound burnt to the ground. The official report said that Benefacio, out of shame and frustration, had set himself on fire with gasoline, and when the fire spread it burnt all the little *chozas* down, killing Benefacio and destroying all his money, every penny of which was missing.

"But Benefacio did not kill himself and he loved Doña Chona and his family no matter what. What we all know is what happened, that somebody from the Big City had been called to burn them out for good.

"That was eight years ago. Hipolita was almost eleven then and now she wants to go with that milk-skinned, eggless gringo and I think she probably will. Who could blame her, after all, for she saw everything. Old enough to remember and too young to understand, she wants nothing to do with being an Indian, wants nothing of this country, wants only to escape, to get far away and get lots of money to bring her mother to the United States, though her mother would never leave her home.

"But Hipolita's employers and future in-laws are blood kin with those who orchestrated her father's death. Her mother knows this and hates her daughter for it, but doesn't have the heart to tell her.

"I gave Doña Chona my family's old coffee warehouse where she takes in laundry and tries to raise all of Benefacio's daughters without the bitterness that her antagonists, from their completed family summer homes, so thoroughly deserve. The father of her new baby boy, Benefacio, is well-known to be me, but it would be a breach of propriety to tell you without Doña Chona's permission.

"These flowers that you barely stole and now find you didn't have to are Benefacio's roses. Everybody calls them that, not Don Gustavo's roses or anybody else's roses, they belong only to Benefacio, they are Benefacio's roses and they are free to anyone who knows why."

Carefully standing and hobbling about the perimeter of the inside wall, Don Gustavo picked about two dozen roses, which seemed somehow to have their own strange dark light in the very dim purple night. After placing them inside a red clay jar half-filled with water and handing me the lot, he fetched and lit his tin and glass candle lamp and walked me to my hut, where all the people came out and kissed the little silver ring on his middle finger before he left.

Onto the floor I dropped to sleep, drifting on the tossing sea of my aching heart in a little canoe of Gustavo's friendship, into dreams filled with the unkillable perfume of Benefacio's roses.

ten

MOHAMMED'S CAMEL, BISONIA AND LA SEÑORA'S UNDERWATER HUSBAND

Though I couldn't get accustomed to living in this anxious and ironic stew of beauty and cultural destruction, carried out by what seemed to me to be the very syndrome whose heartless crushing hold I'd fled away from in New Mexico, the nostalgic reedy waters of the lake, Doña Chona and Gustavo were now my friends and for them I didn't leave.

Our conversations never again included Benefacio, but I never exited Don Gustavo's courtyard with an empty belly or without an armload of Benefacio's roses, which was fortunate for I'd been blacklisted by the rich boy's parents and their friends and I'd waded through the next three weeks unable to feed myself with songs until one night I too was rounded up and driven stumbling at the end of a heartless nightstick into a herd of unwashed American hippie kids, a French couple and a German man.

After forcing us inside the blue painted stone walls of the tin-roofed building of the National Police, whose small calaboose sat reeking out back, they held me until the last which was always the worst of omens.

I watched them one by one clear the room, after going through the same morose procedures of extracting fifty quetzal bribes from everyone, who after they had paid were uncharacteristically released back onto the street one by one, instead of rudely loaded on to late-night buses and sent away. Only the French woman of the couple gave them any trouble, blasting them with a very justified earful of angry French and indignant spitting, as she was pushed like a belligerent colt, unwilling to return back to the tourist pastures of the streets, no longer certain of its alleged freedom.

One of the policemen immobilized my arms by twisting them into my back, while the other of the three pulled my pants down and jammed a stick into my crotch. Then tearing off my only shirt, someone grabbed a fistful of my hair and mashed my twenty-one-year old, sweetheart-searching face sideways onto the seated sergeant's desk.

It was strange to me how big city people or spoiled people from any-where expected that their money should get them anything they might want, assuming their lives should work out according to some rational plan of self-defined decency and comfort. I, on the other hand, knew that what was happening to me now had been coming for a while. We'd been treated similarly in grade school by American teachers on the reservation, so I moved into that well-practiced glaze-eyed trance; what we students used to call the "rubber skin exam," where we would survive such onslaughts of humiliation by retracting our souls from the surface of our skins, pulling into an almost dead reserve, leaving our assailants with a nerveless sack of nothing, while hiding our still vital life fires in a non-corporal form, in some natural indigenous place that existed before we'd been born, a place too subtle for the abbreviated thinking that hate demands and too great a dis-tance for tyranny and greed to follow.

The precious and imaginatively concocted atypical traveling docu-ments which I'd been given upon my entrance into Guatemala by the chief of immigration on the border to replace others that in Mexico I'd legitimately lost; papers that had served me so well up until now that stated I should be accorded free transport and open access to all privileges and that I was the friend of such and so colonel, what's his name, the relative of the president's wife and so on, the same papers which had been honored by all officials everywhere, were here, in this gathering, pulled out of the bag that hung from the leather string about my neck and tossed about, unexamined, flapping like a slaughtered chicken.

Jerking my head up, pulled by the same fist clamped into my curly hair, the mustached sergeant, with his face right on mine, informed me that I was to produce by tomorrow at 2 P.M. one hundred quetzales, at which point he would return my documents, after which I should be out of town by the following dawn. If they rounded me up again I would be imprisoned and deported if I were lucky. Then the three of them lifted me and tossed me into the stony street where, skinned up a little more, I wandered to my hut where I sat and shivered.

If I fled and was caught without documents in another part of the country I could still be imprisoned and maybe deported, but one hundred quetzales on the other hand was a lot of cash and ninety more than I owned. In those times a schoolteacher earned sixty quetzales a month, an architect a hundred, and a normal working man made forty, therefore one hundred quetzales was at least two months' wages for a man with a job and I didn't have either. Wondering if Don Gustavo might shelter me in Chichicastenango, or loan me the money or have another idea, when I stiffly limped at dawn through the wrought iron gates of his garden, though the roses were still intact, his things had been thrown all about and Don Gustavo and his dogs hadn't been there for at least a couple of days. Something wasn't right with him either.

So, I went back, picked up my guitar, packed up the little that I had and avoided the entire town by cutting up the river, past the hot spring on the hillside, up and over on to the highroad by the waterfall, to hopefully hitch a ride any direction far away from here before the cops came looking to collect.

After waiting for a long spell in which not a single vehicle passed, I took out my instrument and started to sing. A short man, a tourist, casually strolling by smoking a cigarette, stopped a bit to listen, then producing a harmonica began to sing and play along in beautiful harmony.

A few more tunes and a cigarette later this fellow, after listening to the highlights of my problems, gave me a job with a one hundred and fifty dollars cash advance. He urged me to go to the police station right away, pointing out that the bad cops were no doubt sound asleep somewhere else, pay the hundred bucks to the morning secretary, retrieve my papers, then go to the market and buy a shirt, where he'd meet me with his automobile.

Because there were no other choices showing, I took the one he offered and once his plan of getting back my papers had worked, we loaded ourselves into his brand new canary yellow convertible VW bug and drove ninety glorious kilometers away from Panajachel to Guatemala City to fulfill the contract I now had with my new boss.

This man was a professional singer who had been brought specially from the States to perform four nights a week in a Guatemalan City nightclub, but speaking only English had been unable to communicate with the house band. My new employer hired me to be the new band director, translator and arranger, in which position I could work off what I owed him at ten quetzales a night, then continue on with him at regular pay or by then no doubt find more work as an American guitarist somewhere in the nightlife of the city.

As we drove away I felt remorse at my helplessness and defeat once again in the wake of a monster business culture whose people accepted as normal procedure their persistent need to crush, control, own or manicure anything that was subtle, natural or indigenous.

What I would need to wrestle such a dragon in the future besides more strength and better understanding of that spirit-crushing syndrome was beyond the experience of my slowly dwindling naïveté to imagine, but it would come later from other people like Doña Chona and Don Gustavo, who now gave me hope that the natural human heart could actually exist on earth, for whom I now prayed were well and who I sorely missed.

The relief of leaving so much hardship physically behind slowly eroded my recently elevated need for caution and as we distanced ourselves over the winding trail up past Godinez, the irrepressible freedom of my youth burst its dam, rising into a euphoria that the possibility of a new start always brings.

I knew very little about my new employer, this American I was riding with, but his character was gradually exposed as I watched how he negotiated the unexpected which in Guatemala was the only thing you could expect, where stretch by stretch we neared the Big City, which I had never visited.

About twenty-five miles out of Panajachel somewhere between Patzun and Patzicia, an elegant middle-aged Mayan man, wearing beautiful, complex ceremonial clothing, showing him to be a member of some sacred hierarchy of his village, lay stretched out on the road right at the intersection where we met the big trucking traffic of the Pan-American highway.

My benefactor didn't like dead people and it took some strong convincing to make him pull over and let me out. He wouldn't help me pull the beautiful man's body off the road so that his relatives, whomsoever they were, would have something left of their kin to bury when they found him, for in the impending dark the truckers heading to the city never stop for human or beast, alive or dead, and would most certainly have crushed him into nothing. I'd seen it many times.

He weighed as much as all the mistakes I'd ever made and when I'd situated him properly, rolled under a swaying *izote* plant well off the road, this dead man's eyes popped open and he pulled me to his face with the grip of ten-thousand howler monkeys. With a flammable breath more *cuxa* than mountain air he whispered into my ear,

"Father, I finally arrived at your house. Jesus, it's good to see your face."

Like we'd thought to begin with, this man now thought he was dead. My blond hair meant that the Catholics had been right, and he'd been somehow let into heaven at the side of their blond-headed Christ. By the time I thought I'd convinced him that he was still in this world, my boss started honking. Horribly disappointed that he was yet alive and facing a hangover on this Earth, the beautiful man rolled and snuggled sideways to the tree and started snoring.

When we arrived into the city it was past 2 A.M., at which point I discovered my boss had nowhere to land, and because all the world's petroleum companies had representatives in the capital of Guatemala to meet with U.S. and Guatemalan government officials about how to soften the restriction on their nationalized oil, every hotel, pension and boarding-house was filled, leaving us to search the harder districts next to the Lemonada or El Gallito for a bed.

We had no luck until rolling down an alley I saw a hanging sign that simply read "cuartos," or rooms. The once whitewashed windowless front had a shut, big, red carriage door with a smaller door that sat tightly closed within it.

Because part of my job was to translate for my new boss, I knocked on the closed steel door for longer than he would have, until a clattering and stirring was heard within, followed by a funny, irritated, nasally, sleepy voice that sounded like a magpie who could speak Spanish.

"¿Manda usted?" the voice asked, without even opening the tiny latch window set at eye level. "¿En que le puedo servir?"

"Do you have any rooms?"

"Yes," the magpie voice croaked, resounding in the unseen courtyard.

"How much are they?"

"One and a half quetzales a bed, per night."

"That was expensive, but we could look for better accommodations the next day."

"Good, can we have a room with two beds?"

"Yes."

But the door didn't open and the voice didn't speak.

"Hello," I spoke out.

"Yes?"

"Can we come in to our beds?"

"Yes."

"Can you open the door please?"

"Yes."

But the door didn't open.

"When are you going to open the door?"

"When you show me your money."

"Where do you want me to show it to you?"

The tiny latch door crashed open, behind which a rumpled face with a big nose and two dark eyes and bushy eyebrows glowered out.

"Quiero ver." "Let me see your money."

I held up a five quetzal bill to his face, at which the bolts started unbuckling and the regular door in the middle of the big door swung open inside, behind which the magpie voice without a body sounded, "Come in please, quickly."

When we entered, the door was shut with an emphatic clang. When I turned to pay our hotel attendant, a dwarf wearing a little suit with a small pistol in a shoulder holster was jumping down from the chair he'd been standing on to peer out at us from the little window. After rebolting the locks and stays, he turned to us, took our money, showed us the room and we all went sound asleep.

Some cooing sounds, the cries of little babies and some hoarse cackling mixed with a sloshing echo that rebounded off the plastered courtyard walls woke me from the depth of my dreams after sleeping like a fossilized fern in a coal seam until about 9 A.M.

By ten I'd revived enough to discover from Señor Canuto Mazariegos, the little man with the pistol who was playing checkers with Maritza and Gladys, that my employer and I had taken a room in what was by night on the ground floor a bordello and by day a laundry, where the unpregnant women took the night shift and those with small babies or expecting did the daytime washing.

Thirty-four women from the ages of sixteen to fifty-three, the younger ladies all with children, lived out of harm's way up on the second and third stories behind the wrought iron verandas, where the morning's washing of sheets taken in from expensive hotels fluttered drying in the morning sun framing for three stories the courtyard in whose center stood a *pila*, a carved water tank with eighteen separate concrete washing troughs, where with babies strapped on their backs in shawls knotted over their shoulders, the women did the back-breaking labor of washing by hand every size item for the "laundry."

Canuto was the manager for both daytime and nighttime operations, which he ran for his absentee employer, a highly-positioned detective in the secret military police or judicial, whose diversified investments included several of these houses where women of every race, compromised by life or for other reasons only they could tell, had no other way to stay alive.

Disgusted by what to him was human trash, disposable women, women beneath his station, together with his inability to communicate, my employer, like a flea ditching a sick cat, fled to better digs, while I, a fool forever and almost as broke as the girls, remained in this "hotel" for free after making actual friends with two of the women who unofficially, but in reality, were in charge.

Golden-legged Maritza and blinkey-eyed Gladys were assumed by the detective owner to be his personal property, but he was unaware that both of them and three other women in his establishment were happily married to one of a five-member group of well-known bandits, the precursors of the guerrillas of the 1980s, whose success at robbing banks, armored cars, rich folk and the military were so popular that they were reported next to the sports scores in all the major newspapers and on the radio.

There were three major reasons for the uninterrupted years of triumph these machine-gun toting thieves enjoyed, not the least of which was the drunken bouts of macho hubris that Gladys and Maritza inspired in the detective major, who spouted secret information to impress them during his visits and private orgies, by which means the two ladies gathered very accurate inside information about the activities of all branches of government including the whereabouts of checkpoints and undercover efforts against their husbands.

Another good reason must have been the bandits' policy of distributing their earnings among the starving public of the smaller villages, keeping back only enough to give generously to their wives and children.

And lastly, because they preyed upon the Guatemalan army, of which they'd all been members to begin with, gathering up weapons and ammunition supplied by the Americans, they were armed at least as well if not better than anyone who they'd encounter.

Though Canuto was there to also ensure that Maritza and Gladys never sold themselves to any other men besides the detective major owner of the house, it was never made an issue, for the two of them were in love with their famous bandit husbands, with whom they had children, and Canuto knew that they both knew how much better off they were by the standards of the surrounding conditions and the two twenty-eight-year-old women actually bossed the willing little man to make very certain that none of the youngest girls were offered to the stream of men who came for women in the night.

Visiting their wives in the dark four or five times a year, staying only for a night and disappearing before dawn, the bandits came in pairs or threes so in case they were discovered, not all of them would be killed. These fellows were always armed and one of them left awake, having decided never to be taken alive by the authorities, which given the certainty of torture, the ghastly conditions of the prisons and the certainty of execution if any were ever captured, was the only alternative to adopt.

During those two weeks of working off my debt to my musician benefactor I managed to get hired for three times what he paid me working
alone in an art gallery-cantina-restaurant in a much friendlier atmosphere,
where I was allowed to play my own combination of flamenco, blues,
mambo and reservation Motown favorites done in samba rhythm. This
afforded me the ability to continue a little longer living in the city, for
another month after my original two weeks were done, which had started
up with me directing nine fifty-year-old male musicians wearing matching
brown suits and ties, combed pomaded hair, playing the worst sort of audio
wallpaper music in an almost 1940s atmosphere.

My benefactor had wanted me, in one hour before we went on stage the
first night, to somehow coerce these nine very able, thoroughly trained, but
inflexible musicians into an American-style 1970s rock band, backing up
songs of which I myself had no knowledge, much less any interest.

The club itself was an enormous dive dedicated to dancing, selling
lethal drinks made with illegal liquor and serving small amounts of very
risky food. It was a place famous for upper echelon military officials and
rich business men to bring their fancy purchased women or mistresses
where they could sit at round tables with table cloths to have an evening out
dancing, far enough away from their normal lives where there was no one
to tell their wives.

Overnight I became bandleader, a gangly, curly-headed, blond half-
breed standing in the front counting down the band. I knew for sure that as
soon as I could, I must head somewhere far away from this particular chamber of mediocre hell, when just as I was expecting to be heckled, all the men
and women seated at their tables flooded to the smoky floor dancing as if
the music were exactly as it should be instead of what it was; like a Guy
Lombardo Band doing Purple Haze in a foxtrot with a trombone and a
flugelhorn doing the guitar parts after my benefactor "kissed the sky."

As a gift to the washerwomen and girls of every age who had become
my friends from the house named "cuartos," I decided I would take the
entire adult population dancing on my last night as director of the band.

Knowing nothing of my plan, my boss, who only woke up for the night,
didn't notice when I borrowed his canary yellow VW convertible for the
evening, which I used at sundown to shuttle nine or ten of the thirty-six
ladies at a time the three miles to the club which for some of them was the

first time they'd ever been in a private car. Like parade queens in their fancy borrowed dresses they sat on the edges of the doors fluttering down the road waving and laughing to the world as we floated to the club.

On the last run, blinking-eyed Gladys in her puff-sleeved long dress and golden-legged Maritza with her long sparkle nails, purple eye makeup, mini-skirt and shiny shoes sat in the back with their arms around little Canuto in his suit and pistol seated between them, with me driving.

The band was ecstatic with my scheme and the staff agreed that I could pay slowly for whatever my friends consumed with money from my next job which turned out very satisfactorily as this place was burned to the ground two weeks later by some thugs at the direction of the owner so he could use the insurance money to build a better club which he did, but it wasn't any better.

Only the oldest prostitutes had ever been taken out dancing and the younger girls and mothers were very shy. But once we got the enthusiastic band chugging I started to dance with a sixteen-year-old named Chava del Galvon who everyone called Bisonia who was as dark and straight-haired as a Dravidian but who was half African and half Pipil native from the coast. I don't think Bisonia actually liked me, but she strutted like no one I'd ever seen and because she had a tiny starving baby daughter that I'd been feeding in my off times she danced with me out of courtesy. But I fell in love with her grandness and with what I'd always searched for and never found.

My benefactor and the owner of the club, who always sat together at the table in the center, nauseated by the affection I showed this girl and my friendship with the rest, whacked the table with the bottom of their empty Cuba Libres, stood up and marched away taking our precious transport with them just to cause us a little more suffering.

But the girls, on the other hand, when they saw Bisonia and myself dancing, poured onto the floor, girls dancing with girls and Canuto waltzing with them all like the entire flower section of a Guatemalan market, their peach and purple dresses and copper ankles whirling and swaying. Sometimes glazed and peering into the distance they held each other close, dancing the slow songs like the hopeful brides of some underworld God.

At some point the waiters, entranced by the magic of these street girls, transformed into a twirling mass of visiting queens joined in and then after a while only half the band played at a time while my musical companions took turns in their bad brown suits, dancing with us until two hours before dawn.

Sitting on my shoulders, straddling my neck, his hard little shoes pounding on my chest, I carried Canuto, who had gotten fairly drunk, but not enough to stop his singing, into which all the girls joined, laughing, still dressed up, but holding their shoes, barefoot again in the street on our way back to the "cuartos," our beds, their babies and little children.

Like white Baraqa carrying Mohammad towards his heaven, the dwarf drove me as his ecstatic pale camel through this paradise of singing flowers, rustling dresses and laughter, in a paradise that moved along with us. Some of these flowers were tender and others of them were tough, but the flowers of this paradise though rooted in the underworld, blossomed in unexpected moments beyond the grips of hell and its demand for righteousness and gray normalcy. And in the momentary infinity of ecstasy, in which this particular paradise moved, at the oozing speed the universe moves, through ecstatic space steadily toward our house, we drifted out of time and no one would ever remember how we got there.

After my month-long engagement at the gallery cantina, I was determined, like some half-baked Sir Galahad, to take Bisonia away from her washer-woman's drudgery and her inevitable slide into a life of prostitution, while feeding up her sickly child whose little head wouldn't stand up. I thought to take my newly earned two hundred quetzales and live in some cheaper mountain village, begin painting and try my luck at selling them.

Maritza and Gladys slapped me and kissed me, applauding my intentions because they knew what no one else could know, that the detective major and his outfit would be killed by their husbands in three months' time and their house would pass into other hands or disband, leaving all the girls with a worse situation or no place to go.

Bisonia was willing to follow me, but only on the condition we go to Panajachel, and Panajachel alone, no other town would do. Though at first I thought it prudent not to tell her about all my history in that place, for she was bossy, temperamental and didn't for sure want to be with me, but I kept hoping for her beauty that she might, when she saw how well I treated her and Maria Natividades, her six-month-old child.

Though I would never know much about Bisonia, in the end I told her everything about myself, in which she wasn't interested much at all, but to the accounts of my disgraces at the hands of them and those she made loyal sounds denouncing my antagonists, which gave me to understand how deeply in love she really was with me, her savior. Nonetheless after hearing why I didn't think we should go to Panajachel she was even more emphatic that she would stay with me if only I would take her to Panajachel.

Not only was I under the spell of my desire and inebriated with a heroic revolutionary urge, but also because I feared losing again the possibility of love, when the time came and I'd been paid, with Bisonia I packed up what we had, my guitar and little Maria Natividades, and took the road back the ninety-two kilometers to Panajachel on a highland bus, in which we were strangely the only passengers.

Even odder still, by halfway to our destination, nobody else had boarded, and at lunch the driver pulled into a empty *comedor* at the bottom of a gorge over whose one-hundred-foot high edge a waterfall crashed into a churning river in front, but whose eerie mist practically hid the restaurant, which was always dripping.

After running through the pounding spray, once inside, besides the bus driver, Bisonia, myself and Maria Natividades, only the owner-cook was to be seen. In countries like Guatemala all buses and businesses have to be crowded for their owners to continue, and they always were. This was odd.

Within four years this peculiar and enchanted place would have disappeared after being filled in by a million tons of stone, buried like Los Robles in the devastating earthquake of February 4th, 1976, backing up the river, damming it enough so that when it broke, it rerouted the whole area and swept it away with an entire other village farther up as well.

But that afternoon while we were eating in the canyon's eternal shadow under the slapping din of the waterfall, a balding man came walking alone and nonchalantly sat down next to us after ordering some deep fried plantanos stuffed with black bean paste and topped with sugar-dusted sweet yogurt. He watched us awhile, listening to how we were, then introducing himself we took up a conversation, practically yelling to be heard over the water.

This was Pachito Paredes, the Catholic priest of Solola. We spoke of Guatemala, Spain, about life and being married, in which state I brutishly pretended Bisonia and myself to be, which any one-eyed, half-drunk *burro* would see was not the case, but I was hoping that by hoping my insistence might make it so.

Involved in some errand of his own Pachito, driving his own parish Landrover with the cross and little sheep emblazoned on the door, was headed in the opposite direction and when our driver started his engine and blared his horn for us to board, though we were his only charges, Pachito handed me his address written down, declaring if he could ever be of any assistance that I should not hesitate to find him in Solola which was just a couple of miles up the hill from Panajachel and the capital of the department.

When we arrived the rainy season had returned, the flowers were all out and most of the resident tourists had gone back and the mood had lightened up considerably in this tourist town.

Since I looked different now, with my sandals, new clothing, some money, a baby, girlfriend and a rented stone house on an obscure corner next to a diesel-driven corn mill that roared and quaked the ground for an hour around dawn, I reckoned the police would not remember me specifically out of all the thousands of tourists they'd harassed over the years.

Natividades's little neck got stronger, her little head stood up and began to look around and she started to grow and laugh, but Bisonia just slept and napped all the time. I even had to rouse her to eat the meals I prepared and get her to suckle the little girl.

With paint, brushes and canvas I'd brought from the capital, I started painting pictures. Probably thinking I was some kind of Gauguin I painted everything I felt about Bisonia that I could, fabricating nine tenths of it because I could draw her only while she slept.

After a month or so she began to wake up a bit and took to visiting the market and we started to almost live a somewhat happy life. One of those days when the rains began to diminish, when she'd gone to the open market with the child to buy some little shoes and food she felt like cooking, a crashing rap was heard to hammer on the double doors, accompanied by what I too well recognized as the police sergeants croaking official command.

"Ábrise esa puerta por cuenta de la Policia Nacional."

"Open this door by authority of the National Police."

I didn't respond, hoping they'd wander off, but they started prying off the hinges with a wrecking bar and so I unlatched one half and said hello cheerfully from the shadows. These were the same three fellows who'd chased me out of town and they didn't recognize me in the least. Like hyenas following migratory grazing beasts, it was tourist-skimming season again.

Holding up a wilted three-foot long marijuana plant, the kind they used to make rope, the sergeant let me know: "We found this growing outside your door, we are going to have to arrest you."

"That plant is three months old at least," I said with great unfounded authority, "We just moved here, so it couldn't be ours, plus I hate marijuana, I'm glad you're getting it all out of our neighborhood."

Expecting the worst at any second, I was astounded when the three looked at each other and were suitably detoured from their ruse, cocked their hats and meandered off. They ended up getting a lot of mileage out of that poor wilted hemp plant having discovered somehow the pickings were better when they went house to house scaring the richer Californians right inside their rented chalets who, since they were avid users of the stuff, would hand over regular protection pay every month not to "go to jail."

Those plants grew everywhere as roadside weeds and nobody except paranoid suburban tourists could be impressed by such a weak threat, but these particular three cops were always thinking up new schemes to extort people.

About a week later, walking home one sunny afternoon from a trip to the post office to pay my rent by mail, I saw that one of my purple doors had been pried off its hinges and tossed carelessly splintered to the ground.

Rushing inside, my eyes unadjusted to the darkness, I could hardly make out the source of the muffled cries, but when I'd focused sufficiently in a second, I saw Bisonia, the top of her dress torn off exposing her beautiful but bruised chocolate breasts held between the same two flunky sidekicks of the sergeant who himself was standing right next to me watching as they beat her with the back of their hands, alternating fondling her while spitting the word "puta" at her face.

His big belly excited and shivering, the sergeant, when he noticed me, grabbed my arm and mildly said, "She doesn't have any papers, no documents. She's a whore; they need documents. Give us two hundred and fifty quetzales and we'll go."

In a split-second with every possibility of every alternative rushing through me without thinking through any of them all the way, I quickly did what I would never advise anyone to do; while agreeing in Spanish to pay, I reached into my back pocket and instead, with both my hands, quite easily removed the fat sergeants nine millimeter semi-automatic pistol from its holster and stuck its muzzle firmly into the folds of his bulky neck.

Though I had no idea how to shoot or load such a gun, having fired only revolvers on the reservation, the safety looked off and from the looks on all the policemen's faces it seemed as if I was holding it exactly right.

"¿Sacase estos tu perros serrotes cobardes sino te soplo tu oçico hasta la chingada! Oiste serrote cabrone?"

I told that man in good Guatemalan slang to stop those men from beating poor shivering Bisonia whose baby was screaming in the other room.

Instantly the men stopped. Having never done such a thing before, I ordered them all to remove their gun belts just like in those old idiotic westerns.

I was scared, humiliated and angry about poor, beautiful, little strutting Bisonia all beat up and torn. Were these men the same ones who raped Doña Chona and burnt to death Benefacio? I didn't want to kill them; I'd just wanted them to stop and was glad then and ever since that the gun didn't go off.

I hadn't thought any further than that. What was I to do now? No matter what happened to me I had to get Bisonia away before something worse erupted. I asked Chava de Galvon, la Bisonia, to gather up her baby Maria Natividades, then after giving her money from my pocket, wrote out a note to Pachito and told her to give it to the bus driver of the first bus she saw going towards Solola which she should board, then watched her leave out the door, rushing up the street.

I handcuffed the three of them back to back around a post in the center of the room, took their guns and keys, i.d.s and wallets and put them in a string bag and, shaking like a new-born calf, caught a bus to Solola where I went straight to the prison, gave up the guns, checked myself in for protection and writing him another note, I waited for Pachito.

Miraculously, I only had to spend one night inside that horrid one-hall stone wall dungeon where you defecated in the cracks in the stone and ate only if your relatives brought you a meal.

By dawn Padre Pachito Paredes was there waiting with food to hear me describe my predicament, which caused his already bulging eyes to compete heavily with his bald head for space as he stared at me open-mouthed, in utter disbelief at what had happened and what I'd done, after which I went on to emphasize how someone, preferably myself, had to find Bisonia to make certain she was alright with her baby. Pachito listened as I expressed how remorse-filled I was for putting her in such jeopardy and how I knew she must be hating me and all men, right about now.

Asking for my documents so he could present my situation directly to the governor of the department, Pachito was unexpectedly impressed by all the wild testaments to my worth written by the border immigration chief and all the brass eyelets, rivets, stamps and fluttering ribbons that accompanied what normally was a small single gauzy paper.

Thankfully, Padre Pachito returned exhausted to the prison on the same day, but in the twilight, bearing a writ directly from Colonel Jaime Crespín Arriaga Molino, the governor of Solola himself, which exonerated me of any malfeasance and effected my release.

Handing me one hundred quetzales to live on and returning my special visa still festooned with ribbons, Pachito walked me to the steep cobbled street.

"As far as the governor is concerned you were never in this jail and there are no charges pending, so you are free to do as you please. Jaime has been trying to trap these policemen for years and he has them now under arrest. My advice to you is to get out of town for quite a while, because when the colonel's men are finished with them the sergeant and his little flunkies will be mashed bananas. The two privates will be expelled from the force, not for what they have done to you, but for some offense having to do with territory. The sergeant, if I can be allowed to make a divination, will most likely retain his post as the constable of Panajachel.

"In any case, they'll all be released within a day or two and I'm sure they'll come looking for you. So, please Martincito, go far, get away from here, at least until they've all disappeared and the dust has settled down and if I were you, the sooner you forget about Bisonia, the better off you'll be."

To be set free was not the same as knowing how to be free and both of these were unexploited luxuries for me, for I was so agitated for missing my beloved Bisonia that I discarded any freedom for the tyranny of my heart's desire. Wanting nothing more to do with these horrible places I would heed most of Pachito's advice, but when I left it would be only to tear up every root and cinder of this country's volcanic turf until I found my Bisonia, hoping when I did, she would still have me and we could start over in a better place. For my loyalty to what I'd thought I loved before, I'd always ended so utterly alone, but this time I would find it and for that I returned immediately to the ill-fated little house to gather up some things I would need to go searching the world for Bisonia.

The door was back on its hinges and I was locked out. The caretaker explained that I didn't live there anymore because my "wife" Bisonia had returned with someone driving a little pale yellow truck, who had helped her load up everything inside the house including my guitar, what money had been left, all our furniture and most likely my paintings and materials. Bisonia hadn't left word, of course, where she might have headed, for fear the police might follow. She was only barely learning to read and write and would not have left me a note regardless, once again for fear she might be pursued.

Locked out with no belongings and no idea where she had gone, I plopped down beneath the huge sticky leaves of a moon-lit tobacco plant holding my knees to my chest and wept alone, singing sad songs to the earth asking how I would ever find her again if she, like myself, was to leave no trail, until shivering halfway to midnight I realized that in her panic she must have fled to the safest and most familiar place where she'd figure I would find her, which of course would be with Maritza, Gladys and Canuto.

In my present exhausted and weakened state I ran toward the little open market, where a few Mayan venders sometimes held on until 11 P.M. and with the cash Pachito had generously afforded I bought myself a wool jerga jacket, two grilled longanizas, five tortillas, *chirmol* and a cup of hot sugar-sweetened coffee, all of which I was still chewing and gulping when, unburdened of every possession I'd ever owned, I ran and mounted the still-moving last little bus of the day heading toward Guatemala City, whose chauffeur was the same man who'd driven Bisonia, Natividades and myself here three months previously. This time the transport was packed with crowds of Solola Cakchiquel Mayans on their way to the feast of Patzicia, meaning the Land of Water Dogs, the Town of Otters.

In every village along the route, to everyone I met, I showed a badly rumpled street photographer's Polaroid picture of Bisonia holding her new baby, taken before we'd ever met. Nobody had seen her and if they thought they had, they were pretty doubtful, but were certain that the person they thought they'd seen was not traveling with our belongings in a truck.

Twelve or thirteen villages later we came into the noisy grinding capital city an hour after sun up. Several miles from the terminal market where the bus let off, walking impatiently and swiftly through the hardest parts of the city to the street where the "cuartos" would have been, I passed my hopes and speeches back and forth, praying Bisonia would be standing there next to the *pila* with her old friends, maybe even washing laundry. I'd talk to her beautifully, showing how well I'd fared with the cops and how we should try again, but when I came to where the sign "cuartos" used to swing the place was without a door, the rooms demolished, the *pila* gone, a large pile of rubble standing in its place. Not one room nor living person, nor even a rat was left behind to give even a hint as to where everyone had fled.

Standing in that demolished whorehouse-laundry courtyard on that cloudy frigid day would not be the loneliest of my life, though now I wish it had been. Then, it was the worst I'd ever known.

If some days are there to crack the hard seeds of what we think is real or true and moistened by our tears, bake us into a bread that feeds more the world than just our own desires, then that morning I was standing right inside the assumption-crushing gizzard of a monster, the dragon of Guatemala City, whose insatiable hunger could be smelled in every puff of diesel and heard in the yelling and churning foment of the city's hard relentless streets as it crushed and digested its daily diet of poor folk, tribal cultures, transplanted families and younger people's dreams, and in whose gaping mouth I most likely would have been trapped, had I not kept moving.

But miracles being what they are, a little five-year-old daughter of a bandit, the child of golden-legged Maritza, rounded the corner running, flapping in her new jacket, recognized me and jumped up into my arms, clutching me close like an organ-grinder's monkey. Within fifteen seconds Maritza came lunging in behind her, out of breath but not enough to halt the steady stream of alternate swearing and kisses of gratitude on the child's head until Maritza noticed who I was, for which we both began a steady stream of banter. With Maritza chasing, the lively little child, like myself, was trying to get back to the familiar and what to her had always been a happy time.

She hadn't seen Bisonia, but Maritza was her cousin and thought that for safety she must have headed toward her brother's house who lived where they'd all been raised in the smothering heat of La Gomera, a rough plantation sugar cane and cattle town of shacks on the southern coastal plain.

One hundred kilometers south and west again but only fifty kilometers south and east of highland Lake Atitlan, this town was in the former land of the Pipil, a proud non-Mayan, Nahuat-speaking people who once tapped all the latex trees and made the first rubber balls for the ritual ballgames called *Kiq* in Mayan, or *Olliin* in Pipil. When the Europeans came they used the same methods to make rain capes and marimba mallets. Bisonia, by blood if no longer by culture, was Pipil by her mother and African by her father, descended from the "washiman" or United Fruit Company field foremen brought in from the Atlantic coast to oversee Indian laborers between the 1920s and the 1950s.

Of course no one would tell me anything when I arrived in La Gomera. In the *aldea* where a couple of people said Bisonia's people were thought to reside, my questioning had irritated a crowd of angry-eyed dark cattle servants. A young man I took to be Bisonia's brother for the gold and black of his skin, machete drawn, with five friends just as emphatic and fierce, convinced me I had no business bothering them or looking for anyone there, which gave me some comfort, for I took this to mean that the girl was well and doing alright having been hidden there somewhere and cared for by relatives.

Reckoning that these men must have assumed I was nothing more than one of her antagonists, I wrote a love letter to Bisonia, put it into an envelope and paid the keeper of the booth-like general store to read it to her when she appeared, after which I fled away from the bananas, humidity, Hindi cattle, heat and angry stares to go straight back to the highlands, right back to Panajachel, where I'd wait for a letter or some notice from her.

Not thinking altogether very clearly, I'd taken the notion that what must have happened after I'd sent Bisonia and her baby fleeing to safety on the bus was that she must have come straight to the coast to her brother's, avoiding the capital altogether.

The caretaker, the owner of the mill, must have stolen our possessions, thinking she'd never return and I'd be in prison forever. In light of this late but intelligent deduction, I'd returned for the third time to where Pachito said I shouldn't, to look for my guitar, to find our bed and wait until Bisonia found me and then we'd go somewhere else and start up again somehow.

But when I snuck into lawn-studded, entrepreneurial Panajachel of the beautiful canyon, Panajachel of Benefacio's roses, Doña Chona's rape and burning corncobs, Panajachel of missing beds and lost guitars, lovers gone and Don Gustavo missing, nothing much had changed except that the police were nowhere to be seen.

I spent days alone weeping on the beach where the river oozed into the breezy lake, which was better than always searching. When I'd done too much of both, I sang my tears into the water, wondering every day where she was and how I was supposed to ever live again.

A small hidden *comedor* in which mostly truckers and bus drivers took their meals and which served the best market food in town was owned and run by a big Ladina lady who hadn't ever seemed to like me very much. I went there now once a day to eat, not only because the food was very good and cheap and tourists never found it, but because, for reasons I was never told, the police wouldn't enter.

The chubby fifty-year-old matriarch wearing all black, in mourning for her husband who'd passed on long ago, after watching me in my inconsolable sorrow, sat down beside me one day and listened like a fortune-teller to my plight. Her eyelids on her big face, like honorable, milkless, old-lady breasts that had fed generations, sagged almost to the side but held in their creases the bright, clear emeralds of her eyes.

After spending the time it took to drink our coffee trying to convince me that the girl I was waiting for now more than three weeks was not going to come and wasn't therefore worth all this heartbreak, and seeing I wasn't taking her advice, the lady began to talk about the Gran Judio and the south side of the lake.

"When my man, Manolo," she crossed herself pretty much like a Catholic but then reached down to the earth, retrieved a pinch of soil and kissed it as Mayan traditionalists always do after giving the heavens their due, "when he disappeared out on the water, I went to visit my sister, Doña Chica, who has a fairly big store in Santiago Atitlan across the lake to find out if my husband was dead or alive, living somewhere or drowned in the lake, because God, *Santo sea su nombre*, left us no sign one way or the other.

My sister Doña Chica took me to visit a scary old Tzutujil zajorin who looked into his little bag of magic things and made a divination after which I returned to my sister's store to pick up esterina candles, cigar puros, aguardiente, silk scarves, silver money and chocolate, and then we went to see el Gran Judio, the Holy Boy, and made a big *costumbre*, a ceremony, during which this old cabalista was informed by the *santo* that my poor husband had indeed been drowned and now, may God assist him, he lives with the *santos* at the bottom of the lake. So, I didn't wonder anymore; it wasn't his fault he hadn't come and when I see the lake now I don't feel that I've lost him but, like all of us who have to perish sometime, I feel him close by in the water.

"If you want to go to Santiago, my sister, she could help you find a zajorin to take you to see this *santo*, the Gran Judio. I don't know how he works because you know how Indians are, they hide everything from everybody, but Jesus doesn't mind him either, though don't tell the priests... Anyway, you have to go there, Holy Boy will find her for you, he'll put your heart at ease, this saint is miraculous, the things I could tell you that he has made come true... Whatever it is your heart is longing for, he'll bring it to you. You will go there, won't you? Because if you continue like you have been up to now you're going to die of longing right here in my *trampa* and I don't want to have to bury you!"

Then leaning over, the vital old woman whispered in my ear, "You, *jito*, did very well with those evil policemen," and got up and went about tending to her stone and plaster, smoky, earth-floored diner. She never again charged me for any meals for as long as I remained on the north side of the lake.

If you are not very tall and have been living, walking, riding, eating and weeping with people who are shorter still, you are always startled by the enormity and length of individual tall people when you meet them.

Though I never knew his name, a very good-natured, very skinny, tall Belgian hippie with a striped, factory-woven Guatemalan tourist shirt, a big nose and floppy straw hat strapped on beneath his pointed, dimpled chin was recruiting workers on the beach, men strong enough and willing to help him load handmade Atiteco log canoes into his big Dodge pickup truck.

The Tzutujil Maya of Santiago Atitlan had an ancient guild of canoe carvers from whom this wealthy but amiable Belgian boy had commissioned five hand-adzed *cayucos* or what Mayans called *juqu*, hollowing the entire length of jungle cedars or wild avocado trees into elegant, log canoes.

Despite the fact he was paying ten quetzales for one day's work, over seven times the Guatemalan minimum wage, because the tall fellow's spoken Spanish and Mayan were very poor, he ended up with English speakers, of which I was one.

Though he could have had the men who'd carved these magnificent little boats simply paddle them across the nine miles to Panajachel, then send them back on the mail ferry for seventy-five cents apiece, he was determined with his much deliberated plan to drive the thirty miles of hard, deeply rutted, bumpy, not always passable road around the lake to load into his truck bed five two-hundred-pound canoes and slowly bounce the same distance in the same ruts back around the same twisting and rising roads, circumnavigating the same lake, all in the space of a single day.

But, I needed the cash and he was going and so I climbed into the truck bed with the others, wondering if I could find a zajorin to take my case to the Gran Judio, the native *santo* and god who could find my heart's desire.

At some point in the journey, a geographical position in the ground below the chalky bluff I would later know was called Psacab on the cliff of talc below *Iq´utiujuyu´*, the Black Coyote Mountain, a line was passed after which the forces that had made a prisoner of my vision locked behind the sorrows of my life, were stymied, deflected, left behind and unable for some reason to cross this magical boundary in the earth along with me, and for whose absence I began again to recognize from dreams the land that would come to be, as it gradually dawned on me increasingly throughout the duration of the ride, the home for which I'd left my land of birth to find.

There was the pier where the God had stood up from the water. I knew perfectly the landscape of the western edge of the town. All the wild birdlike chattering of over two-hundred women, their blouses tucked into long wraparound skirts, rolled up when they washed their clothing above their knees, bent over plank-like family stones where standing in the water they kneaded, twisted, slapped and wrung out with their powerful coppery wrists their family's hand-woven tribal clothing, stretching out for half a mile along the basaltic boulder water's edge.

I forgot my earlier pain, and distracted by an even earlier longing, I had trouble just remembering what Bisonia looked like or what was her real name, conscious of my indigenous memory racing through my bones, bones I'd had before my ancestors had been born, a memory that the dreams I'd dreamt in that Taos blizzard had used like a horse to bring me here to Santiago.

Leaping from the truck, running up the shore, I disappeared into the convoluted pathways of the town. I forgot about five canoes, about ten quetzales, about a Belgian hippie, about my lost bed, my guitar, about my losses, almost about my heartbreak for Bisonia.

This village was not a good place or a nice place or even a friendly place, but it was here that I first felt at home.

This lakeside village was my heart's desire, the sweetheart I'd never had. Her eyes were the wild intact gaze of everyone I met, her voice was in the sounds of water birds rising up at dawn and in the village chattering and panting struggle of forward-leaning men returning from the volcanic ridges loaded with firewood on their backs.

She was in every stone, every particle of corn chaff, in every pot chard or old jade bead, in the musty shoreline muck, in the closeness of her people's village compounds. She was everywhere and everything.

That was how I got to Santiago Atitlan and my first moment in the village, the rest of which has been told in other places. After three years of serving the "zajorin" Old Chiviliu in his rituals, becoming fluent in Tzutujil and the secret elevated prayer language, and was myself initiated by him, I inherited his career. Then after three years of playing flute for the sacred hierarchy and on the verge of my appointment to the position of Najbey Mam in charge of youth initiations and the guarding of the Village Heart, I was visited by the old Ladina lady who had the diner on the opposite shore, who now sought me out in my capacity as a "cabalista and zajorin" to communicate again with her missing, underwater husband with whom she'd more or less continued speaking and being married to by talking to the lake. She wanted me to formally ask him, in his underwater state on her behalf, for permission for her to marry an old timer with whom she'd fallen in love. In the course of our alternate seriousness, our laughter and our banter the conversation turned to the subject of Bisonia, Chava del Galvon, from whom I'd never heard again. The old lady, of course, was privy through her connection with the truckers, to the entire story.

On the day after her beating by the police and the day before I'd been released after being blessed by their arrest, Bisonia really had returned in a little Datsun truck and had loaded into it everything we'd owned together, our bed, pots and pans, our money and my guitar, and after collapsing all my canvases and throwing away all my artwork and supplies, she moved herself into the house of the brother of the town baker, not seven blocks away, right in the middle of the town.

This "panaderia" bakery was the best thing in that tourist village and the younger brother of the baker who worked there in the family business had made Bisonia pregnant on a sugar-buying trip to La Gomera on the coast, a year and a half before. He was the father of Maria Natividades. Though Bisonia and her baker lover Emilio Galvon had wanted to get married at the time, Emilio was still attached to another woman, from whom he eventually severed relations. Bisonia's insistence on coming only to Panajachel was the result of hearing that Emilio was now single. But the estranged ex-girlfriend of this brother of the baker paid off the town police to get rid of Bisonia after noticing her visits to the bakery, which I'd taken as visits to the market.

When my naïve, heroic antics had rid the town for a time of these particular corrupt police, Bisonia and Señor Emilio were free now to openly unite and did so when they assumed I'd been sent to prison. The two of them were married and Bisonia worked happily in the bakery. Her strategic abilities with business were so acute that by the time Natividades was five, Bisonia, wearing polyester sweaters with false pearls sewn on the neckline, was the sole owner of the very successful bakery where all the tourists came to get their doughnuts and her famous Guatemalan coffee.

Because priests, like cops the world over, love baked goods and to fetch some of her very fine coffee, after negotiating all the landslides and driving the beautiful miles down the forested canyon hills, what for these priests had been preparation for the trial and for me miles of remembrance, Padre Pachito, Stan and Gaspar Culan the grandson of Swordfighter stopped the parish Landrover at Bisonia's bakery, the one and only bakery for miles, on the main thoroughfare running through Panajachel, that would take us to Solola and this time to the seminary.

This was the first time I'd seen Bisonia since before I'd lost my bed and my guitar. She had five children now and was doing very well. Of course she didn't recognize me anymore and I didn't say a thing, but besides her strut and her beautiful skin and the long look her nine-year old daughter dressed in her white blouse and red tartan school uniform gave me as we got back into the truck, I couldn't remember what had pulled me so close to her and caused me to risk my life. But, I did know that with stubborn lonely people like myself, the Holy Female Spirit that did want me and brought me to Atitlan had probably used Bisonia to drag me toward herself, like Bisonia had used me to bring her to her husband.

The Divine woman whose face was in all things was the very same holy thing that Padre was accused of worshiping and about which, because he didn't respect the story, he knew absolutely nothing. But a trial was prepared to prove that the kind of worshiping he'd done alongside his unbaptized wife, who did know the story, had somehow made him a better Catholic and not a Pagan like myself.

eleven

PADRE'S INQUISITION:
THE TRIAL OF HOLY BOY

I f Holy Boy had not given me his flexible armor of the wind whose invisible protection caused me to remember, in the most spirit-killing situations, what it was I really loved, then anything indigenous in me would have been spiritually defeated in the instant I passed through the seminary's aluminum sliding doors.

With an unexpected Marxist concession to rationalism that would not admit of the spirit that is either given life or killed in certain shapes and spaces or even the holiness in matter, this order of Catholic Christian priests, in their artless effort to close the distance between the altar and the "regular" people in their flocks, had mysteriously neglected to examine "the regularness" of the people and land where they were seated, and imported what for the priests was "regular" from their own Midwestern American lives, over whose cat-vomit colored wall-to-wall acrylic carpet Padre, the grandson of Swordfighter, and I shuffled in this dry-walled, pre-fabricated house from Des Moines to be seated behind a rickety gray plastic desk in front of a crowd of seated white men in short-sleeved shirts, hairy arms, wrist watches, polyester slacks, coffee cups in hand, all priests, monks and bishops who were here to judge our spirituality.

This aluminum-sided monstrosity was built into one of the steep forested volcanic hills in the middle of Cakchiquel Mayan territory that had always been called by all the country's indigenous peoples the *Ruchiuleu Aj Tzotzila´*, the Earth of the People of the Bats, whose "regularness" consisted of hand-adzed boards, oak and spruce cooking smoke, thickly riveted sandals, red, brown and cream embroidery-covered hand-woven pants and blouses, clay roof tiles, misty hollows, hillside cornfields, women in bright ribboned braids, earth floors, big-bellied clay cooking pots and water jars, high mountain cave shrines and large, beautifully dressed, complex sacred hierarchies of men and women whose rings we Tzutujil kissed when we saw them in our villages as they kissed our hands when we visited their towns in mutual recognition of our love and service to our unique forms of the Holy.

Today in this carpeted spiritual morass there was no hand-kissing, but a wrestling match of sorts where as a coach, I was here to help Gaspar escape being thrown out of his circle or pinned down with a stigma of paganism so he could continue in the grace of those who had to live inside this myopic dry-walled bubble.

It's impossible to beguile through the use of subtle understanding those who are not conscious beyond the dogma of their cause. I felt somewhat like a martial artist trained a millennium before, accustomed to doing battle with dragons using wild supernatural moves and sophisticated spiritual shifts of vision, who had agreed to spar with a comfortably-seated row of passive-aggressive Midwestern American couch potatoes only to discover that their apparent good natures camouflaged an unconscious ethnocentric arrogance which judged everything from that core. In order to assist Padre, I would have to make myself unintimidating, smaller than I was, narrow my apparent focus, shrink my vocabulary using their own arguments to win,

while pretending not to want to win, all without any sort of flippancy, toler-
ating their numbness and sarcasm without the luxury of expressing mine
and still not lose my direction or my temper for being intimidated as I was
by my anger at these men who espoused a religious direction whose ancestral application had been dedicated to the utter destruction of the elegant
spiritual understandings and many Gods and Female Deities that I with all
my heart did truly serve. Serving the village that day in the seminary meant
keeping most of the big picture hidden so that we could all get home in one
piece to continue living in the exuberant flowering dogfight that was life in
Tzutujil Atitlan.

The referee in this wrestling match would be Padre Pachito, who mysteriously ended up appointed by committee to be the keeper of the rules and
mediator during the debate.

All interrogations, oral examinations, quarreling and debated back-
and-forth discussion, Pachito informed us, would take place only after lunch
and end at sundown. The mornings would start with mass in the chapel
after which everybody, no matter who they wanted to win, would have to
grab their own baked goods and cups of coffee from the board back in the
carpeted inquisition chamber to listen to formal presentations from Stan,
Padre and myself.

The chapel, on the other hand, was the only part of this place of monks
where you could tell that the unseen Holy could actually find a place to
come inside and take a seat. Tunneled cave-like into a soaring cliff of soft
volcanic stone at whose base the seminary sat in some great evidence of
faith, tempting landslides, it was here inside the sparkling stone and earth
chapel, where the priests sent their incense vertically up toward their only
God, that without their conscious understanding they also blessed and fed
the deities that sustained them in the earth, the sweet smell of their frankin-
cense only adding to the powerful musk of the Holy Earth's humidity who
all villagers knew to be the scarred, dark-skinned daughter of the ground
who pushed her holy water into the sap of the sunlit trees above.

Like a big city man on a date with a girl he thought he'd never get, Stan
started off the first morning by boring the entire board of examining
priests, the Bishop and one hundred and thirty monks and students by talking very slowly for an entire hour about himself and his mission. As with
anything that had poor Stan in it, there was a lot of sleeping going on, but

he finally brought it all to a close, raising my blood pressure by introducing me with several derogatory remarks about my mixed heritage, calling my wife my "tortilla-making woman" because we weren't married in the church, while expressing his worries about my poor unbaptized older son, who ironically enough actually was baptized, and commenting on the "secret study" he thought I must be making of what he'd hoped was the dying practice of Mayan shamanism.

I let all his unkindness slide, for my goal was not to be right, but to get Gaspar and I back into the arms of the things he mocked, by which he'd never be held and myself away from this terrifying collective lack of vision. So I thanked him as a brother and let Gaspar begin his *charlada*, his discourse.

After standing like a rector, putting on his horn-rimmed eyeglasses, Padre pulled out a plastic snap-ring binder from his backpack, unlocked a couple of laminated leaves and began speaking in a deep, aggressive, open-jawed, non-Mayan voice, not unlike orphan Indians do when raised by Norwegians or American missionaries; a voice that didn't match his face, a voice I'd never heard before. Like a pushy socialist church historian, he cited the data of certain anthropologists and the conjectured opinions of some scholars about Mayan ritual, blaring on about the grandness of Mayan spirituality before they had become acquainted with the advantages of the modern Catholic church, which took the better part of an hour. For the next hour, he expounded unimaginatively but with great detail on why he was disappointed with the Catholicism of the Spanish conquest and how all of what the Oklahoma Catholics were doing to rid the highlands of these vestiges of damaging spiritual superstitions and the people's persistent veneration of idols through their mistaken understanding of the statues of the Spanish Catholic saints left over from the sixteenth century was very laudable and slowly having a positive effect, as far as he could see, and of which he was an avid supporter and so on, and so on and so on.

With his coffee cup held on his thigh, the Bishop tried to look as serious as his position demanded, but every hungry monk could tell he was pleased with this clear, positive delivery of his party policy by his prized Indian candidate.

I think there was a great longing for what they knew as God among most of the monks, seminarians and a couple of the priests, but for them God was not in the ground, in the whiskers of jaguars, or in the utterances of mad street women; God was only in the caring that humans had for one another and was therefore a deified institution.

The remainder of old boy curates from the American middle corridor, who were the hierarchy and core of judges here, feared what the others desired; God for them was a stack of rules and rightnesses, a place for their conquering football instincts to gain territory for the church.

Almost all the seminary students here were young Mayan men from various villages and linguistic tribes, some of them Quiché, Ixil, Mam, Cakchiquel, Kekchi, Pocomchi, Pokoman and Tzutujil and everyone of them spoke their mother tongue.

Made to stand as a crowd behind the seated bishop, Pachito and the old boys embedded in the couches, the only seminarians not present at this welcome flamboyant interruption to their predictable daily routine were the youths assigned that day to bake the bread and cook the meals, who every chance they could get joined the ranks of the wide-eyed, loyal audience, bronze-faced would-be priests with their *delantales* still tied on, everyone dispersing to eat their lunch when Pachito finally rang his little bell.

But in the afternoon the wrestling began and the first words that were aimed at Swordfighter's grandson came from a known enemy of the Bishop's, who, in tolerable Spanish with a bad Okie twang, matter-of-factly blurted out, "What about this image of San Simon you were out there worshipping? He's anything but God; isn't he an image of the Devil?"

"I wasn't worshipping this idol," Padre retorted with his strange non-Indian voice still in place, "I was kneeling at its feet, praying to Jesus to help my people to see the way and come away from such things into our holy church. What better place to do this, as Padre Francisco says," pointing to a very worried-looking Stan, "but in the very places where the people have laid their mistaken faith?"

Though I couldn't endorse either side of such an argument, as far as Christian spiritual wrestling went it seemed that Padre had the edge, but the big guy from Oklahoma who was sitting on the edge of the couch now wasn't about to give in. "Even if we are to believe that you could keep your eye on Christ surrounded by such a presence of the Devil, isn't it true that the idol at whose feet you knelt is considered by your people to be a God and that anyone who worships him has more than one God, and don't they call this idol the 'horned one'?"

Finally, I found a loose brick in the wall of their mediocre dogma and in an attempt to earn and be a worthy keeper of the story of The Toe Bone and the Tooth, I spoke up, not only in defense of Gaspar Culan, the grandson of Swordfighter, but in defense of Holy Boy.

"This deity you speak about is indeed an ancient God," I finally spoke, my voice also not sounding entirely like my own, "but was never called the 'horned one' by anybody until your religion showed up to show the people what to call him. Before the coming of the Spaniards and the arrival of Catholic Christians he was called the Lord of White or the Clear Unblemished Boy or Holy Boy, all names still used today. It was before this God of both human frailty and possibility that people had always gone for alleviation of their hard lives, as they still do today, and more importantly for you to recognize, they went to this Clear Youth to be given the blessing of forgiveness, the forgiveness that people are not so good at bestowing."

This large priest who I stopped short of calling Buba was getting fairly excited and, widening and bracing his seat, he severely crowded little Pachito, who sank back involuntarily into the hollow wake of cushions created by Buba's forward lurching.

"You're just trying to whitewash the Devil," he yelled out in his Oklahoma-accented Spanish, the Indian men wide-eyed and open-mouthed, taking it all in.

"Isn't it true," Buba continued, "that the Tzutujil and every other kind of sinner, go before this devil with pagan shamans, zajorines, to which they give all their hard-earned pay and sell their sins to this demon with tobacco and liquor, finery, money and licentious words for which he adopts their sins for them and which they continue making, so they can live in this world unaccountable, having traded, like Mephistopheles, for an eternity in hell where this devil rules when they die. Isn't this true?"

In a policy I learned from Chiviliu when he'd been confronted for his habits and understandings, I took up where I'd left off instead of biting on the barb and baited hook of his interruption.

"Before your people came here, I mean white folk from abroad, this God you call the 'horned one' was the Mayan equivalent of Jesus; an unmarried, magical boy whose annual sacrifice caused the world to flower and the earth to provide again; whose disappearance every year, like Jesus' crucifixion, caused the people to grieve and weep; whose tears fertilized the earth, his mother, whose womb brought forth a new 'clear child,' like Maria does every winter... "

I hadn't wanted to explain the intricacies of how this deity transformed annually thirteen times, and how because there was no verb "to be" in Mayan language there was no issue of one-ness and because of that sometimes he was a woman, and that he was built of lightning thought and ropes of two hundred and sixty Gods of deified Time from the Tzutujil version of the more generally known Mayan calendar, whose knots created a supernatural net of fire who were the stars, which in turn were the spark souls of a million types of life and life to come, but pushed by this angry, not very subtle Oklahoman enemy of the Bishop I proceeded, against my better judgment, to do exactly that.

The hundred nodding heads of young Indian novice priests, who recognized in what I'd said their own spiritual dilemmas, of wanting as Indians to love some part of their people's traditional ritual and faith, but having had it demonized or trivialized by the church who called their beliefs childish, upon hearing the Tzutujil version of the same, explained in terms of its splendor and spiritual depth, allowed little hairs of Indian pride and doubt about the Christians to be planted in their hearts, all of which now terrified the priests.

Buba, though seeming by then to be more of an embarrassing liability than an ally to the other curate's cause, was so wound up by the hatred he felt toward me personally and the ground he'd lost on my account that he now jumped to his feet and forgetting to speak in Spanish so everyone could understand, blurted out accusatorily in English while shaking his mutton-fisted arms my direction, "Then tell us, smart guy, if this manifestation of Satan, that you call 'the clear white child' is so glorious a thing, why is he known far and wide as the 'Big Jew'? Wasn't it the Jews that killed our Jesus? Huh?"

Unaware that Pachito understood and spoke English as beautifully as he spoke his native Spanish, along with Latin, Greek, Italian and Cakchiquel, I now listened as he very carefully translated what the American Buba priest had inquired into Spanish for the crowd, his eyes bugged out, eyebrows wrinkled up to his sweating, bald head, staring in horror at the Bishop, whose rising blood pressure was already in heaven and whose fist thumped his jittering thighs.

Padre froze with the rest, his arms folded and looking straight down at the plastic desk, while I on the other hand responded before anyone could stop the session or interrupt, starting before the last words of Pachito's translation had dropped from the air.

"When the Spaniards came they were divided between clergy and civil colonial bureaucracy. While different religious orders were assigned to different districts, here in the southern highlands the Franciscans won the appointment.

"After fifty years of forced building, proselytizing, saying mass and instigating their cults of saints and *cofradias*, this more human-sounding Mayan Jesus, 'Clear White Youth,' was still just as difficult for the Franciscans to eradicate as he has been for all of you.

"When the Tzutujil people were increasingly punished and further harried for their veneration of this more visible of their many deities, they started to call him Saint Simon Judas Tadeos, considering him to be Jesus' older brother, which was further confused over time by the Spanish priests with Judas Iscariot, the one who sold your God's son to his persecutors.

"By the time the Catholic Holy See, the Dominican Inquisition feared by all people far and wide, sent their anemic, sadistic officers to what is now known as Guatemala, they had as their prime directive to rid the Earth of all heretics, Protestants and heathens, all of which were known collectively as Jews.

"The Inquisition could not legally try Indians in their courts for heresy for the greater faith they showed for the 'Clear White Youth,' or San Simon, as his newer manifestation was called.

"This was because in the human ranking system of Europe, the Indians were ranked as a subhuman caste with a status equal to the beasts, which Christians, Protestants and Catholics alike saw as not having a soul and therefore exploitable as dead matter.

"Of course, everybody knew they were people, but they weren't legally people. To make them into people legally, so the Inquisition could have domain over them all, the Holy See set about proving that Mayans were actually one of the lost tribes of ancient Jews, from the time of Gog and Magog, before the Jews had a temple, much before they'd lost their temple and adopted Rabbinical Judaism. If they could convincingly show that Mayans were genetic Jews, then the Inquisition could have at them.

"So, like the council and Pilate that judged and sentenced Jesus, the Inquisition, just like you seem to be doing here, tried and sentenced the Mayan Jesus, proclaiming the 'Clean White Youth' to be the 'Gran Judio,' so they could eradicate their God for being a Jew and crucify the Mayans for being Jewish, forgetting of course that the Romans who later became the Roman Catholics crucified their Jesus who died not a Christian but an Aramaic-speaking Jewish Rabbi."

Then finishing up like I thought a lawyer might, I added in conclusion:

"If this council has been called to determine the purity of the faith of the prospective priest Gaspar Culan by trying and passing judgment yet once again on another people's God, then I say that even if he had been worshipping what is holy at the foot of the Grand Jew, or the 'Clear White Youth,' or conversely if he was only accompanying his relatives who were, no matter how you cut it, you have all ended up looking a whole lot like a tribunal of jealous, unforgiving people trying Jesus all over again, instead of practicing trying to be like him. In that light I submit that Gaspar Culan has as good a faith as anyone else in this carpeted room."

Though I was hungry and could have eaten, the dinner was late, for every single cook, monk, novice priest, student, delivery boy and visiting Indian parent had forgotten what they were doing and had converged into the crowd mesmerized by the argument, which at this point was immediately and emphatically halted by the Bishop, whose hierarchical cronies called for a huddle which all the priests jumped up to join, whispering like a football team after their last down who was going to have to punt, throughout which Gaspar and I, uninvited, patiently waited.

When the knot of priests unfurled, Pachito loudly announced with his little bell and clipboard in his hand that Padre was exonerated and back in the graces of the church and that two more days spent discussing what was obvious to everyone would be a waste of precious time away from their parishes and all our work. Which meant to me, best of all, that tomorrow we could all go back home to our families in Atitlan.

In the months that followed more than sixty percent of the Mayan seminary students would have renounced their ambitions to pursue a Catholic priesthood. What had happened to them all, only they themselves could tell, but not a few of those young men ended up as left-wing guerrillas.

Father Stan must have known what was coming. On our way back in a borrowed Landrover, having refused to take the boat, squeaking past the makeshift tracks around the landslide, past the waterfall, past the Black Coyote Mountains, past Palpoj, down to the south side of the lake, Stanley talked to me for the first time in English at a desperate rate not common in the normal friendly drawl of Oklahomans about what we could do "together" to head off the suicidal tide of hot-headed Catholic Mayan youth who were arming up, holding trials and passing sentence on absentee defendants who were then declared "enemies of the people" to be executed in efforts to be seen as serious chapters of liberation guerrillas in Atitlan, dedicated to removing all old vestiges of Guatemalan Mayan life-ways that were at odds with the "people's revolution."

All the young men and women in the Catholic Action group set up by his American Catholic order to rid local Catholicism of idol-worshipping had instead become a secret government for "liberation theology," which would no doubt end up getting all his people killed for their inexperience, who had no awareness of the depth of the horror that would ensue when the Guatemalan right wing sent their highly-armed hit-squad goons and illegally-conscripted army to rid the place of these young people as enemies of the state.

Before I could make a reply to this startling plea for help from a man who'd never taken me seriously before, Padre, who would be ordained within a couple of months, sitting with me now on the jump seat in the back whispered to me in as elevated a Tzutujil as he could manage,

"A Martinach, nketnaquin nacoma´ chwa je q´aq´ jeah ta?"

"Martín, Lord, could you possibly bring us some fire here, father?" By which he meant, could I supply him with guns.

"Guns? What kind of guns? And for what do you need guns?"

"We want any kind, every kind. We need guns."

"What makes you think I can get you guns?"

"All Americans have guns, tucked away in their house, beneath their beds, everybody knows, even Padre Francisco here has one in Oklahoma."

And then he explained his revolution to me, even offering me a spot in all the action, realizing that many anti-government groups were starting up and his original revolution would now be swallowed and misinterpreted by incoming political revolutionaries, which didn't have his dedication to the church.

Like a strange Raggedy Boy who refused to live out the remainder of his story, Padre was determined to remain on the ashpile of his original desire, asking me, like one of the older hunters, if I could get him weapons. But Padre wasn't really from our village anymore, he'd caught the priest's disease of needing to erase and conquer evil and having to be right. He didn't want weapons like Raggedy did, to find a way to be admired or loved, Padre wanted to fix life.

But like one of the older hunters in the tale, I told Padre, Gaspar Culan, the grandson of the fighter against swords, that I would not give him weapons even if I had them, which I didn't, because Padre, unlike his grandfather, refused to hear and understand the Story.

twelve

MAN-EATING BIRDS, PLOTTING TOADS AND A VISIT FROM THE GREAT REMEMBERER

E ven though we came home without any warning, no one in the village was surprised when the three of us showed up back in Santiago two days earlier than we ourselves intended.

In the usual Tzutujil way where everyone seemed to know magically more about what their neighbors were doing than they knew about themselves, when I walked into our compound yelling my salutations into the wailing crowds of leaping, happy dogs and squealing little children, I found my relatives already seated around the fire waiting just for me, with hot food still bubbling and toasting being laid out for the feast of my return, everyone eager for news of what they already surmised had taken place with Padre.

The way that most of the old folk, bustling girls and working adults almost always knew where anyone would be and how and when they might return was a tribute to an indigenous capacity once common among all humans to read their intuitions in the sky, water and ground, in the flight of birds, in dreams, in twitches in the body from which most villagers could accurately plot a course between the hard-laid plans of human desire and the more subtle nudgings, storms and miracles of what on the surface seemed like a randomness but was nature's bigger mind, by which they navigated their canoes of everyday life, paddling half-dreaming and half-awake through the water-like nature of village time.

At that homecoming feast we were joined by the head chief of the village and his lieutenant. They were called respectively by the titles *Najbey al* and *Rucab al*, or First Born and Second Born, which referred to the fact that as long as they served the village in these capacities, they were understood to be the living representations of the first human males that had ever existed on Earth and who had been born as twins, making plenty of mistakes and who just had to keep on trying, no matter how much they failed.

These struggling chiefs, along with their wives, "the first human females," and six other sacred house leaders, had been waiting for my arrival with my family in order to solicit my help, mysteriously calling on what they claimed as my newly proven capacity to deal with the non-Indian world beyond the village, which in this case turned out to be a troublesome land dispute.

After patiently listening to my story about Padre and courteously talking about everything except their intended mission, the conversation after the meal gradually digested the last days' events until we found ourselves directly discussing the object of their visit.

A rare, flat piece of corn-growing land at the bottom of the bay had been planted and tended by the family of the present First Born chief for over two hundred years. Thirty years before, however, one of the relatives had pawned the cornfield to an unknown non-Indian man from Chichicastenango to gather enough cash to effect the release of his fifteen-year-old son from an illegal imprisonment and pending conscription at the hands of the local military commissioner. Though never seen by anyone but the chief's now deceased father, the new owner had no designs on the land and had compassionately allowed the chief's family to continue farming and harvesting, sending a man down every year to fetch a small sack of shelled corn as rent.

But this year when Ma Tacoxoy, the chief, and his sons went to burn the stubble and turn the beautiful rich shoreline earth with their foot plows, the great Mayan hoes, they found a tall, unhappy *mos* or non-Indian, who said he was yet another new owner unknown to anybody in the village, who with a large crew was flattening out the land, explaining to them in angry condescending terms how he was intending to pave it all over as a landing strip for small airplanes.

When pressed by the stunned family whose survival depended on the use of this land, the mysterious, irate, non-village man shot a gun in the air as a reply to their pleading, yelling how the land didn't belong to them and how they shouldn't show their faces again or he would have them shot.

The old people wanted me to accompany them to Chichicastenango as an advocate and a translator in their search for the original owner to discover what had gone wrong and to determine if any arrangements could still be made.

We all knew it was unlikely that we should succeed, but as I could not refuse, by the next morning all fifteen of us, finely attired in our best black wool ceremonial *q´u*, sparkling *xcajcoj*, official hats and staffs, each according to their rank, filed into the worn white van of an American visitor, a professor who had generously agreed to haul our venerable team back up the steep hill to Solola, past the seminary and the old whitewashed colonial town, grinding up into the pine-topped mountains another thirty miles into Quiché Maya territory and down into their cold and cloudy hilly town of Chichicastenango, the ceremonial capital of the region, whose name was a Tlaxcalan translation of the Mayan name by which it was still called but never written, *Pan Yel*, or the Land of Giant Nettles.

The route pursued by the American professor over the steep river-stone cobbled roadways of the ancient town took us straight into a ceremonial patrol of barelegged, finely dressed, headcloth wearing, staff cradling Quiché sacred house hierarchy, in front of whom we tumbled onto the mist-slicked rocky knobs of the street. These lower echelon officials, recognizing us by our clothing for who we were, though none but two of us had ever passed this way before, were obliged by custom to exchange hand- and ring-kissing salutations, ritual embraces and a welcoming toast carried out with the powerful *cuxa* of this town.

Chattering in the speech of their position, a more eloquent and antique version of their already magnificent everyday Quiché dialect which differed from Tzutujil in that they pronounced all the vowels that the bird-speaking Tzutujil had dropped centuries previously, it was they, joining our ranks, who led us straight-postured and proud to the threshold of a stone-walled cluster of clay-tile-roofed colonial houses in which resided the wealthy landowner, whose name our chief Ma Tacaxoy had on the yellowed hand-written official land agreement, which he had shown to the youngest of our guides whose position required that he could read documents.

This young official clinked his cane on the flat threshold rock and disappeared into the courtyard through a small door in the whitewashed wall, emerging a moment later with a servant who ushered us to some hand-hewn benches under the tiled eaves against the walls of the three wings of the grand house terraced into the cold foggy mountainside.

Uniting wildly with the deep and delicious aroma of the region's thick little *pixtun* tortillas and boiling coffee, carried into the courtyard on the smoke of an oak-wood cooking fire somewhere within, the intoxicating mix of several different *copal* gum incense smokes from multiple rituals held somewhere over the walls almost disguised but could in no way keep out the nostalgic perfume of something else, that caused a sleeping fish of memories from a time of loss whose thrashing and whirling of painful nostalgia prevented me from fully hooking and pulling the slippery remembrance out of some deep water nook of preferred amnesia, which continued until I saw what I was smelling lay just beyond the wall and became apparent in an instant when the servant led us into another chamber of the courtyard, which was lined corner to corner with bushes holding roses as big as two fists. That fish of remembrance flopped out of my chest and into my arms causing water, salty ocean water, to mist my eyes as I realized the full weight of what I'd been hiding but couldn't carry was that these were the roses of Benefacio.

And in that moment of turbulent remembrance before I could savor what it fully meant, coming clear in on those of us standing there, from some deeper place inside this king-like, rose-studded abode, a boisterous old voice, both laughing and ringing, whose source was yet within but which during the course of the increased volume of its outpourings, soon came into sight, yelling out as it did:

"¿Aha, por fin, el Ladron de las Rosas de Benefacio te tengo en mis garras. Mañoso, cabroncito el gran cuatazo Martincito, que es que te has hecho, que ni una palabra has reservado pa el viejo Gustavo?"

These were the roses of Benefacio and it was Don Gustavo Rodas who had owned the land we came to talk about.

Embracing like two war veterans separated by life, each thinking the other must be dead, remembering out loud in seconds the mad plans and trials of the past, we shook and punched each other until we were laughing so wildly and unabashedly that the rest of the Old Lords on whose behalf I'd actually come were so tickled by the sight they were shaking and laughing harder than Don Gustavo and myself.

We were feasted in the house of that fine old man Don Gustavo, who kissed the rings of our chiefs and ladies as they kissed his, all sides speaking a delicious banter of ceremonial Quiché phrases for dessert, between grand cups of cool *nantze* wine.

After explaining how his sister's grandson, who worked on commission for a Guatemalan military family as some kind of *tramatista*, made a living by terrorizing people off their land in the first phase of certain military money-making schemes, Don Gustavo, still barefooted, rich and in love with animals, on the spot signed his entire landholdings in Santiago back to the people of our village.

Because our zealous gringo driver had not returned from the market, Don Gustavo insisted we spend the night. At the dawn half our party went searching for the American and the rest of us went up the hill behind the town to make offerings at a series of Quiché shrines, to feed the local Time deities with chocolate, fat candles, liquor, tobacco, food, *pom* incense and magnificent words, raising a delicious smoke that rose and disappeared in gratitude for our lucky journey, pleading for the health of our people, the land, future time and people like Don Gustavo, and Don Gustavo himself who'd come along. More specifically, we gave gifts at these mountain-top rock shrines to feed a particular part of the Holy Female, dismembered by our forgetting, that this place held, which annually sent us a certain type of weather that made the earth around our own village live.

We found our patient driver more easily than he could find himself. Beguiled by the exuberance and richness of this town's world famous market, he'd been swallowed into its belly on the trail of his desire to acquire the place and the things that lay for sale on the tables and cloths, while we were busy giving gifts away to the powers that bestowed everything, life to every form, including his possessive folly.

Though on the surface, the entire market appeared to be created only for trade with tourists, of which there had always been a great deal, beneath the benches, behind the cloths, under the tables and hidden in other parts of the town an entirely invisible native market existed for those shamans and traditionalists who knew, and which also did a brisk, covert business. This, however, was not the market in which our driver got lost.

When Don Gustavo Rodas had finally released us from the blessed grip of his endless kingly generosity we were again full of food, waddling into the van unsteadily, both from the effects of his *nantze* wine and from the loads of cigars, cloth, chocolate, petates, bottles of *nantze* wine and basket-loads of Benefacio's roses.

It was my relentless search for the love of the Divine Female that had led me years before to steal Benefacio's roses, in whose perfume Benefacio's love for his sweetheart, his people and his land lived on, which then as today pulled me behind the fragrant wall to find friendship with the likes of Don Gustavo, a man more earth than human, whose admiration for that same love gave him the courage to live barefooted and to keep alive these roses as gifts to that love we almost never find, whose search had given life to us all on that day, and for which we left holding our land and his roses in our arms as we returned home from the Land of the Giant Nettles.

Packed tightly into the van we dozed half-drunk with our stomachs full. Tied into their red headcloths, our heads bounced and bobbed in a relaxed familiar unison like *tule* reeds in a windy pond as we descended the mountains, until our driver woke us with a laugh and the abruptness of his brake, jolting us all awake to witness the terrifying sight of tall blond men jumping off a cliff overlooking the lake, a hundred yards from the waterfall.

The entire hierarchy in the van screamed and gasped as twenty men voluntarily leapt over the five-hundred-foot drop straight into the steaming forest canyon below.

Our complete group of sacred house chiefs, ladies and village headmen, blankets flapping, headcloths falling, sashes waving, rushed out of the vehicle to the edge of the cliff to see what they could do to help as even more tall young tourist-looking youths dove off the cliff to what for us would have been certain death at the bottom of the ravine.

Even stranger still was the crowd of tan non-Indians wearing machine-made shorts of every color peering unperturbed through their sunglasses at the ghastly sight, who chuckled at the concerned horror of the old people who along with myself had never heard tell or ever seen someone flying a hang-glider.

But upon our arrival at the edge of that cliff the men we'd seen disappear lifted and banked like twittering butterflies up and out of the *Siwan* under their garish, synthetic kites.

These men were members of an Australian club of what seemed to us gigantic white men, who were engaged in testing the suitability of the air currents off the northern cliffs overlooking our Mother Waters in their search for a place to convene an international hang-glider tournament.

Slipping off the steep promontory, their great Kool-aid colored wings held up over their helmeted heads and sunglassed eyes, they'd sink like fluorescent pennies dropped into a tub of honey, down into the misted crack where just before splitting their bellies on the trees they'd slide forward, dropping toward the Mother Lake like shaky vultures who are always at the mercy of the water, air and heat.

But then the rising thermals of the lake surged them up and away from that holy water before they could touch her sparkling face, thrown and pushed aloft by her fists of rising air until circling and wheeling like synthetic ospreys with humans in their clutches they hung above the forests and volcanic slopes unmelted by the sun.

As yet unable to serve anything other than his craving to feel important to others like himself, our driver mined his well-funded travels for little nuggets of meaningful "experiences," that he would later parade back in the States and in his suburb; experiences, interesting people and celebrities about which he could boast a closeness without the burden of any slowly earned knowledge or ability toward any single pursuit or object of his love.

Though the old men and old women leaders had all along been planning to make gradual friends with him at a feast when we arrived back in the village, our driver was now finished with us having extracted all the "feeling" he wanted from his nearness with some Mayan chiefs, dumping us ungraciously like mine tailings in Panajachel. We were forced to find our own way back across the lake to our homes in Santiago Atitlan on the southern shore some ten miles away, while our former driver attached himself, uninvited, to the flyers, to drink and be part of something he could tell someone else about later.

Just barely arriving at the dock on time to be squeezed into the crowd on the afternoon mail boat, we watched the hang-gliders flying, this time from below the cliffs as they hung over us above the water. Our gradual distancing made them eventually look so small that they could have been mistaken for shrikes dragging off big, bright yellow grasshoppers beneath them in their talons if we hadn't seen them closely, knowing them for what they were.

When our mail boat chugged into Chinimya crowds of villagers were lined up on the basaltic cliffs, straining their eyes looking north. Nobody in our town would believe us. It seemed absurd to them that people should fly. These were huge, man-eating birds whose coming had been promised in all the stories.

Not having spent their entire youthful days indoors, in artificial light, focusing on texts or television screens, some of the people had the eyes of birds themselves and could actually see that far.

The teenage girls had the best eyes of all. They perched on the highest rocks above their washing stones at Tzanjuyu and Chinimya, yelling out like flocks of agitated water birds, reporting the disturbing sight of what they were seeing down to the thousands of people filling the space between the young women and the lake along the black-bouldered talus slope.

Gazing lakeward toward the cliffs opposite, barely visible beneath the hilly crown above Solola, nine miles away where the hang-gliding was taking place, the young women who were now the eyes for the remainder of the village who couldn't see that far, concurred in quite explicit and terrifying terms that since mid-morning they'd seen endless flights of enormous, peculiar birds of different, scary colors spiraling out of the canyons over the north side of the Mother Waters, after diving down, carrying people away in their shiny talons.

We were questioned by the crowd who, oblivious to our successful foray to retrieve the land, knew we had come right through that area and though they were all thankful we hadn't been carried away, the village wanted to know if we thought those dangerous human-eating birds might find their way to our side of the Great Mother Waters.

When the chief Ma Tacaxoy and his wife Ya Zunit replied laughing that what the girls were seeing were actually big kites under which tourists were voluntarily hanging, jumping off five-hundred-foot cliffs to sail around in the Holy blue sky above our Mother Waters, the whole tribe groaned and roared in disbelief.

"Imagine," said Ya Tzar Tzac, the most outspoken of the young girls who were seeing for everyone at the great distance with their own sharp brown eyes and undisputed vision, "big people flying around on their own like birds! You old trees and vines, you old people, have been drinking foreign liquor again. The old knots of the net that binds you together are coming unwound. Fathers and Mothers, I hope you can reassure us that those killing birds falling out of the sky that carry folks away to feed their young don't make it to our village. What would we do? We'd all have to disband and run away."

Although stories ran from hut to hut, compound to compound, field to cooking fires and back again for days, all differing as to what the appearance of these birds really meant, the chiefs and all the people stopped laughing at each other, knowing in their bones that no matter what the story really was, somehow what the girl had said was right.

The Tzutujil never assumed that the sun would shine again the following day or that they wouldn't disappear and another life form take their place. They did, however, know that if they were to continue on the Earth, the losses that they as humans caused to Nature and their own natures were voids that dangerously undermined the very matrix of the universe of which they were part and which gave them life.

The villagers knew that what defined a person as a complete human was our ability to fill those hollow places with sacrifices equivalent to the chunks we pried from the surrounding nature to feed our children.

These sacrifices that shored up the timbers of the universe were not the sacrifices of blood, of cutting heads, killing turkeys, splitting chests and removing hearts, for all of those offerings nature had created as well, and while these kind of sacrifices filled some gaps, they only created the need for more offerings to make up for having made more voids.

The sacrifice that made humans useful to the world were the sacrifices of offerings made with what only humans had, namely the product of their magnificent opposable thumbs and the songlike eloquence of their human speech, upon which the Gods who also magically made tangible life with their speech were fed and made drunk and ecstatic. The ecstasy of Nature and the Gods was the fertile tree-filled exuberance of the land.

The land was made to live when fed on the inebriating quality of human eloquence and the beauty of their creations when they were spent only on the Gods as deified nature of the life-giving universe.

This meant giving the best that humans could create to the Unseen powers behind the natural world that sustained us, which also meant leaving certain canyons unexplored, some mountains left unclimbed, certain buildings to decay, fat to burn away, handmade weavings to unravel, carvings to melt, flower arrangements to wilt, songs, dances and esoteric understandings expressed in elevated language that floated off, none of which was to be given later to humans, but only to the universe, to be consumed as we consumed it. Otherwise, humans would end up as the sacrifices.

To the Tzutujil this was not a philosophical notion or an esoteric day-dream, but a pragmatic and scientific fact: that if humans did not consciously create and sacrifice a percentage of the very best their human artifice could make in sincere, elegant, ritual fashion, then generous Nature already plundered, wounded and in grief from our agricultural sucking, recreational raking and mining of her bones would be forced, in order to survive, to magically inspire such forgetful humans into inventing what might seem to them as some rational project, but which in the end would cause a quota of human suffering and death equivalent to what Nature routinely experiences at our hands.

The old Tzutujil knew that Nature would always come to collect for what humans refused to deliberately give and that was some kind of blessing, for if the Earth were to continue to suckle us it had to stay alive.

Humans cause wars and revolutions, ethnic cleansings and epidemics by forgetting what gave them life. That forgetfulness caused the voids that forced Nature to invent weapons of mass destruction, pesticides, nuclear waste and a myriad other things of which humans in their conceit thought they were in control.

The only things that humans had in their control were their abilities to bless and give gifts. All else was rape and war.

So when a war, an epidemic or mass depression rolled in on the village, the villagers knew that the Gods of deified Nature, Time, Sound and Earth had been forced to engineer the conditions for another lottery of human sacrifice to close the gap caused by human conceit and amnesia somewhere in the world.

That's why stories of remembrance like The Toe Bone and the Tooth were kept so special, because the stories were the memory of the people and it was the remembrance in the stories that kept the people awake enough to remember to fill the voids long enough to keep the world alive and to remind them that they shouldn't take more than they could pay for.

Every child, old lady, ancient man, working middle-aged man and woman knew that our human bodies were the Earth and that whatever happened on or in the surrounding Earth, good or bad, ended up being played out in our bones, blood, flesh and feelings. When the Earth was blessed, we lived, flourished and died and fed the next generation with our passing. When the Earth was riddled, mined or warred upon, our bodies were made sick, our subtle understandings stunned, depression became a norm and spiritual amnesia a way of life.

Because the Gods lived in the Earth as functions of Time and Nature on the Earth, before and through the Earth, Gods were also always jumping in and out of people whenever they felt the need or inclination. The people that this happened to would have moments of strange understanding and behavior, conforming to the nature of the deity that was visiting. The Deity of Crabs could make a person head towards the water rolling along the ground, hiding behind rocks until the Deity had fled into another thing.

There were other deities, powerful life-giving spirits who lived naturally as rocks or wind, rain, flowers, birds, fish or trees, whose singing voices were the tumbling erosion of the wind and the sparkle in the stone, the ant-covered opening of a sticky blossom, the frantic flight of alarmed birds, or lively shoals of cold, scaly fish, and the long, silent groan of cracking bark on slow-growing trees, one of whom one day might secretly become enamored of a human, make love to him or her inside a dream and come alive nine months later born from a human womb, looking like a human child, born speaking and thinking strange holy thoughts out of a little human mouth.

We called these people "those who can never forget" or the "Holy Rememberers," because like the deity that filled their human body, they were constantly trying to speak the world into life and half of the words they spoke and mysterious things they did were the direct messages and activities of the Holy while the other half were the sacred stories the rest of us were forced to slowly learn, but which they had innately waiting in their bones.

Though the outside world might have seen these holy people as handicapped, having Down's syndrome, or crazy and impaired, for they usually were missing either a limb or the over-confident arrogance of regular people, the village knew that their ability to remember kept the village alive. They were unanimously recognized by thinking folk as singular, disturbed, ecstatic and grief-stricken members of the town who were pieces of the Earth walking around as humans, who were forced to live painfully awake and conscious among the banal sleepy tread and natural spiritual amnesia of the everyday village. No one knew more about that than Yalen Shuruy, the mother of Malip Qoquix.

But Yalen Shuruy, as everyone knew, had a big problem with toads, which I'd assumed was why, as always, she was sitting in my hut waiting for me after my return from Gustavo Rodas and the man-eating birds.

Yalen was an upright-walking, big-boned, beautiful old woman, a kind of female Chiviliu, whose deep melodious voice was so well-spoken and her experience in rituals so thorough and vast that although officially retired from decades of ceremonial service to the village, the sacred house leaders always made every effort to include her in some part of the sacrifices of delicious speech, if only by laying out elevated phrases of real gratitude to her for some favor she had rendered in hopes she would in kind reply, knowing that the Earth was so entirely revived by her delicious and powerful responses that the corn would probably grow again and their children wouldn't starve.

Coming from a family of strange and miraculous people, Yalen Shuruy was also the cousin of Swordfighter and considered by the village reckoning to be Padre's great aunt. Her only brother had been the old man named Ears who'd died and come back alive at the bottom of his grave just before they'd buried him, who'd punched his way out of the box; then, after living in the coffin up in the smoky rafters of the hut of his son-in-law, who'd been my whispering instructor on how to be a chief, finally danced off and disappeared from the Earth only to return and die again two weeks later, married to a pretty sixteen-year-old Cakchiquel girl. And of course the God of Fire had fallen in love with Yalen, for whom she had given birth to an enormous baby boy who'd grown to become the tallest and one of the most scary men in the village. Because his father was the Lord of Fire, the North Star, the Lord of all stories that spoke and remembered this world back into life, Yalen's son, Malip Qoquix, wandered the village and the mountains seemingly talking to himself, but he was actually in the constant activity himself of remembering everything he passed over, back into life. He was our village's tallest and most forceful child, the human embodiment of the memory of the Earth; he was the "Great Rememberer."

No one knew why, but everyone surmised that the fondness the God of Fire had for Yalen Shuruy was somehow at the root of why all the toads in Atitlan had conspired for forty years to pee on her old dusty toes every time they saw them poking out from Yalen's old-fashioned, untinseled, red wraparound *uuq* skirt that snapped and rustled as she bustled about the village on her errands, trying to avoid the toads.

It was considered very unfortunate to be peed on by a toad, especially if you were a woman. And it was not the welted, painful rash that the milk oozing off the back of certain brands of toads could raise upon your skin if touched that bothered all the women; after all, half the plants, most of the caterpillars, a third of the snakes and who knows how many insects either stung or bit, burned or burrowed, sucked or itched or could kill you or make you wish they had. What made the women fear the toads was the coldness of their bellies and the coldness of their urine, the coldness that once it got inside your bones through their pee would never leave and cause your warm womb and milky breasts and happy fertile heart to harden and cool.

All the village women feared the toads and avoided them, which for most was not so much trouble, for although in certain seasons toads were fairly common, they were almost non-existent the remainder of the year and could never be classified as something of a plague. All excepting, of course, eloquent Yalen Shuruy, the mother of the giant babbling "Great Rememberer" and the lover of the God of Fire and stories, for whom everybody knew the toads had some kind of vendetta, actually pursuing and ambushing her at every unlikely place, leaping unseen from where they hid, flopping clumsy but well-aimed to rest their cold bellies dead center on the poor old woman's foot with a big-chinned, self-satisfied, ecstatic look upon their faces for the long particle of a second it took for Yalen's thighs and calves, made strong from so much practice, to punt the toad like a deflated soccer ball into the bush to either die from the effects of the mighty kick or patiently wait to hunt her later when she returned.

The effects of toad-piss poisoning among menopausal women and unmarried girls were a reliable source of income for many male shamans, for it was considered a problem that only men could help. But lately, for almost a year even the pharmacists had been baffled when overrun by women of every age complaining of symptoms of toad-piss coldness coming into their bones, women who hadn't even seen a toad, for which they were sold everything from vitamins to sedatives to cure what the pill peddlers couldn't comprehend.

Because of Yalen's eloquent and relentless promotions of the effects of my cures, my family's compound was particularly popular for women who'd run into a toad or who were experiencing the effects of the recent plague of cold, electric numbness in their wombs, bones and feet, whose symptoms they associated with the toads. And, since those diabolical amphibians were always on her trail, the eloquent old woman herself practically lived in my hut for at least three months of the year.

But for all that, this evening of my return would be the first time Yalen Shuruy would come to see me for something other than the toads. She had heard that hard times were near and almost on us here inside the Canyon Village. The person who knew the most about some of what was supposed to happen was her son Malip Qoquix, who had told his mother that he wanted to speak to me.

Yalen Shuruy had not come to help herself, she said, for knowing a lot was going to change she thought not only about the possible safety of my little child Jorge and Yalur, who was expecting our third child after the last one had passed away, but also, as Chiviliu had said before his death the year before, she wanted me to keep alive what I now embodied, so that someday in seed form it could perhaps be replanted here again, inside the cultural ashes, after what was to take place had transpired, and somehow regrow a culture that could once again know how to feed the Flowering Earth.

Unlike other villagers, Malip Qoquix was not a man you could find by simply looking for him, for he wandered constantly talking out loud to the ground, besides which only a very few ever deliberately sought out his company.

Being half Fire God and half Yalen Shuruy he'd inherited the fine speech of both, but had the unnerving quality of jumping from his incessant eloquent banter addressed to the wind and stones to all of a sudden looking at you a millimeter off, straight into your eyes, and blurting out very loudly and in public exactly whatever you were thinking at that very moment in an accuracy that was beyond disarming.

Though he was not a bad man, if he was a man at all, none of the villagers ever felt easy in his presence, fearing his unexpected visits as they would an earthquake or a straight-line wind, neither daring to shoo him off nor humor him too much for fear of what strange thing he might say or do, not wanting to disturb him knowing that any insult to him was an insult to the God that rode his body as its horse. So, they emptied their minds and bit their tongues when he showed until, like a storm, he left bantering to the ground. On the other hand most shamans, like Chiviliu and the entire hierarchy, along with several deep-thinking Mayans from other villages, had always held the wild man in very high regard, for above all else, Malip Qoquix was the best storyteller the village had ever known. He had the knowledge and the unanimously-endorsed right to tell more sacred stories than any living Tzutujil, for he had the terrifying ability of actually becoming anything in the story he was telling, especially the God or Goddess that was speaking. This made many people shiver when he told a story, but he was the very best not because he was acting, because that he couldn't do, but because like the Fire God, all things of the world could sit inside him when they chose.

He had whiteless muddy eyes in whose centers tiny red fires smoldered like those of an armadillo, that very fiercely peered out in every direction from a big healthy wide bronze face that refused to age beyond the age of thirty though he was over fifty. Everybody, especially the middle-aged men, envied his clothing, for unlike most babbling street derelicts, Malip Qoquix wore only the most intricate and beautifully woven five-colored *jaspeado* shirts, thickly embroidered rich man's *scav* pants, cerulean blue and canary yellow handwoven sashes filled with multicolored tinseled threads, and on his feet buckled sandals made of densely riveted harness leather, soled with Michelin tread.

Though he never seemed to sleep, when he did, he would curl up next to Yalen's cooking fire embers without a blanket or a mat, directly on the ground, sleeping without breathing as if he were dead, for sometimes three days laying motionless without so much as a twitch.

I never once saw him wearing the same hat, but they were always felt fedoras and of the most expensive Italian brands that even rich cattle men saved up to buy and the greater population could only long for. He wore them on his head in total disregard, soaking them in water if he bathed, putting baby chickens in them or puppies or stones or whatever the divine thing within him directed him to do until his hat was rumpled, ruined and fell off and another new one took its place.

Yalen did not supply him with any of his clothing and no one I knew could guess where he got all his wealthy look, for he was never armed with the requisite machete or any of the hoes, axes, ropes, burden bags, canoe paddles or jugs like other village men and he rarely visited the fields and if he did it was not to cut the trees, dig the soil, raise crops or to make a living, but to have a deep conversation with the ground.

Everybody knew he wasn't human, for one of the salient characteristics of being human was the ability to forget and Malip Qoquix never could. Of all the things he did, the one that made the people most nervous was the fact that he never forgot any story, person, name, detail, event or nuance of any side of any situation that he had ever witnessed and he could bring it into his present conversation at will.

It was all a mystery to most and the village left it that way, but I could never determine for certain if he was really all that much more massive, open-faced, powerfully built, and taller than all the people in the town or if it was just the enormity of the mark and burden of all he had to remember that caused him to invisibly cut a wide swath in the spiritual waters underlying the village's everyday life, which left us all in the swelling wake of his constant grief as if a big canoe of memories had just paddled by.

His mother said he wanted to speak to me, but where would I find such a man? I would have to be found by him in a place and time that something bigger than my will would choose.

Very late one night while returning alone from my duties with the hierarchy during the feast of Santiago in July, I ambled stiffly down the cobbled incline of the Nimbey towards my home in the breezy dark when Malip Qoquix, like one of his mother's toads, ambushed me unseen from the shadows beneath the tin-roofed whitewashed stone house of the local baker. After jumping up while madly spewing out at me in Spanish, which none of us had even known he could speak, he grabbed the back of my neck with the inescapable grip of a gigantic monkey, by which means he forcefully steered me toward the lake a half a mile down by Tiosh Abaj away from any late-night village ears.

While we walked he kept up a crazed chatter in Spanish with an accent and mannerism identical to Guatemalan City street hustlers who hawked homemade vitamin elixirs and tin-can kazoos until we were out of earshot of anyone but the earth.

When we arrived at the horizontal washing rock of Ya Sar Co, against which the dark water of our Mother Lake rippling out under the moon rose and lapped up from the reeds, he commenced to speak in a straightforward, sane Tzutujil male voice which I surmised may have been the first time I'd actually heard him speak, in a sound that was his own.

"*Kinwutkij anen nawetkij conjilaaltet ruman aqaxan conjilaal nimlaj taq tzij. At cotzratet najbey, nix nataj jilaal tet?*"

"I know you know because you heard all the Big Words, the grand stories, you know the Story. You were there when it all happened. Do you remember?"

He'd always said that to me every time we'd met and expected a reply as well, especially in the past after visiting us in the ceremonies. Like some strange, unscheduled, wild holy visitor, a messenger directly from the very same Gods we would be feeding at the time with our rituals, Malip would sit on the bench with all the *Ajaua*, chiefs and woman priests, where he'd tell the story in such moving beauty as to bring us all to tears, but he'd always punctuate his vivid narrative every couple of minutes, usually turning to me while blurting out, "Isn't that so, father? You were there, don't you remember?" The strange part, of course, was that there were dreams and times when I did remember the things he meant, but never the way he could.

But tonight he interrupted himself, flying into yet another voice. While scanning the diffused moonlit sky, the stormy cadence of multiple, angry voices talking back and forth, some claiming to be members of different secret committees, a confidant of *guerrilleros* or distant non-Indian intellectuals in charge of planning the coming revolution, while other voices for which Malip Qoquix now spoke from one corner of his otherwise closed mouth whispered about their horrid intentions as members of certain squadrons of clandestine right-wing killers in such detail as if he'd been part of their private meetings; all came gushing out of the man, trampling over his tear-filled heart.

"They are idiots," speaking once again back in the voice I thought must be his own, "they don't know the story, none of them. They cannot remember, they are lost unto the ground, these jaguar-skinned fools who will soon arrive at your door to take you away." The Tzutujil called soldiers jaguar skins, *bajlam kij,* in reference to their camouflage.

Then he turned and grinned, snapped his fingers toward the moon, bellowed, then bent over double in pain, after which he slowly straightened out. "They want to drag you all to death, to take you and your wife and little children and pull you all into pieces, but they cannot and you cannot remain here to let them, because you remember. You were there, don't you remember?

"None of them can remember, none of them can put things back together, they can only dismember, tearing them all apart. None of them can understand anything about the story, none of them will take the time it takes to try to put her back together and failing, live as regular people, none of them can remember, but you remember, you were there, don't you remember?

"None of those who are coming to kill you, and there are those here tonight planning your demise, some from faraway, talking to the baker, to kill us all, none of them even have the courage or could take the chance to even try to remember, so like Chiviliu now says from his throne underneath the Sun, 'You, Martín, must keep it all alive, carry the babies and the seed heart and especially take the story, take it through the storm, the hoop of fire.' You remember, you were there, don't you remember?

"Keep it all alive, take it far, far away from here into the land out of which you came, right underneath those who can't remember, plant it directly in the body of their forgetting, plant it, go, get going. It's true what I tell you: the baker plans your death and the rest as well. Go. You remember, remember the story, you were there, don't you remember? You remember? Remember her back to life."

Pulling up my chin with one hand and glaring with his whiteless armadillo eyes into mine, his teeth clenched only in the front, as earnest as a deersnake dragging out a rodent he hissed: "Never, never, never, never disregard your divination bundle, always listen, count the beans, roll the finger bones, read the news, listen to its story and the story it tells; like the story you must live, it will help your family to escape what the amnesiac jaguar-skins have planned. Your leaving with the seeds of remembrance is the only remembering some of us will ever have again if their seeds can be kept alive. Promise, then, to grow the fruit of remembering of what we will soon enough lose. Promise; always use your divination bones. Promise. Remember. You were there. Promise. You remember?"

And he was gone, my jaw released, his big scary head bobbing back and forth carried rapidly away from me in the pale moonlight by the forceful, long ground-covering stride of his heavy bones. Hitting boulders with a stick I hadn't even noticed until now, he was almost out of sight by the time I whispered, "I promise you, Malip Qoquix," tearfully wishing I could somehow take some of the constant pain from his hurting heart. But in the instant that I spoke he leapt back, flying up into my face again like a slingshot, blurting out, "*Majun kin na tzuj ninanic saquul!*"

"Don't pity me, you dumb banana!"

And this time he was really gone, back toward his relentless wandering and constant spoken remembering of everything he walked over, disappearing into the dark.

thirteen

TIPTOEING
INTO EXILE

Though the great dark tongues of turquoise waves from the mouth of our Mother Lake still tried to lick and grind the bronzy black patina off the basaltic boulders of the shore and all the dogs still barked and teething baby's bottoms still got too chapped and made them cry for two reasons instead of one and though errant turkeys still played dumb yet carried out their long-planned raids in which, behind our backs, they snatched food right from our cooking pots and a million birds yet twittered, flapped and screamed throughout the flowering trees and in the reeds, the world we knew and loved hung suspended between a big hill of hope and a small valley of possibility, while what was going to happen hovered above us like an angry metal eagle in a dream who could wait up in the air for almost a year before he dropped to destroy the village as it would a shaking rabbit in the grass.

Like families at the deathbed of a tenacious grandparent, waiting patiently but honorably for the old tree to die and fall, who in their efforts not to make things any worse carried on their lives as if the old-timer would recover, but always knowing a hard loss and change was soon upon them, cherished the constant moment of what was still their everyday existence, in like manner, the village now continued thumping, laughing, arguing and squeaking along in the old familiar ruts of their living out their story, while taking more shallow breaths than usual to make room beneath their heart and lungs for the swelling anxiety in their bellies, for what everyone knew was nearly on them.

There were two bakers in the town, both of them Ladinos, one of them was a woman, but the other was a man who had the same first name as me.

Martín Sosa had lived and baked not far from us for twenty years before I'd even come here on the heels of my desire. He was well-known and friendly to my family and became friendly to my wife and to my little son. He was even helpful and friendly to myself until the political winds he represented obliged him to matter-of-factly arrange the capture and execution of several prominent Mayans and their families. Though we'd all known him for years as a baker of good *casueleja, xecas* and *quesadillas de arroz,* a man who was fat, compact, almost friendly, always sweating and the only man in the village to wear a tank top, he'd actually been stationed in Atitlan years back in a more indolent time to serve the Central Army in the capacity of the local conscription officer and military commissioner.

This should not have been such a surprise to me, for Sergeant Martín Soza was the exact double of the sergeant in my dreams, who with a crowd of well-armed people had been shooting at Chiviliu, me and the beautiful lady who I now knew was the village and the Earth herself. At home in the village with so many of the extraordinary people about whom I had dreamt about years before I'd even met them, like Raggedy Boy, I would become so entirely overwhelmed by the inebriating spell of finally being at home, living out my dreams in the balmy reality of the village, that sometimes I would forget the overall content and warnings of the original dream.

Even the baker himself, who had become such an integral part of my Panabaj neighborhood of compound walls, huts, dogs, chickens, turkeys, children, orchids and loyal Tzutujil lady clients who, with their tiny bits of money, bought his *xecas*, forgot himself why he'd been sent and by the time the heartless order came from faraway, commanding him to direct the military secret police now assigned to him as an undercover squad, showing them which of us to kidnap and kill, which of us to be thrown into streams in pieces, which people in town should be simply made to vanish by throwing them from helicopters into active volcanoes, this poor baker Sergeant Martín Soza succumbed to the contradiction forced upon his now too-opened heart, dying a bad, shaking death much before his time, but only after arranging three horrible murders, one of which was Padre, the other Padre's wife, the third their little child.

After his ordination as a Catholic priest the entire Tzutujil nation, including villages beside our own, came to hear Padre say his first mass as the first native Mayan priest of the country. In the entire history of the enormous colonial church and to the great delight of the Bishop, there had never been that many people to attend a mass.

But in the months that followed, the attendance once again dwindled, for even though Padre said a lot of masses, most of which were not as boring as Stanley's, and though his sermons were more stylish and in an impeccable Tzutujil, they also contained a lot of political rhetoric and allusions to a Christian endorsement of revolution which until Padre was killed kept most people far away from the church, out of fear of being marked as supporters of what the right-wing government classified as the "Catholic Left", or the adherents of liberation theology about which most villagers knew nothing, but knew enough that it could get you killed, which is exactly what happened to Padre who was carried off, killed, dismembered, brought back and dumped in pieces next to his beautiful murdered wife and baby.

It was all more than the village could bear and we who wept for three months would have continued weeping for another thousand years, weeping for Gaspar Culan, weeping for the grandson of Swordfighter, for Padre, for our friend who wouldn't listen to the Story, weeping for Yachat and her baby, but our weeping was cut short, our grief postponed when *guerrilleros* from the left appeared as predicted, stupidly killing other unarmed villagers to avenge Padre's death, which only brought more clandestine right-wing killers to retaliate in turn and escalate the horror. Neither side was actually able to find the other, both killing civilians out of rage, civilians who were fingered by the grief-soaked relatives of the dead, until the government army itself was sent, bivouacking permanently just outside the town, past Xecasiis on the trail to Chicacao. Comprised of flogged underage Indian youths of mixed tribes and villages whose relatives could not pay the ransom demanded when they'd been brutally shanghaied in an illegal conscription by the likes of our deceased town baker, this "army" was armed with Belgian, Israeli and Italian guns, ammunition, uniforms and transport, paid for with U.S. dollars and commanded by non-Indian officers who ordered these humiliated Mayan soldiers to kill even more of us, burn the fields and eat up all our food.

It was during the space between the killing of Padre and the entrance of the army that every family's handmade cedar or wild avocado canoe, two thousand of them at least, was mysteriously dragged unseen into the middle of the bay and set ablaze at night, burning down to a flotilla of carbon film and smoking pitchy logs by dawn. During this hard, smoky time foreign aid officers from the U.S. came to enlist my help as a ruse to gather information for the CIA but got nothing, while emissaries from various right-wing hit squads pressured me to point out likely "communist" members of the village who they said needed assassinating, but went away angry and empty-handed, after which, seeing how I'd sent away the right-wingers, leftist *guerilleros*, now assuming I supported them, made a scary visit to my hut as well, but in broad daylight, to get my assistance to bomb a Guatemalan army colonel, but were themselves enraged when I refused. No one, especially the traditionalists, had any notion of why any of this was happening beyond the needs the Gods had to make humans sacrifice for what certain humans would not give of their own free will for the terrible things done to Nature in the name of human will.

None of the political entities, left, right or otherwise, had any comprehension that my leadership in the village was a leadership of flowers in service to the Story, to the non-human world that feeds us, and that the reason it appeared that I could raise army-like crowds of twenty-thousand strong to follow me had nothing to do with me or any politics I espoused, but to the annual cycles of initiation and ritual gift-giving that I led as part of my responsibility as a young chief. Rituals in which the entire population of the village enjoined to help remember and reanimate the deified world of Nature. Huge crowds of people always came to participate, no matter who was at the head.

But, when all was said and done I was branded by every faction, left, right and otherwise, as an uncooperative traditionalist who didn't support their side and who therefore was an enemy and needed killing. Though unarmed and no physical threat to anyone, my name was placed on every team's wanted list, the most serious of which was one which was publicized weekly in a right-wing newspaper. This paper printed upgrades on who should be eradicated on a scale from one hundred to one in which they removed those who were killed during that week, moving all the names on the list up a notch, and bestowing some very substantial bounties for the heads of certain of us who ended up being harder to catch than others.

In Santiago, every day, between one and ten more people disappeared or were killed out in the open. Houses were burnt; people were hauled away at night, poisoned to death, raped, sliced to death or burned alive. The village world was on fire. A place that hadn't even seen a machine gun or a bomb before, whose language didn't even have words for such instruments, now lost so many people that the toll in our village alone reached close to two thousand.

The men whose bodyguards had nearly shot me for my cigarettes at the party in the Israeli ambassador's home would be responsible for over 100,000 Indian deaths in the country until another man was made president, put in charge by the United States, who would then bring the total of unarmed civilians illegally murdered up another 80,000 by their own tally.

The country would never spiritually recover and the village I'd known and in which I'd found a use, a home and actually sat with people whose parents were deities, began to fade away to eventually live only as another part of the story.

But there was then no time for elegant armchair moralizing or time to grieve for all our losses, for during this era, one dawn as I stood gazing at the shimmering lake, recovering from the daze of an early morning ceremony, three armed men tried to shoot me practically at point blank and thinking, as I did at the time, that they'd accomplished their mission, for the blood that leaked from my sternum, ran fleeing to the bottom of the bay.

Their bullets had missed me altogether, save a little curl of lead that had ricocheted off one of the mossy orchid-covered basaltic pillars that towered over my lakeside hut at Xexhivoy, and that only pierced my skin and knocked my sternum out of line.

Nineteen young men of my generation, several of my friends, some initiates and married-in relatives were lined up and shot in the center of the village at the same moment, only all of them were killed.

Malip Qoquix and Chiviliu had warned me in plenty of time, but I hadn't departed and was almost killed for my belligerence.

But even then, I dawdled on.

I couldn't seem to figure out how to leave the village which had become for me, by then, the only real world worth dying in, where I'd finally become a part, where I was remembered every day not only by the people but by the land itself as I remembered it. Like a lot of villagers, something in me wanted to think all the horror would eventually run its course and leave and life would resume as always.

At a time when I should have wrapped up my bundles and run, instead I stood, stunned, willing to perish in the only land I felt I'd actually truly been able to live. I was immobilized by my unsureness of how I would ever live away from people who personally knew the Gods, where everyone was a king, a queen and I a prince in a land of eloquent speakers; away from the land's living story, wondering if by leaving we weren't heading for an even worse living death. Could I live again among people who'd forgotten their stories, who laughed at things that weren't funny, who didn't smile as a matter of course, whose forgetful and unconscious way of life was filled with mounds of unloved, unstoried dead matter, a way of life away from which I'd already fled to finally live and die here where nothing was dead?

For Yalur with our soon-to-be born third child still in her belly it was even more incomprehensible that we should leave, for losing what you've come to love is horrible but losing one's ancestral homeland is akin to losing a child. Though we never thought to flee, never to return, every villager knew without speaking that should we even survive long enough to escape the village, we would still have to leave the country, for in our case they would hunt us down, and if we left the country there was always the looming possibility we might never return, having been consumed by the place we fled to, especially if the war didn't subside.

Even so, the village to which we might some day be able to return would no longer truly be ours any more, our having left it and its people to fend for itself to save ourselves. For these reasons and a thousand others we dawdled on.

Fleeing with her children and me, away from the certain torture and death assured us by the mocking and chilling contents of the profusion of leaflets dropped at night on the village from the sky, or from propaganda cannons, or in the numerous newspaper articles and radio programs that named me by name, or by the sight of refugees filing in from villages in even worse condition who told us so, meant for Yalur what it has always meant for every indigenous people or people who have ever been truly at home, then suddenly displaced into a diaspora away from everything they know; it meant learning how to change shapes to survive, it meant learning how to remember while appearing to forget, it meant losing your throne, it meant being willing to risk being forgotten. For some, death at home seemed better than the endless generations of tears wept and unwept one would risk by leaving the center of the universe.

But the Umbilicus of the Earth had already been invaded by political and religious idealists from societies of spiritual amnesia whose own indigenous ancestors had been terrorized and melted in the rationalist furnace of the last thousand years and pounded out of their natural forms into hard unforgiving square bars of being right. Our home was already becoming a refugee in its own landscape. But still we dawdled while the horror raged around us everyday, until Yalur's father shook us from our trance.

Yalur and her father were autocrats and so evenly matched in stubbornness that both of them would rather die pulling away from one telling the other what to do, even if the idea was their own to begin with. To make things worse, the two of them hated each other. He was a heatedly opinionated, unpredictable, potentially violent man who some people feared and others knew as a good companion.

He'd been taken in with his only brother at an early age by Catholic nuns when their widower father had been hauled away to the unpaid labor camps of the 1930s to where all highland Mayan men were conscripted to serve Ladino overlords to "develop" the country, building railroads for American agricultural corporations and wealthy Guatemalan oligarchies.

The nuns poisoned the boys against all indigenous traditions and instilled a repressive self-hatred into their hearts, which forty years later blossomed into their allying with the liberation theologists, some of whom were the authors of various guerrilla groups taking turns shooting us with their supposed right-wing antagonists.

In the horrid bubbling foment of grief, hysteria, hatred and fear of the time and during one of their never-ending bitter clashes, Yalur's father blurted out to her with some glaze-eyed sense of triumph how he would not have to bear the smell and sight of us very much longer as he'd voted in his secret Marxist committee meeting that his daughter, son-in-law and grand-children should be executed by his left-wing Catholic cronies, who, know-ing full well how mercilessly I was hunted by the right wing, wanted to be the first to take my head. His strange maniacal elation at the thought finally propelled both Yalur and I to make secret plans. Leaving our blankets stuffed so they looked like we were sleeping and the cooking fire on, we tip-toed into exile on a 2 A.M. bus without telling a soul where we were headed, in hope we made it at least that far without getting shot.

Her father in his rage had inadvertently saved our lives of course, but in that instant we didn't know it, for now to us the village was dead because we could no longer even trust our blood relatives. With my bundles on my back, my toddler in my arms, Yalur and the child inside, we bumped and lurched away from all we'd ever loved, away from our friends, our hut, our ceremonies, our families and our dead, the little bus grinding down from the cool highlands, down to the hot coast picking up passengers every cou-ple of miles.

Though we would end up, as always, three to a seat with someone strad-dling his acrobatic bottom over the aisle making seven to a row, no one but my little family had boarded in our village, which I felt was lucky for there would then be no one to report our direction or whereabouts to those that would do us in. But by the time we had turned south, lurching past the little hill of Pakaman, Xescut and Ch´ejuyu, and left their ancient stories and kid-ney-cracking unpaved ruts that ran between them and the lake, the bus was packed to bursting for all the passengers that had been picked up in between.

Once we hit the smoother asphalt of the highway descending through Xejuyu or the piedmont on to the Pacific coast, the Sun Father shot his grassy arrow, as the people always called his first emergence from the gradual clarity of dawn, for to them each day was something grown like a plant where every dawn was a sprouting from the Sun's seed, nightly hidden in the dark, whose first shoots at sun-up were his arrows with which he forced his birth out of the tenacious womb of ground.

By then we were pointed east straight into him on the coastal run rushing toward Escuintla. Along the road the gigantic lowland trees were all a-blossom, some against their green or shaggy brown bark blooming as red as *cotinga* breasts while others looked at first to be yellow and literally on fire for the peculiar quaking orange that was interspersed, but which turned out to be a million nomadic butterflies resting among the flowers and covering the trunks, while others rose up in lazy clouds to settle again in a different tree, resuming in this casual way their migration further south.

We, on the other hand, were not headed toward a place, a people or any friends, but only away from what would kill us.

I was far too scared, protective and on high alert to as yet be devastated by the profundity of sorrow and loss that was gathering in my chest; though I knew that just as many people were being shot and hauled off buses as were being killed in villages and towns, I still attempted to keep the dignity of calm that men like Chiviliu had inspired in me when under fire, in whose spell Yalur and Jorge drifted off to sleep, their tired heads bobbing in the dawn.

Because people felt that the damp night air contained the substance of "cold," a cold that could cause them to fall ill if breathed in through the lungs, throughout Guatemala all night-travelers waiting on the roadside where the transports ran were in the habit of covering their heads, throats and faces, often wrapping them right over their hats or headdresses, looking a lot like Tuaregs, until the day had warmed.

Yalur, Jorge and myself were wrapped up as well, ostensibly for the same reason, but more so as to avoid being recognized. The *guerilleros* and their opponents, the right-wing hit men, very often did their killing covered up to keep their faces hidden.

The rolling bus was filled one-hundred percent with wrapped up individuals, all of whom had boarded in the night. Now at mid-morning on the coast the air was actually very muggy and hot, yet no one in the sleepy bus had unwrapped their heads, not one nose was poking out.

I seemed to be the only person sitting up and wide awake until one man seated directly behind me quickly thrust his huge hand under my handwoven scarf, jerking it off of my head, while yelling out as he pulled off his own, simultaneously jumping to his feet, jostling his fellows and bumping his head with a loud thump.

"Surprise!" he yelled. Everybody jumped, headcloths coming aside and the entire bus turning to look in terror at what in a split-second could mean the end, but in that millisecond, starting before I could turn to look and ending when I had, a singsong voice chortled out clearly over the grinding of the bus, "*Amartin ala nix lutzawach ach, nwutqin conjilaal najbey, xin bijchewa, wavie at co chic tet nix ntaxa?*"

"Ah Martin, little boy, how's your face? We can see you know everything. Well, I told you and here you are. Do you remember?"

Like a big bear playing peek-a-boo, beaming and giggling like a laughing falcon, and oblivious that he was too large for the bus, it was Malip Qoquix.

With a new, luxurious, charcoal-blue felt fedora from Padua, Italy, sitting sideways on his massive head, he crammed forward with his face a hair off from hers and attempted to wake Yalur, who, probably having slept through her own birth, refused to even twitch, though her strange and thorough hatred of the man might have made her fake slumber in hopes he'd go away.

But in that moment all the headcloths came flying off amidst a collective roar of laughs and hysterical relief which for many ended in tearful weeping, for not a single person on the bus was unknown to us and all had boarded fleeing threats of death from one side or the next, all of us hated by some faction, fleeing all we knew, happy at least that Malip Qoquix turned out to be himself and not some thug sent to end our anxious lives.

Though none of us could know it yet, within the next five years, of all the people on the bus including the driver, only Malip Qoquix, I and my little family and one other tall Tzutujil man allied with the left would survive.

All along the coast and as we started back into the highlands the hill toward the capital, people had the driver let them off, sometimes in towns and others in the bush, where everyone including little kids and ladies would hope for life unrecognized beneath a cliff, behind a tree or in the outskirts of a plantation town. If they had the cash, they'd discard their clothing to dress in the standard poverty of such non-Indian towns, trying out any ruse to save their lives until they could return to their much longed-for village. The whole country was displaced within itself.

The "Great Rememberer" was fleeing nothing but the burden of his having to remember what was going to happen, which he could never do, to ease his crazy heart and to cause me to remember what I would need to keep in mind to keep alive what really mattered for the next two decades and especially the coming year. Malip Qoquix badgered me into telling Swordfighter's version of the story The Toe Bone and the Tooth. Although most of the adults there knew the tale well, none of them had heard this version and soon the entire bus was engrossed in the story that we all in some way were now forced to be living out, albeit that telling was the wildest ever done because Malip Qoquix kept expertly turning himself into frogs, coyotes, mice and snails, as only he could do, which kept all the exiles laughing out their heartbreak until the tears began again, most of us knowing like Raggedy Boy we would never be held in the arms of Her, our village and Flowering Earth again.

With my bundles strapped on my back, baby Jorge under my arms and sleepy Yalur in tow, I had the driver let us down in the middle of a poorer commercial barrio of Guatemala City, before he arrived at his destination at the enormous, bustling terminal market well-known now for its abundance of assassinations.

We walked through several neighborhoods and a couple of different open air markets to make sure no one was trailing us through the smells of onions, corn tortillas and the sounds of ladies washing with their babies lashed on with their shawls criss-cross on their backs. Coming to an old colonial park where after eating a ceviche, we took another bus to San Pedro Sacatepequez, dismounted and boarded another for Antigua where instead of getting down in front of the sixteenth-century powder-blue-painted old Spanish capitol building, we prematurely got off at the very edge of the old capital, pushed our way through the muddy forest over a creek and into some *cafetales* until we came out at the opposite side of town right at the corner of the house and hostel run by an older German woman that was set off a-ways from the mostly quiet colonial city.

From previous experience I had from some art shows in this town, I knew Helga Werner thought most Indians were backwards and their spiritual beliefs to be superfluous theatrics that they used just as an excuse to have a party, but her monorailed Lutheran thinking, as limited as it was, included a straightforward kind of courage and an inability to betray.

Without requiring any details she gave us a little house hidden in the coffee groves with a strong gate from where one could survey the grounds around without actually being seen. I was sure she recognized me from the newspaper and events from years gone by, but she pretended not to know me and called me by the assumed name under which I registered. We were already changing forms.

Our first three weeks of trying to get used to non-village life, holed up in our *cafetal* bungalow hideaway, were nerve-wracking, because in order to get situated and eat, I had to make speedy forays into the town market to obtain cooking implements, food, blankets and so forth without drawing attention to myself. Yalur couldn't help because the people would instantly recognize her tribal dressing style, which I didn't have the heart to ask her to abandon, as none of her people had ever done until now since the beginning of time. In Guatemala, when a Mayan woman gave up her native dress it meant her culture was dead or she had ceased to be an indigenous person. To go into the public, on the other hand, I cut my hair into a crew cut, grew a short yuppie beard, began wearing dull-colored sweatshirts and slacks and shed my fancy Atiteco sandals for white-man tennis shoes and socks, all purchased with the help of a young semi-acculturated Cakchiquel woman named Antonia Ziis. Antonia was Helga's *criada*, or maidservant, and grounds manager and though she dressed in the usual non-tribal, pan-Indian uniform of the Guatemalan Indian maid she came from a very strongly traditional Mayan family. She became a loyal sympathizer and our only confidant more quickly than prudence would have endorsed, when we recognized, rightly as it turned out, that we could trust her and shared with her the long details of our plight.

Antonia wept and played with Jorge and to keep us from being seen by the numerous squads of soldiers that regularly patrolled the streets or anyone hoping to cash in on the now rather substantial bounty that rested on my head, she generously bought what we needed to keep us off the streets.

From her we got news of any political changes, suspicious people who might be dangerous and the rumors of things to come.

Though crawling with my antagonists and people who might have killed my whole family if they'd known we were right there under their eyes,

Antigua was not populated by resident Mayans or indigenous Guatemalans, but with elitist Americans, Europeans and a few wealthy non-Indian Guatemalans, most of whom knew of me only by rumor, and though most of them detested what they thought I represented and what I did, none of them could have picked me out in a crowd of people like themselves.

Though the town was surrounded on all sides by agricultural villages of Mayans and Tlaxcalan Indian descendants from the initial Spanish shock troops in the 1500s, Antigua's core actually housed some of the people whose families were behind a great deal of the corruption and the present repression in the country, most of which was not carried out through direct government channels. Of course, there were also mobs of tourists, missionaries and academics stationed there as well.

Whereas in Atitlan I'd been too tall, too blond, too overly well-known for better or for worse and simply too publicly involved with the fancily-dressed hierarchy to hide, here in Antigua, after having my hair cut and donning machine-made clothing, I could blend right into the crowds of the same judgmental people I'd fled from in the States, only to flee them here again in a more serious way, by standing amongst them looking just like them.

Yalur was due to give birth by the end of August and this was June. So before she got too large to make it dangerous for her to go, she convinced me we should sneak back into the village of Atitlan to see her dying grandfather one last time before he swam into the next layer without having said goodbye.

Leaving Jorge with Antonia Ziis, we were driven by an American woman staying at the pension who didn't know we were hunted. We snuck past the government checkpoints very easily but it was the guerrillas I knew I wouldn't fool if they caught us because they relied on tradition-hating "new" Catholics who knew me very well and would inform them of any movements in the town. We arrived only just in time to speak one phrase to the beautiful old man, who unlike his hate-filled son, thankfully held off on reporting us and died cuddled in our arms repeating, "Tell the children not to fight."

We could never go to bury him, the army patrols would shoot us at the grave-site, a danger made more probable still because some of our old heartbroken friends, forgetful of the danger, began to converge on our old hut when the body-binders told them we were there, drawing added attention to our presence. For their sakes and our own we were forced to tear-fully flee before the dawn, back to our hiding-place in the *cafetal* cottage out-side Antigua.

When we were sure no one had followed us, we rushed through the trees to see our little boy and were greeted by a weeping Antonia Ziis who'd been told we'd been seen in Atitlan and slain, which for her had been a grief, but for me, at first, was a relief, for we'd be less likely to be hunted if our pursuers thought their quarry had been bagged. But then my easiness fled, as I realized that this news had traveled the hundred kilometers to her faster than we could drive, which meant someone was using radio equip-ment and that someone else had probably been killed at the graveyard, for there had been another lady who'd been murdered by the hit squad whose relatives had gone to bury her and most likely one of her companions had been killed trying to bury her, by the soldiers waiting there for me.

The *cafetal* was secluded and no one save an ancient male coatimundi, beautiful and black, and a thousand twittering birds ever found our rainy for-est path. When August finally drifted in and the rains held off a bit, the air was streaked golden and anxious through the thick canopy of leaves, every moment hanging precious to us as every second could have been our last.

Chiviliu, before he died, because he knew the story and the hardship we would pass trying to keep both our children and the knowledge of what the bundles were alive, had, like Malip Qoquix, admonished me to rely and act upon the responses of my small and treasured divination kit for guidance like a trustworthy friend.

Divination, the way we used it, was not fortune-telling in the strictest sense, but was a way to hear the gossip of the Bigger Picture of Nature that saw the world more completely through the composite understanding of roots, eagles, beetles, deer, wind, stones, weather, mountains and the like. Our divination bundle didn't tell us exactly what would happen but what was hap-pening and could happen if such and such was done in such a time in such a way as regards the thinking of the whole of life as represented by its pieces.

It was a highly intelligent and imaginative friend who was an ally of all that was holy and gave us life. The trouble with it was that one had to be as able as the bundle to understand it.

As a shaman in Atitlan I'd lived with my divining bundle for years on end, not doing everything it suggested or acting on its every response, but rather discussing and consulting with the other worlds as advisers to help me make decisions.

But now, with month after month of hunters hunting my family and my friends, and news of their daily kills drifting in, I called upon my *qijibal*, divination kit, like I would upon an old couple, like a trusted neighbor to help plot a route of future life for my family.

And from one of those divinations I knew something bad and unexpected was coming our way, which immediately appeared toward the end of August when Yalur was actually due to give birth. An alcoholic, wealthy, white-haired American woman had recognized me while she was drunk, just out of one corner of her eye, after having staggered in to make an unwelcome visit to my gracious hostess, who to her credit had never revealed our existence or whereabouts to anyone at any time.

But this angry inebriated woman, speaking in the trend of the hate-filled conversation that her other cocktail associates seemed to keep, was horrified that a "disgraceful Indian-lover" such as me should be housed right here with Doña Helga, and growing hysterical, the woman ran about the town announcing it to her world.

Nothing could be done about it, for the next morning all of us, Antonia Ziis, myself and Doña Helga, could see that the baby was soon to be born, or to "give light" as all Guatemalans call birth, though Yalur was not convinced. All our midwives had been back in the village and Antonia Ziis, try as she did, was unable to find one that both she and Yalur would trust with the birth and our safety.

Little Jorge stayed with Antonia Ziis while Yalur and I pushed through the thick morning mist that was rolling off the earth, soggy from the pre-dawn storm. Yalur's water broke just as we arrived at what would have been sun-up at the door of a birthing house at the outskirts of the town.

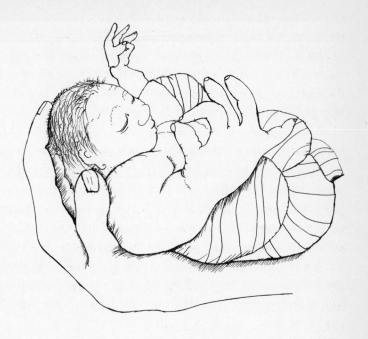

fourteen

UNDER TREES, UNDER VINES: HIDING THE NESTLINGS FROM THE EAGLE

Haphazardly set in conditions whose underfunding kept them in the general condition of over-crowded, semi-urban squalor, these birthing centers had usually a non-Indian midwife and an assistant who served expectant Mayan mothers far away from their native villages, homes and extended families; women who harvested coffee, cut sugar cane or picked cotton for cash alongside their children and husbands on the *fincas* or plantations of the rich Guatemalan, German, Japanese and Americans that engulfed the surrounding areas.

The Toe Bone and the Tooth

267

Though they did so for less pay than the men, these expectant mothers labored as valuably and intensely as anyone else and they worked out in the hills right up until their water was ready to break, when just like Yalur they came into a place like this to perfunctorily give birth far away from the nest-like reception they might have known back in their familiar mountain villages and valleys.

When they finally answered the doors, the midwives looked like two old-time Soviet immigration officers, more interested in keeping something out than letting new life in, whose bulldog stances and condescending Indian-hating attitudes made certain Yalur knew they were the birthing bosses, while they carried on in a strange obsequious manner with myself, convinced that Yalur was just a "dirty Indian menial worker" with loose morals who'd been made pregnant by some white plantation owner's son, who they figured I must have been. They told me in very reassuring terms that I could vanish now to forget it ever happened and they would make sure nobody would hear about my misdeed and my "illegitimate" child which they could arrange to be given away if I so desired!

While this unhappy parlance was causing my jaws to clamp and my teeth to grit, Yalur had staggered over and lain down on the birth bed, the only bed hiding among the crowd of some twenty new mothers who were resting on reed mats radiating out from beneath, suckling their babies on the ground. Before I could vent my indignation at the racist horror they proposed and remove us from that place, Yalur began to crown.

The little boy to whom she gave birth like a mother deer in her usual easy soundless style was a hungry beauty of a son who was already sucking angrily on his fist before the biggest bulldog midwife cut his cord with boiled scissors.

His first, gurgling, whiny cry caused his arms to raise and his tiny long fingers and hands to dance, which kept opening and gyrating like a flamenco dancer signing for the deaf. All our hatred, fear and heartbreak now knelt before those dancing fingers of the boy whom we would name Santiago, whose sound and little dance joined forces with those of twenty other babies suckling while their fathers from five different languages and tribes sitting by their wives and newborns, back against the wall, carefully picked bits of food from their string bags to feed the resting mothers, all of whom congratulated us in languages we could all understand.

With his little hands still talking to the air, his big muskmelon head still looking for a breast to suck dry, all the world was in that moment happy.

Because they had no funding and we'd come walking with just what we could carry, I was asked to bring back clean rags, blankets, food and other sundries, while Yalur remained to catch her wind.

The midday sun was out now, all was bright and I could have been easily observed, so the route I had to travel to remain unseen to Doña Helga's house, where Antonia Ziis and little Jorge waited with the things Yalur now needed, led me past a three-sided, abandoned pig shed on the inside corner of an orange grove in which I'd never seen another human, but where this time, while crossing the corner past its open side, I ran head-on into three soldiers who had just finished beating to death one of those that they daily hunted, who now lay dead inside the crumbling shack.

Seated on the ground, lacing up their military boots over the bottoms of their fatigues, all three killers were just then frantically slipping out of their civilian "disguises" back into their uniforms when in the instant I came around the trees one of them unfortunately looked up and right into my eyes, which were still filled with the joy of my son's dancing hands and Yalur's valiant birth and though for survival's sake I tried to keep my eyes vacant when he looked, I was instantly recognized, at first as a witness to the crime, but immediately after, for who I was.

Their boots not yet tied on properly and their handguns in their holsters on their belts still hung up in the branches of the trees, I had a tiny head start in the desperate chase on foot that ensued.

By the time they got their pistols, running with them pointed at the sky, their boots still trailing laces that sometimes tripped them, I ran like a deer; dodging, jumping, stopping, then darting off.

I was very skinny in those days and wasn't even running very fast at first, for I wanted them away from our nest and the remainder of my family, for if they were to kill, they should kill only me and I wanted them to shoot and not torture me to death. So I ran, remembering my two babies, Santiago's dancing hands and melon head driving me like the wind, so I ran as I remembered old Chiviliu's bundles, and my knowledge of the Flowering of the Mountain Earth, and I ran remembering the roses of Benefacio, Gustavo Rodas and my love of the village who was my true love, and like the wild animal, one half of which I am,

I'd doubled back to where I'd started running and ran again in another direction.

But they were hard on my trail, so I decided then to streak back into the sixteenth-century cobbled carriage roads that led like a maze around the profusion of high-walled whitewashed colonial palaces, monasteries, convents, mansions and fortresses running straight through the town, twisting into alleys and up narrow streets until, pursued more closely than before, I noticed one wall bristling with broken bottles embedded on its gabled ridge, somewhat shorter than the others, but still some six and half feet before the razor glass, where, invoking poor burnt Benefacio and the similar wall I'd jumped so many years before to steal his blessed roses, I suddenly recalled the look that Morning Star the mare had in her eyes the last time that I saw her but which now had the face of She for whose love I could continue living, without the village, if life would allow me to live, all of which gave my thighs a leaping strength that only the Holy could explain, with which I jumped, folding myself right over the razored wall, rolling onto my ribs and shoulders across the hard courtyard ground right onto my feet again, which kept on running only to climb the neighbor's inner wall that separated the monastery from a private residence.

Having let myself carefully down into that second courtyard and dropped easily to its base, I ran nimbly over a large sleeping mastiff, landing in his unpeopled master's kitchen, from where I found the stairs, climbed up into a bedroom, peeked out the balcony to survey the motions of my angry pursuers, who, too heavy to leap the wall, were still occupied giving each other a boost, leaving the third man in the street. By the time the remaining two had dropped into the second courtyard, the dog, God bless his determined soul, slowed them up by chasing them back into a corner with a vicious charge which caused the brutes to finally shoot my brave defender, but by then I'd already walked calmly out the front door of the mansion on to a parallel street one block away and hidden from their view.

I didn't run now until I was certain I wasn't followed and then sprinted like a colt a couple of miles into my *cafetal*, never slowing until scared and out of breath I collapsed on the kitchen floor of Doña Helga, who was gone, but where Jorge, not so happy to see me as he might have been, was whining to get another sesame-studded sugar pretzel from an exhausted Antonia Ziis, who soon learned the desperate story of my flight, Santiago's birth and

Yalur, who was where I couldn't go for fear someone might follow me and kill my entire family, as was the custom of those sorts.

What we all feared might happen had begun and Antonia and I arranged an emergency plan where she would run off to convince a group of Basque separatists, themselves in exile from the Pyrenees, who she claimed were supposed admirers of mine from the rampant gossip they had heard about my life in Atitlan, and have them fetch Yalur and Santiago to their house to where afterwards Antonia would take Jorge.

Though there was no way for us to know or time to hang about conjecturing as to what degree they would continue their search for me after the word went out that I'd been seen, but assuming that this might be the case, if I were to be hunted I decided it would be safest for my family if I remained *xe che xe caam*, or underneath the trees and bushes, as all the Mayans called staying hidden out in the dense river bottom thicket, until midnight or so when I could use the mists of night to more calmly return to Doña Helga's to get an update on the movements in the town, the welfare of my little family and to make some further plans.

Shaking and hungry in the late evening rain, under the chichicastes along the pitch dark of the rain-muddied creek, I tried hard to keep from getting lost inside my stunned disbelief at what humans could do to one another. I could not at this point afford to indulge either my grief or any moralizing hatred I felt for all the thousands of years of how what I represented had been always chased, harried, hunted, annihilated and consumed by the armed henchmen of comfort-oriented peoples who, though their top-heavy lifestyles had bought and sold the Earth, were as far away from their own souls as from the indigenous ground, animals, plants and people that their lifestyles caused to be mined, unaware and unfeeling that the very copper in their lamps had torn up the Ural mountains, that the plastic in their shoes came from petroleum that ruined the Peten rainforest, killing thousands of Indians who lived in the wake of the placement of the illegal pipeline to Belize into the ships; that every motion, consumption and exploitation done without a tear shed for the shame left the world, animals, plants, and humans trembling in hunger, homeless, in the dark; like I myself, who now, with very little possibility of relief, a person who'd always been unarmed, had never led a rebellion or advocated any killing whatsoever, was chased for what he loved. Now, frightened for my family,

I couldn't even afford my love, much less my hatred. Now, for me to be able to keep alive what I loved and the little I was left with in the teaching of the bundles, to protect the lives of Yalur and my two beautiful, ornery baby boys, I couldn't afford to falter, to dwell on rights and wrongs, preferences or hates, happinesses or comforts, for me at that moment to continue unarmed and still in love with the memory of the look in the eye of She that had always loved me, as a beacon, I, with no tribe any more, or even a place that felt like home, had to concentrate only on possibilities of how to get to a land where we would be unknown, unnoticed, so our antagonists would have forgotten. Only by disappearing could we begin anew.

To ensure I was keeping what really mattered alive in this shifting of forms that we had to do in order to flee that angry monster chasing us from the land that had always fed us, I now pulled out the miniature *qijibal* sack I'd always carried in my sash, and more recently inside my pants pocket, and commenced through my shivering to speak deep, elevated, phrases of antique Tzutujil eloquence and praise to the substance of the rushing water which we know to be the Mother of all Life, and at the base of trees where the spirits of possibilities unseen might hide. I watched the words leave my lips riding horses of curling steam straight into the unseen, merging with the soft blanket of misting fog. When my gift of jeweled speech was done, with a breath, I left the only piece of polished jade I had with me in the bush. Once a lip plug of an ancient royal Tzutujil lady and now an offering to the Holies that gave us life enough to feel both the teary grandeur of newborn sons and this soggy hunted misery, I gave it as a pledge as well to ensure at least that this moment would not be any kind of victory for my assailants or any enemies of life, by not letting them drag me by my hate away from my ability to make a gift of beauty to Life's Bigger Picture, into the cynicism of those who refuse to feed what gives them life.

Then, with my eyes well-adjusted to the dark, I climbed out of the miry riverside thicket back into the *cafetal,* where, shaking, I made my way slowly back towards Doña Helga's high-walled pension, arriving sometime after midnight.

Silently and always in the shadows, I closed in to squat under a tree in an open area behind the portal of Helga's house, which one had to go past to get to the pathway that led to where we'd been staying.

Besides speaking secretly with Antonia Ziis, I'd hoped to gather up my bundles and some things I could use if I had to continue disappearing into the hills. After watching for three quarters of an hour I figured it was safe enough to proceed down to the bungalow when something tightly grabbed the top of my head by the hair and another onion-smelling hand covered my mouth, while a voice whispered into my ear in a beery-smelling breath and German-accented Spanish: "You're looking for your death, young man. I suppose that's why you're lurking right here."

Of course this was Doña Helga, who continued whispering, "Look over there in the corner in the shadow... Two men are watching the entrance to your *casita*. Their boss is drunk in my kitchen. Take a look."

Helga handed me a pair of octagonal pearl-inlaid opera glasses with which I peered the hundred yards into her yellow-lit kitchen window, where past the ruffled drapes, sitting at her table, a kind of European-looking man with an Uzi slung over his left shoulder sat drinking from one of Helga's painted porcelain cups.

About forty years old, his balding head shaved and shined, the short sleeves of his khaki shirt rolled completely to his shoulders, he looked like a combination of Moshe Dayan with both eyes and a sinister Mr. Clean.

This was even bigger trouble yet, for neither this monster nor his pistol-brandishing mestizo assistants waiting for me in the shadows of the court-yard were soldiers or among my earlier assailants, which meant that more than just the secret military police now were aware that we were here.

I knew this because I recognized this man. Two years previously in my capacity as a chief, I had hidden an elderly Guatemalan religious woman, to return a favor to her for having fed me in the extreme poverty of my earlier days. She was mercilessly pursued herself by these very same thugs who had wanted the old lady dead for having exposed their organization as authors of certain political murders. The very same bald man had forced his way various times into sacred house rituals where, after sitting down by me, I was questioned about politics and the whereabouts of the nun who, on account of our ruses, thankfully survived.

Helga said he stormed in, livid that I was in Antigua and in some kind of idealistic zeal kept repeating as he shook his shiny head, "If they only knew he was here, I'm telling you, he wouldn't last a second," by which I presumed he must have meant the secret police or even their opponents from one of the many Marxist *guerrillero* groups; however in the instant that I thought this I realized that none of that could be the case.

These men were members of a clandestine right-wing hit squad sent out to assassinate so-called "communists." This bald man, though fully aware from our previous conversations that I was neither a left nor a right winger, knew about the large bounty for my death and must have decided to independently kill me, for the cash, all in the guise of doing his duty.

He was angry because he didn't want his competitors to find me before he could get the bounty, for which he now guarded the place of my residence to ensure he'd be the first. How did he find out where we lived? The soldiers earlier in the day would have not discovered that as yet or they'd have been here.

"If I don't miss my guess," Helga continued in a whisper, "this man is rather determined to get you and will wait here at least until tomorrow. That drunken Miss Elizabeth told him where you were. You'd better hurry now to your family with the Basques before they lose their nerve to hide them. Make a plan boy; get out of the country. Make sure you write us," whispering and poking my skinny ribs with her big sausage finger, "please tell us how it all turns out. I apologize to you, I never thought an American would have turned you in to these *matones*."

After giving me directions to the stone house of the Basques, Helga returned to entertain her armed visitor.

But by the time I arrived, the Basques had been warned by an overwrought Spanish lady, a former Catholic nun married to the former Catholic priest of Santiago Atitlan, who convinced our recent hosts that harboring my family in their house constituted an enormous jeopardy to their well-being and we should be quickly pushed away for fear they'd all be killed as well.

I found my family well fed and resting, Yalur propped upon a couch and little Santiago and chubby Jorge sound asleep on either side.

Apart from one big, scared, long-haired, bearded boy who was disgusted with their cowardice, the remaining Biscayners voted, then politely suggested that we, that very night, find a way to get as far away from them as we could.

After speaking on a telephone, for the first time in more than a decade, to over twenty different parties, I convinced the younger, braver boy to drive Yalur, Santiago and Jorge to the house of Peter Grinnell, an old-time American friend who loved to play guitar with me, who'd married a Guatemalan Ladina woman of great bearing, class and courage named Irene. They were the only people in the entire country, out of all the non-Indians that knew our situation and had the means to help, who out of love and friendship were willing to hide my little family, at great risk to themselves, for they lived in Guatemala City in the middle of the very neighborhood where the political bosses and wealthy families who ran the country had their well guarded homes, Guatemalan and foreigners alike. If we had been recognized, Peter and Irene could have been killed with us for affording us sanctuary and aide.

Peter was the foremost and most reliable electrician in the country and was himself killed mysteriously not so many years later by a sudden gust of wind which swept him from the top of his tall, well-known business building he'd established long before, while inspecting some of the wiring. He will always be remembered as a loyal and courageous friend to us in those hard and unsure times, and it was at his house that Yalur, Santiago and Jorge were to remain while I would live some miles away under the small, tired trees and struggling new growth of bushes in the mountains ravines of nearby Acalan, cooking my beans and coffee, moving my camp every day, pondering how to get an audience with the American consul to seek possible asylum for my family, or at least arrangements for getting us out of Guatemala.

The previous U.S. ambassador had been killed in Lebanon and because of the present danger in Guatemala no one could be found to replace him. The consulate, which of course was housed inside the Embassy building, where everybody had to go to arrange visas or get their passport for entrance into the U.S., was closely watched by Guatemala's military intelligence both day and night and they sometimes had lethal shoot-outs right in front of the Embassy with members of various guerrilla groups, all of whom were casually after me. The consul himself, just to get to work, had to be driven in one of two simultaneously leaving bulletproof cars, with lead-lined doors that took two men to open, on a differing route every day to and from the Embassy, where, to take an elevator to his work on the first floor he was driven into a subterranean disembarking chamber, where steel doors closed on all sides, at which time he got out of the car and rode the lift to his windowless office inside the solid steel plate and concrete building.

What chances did I have of getting in and out of the American consulate without being spotted by the hunters parked across the street, not to mention the unlikelihood of getting a face-to-face appointment in this, my one-shot attempt to see the consul?

I couldn't tell, but that was the only course with which I was left, as I couldn't live in the ravines forever, freezing, alone away from my family.

Hiding my appearance as best I could and knowing that with prostitutes, bankers and bureaucrats the world over, if you have good shoes they'll overlook the rest, I bought a pair of shiny leather shoes and proceeded on foot alone through the hardest barrios to the Embassy to see what I might arrange.

When I arrived, a queue of petitioners a quarter mile long stretched around the corner, filled with resident Americans indignant they had to stand in line, people married to them, and others trying to straighten out their documents to get into the States.

I repeated my magic praise poems, prayers and incantations to Holy Boy over and over while holding my *qijibal* hidden in my left hand, hoping the magic would work to make me invisible to the judicial across the street having lunch in his big Buick with tinted windows. I walked past the entire line of people, straight to the big glass doors with brass handles and told the marine security guard, while he looked briefly at my shoes, who I was and that I had an appointment to see the consul in person, hoping, as I lied, that my prayers would work and that the consul was not off lunching himself.

The marine guard returned with a very tall suited fellow who without much questioning looked quickly at my shoes and led me miraculously to the consul's inner chamber.

When he arrived, the consul was at first a friendly, cigarette-smoking bureaucrat whose suspicious eyes looked afraid and who talked a great deal to keep everybody thinking he was confident. After hearing my tale, about which he was not as surprised as I'd wanted him to be, he reassured me that if I needed any help getting out, he'd have me helicoptered to Panama, where I could catch a military transport back to the States, having done this just the week before for some Peace Corps workers threatened by the *guerrrilleros*. But his offer stood for me alone, for as he put it, his government did not recognize my Indian marriage and my children would have to stay back as well until I had marriage papers arranged, then birth certificates, passports and visas, all of which needed photos, translations and stamped district notarizations. I pointed out to him that the details of all the bureaucratic paperwork he demanded would take us at least six months, in peace time, to collect and process, and would now put my family and myself into great jeopardy as we exposed ourselves to the secret police, soldiers, national police, certain guerrillas and bounty hunters, not to mention that anyone in the many agencies who saw our names on the papers they might be processing, might try to catch a piece of the reward offered for my head and report us to whomsoever was paying the highest rate.

The consul suggested in that case I should abandon my family and save myself. "Who knows," he said, "this might all blow over and you can come back and deal with it in a more relaxed atmosphere in a couple of years or so," after which he went on to compare my life in Guatemala with that of American soldiers he'd seen on his diplomatic stints overseas in South Korea and South Vietnam, who had children with "foreign" girls whom they'd left when the G.I.s returned to the States.

To save my family and the knowledge of my bundles I had to bite my tongue, swallow my humiliation, saving my disappointment and hatred about humankind for a later time while I entreated this unimaginative man again if he could think of any other channel we could use to get my family to safety.

"Well, as far as we are concerned, you don't even have a family, unless we have a paper from government institutions that we recognize that says you're married. On the other hand, if you get it in writing from the people who want you dead that they truly want all of you dead, signed and addressed to the consulate, then we 'might' be able to give your family sanctuary, but only after the U.S. State Department okays it."

The fact that one of the most commonly sold right-wing weekly papers had published a bounty on my head now for over six months on an updated hit list of who'd been killed was not admissible, he said, because it was not clear that any officially recognized political entity was verifiably responsible for the statements in the paper.

Having been asked too many times to describe exactly where we were presently keeping ourselves, to which I lied, explaining how we had a house on the Pacific coast in Mazatenango, I began to feel the massive numbing thickness of the concrete and imported steel walls and how much this man resented me. This man who hoped he held my fate inside his palms actually envied me my problems. His admiration for the life I lived beyond the book he followed only fueled his hatred. Instead of taking courage to bless us by moving beyond the rules, he was only jealous of my dilemma in some bizarre way and for that, the animal in me that felt every subtle smell in the shifting breeze knew that he'd betray me to my pursuers and failing that he'd counter me in any way he could, just to feel that he could ride and crush my wild, unassuming nature with the over-domesticated remnants of his own, already broken and chained to the monster that he served.

As I rose to leave his office to return to my rocky cliff out in the hills, he patted me on the back, speaking his final words to me which confirmed my suspicions of a deeper study of my case, when he referred to something I'd said almost a decade before, "I thought you were going to live and die with those Indians you've always said you loved so much."

I fumed along the city streets, striding away from the consulate, the words he'd said rankling in me like a dog bite that breaks the bone but doesn't pierce the skin. I'd never leave my family or my little ones to be eaten by killers or to fend for themselves with no one to feed them, so far from the village and any semblance of home. And as I groused to myself working my infuriated jaws, I lost awareness of my surroundings and was soon overtaken by a long American car with tinted windows, and just as I noticed and was leaping to bolt, a voice I knew rang out over the sound of the window being lowered, "¿Martincito, hoy no, todavia no, espero que no te veo nunca mas, p'ca, oyó?"

"Not today, little Martin, not yet, I hope never to see you again back here, did you hear?" And the window locked closed again as the car squealed past, speeding away from me and disappearing around the corner. It had been the voice of Ishmael Daud ben Galeb, who let me live this one time, probably because he liked my blue paintings just that much.

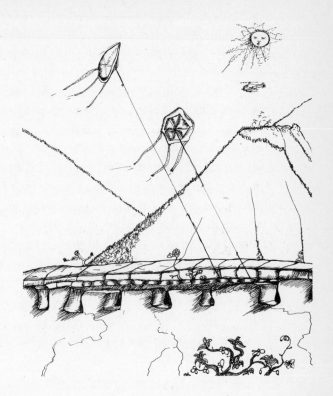

A LITTLE BLUE WIND
GOD, KITES, FROGS
AND THE ISRAELIS

P eter's cook, Doña Costa, was from the very same *aldea* of the same
Mayan town as the family of Antonia Ziis and, like all maids the
country over, they kept such close contact that when Antonia found
out that the three men who'd been trying to trap me at her employer's six
weeks previously had just been killed below Cuchummaqik, heading
toward the Cliffs of Black Coyote, when one of the girls' relatives, a guerrilla, tossed a bomb into their jeep, Yalur, whose insatiable appetite for gossip was deeper than mine for *chicharron*, already knew about it within the
day though we were many miles away.

The late summer rains had lifted; fall was here, the colder, dusty winds were getting to my lungs, which had finally fanned into the fevers of pneumonia. I needed to get under shelter, to eat regular hot food and rest for a week, and decided to go to Peter's to convalesce. But during my latest absence, for I'd been visiting in the dark a couple times a week, Yalur, who'd never fully cared or comprehended how much danger we were in and who never totally liked me to begin with and now actively hated me off and on more than ever for all the adjustments she didn't think she should have to make, had now fully recovered the original spoiled attitude that had caused her so much trouble among the village women long before we were married and which now resulted in her having violently quarreled with the only friends we had along with everyone in Peter's house, including his right-wing neighbors who were not supposed to even know we were there, much less who we were, of which there was now no speck of doubt, thereby endangering everyone, including our hosts.

After Santiago's birth and during the scramble to get away from the killers at our door, Antonia Ziis had wanted to hide us in a high, stone-walled, windowless, fortress-like sixteenth-century hacienda for which she had the only keys and which she looked after while its absentee owner, an American rug dealer, was off peddling his imports in the States for more than six months of the year.

Therefore, because the only pursuers who ever actually found us had now been killed and those who had turned us in would probably assume we were now hiding in a town on the Pacific coast, and because our relationship at Peter and Irene's was strained to say the least, I, for the sake of safety, decided to move my family and myself straight back into Antigua into Antonia Ziis's thick-walled palace, where I hoped Yalur wouldn't start any fights.

Peter generously drove us one night to the north edge of Antigua, next to a thicket where Antonia Ziis was waiting. Only she and Peter would know where we were. That would be the last time I ever saw Peter Grinnell.

The entrance to the palace was through a tiny four-foot door cut in the massive timbers of double carriage doors which were bolted with steel and studded with ancient hand-swaged, square-headed rivets. The door opened onto a covered cobbled corridor, which came out onto a courtyard lined on one side with roses and on the other with several rooms, including a kitchen behind a long veranda with clay-tiled overhanging eaves.

Thirty feet high and eight feet thick, the surrounding walls could be climbed only from inside the courtyard by a narrow strip of tiny stone steps that came out on top to a low row of merlons and embrasures as in a battlement of an old Spanish bastion. There was plenty of room for Jorge to run around down inside the courtyard, but I disallowed any of us to climb the battlements to ensure that Jorge wouldn't fall over into the thicket below and to make sure we weren't seen.

From then on out, in all my communications between ourselves and our angel, Antonia Ziis, I would be referred to as Helen in case someone should overhear. Every two or three days, unbeknownst to anyone including Doña Helga who assumed we'd already made it to the States, Antonia Ziis would bring us baskets of food and cooking fuel from the market, banging on the steel banded door with a fist-sized rock, while yelling out my newly adopted name for the benefit of anyone who might be listening in, as if she were a worker delivering market purchases to the cook of a wealthy household, then unlocking the door she'd deposit the basket just inside and leave, locking up again.

We hardly ever spoke unless something concerning our survival demanded it, but Antonia walked by every evening and if we lacked anything I'd put a little broken cup outside the massive locked doors and she would know to approach later in the night to hear what we might need.

From our remote position I tried to develop a way to process the necessary bureaucratic papers that we needed to get Yalur and the children visas, but it was only after Antonia Ziis had commandeered the services of a young zealous American archeologist lady friend of hers staying at Doña Helga's that anything got done. Though this woman probably had no idea where we were holed up, she followed my every written instruction and bravely and assiduously pestered all the necessary agencies and people, even in the Guatemalan immigration and the U.S. consulate, into stamping this and that, accompanied with the customary bribe, all in the correct bureaucratic sequence just in time, for shortly afterwards Guatemalan authorities had my land and money frozen and made my name an anathema for anyone to do any kind of business with me.

We had no more money left to buy food, pay bribes or proceed forward and no way at first that I could see to earn any. It was faced with this reality that I began to make paintings with paints Antonia had bought for "Helen," painting under the courtyard eves, in a style very different from what people were accustomed to expect from Martín Prechtel. I signed them with the very respectable Mayan woman's name "Maria Poq", or Mary the Grebe.

Antonia Ziis took them to galleries, which used to sell Martín Prechtel's paintings where they became a craze, selling at a tenth the value of anything signed with my real name.

When the public demanded a gallery show, Antonia Ziis, who was now "representing" this enigmatic Cakchiquel lady painter named Maria Poq, very nicely explained how sensitive the painter was and much too shy to appear in public, but how she would be very pleased to put together an exhibition. Which she did, but of course did not attend, and which now brought in the modicum of cash we needed to survive.

All that remained for us before taking the pile of dearly gathered, translated and officially-stamped documents to the embassy and Guatemalan Immigration Service for the first stage of the passports, were recent photos of Yalur and both children and for all of this they had to go in person.

Though this was nerve-wracking for me, Antonia Ziis, without a second thought disguised Yalur in one of her own lace-trimmed Pan-Indian *trajes*, the beautiful garb of highland Mayan parlor maids, from which no one could determine one's tribe or provenance, and led Yalur and the children to all the necessary places, channels and desks, traveling by bus to and around Guatemala City while I prayed and waited alone inside the fortress until they returned in the night, valiantly successful, happy to have been out of isolation for a little while.

All of us had our passports now and every paper necessary to approach the American Embassy with our petition for the entire family's entrance into the Untied States.

If they refused to give Yalur a visa then we planned to make an overland run for Costa Rica, passing illegally through Honduras to avoid the Guatemalan soldiers at the point of exit. Mexico was a possibility as well, if we could make it far enough inside, but on the borders Mayan refugees from Guatemala were being killed here and there and the rest rounded up and turned over to the Guatemalan army where their fate was as can be imagined. Even if the Americans miraculously gave us Yalur's visa we would have to find some cash in order to buy plane tickets, though the chances of actually boarding the aircraft without being recognized by the myriad types of police and paramilitary patrols inside the terminal would be a courageous gamble.

Knowing now how intensely the U.S. Consulate was being watched by various groups, none of whom would waste a second thought about blowing us to dust, I sent our archeologist friend with the power of attorney to the consulate to deliver the bewildering stack of necessary original documents preciously gathered over the previous several months, including all our translated birth certificates, affidavits, police records, health reports, *cedulas*, letters of recommendation from important people in the States, all and more than the consul had demanded.

But, like mother cranes whose hopes are scattered like the down they scratch from their chest to line their nests when marauding foxes crush their eggs and eat the newborn chicks, who took so long to hatch only to begin the long exhausting process all over again, we lost all our precious documents in one heartless blow, when immediately outside the Embassy, two assailants on a motorcycle pushed our archeologist benefactor into the pavement, damaging her face, while snatching every shred of our necessary paperwork away to where these demons roost.

I toast that woman's willingness and bravery, for they might have killed her for her troubles on our behalf.

At news of this, Yalur decided to give up trying to go to safety. As Santiago was eating solid food she would simply walk out the door and return to the village with the children and take whatever fate life dealt them, which in this case was certain death. I commiserated with her rage and desperation, for how could we with the ban and price upon my head ever gather once more what we needed, and who would be willing to do the footwork again? But, still I knew from my divinations that a lot of shifts in the wind, both good and bad, were coming and I refused to let her leave, for which I was screamed at, while taking blows to my head and ribs from her small pointy copper fists. She even started throwing stones and cups, most of which I dodged from so much practice, and was in the process of wrestling a long knife from her hands when Antonia Ziis rushed in and announced that Stanley Rother had been killed and crucified.

What they did to Stanley Rother was too sickening, but the grief of his loss we added to the gathered flood of combined tears for everyone we had lost.

He'd left the village two weeks after we had, when I sent a warning to him from Antigua about how I had it from a source that he took seriously, that he was immediately scheduled to be killed for which he returned, quickly and unobstructed, to his Oklahoma family. But like the rest of us, uprooted from the village, he felt lost and useless far away from the flowers, bright clothing, laughter and his accepted function in the lives of people of Atitlan. After several months, unheedful of any warnings, Stanley couldn't resist his longing and foolishly returned to "take what came."

The instant he'd stepped off the airplane, Stanley was followed and he knew it. Back home in Atitlan he was killed in his bed in the rectory, then nailed up and mutilated in front of the old colonial church where all of us had prayed, albeit to different deities.

Father Stanley was made by the Catholic Church into a martyr, a sacrifice for their cause. Padre Gaspar Culan was almost forgotten.

Gaspar Culan the third, the grandson of Swordfighter, had been a Catholic sacrifice as well, a sacrifice to the growing losses the church had caused the indigenous soul. Both men, just two of more than 1,800 people that were murdered in our village by the same heartless entity, loved the same village whose heart was in the Story, whose telling we were living.

The most horrible perversity of the tense and cautious state of life in hidden exile is that one lacks the friends of the village into whose arms one can confidently drop, unguarded, into the holy bath of grief, inside of which all truly happy men and women must bathe to transform the great losses of life in wars, sicknesses, the loss of homelands and the loss of one's confidence in human decency into a wailing that ends in poetry and elegant praise of the ability to feel. For desire, mistaken for love, without the capacity to truly feel the losses that actual loving entails, is what makes murderers of people who have no home friendly enough to allow them both the complete sadnesses and joys their love can feel.

Occulted as we were, like quails in front of searching bird dogs, our silence caused our immediate survival. The great proper wailing of the type Mayans and all indigenous humans know they have to make at all their losses, deep and true, become when hunted and away from all the friends, a thing put off until a later time, if a later time ever comes; which if it doesn't and the uncried grief of war is later forgotten for what it is, the waiting tears will settle into a violent silt at the bottom of the river of the so-called resumption of normal everyday life, in which the ghost of wars-to-come are sprouted from this forgetting, this grief left uncried for future generations far from the time that made it.

Hundreds of us were dead now: Padre was gone, Stanley was gone, my best friends were dead, Yalur could not return, our papers were lost, we had no money left and we had been prisoners here for months on end. So we did what any self-respecting Mayan would do in such a plight, we made ourselves a kite.

Yalur had always loved kites and like most Mayan kids, both of us could make them from any discarded bits of this and that, tying this string from a weaving to that string from an unraveled straw hat. Yalur flew them high, like a master, while mine liked dancing lower down, all to the delight of our little boys who started laughing up out of the courtyard into the air to where the flyers stretched. Though I feared somewhat we might be discovered by our kites flying over the tops of the fortress – for Antonia brought us notice that someone posing as Yalur's brother had been asking around for us, passing the word that he had important news of her family, but who turned out to be a known *guerrillero* hunting us for cash – we were now at the edge of our sanity and if we were to be killed because of attention drawn to us by our kites then it was most likely only a matter of when and the simple joy the little round yellow paper kites gave us, flown on lines of knotted warp threads taken from a dilapidated shawl, was a better hopeful thing than the constant gut-grinding apprehension that could kill us just as well.

We did, however, listen for the low-flying helicopters and heavily armed gun ships, sold to the Guatemalan army by the Israeli and Belgian dealers on behalf of the U.S. Like little spoiled kids with brand new slingshots who, aching to try them out, shot every bird, squirrel and bug they came across, these noisy mechanical dragonflies were flown without strategy or military plan by only half-trained pilots on a vicious whim, who scoured the mountainside and Mayan cornfields for something to shoot. A lot of unknown or innocent Indians, flocks of sheep, stray dogs and civilians were blown up by cannons or gunned down from the air.

If we heard them coming, we backed like frogs did into their mud, hiding in the recesses of the murky fortress until their rhythmic chug and subsonic flapping no longer echoed in the ground, to once again raise our kites above the walls and roses to the sun, in a prayer of play in hopes he might bail us out.

At that point, to everyone's surprise, our archeologist lady friend remained undeterred and instead of being intimidated, was even more determined than ever to help us beat the odds. She commenced again to gather up the necessary bureaucratic material, first piecing together what she could from copies she had made and leftover photographs and using her own cash, made more substantial bribes until she had put together an even more creative-looking stack of legal folders and paperwork than before.

This time, however, I had to send out letters with a Guatemalan City return address to everyone I could conjure in my memory, petitioning them to write directly to the State Department to ask that they give us some special dispensation when the consul on this second attempt refused even to give our loyal helper an audience.

Several weeks later, even when they did allow her in, under pressure from the State Department itself, which was moved by our letter-writing campaign, she was told by the consul that he was under no obligation whatsoever to assist us due to our "immoral marital" situation and that under no circumstances would they issue even a visitor's visa for Yalur to enter the U.S. for so much as a day.

As a last-ditch attempt, the archeologist called an old stateside boyfriend who was a lawyer involved peripherally in a case involving Guatemalan agriculture and who was somehow able to speak directly to somebody in the State Department who knew something about our troubles. He was informed that the State Department could strong-arm the belligerent American consul in Guatemala City into issuing a short-term visa if we could show that we were only visiting the U.S. for some sort of legitimate event for only a week, during which it could be verified that Yalur would earn no money, but for which the entire family had to be present. After praying, looking at and listening to my divination bundle to find an answer to this fairytale riddle from bureaucratic hell, I wrote a letter to Izzy and Vera Winer, who'd been pestering me repeatedly by mail for a year before the war to make a series of paintings for a show that Vera was trying to arrange in Honolulu through the auspices of her hobby art gallery in Southern California.

Because the army was now in charge of the postal service, opening, reading and censuring any letters that attracted their attention, it became difficult and dangerous to do anything by mail. Like a mother turtle laying lots of eggs in hopes that one survives, I made fifteen copies of my letter and had the archeologist hand the envelopes to travelers returning to the States, who promised to post them on their arrival.

In my correspondence I asked the Winers if they would be so kind as to make a letter that stated what the State Department wanted it to say and post several copies to the archeologist's lawyer-boyfriend in the States, one to the American consul in Guatemala City and double copies to certain individuals in the State Department and so on.

They responded immediately, carrying out my every instruction, but added that it was imperative that I somehow contact Vera's brother, Salo Harshov, and his wife Miriam in the shoe-selling district of the capital.

Antonia Ziis went there on our behalf, returning with fifteen hundred quetzales in every size of bill accompanied by the hoped-for-letter from Izzy, the same one he'd forwarded to the State Department:

"From the crazy Jews of Orange County, for paintings you will some day paint for us, for an art show in Honolulu, for which you and your family had better show up for one week, or the deal's off. Peace. Izzy and Vera Winer."

With that came another note in English, but this time from Rabbi Nehemiah Harshov and his father and mother Salo and Miriam Harshov, which had five hundred quetzales taped across the fold:

"We heard about your land and cash. We can always exchange money for you or advance you some if things get dire. Here's some towards plane tickets we collected from your friends in the discussion group. Peace. Rabbi Harshov."

None of the letters mentioned us by name, for these Jews of Poland, Germany, Russia, the Balkans, Armenia and other places who now resided in Central America, knew better. They could still remember how and were as yet entirely set up, to help relatives and friends escape the multiple oppressions they themselves had experienced most recently in Europe in the wake of Hitler, Stalin and others, having ironically come to find peace in places like Guatemala to elude the horror of the very same mentality that in Guatemala chased us now. But under constant historical threats of death and relocation, their particular Diaspora had been so big and long unfolding that the culture itself was now fitted with an institution of cultural and spiritual survival of which we were now the partial beneficiaries.

Because of this they knew as well that even if the consul acquiesced to State Department pressure and accepted Izzy and Vera's note, I would still be required to show documented evidence of sufficient funds to be able to travel and support us during our "week-long" stay in the States, to prove that we had every intention of returning to Guatemala from our "visit," which of course we did not. For this the Rabbis gathered up some money, knowing what it meant to have your money frozen. I'd often thought earlier about going to the discussion group for help, but beside the fact I didn't want to get them hurt, I worried that the Israelis, who were officially supporting some of my pursuers, might find out through some innocent connection, possibly alerting certain elements who didn't need to know.

But in the end, for all the volumes of letters and calls that different kinds of people throughout the world made on our behalf for almost a year, and all the painstaking, life-endangering gathering of documents, files and evidence, and infuriatingly slow, minute details tended to twice over by Antonia Ziis, ourselves and the intrepid archeologist; the consul, who powerless in his own mediocre life, wielding the little bit of might and toughness he still retained in his official position, was still determined to crush us in revenge for what he saw hatefully as our flaunting of our indigenous pride and love of freedom and refused for the third and final time. Three times was the limit for the refusal of a visa, making us ineligible for any further attempts.

We would have to obtain visas to fly to another country like France or Spain, or flee illegally across an unguarded border on foot, dodging the authorities in either Mexico or Honduras, to "take what might come."

We had been running all the possibilities through our outraged, exhausted, desperate and unbelieving minds on that beautiful, sunny, butterfly-filled, mid-November morning, Yalur and the boys just having fallen asleep when out of nowhere, with no warning whatsoever, the iron-strapped carriage door exploded open with a subsonic, dusty thud accompanied by the smell of cordite that rode a small cloud hanging eerily in the air, out of which over twenty highly-armed soldiers in dark blue uniforms and berets bolted and scrambled, dispersing throughout the ancient palace, until standing in pairs, back to back, they began yelling.

Because both children were asleep in a windowless room with Yalur, I thought to run straight into the street to draw them away from my sleeping family, but in that instant Jorge, naked from the waist down, came scurrying out holding his two hands together over his round little chest. I scooped him up, ran into the adjoining room and put him back into his mother's arms. Then as I proceeded to make my delayed break for the road, two tall soldiers with a variety of grenades dangling from *bandoliers* grabbed me by my arms.

My heart was beating so wildly I could hardly hear them speaking, but the few seconds I figured I might have before they hauled me off, or shot me on the spot, stretched out into a strange quiet, while out of the smoke and between the remaining soldiers outside the door the Israeli ambassador, Menasham Havel, still in a suit, stepped into the corridor with his very tall, broad-shouldered, one expression son-in-law, the head of Israeli embassy security, by his side, both of them looking about, removing their sunglasses, strolling leisurely toward me, just like they used to years back in Atitlan.

Grabbing me by the shoulders he gave me what I took to be a repressed version of an Eastern European hug, then asked me in his quiet and polite Israeli-accented Spanish, "How long have your kidnappers been away?"

"Oh, Mr. Ambassador, I'm sorry to tell you, but we have not been kidnapped. We were trying to avoid just that and had been here secretly hiding, until now of course." I answered, watching his poor, chalky, hound-dog expression shift into a crooked smile of embarrassed chagrin.

"Do you mean to tell us that you are not at this time being held against your will? We were told you were captured and being held and you know we came expressly to rescue you and your family from the insurgents, who as we see are non-existent here."

Menasham knew full well that I was being hunted by every side of the fracas and most intensely by certain notorious segments of the Guatemalan army with whom, because of their terrorism, he was secretly quite disgusted, but more so with himself for having to collude with them by supplying them with the weaponry and so-called anti-communist, counter-insurgency training, using Israeli advisors that the right-wing Guatemalan military used to sadistically torture and eradicate whole villages of people, not to mention evening scores between rival right-wing oligarchies, most of whom were anti-Semitic to begin with, but whose internecine violence was disguised as communist guerrilla activities. As terms of his appointment to the ambassadorship he was forced to carry out such deals made higher up politically, in which Israel had agreed to something like this in order to continue receiving something else at home from the true originators of this unintelligently manipulated mess, which of course was not Israel, or even a particular people, but a syndrome running strong in several paranoiac sections of powerful governments far away from Israel and Guatemala.

Having been a very heroic freedom fighter and later a captain of one of the freedom boats negotiating unarmed through the dangerous waters of Europe, the Mediterranean and the Adriatic during World War II, and afterwards bringing boatloads of Jewish refugees away from the horrors of torture, terrorism and repression, away from the gas chambers, the gulags and the pogroms, Menasham was not cut out for the kind of work that sold the tools of that same repression, torture and terrorism to the oppressor of the unarmed population of Guatemala, most of whom were Mayan Indians.

Menasham loved his people and the idea of an Israel, but hated his position that compromised them both, knowing well the grief of what it had been like to help bring freedom to so many when so many had to be left behind, not to mention all those who'd been lost.

Now stuck for years inside an iron suit of politics that had forced him into an activity unworthy of his real freedom-fighting heart, by pretending to be saving us from "left-wing insurgents" he'd come to deliver us from the brutes to whom he'd been funneling arms, and in the heroic posture of his love, rescue some portion of his soul from the hatred it bore him for his recent life.

After narrating the long tale of what we'd been enduring, to which everyone listened with an unexpected silence, I inquired of the ambassador how it came about that he found us, expecting him to say that Izzy and Vera had initiated the search to save us, but he replied instead that, "The rug dealer who owns this house wants you out so he can have his house back, we met him at an art show, he told us in front of everyone where you were holed up. Now given all that, in what way do you think I really could be of help to you and your family, Mr. Martín Prechtel, since obviously there is no one here to shoot at, or from whom we could save you?"

My little son Jorge who'd been milling around our feet, bare bottomed, like a waddling pigeon, went off to pee over the veranda onto the courtyard plants and, after returning to our knees wringing his little three-year-old hands, apparently went to work, unnoticed, down at our feet, beneath the three of us; the ambassador, his head of security and myself. As we stood there discussing the possibilities for getting us out of the country, we heard a quick click and a pop, as the security man's bomb-proof, tamper-proof, attaché case opened and lay spread out on the colonial stone floor of the veranda.

In this early debut of what would become a life-long talent of being able to unlock anything, Jorge, by fiddling with the tumblers and buttons, had cracked the Israeli security officer's combination, opening the case to reveal gas masks, poison, syringes, gas grenades, small pistols, a phone of some sort and all sorts of little instruments, picks and papers, all with a great ambience of toxicity and explanation beyond my experience.

The soldiers inside still in their watchful positions began to laugh and when those surrounding our hiding-place outside began to chuckle in the thicket I realized just how many armed men Menasham had brought along.

Though he would have liked to, Menasham could not legally give us asylum in his embassy, but he could arrange for us to be transported, free of charge, to Israel that very night on a weekly flight that ran between Guatemala and Jerusalem. He could have us installed in a kibbutz within three days after which we could more slowly figure something out in a "less hectic" atmosphere. At least we'd be out of Guatemala, away from our hunters and have work in the kibbutz and therefore some means of support.

Because of the ambassador's commando raid we were no longer hidden and it would not be safe to hide here any more. There were precious few places left us where we wouldn't be noticed and where a family could survive, but no matter what I thought about going to Israel, and it sounded like the best deal we had going, Yalur, now that the chips were down, flatly refused to go, still hoping to return to her village regardless of whether she died by doing so, which in the end made it so we had to kindly refuse Menasham.

Saddened and embarrassed, I asked an even more disappointed Menasham if he might put any pressure he could think of on the American consulate and the State Department, asking them to give up their hatred of us and issue a visa for Yalur. He just stared for a while and thought, then speaking calmly, "Dolly asked me to ask you if you've been doing any new paintings lately?"

I showed him to the far end of the veranda where my recent paintings were still drying and the sad hero bought two of them, a big yellow one with roses for Dolly and a little blue Wind God for himself, after which he shook hands with his troop leaders, then with us, and we watched the soldiers pile back into their sky-colored Bluebird bus. The Ambassador, waving shyly goodbye, was ushered into his limousine with his son-in-law still carrying his attaché and the entire entourage drove off leaving a cloud of diesel smoke in the heavy evening air. Exposed in the twilight, sad and even more afraid, we huddled together feeling very alone in that big murky stone palace we now knew could easily be penetrated by killers if they knew we were here. And now because of the hubbub of our failed rescue, everybody did.

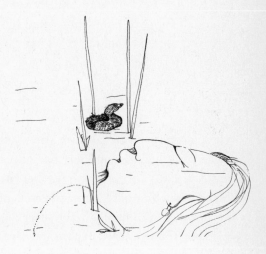

FLEEING OVER THE TOES OF THE MONSTER: NO MORE WEEPING OF THE LAKE GREBES

Bickering and yelling at the top of their lungs, Antonia Ziis and Steven Kuznits came crashing through the broken carriage doors the following morning with a family of five well-off Quiché Mayan blanket weavers from Momostenango who were shouldering the heavy, wool-polished beams of their enormous disassembled floor looms whose massive fragments and delicate combs they continued to unload beneath the veranda, after which they proceeded, without even looking up at us, to pound, pin, bolt and hang them together until two large blanket looms rested where my painting and easels used to stand.

We'd been hiding here longer than any of us had wanted and Steven Kuznits, the legal owner, the photographer, the rug dealer, was back and wanted us to move out and return his fortress to him.

To make it all the more emphatic that we leave he'd gathered up some of the weavers he'd indentured along the way, causing them to take away our rooms and crowd the house beyond what he thought we would tolerate. But, because he'd failed to actually live on the ground with the people he claimed to support, he miscalculated the Mayan love of company and the normal crowded condition of all Mayan family compounds no matter from what different tribe or language they descended and because of that his plan to get us gone failed, for we made tremendous friends with this group of invading weavers who passed the week's first woven blankets on to us as gifts.

Just adjacent to Antigua, still buried deep inside the ground, an older town called just that, Ciudad Vieja, had once been the original capital of the invading Spaniards long before. It was here in the middle 1500s that Spanish documents say a Tzutujil king had been kept in an underground dungeon for two decades, and finally hung, after which the town itself was taken unawares and utterly buried in a rushing river of deep and mighty mud.

Tzutujil tradition, on the other hand, said the Spaniards were holding three hereditary Tzutujil leaders whose bodies were human but whose souls were reincarnating deities, who from inside the dungeons themselves conjured the flood of mud that buried them alive and all the Spanish citizens at once, killing even the *encomenderos* of Atitlan, Jorge Alvarado and his paramour; the wife of his brother Pedro Alvarado, the man who butchered Guatemala, who himself was shortly after killed by the unconquerable Tarascans in central Mexico with an arrow in his heel made of native arsenic bronze that pierced his steel armor. However it happened, the generation of foreigners who stole Guatemala from its people were destroyed by the ground and to this day anyone can stroll on the spine-like roof combs of that extinct town.

The colonial government and numerous religious orders, all of whom quarreled incessantly for territory and jurisdiction over the Mayan populations, rebuilt a capital, which became Antigua Guatemala, which grew into an even more intensely fortressed town containing many smaller fortresses, a center where those taking taxes, tithes and rent off of the land were headquartered, whose owners all had houses in Antigua but who for the most part only came to visit. Though the capital was moved from there later on, this tradition of absentee ownership had continued to the present.

Mr. Kuznits, on the other hand, like a lot of Antigua's present-day absentee owners, was living off a trust fund. The child of a big city, probably New York, he had the hobby of making money without money, appearing to have money, which he did, but never spending any of it.

He was a taker and a user and the entire world was about him, enduring our presence about as much as a poodle would a family of raccoons in the kitchen, unable to tolerate our presence in "his territory" unless we were paying rent or he could mine us for something he could sell. Yalur said his eyelids wouldn't drop an eyelash hair unless he could make a dime.

So, after months of silent hiding, keeping ourselves alive inside, Steven Kuznits', who would not listen to our pleas, left the door wide open, bringing his clients freely by to take a look at the famous exiles, snapping "art" photos of us without our permission, photos of us in our beleaguered postures that he would later sell in his art shows in Florida.

We were still very village-like, scared and overly polite and therefore grateful for having had his run-down palace so long to ourselves as an excellent place to hide.

But, Mr. Kuznits' self-assumed immortality and thoughtless lack of consideration for our situation, that would just as surely have caused his own death as thoroughly as ours, was too unnerving for us and I was just getting prepared for us to change our place of hiding when Antonia crept meekly through the unlockable doors reporting with a great bursting smile that the U.S. consulate had awarded Yalur a one-week visa having finally buckled beneath direct pressure from some very convincing person from Washington D.C. after a thorough badgering from the Israelis!

We all danced and jumped and wept a lot, going to our knees to pray for thanks, all except Jorge, who kept on spinning, and Yalur, who still didn't want to go, while Steven Kuznits with no shame and feeling left out of our relief for having never suffered enough to know what it meant, began to photograph our grief, relief and befuddled exhaustion, which tried my patience and I stared at him in rage, my village spirits jumping toward him from my chest until he dropped his heavy camera on his bare toe and while bending to recover it, banged his head on the lever of one of the heavy looms, his other foot crushing the camera in the process, all of which caused him to fall onto his back holding his toe, making my babies laugh wildly and inspiring them to continue dancing for joy on top of his chest which made everybody else roar.

We weren't out of all danger yet and another tense stretch lay before us. For even though the archeologist and Antonia Ziis had already purchased round trip tickets to Los Angeles, California and back, those that the consulate had required as proof of our intention to return, which had used up all the money we had left, there still remained the unlikelihood of our filtering unrecognized past the mesh of roving national policemen, plainclothes secret army police or the judicial, the many machine-gun toting uniformed military police posted on the catwalk above the airport lobby or any number of clandestine, anti-communist assassins that constantly guarded and kept watch for any disembarking guerrillas or people they were hunting who were trying to leave the country by way of the Guatemala City airport.

Alternately, we could have chanced driving to the border without being recognized in a military roadblock or a guerrilla shakedown spot, take a bus to Mexico City, then fly to the States unhindered, but we didn't have more than a hundred dollars left anyway, and that could have been just as dicey as visiting Atitlan at this point.

The only choice we had if we were going to the States was to change our shape, look, sound and way of walking to appear as modern and non-tribal as possible, to make ourselves seem to be casual American travelers, and hope the immigration officers and airplane company employees didn't recognize us and turn us in.

This did not even take into account the route we'd have to take getting to the airport, which was fraught with killings both left and right and bandits taking advantage of the situation to rob and kill unpursued.

We would probably fail and in our worn-down, exhausted emotional state, bracing ourselves further for all that was overwhelming.

The following morning at about 2 A.M. I heard a helicopter very close over the rooftops, a couple of blocks to the west. After chugging eerily around repeatedly in what seemed like figure eights for several minutes it finally faded away. The dogs began to yip and moan, and I felt something hard had taken place, but I'd probably never find out.

The horror and the truth of what had happened became an unsolicited grace afforded us by the hideous and wasteful death of a man, whose cowardly murder gave us a space of time in which we could finally slip away from what had killed him.

Living in the north central highland mountains of southwestern Guatemala, a young German man, recently naturalized as a Canadian citizen, with a Mohawk haircut, allied with the Canadian Mohawks, but with a German last name like my own, was engaged as a teacher of music and Onandaga understandings to Quiché Mayan children. There were actually not a few distant, indigenous relatives of mine wandering the hills of Guatemala in those times.

The same heartless entities that hunted us, captured and killed this poor boy for reasons no one knows, but no doubt comparably as ridiculous as those for which we were pursued.

They flew his dead body down to Antigua in the night and maybe because the flyers were low on fuel and couldn't make it to the live volcanoes behind the town they normally used to cremate the people they'd destroyed, he was mysteriously dropped only two blocks from Steven Kuznits' unlocked palace.

Though mutilated beyond immediate recognition, for the parts of him that could still be ascertained and a rumor ran swiftly throughout the town, and beyond the town to the next town, until it got into the newspaper in Guatemala City, after which the rumor was out everywhere that this man who'd been killed was none other than myself.

By the time the consulate received the results of the fingerprints they'd taken from the man that everyone had assumed was me, the Canadians had correctly identified the boy and had already shipped his remains back to Quebec. Luckily for us, the original rumor had by then become the country's fact.

Because of this unfortunate man's death and mistaken identity, my family and I were given several days where no one would be searching for us, during which I hoped Mr. Kuznits, who was distinctly sobered by all this, could keep his gossiping American, marijuana-smoking, coffee clutch away long enough to preserve our life-saving secret.

I toast the memory of that Canadian man and all his friends.

The first name everyone called me was not the name in my passport and that would as well be a help, so all that remained was for us was to change our shapes.

My beard was red and well trimmed, my curly hair cut very short, I wore a very tacky, light-blue polyester suit with long lapels, looking all the world like a Dade county door-to-door sewing machine salesman.

The archeologist dressed Yalur in nylon hose, black patent leather low-spike heels, a short, pink mini-skirt, a ring and a polyester blouse. The kids were dressed and combed like little Anglo children, their handsome, hand-woven clothing made for them by their female relatives all gone, and new machine-made denim overalls and funny plaid shirts in their place; though they continued unaffected like the energetic rascals that they were.

This would be the first in a series of years of shifting shapes we'd have to do, but this one could have been our last, as in a few hours we could be dead.

Even if we miraculously made it onto a plane, there was no one waiting for us on the other side, not to mention the fact that the consul in his fury had added damaging handwritten comments in Yalur's passport, the worst of which stated that "under no circumstances was any privilege or exten-sion recommended," and if the immigration officer right off the plane in the L.A. airport didn't like the looks of us or our paperwork, they could have my family deported, without a trial, back to Guatemala, straight back into the hands of death.

If we wanted to survive we had to look like we weren't Indians, didn't like Indians, and weren't interested in anything that had to do with the nat-ural or indigenous life.

We now owned very little, so every little thing we had we packed. We packed my bundles and all our handwoven clothing and small remem-brances from the village in hopes they'd let it all through, for if the customs agents on either side inspected it, my bundles would probably be confis-cated because of the laws regarding antiquities smuggling.

I had to put a spell on myself to rid the air around me of any sign of fright, rage or aversion that might tip off my assailants. For this I made a small ceremony the evening before our departure, making word offerings for the Mother Waters and Holy Boy, the Flowering Earth, the Wind and all the others whose elegant roll-call I sung into the night, making offerings as all harried peoples do from whatever they have at hand.

I asked Holy Boy to help us, to charm temporarily my walk, my accent, and my mannerisms into something that would blend into a crowd of alien people, so that I would not seem the alien; I asked him to temporarily harden the look in the expression of my face, to make it seem like I understood less than I did, was not as awake, and was less informed, at least enough to get leisurely past the predatorial officers, by appearing to merge into the homogenized drone of a crowd of people accustomed to and dependent upon machines without leaking out any of the non-verbal indigenous communication all people still have in their bones, but about which they are usually not sufficiently aware or rehearsed to know more than to investigate an unsolicited feeling.

Not feeling at home in any big city under normal circumstances, not relaxed by nature when immersed into crowds of people I didn't know and not likely to get to know, I would've been on edge in an airport even if there hadn't been a price on my head.

I tried at least to look and act like other people I'd seen in airports, trying to act irritated all the time, with an overwhelming self-interest, manifested somehow through the unwritten mandate of airport crowds of not talking too terribly much to anyone while looking perfectly at ease inside this insane self-imposed isolation, as if it were normal to say everything you thought about nothing and nothing about anything with content, while remaining only mildly diverted by the enormous rolling wave of collective numbness of the milling crowds, which by itself would be scary enough to drive any normal human back to more familiar territory.

When we got there the next morning the hardest part was that after so many months in hiding, having spoken to only three people besides my children, Yalur and the Holy in my bundles, the killing monsters, though thickly distributed throughout the airport exactly as I'd imagined them, after tens of weeks of incessant rehearsal of our escape, turned out, up this close, to be human beings and in my longing for company and friendship I had to be very careful to avoid their searching, human eyes which would have instantly singled me out, for my longing, as being different from the rest and may have recognized me for having even looked. But, also, it could not appear that I was avoiding their gaze. Like riding a hungry horse on thin ice, or pulling the whisker out of a live jaguar's cheek, I had to breathe just right and remember what it was I really loved, for without that beacon, nothing else would get us through.

However, as it is so often in life, what I'd feared the most went suspiciously smoothly. After passing through the interminable stalls, booths, benches, bureaucrats and air company representatives, showing our passports, alternate forms of identification, visas, tickets, *boletos de ornato* and so forth, we sat down alone into the middle of a million unknown people in our polyester and nylon with two scared and over-stimulated little boys, our last days as villagers vaporizing, feeling like a handful of indigestible jade beads swallowed into the noisy stomach of a insatiable ogre.

Gone were the sounds of old eloquent speakers looking for my help, gone the weeping of the lake grebes, gone the days of thirty-thousand people welcoming young people back from the underworld, their souls like orchids on their backs, gone were Yalur's handwoven blouses and my Indian pants with their double-headed eagles, single-headed hawks, water bugs, bats, hummingbirds and lightning embroidered by happy girls whose fathers speared fish from hand-carved, dugout canoes, and died of tuberculosis, mourned and wailed for days like anybody should be, gone were the waddle of the women and strong free gait of the men, the constant obligation to say hello to every soul you met whose own story was part of the Story. Alone, we were beyond alone, no more Antonia Ziis, no more kites in hiding, hatefully alone, trying to survive by flying directly into the madness, inside the madness' machine, to get away from the digesting sacrificing storm that the world's unconscious, greedy heart caused to happen so far from the center of its consummation.

These were thoughts I couldn't think, but were thought as thoughts to be kept alive in a layer too deep for the predator to smell, and then the loudspeakers called us to our plane.

To my great surprise, the children and Yalur loved climbing into the winged titanium tube, which for the first time in my life gave me an initial pounding case of claustrophobic shudders that soon gave way to long, cautious, stifled sighs of relief as we sat on the tarmac, the gangway still crowded with a queue of boarding passengers.

Just when the plane had boarded its last passenger and the gangway ladder was to be rolled back, I was called by the immigration police to exit the plane alone and proceed back into the terminal.

In an instant of resignation to what might come, I was somewhat reassured by the possibility that my family at least might somehow make it away from this particular place whose particular time was so full of danger for us all.

Stunned and fascinated by the profusion of new things to see and try to understand, Yalur was oblivious to what was actually happening and I did not alarm her, for she might have followed me out of the plane into the hands of the authorities toward whom I was headed.

Rising as gracefully as my terror and polyester suit would allow me and feigning an ignorance and patient inquisitive interest in what I was certain was my capture, I passed toward the cabin door, and down the stairway where I was immediately taken by the right arm by a suited immigration authority and forcibly walked toward the immigration podium.

As the two of us rushed strangely unaccompanied across the lobby, a big European-looking fellow in his late thirties wearing very large, dark sunglasses ran into me and crashed solidly down onto the slick floor. The officer didn't want us to stop, but I did and we ended by setting the brawny-looking fellow upright again. My disguise must have been quite effective, for this man I'd tripped was the commander of a very famous Marxist guerrilla group whom I'd known years before he'd become anything of the sort. But who a year and a half previous had sent his brother to warn me, that for the usual reasons, he was going to have to kill me and wouldn't I rather take a trip out of the country so he wouldn't need to kill me, for which they would pay for me, but not for my family.

Any of the guards would have loved to catch both of us in one motion. But nothing happened. He thanked us perfunctorily and courteously and went on his way.

We, on the other hand, resumed our progress towards my own doom, arriving at the immigration counter practically running at the firm instigation of my armed escort. When we arrived, the head officer behind the counter scolded the arm-holding officer for his tardiness and handed me a folded piece of paper, which turned out to be my *cedula* of alien residency that for some reason had accidentally slipped out of my document package, and I would need it, as he put it, to re-enter Guatemala on my return!

They didn't want to kill me, they just hadn't wanted me to leave without all my papers, and in the most emphatic and friendly Guatemalan way he bid me to have a pleasant flight and urged me to sprint back to my plane before it left me behind.

Sort of running and sort of not running, for I didn't want any of the other officers on the catwalk to wonder why I was running and all of a sudden recognize me, I popped into the plane panting, sat down, buckled myself in, pulled Jorge off the aisle where he was running up and down unbuckling everybody's seatbelts, and wrestled him screaming onto my lap, until we went thumping and bumping down the potholed Guatemalan City airport runway, past the tanks and the helicopters at which point Jorge, like Santiago and Yalur, finally sat bug-eyed and quiet, fascinated by the receding ground as we surged up into the roiling clouds.

Within a quarter of an hour, with both children in my arms and my bundles in the hold, we flew over Lake Atitlan, over the Umbilicus of the Earth, over our village, over a culture, over a country which from that mechanically-driven height looked as it had always looked: green, peaceful, gorgeous and sunny, but which lay vulnerable and struggling between terror and hope.

My original sweetheart, the Tzutujil Earth, her people and the flowering body of her hills lay behind us now, Yalur's home, my love and my children's legacy fading as we went streaming, rushing and roaring over the line of Indigenous memory, into the mesmerizing land of unstoried tribelessness, the freedom to forget and the mores of the gray sky people; back to the land from where I'd once fled looking for life, love, home and a certain look in the eye of She who turned out to be what was Holy and Female in the Earth.

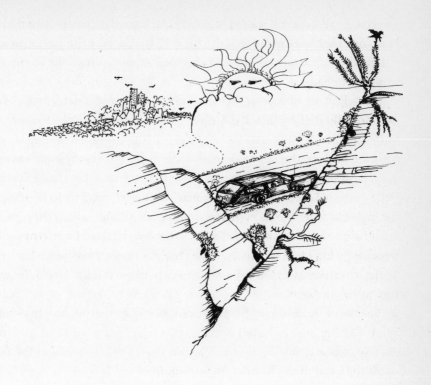

CROSSING THE LAST RAVINE: ESCAPE INTO THE LAND OF GREAT FORGETTING

There were only five lanes open and manned for business on the side marked "foreign" at the United States Immigration document inspection station in the Los Angeles, California airport, out of which five long lines of Hmong, Karen, Mru, Montanárd, Thai hill folk, Taiwanese, Vietnamese, Chinese, Zapotecs, Tarascans, one family of Cunas from Panama, Laotians, Cambodians, Thais, Indonesians, Japanese, Mexicans, Peruvians, Salvadoreños, Chilenos and Ecuadorans and who could say how many more for all the queues, save one, stretched beyond the vision, where for the most part entire families of every kind of people,

provenance and speech waited patiently like ourselves, bewildered and anxious, with their passports in hand hoping to get past the unsentimental-
looking officials seated in the cubicles, one of whom had our fate casually
sitting in his hand.

I watched the lines to see which one had the greater percentage of travelers actually getting into the United States. For at this place many were
refused; some simply turned away to get flights to somewhere else, others
deported back to the very land they were fleeing if on their papers something was missing that the officials wanted there, or if any doubt remained
in the entry officer's well-trained, square-cornered mind as to the "motives
and legitimacy" of the foreigner asking for entry, after which they could be
detained for months as their petitions were investigated. I watched the lines
very closely for I had to choose well. This was the last ravine we had to run
before we crossed the line, chased from where we'd left all we'd known, to
drop into America.

In four of the five booths, four tired, deeply resentful, bulldog-looking,
badge-wearing, white-shirted women sat, a couple of whom had turned several parties away.

At the head of the fourth line, second from the last on the right, a bald-
headed fellow sat, his head bobbing up and down like a wild turkey raking
pine needles searching for some seeds. While I'd been watching he hadn't
sent anybody away, but he did a lot of talking and his line was the longest,
for it was moving very slowly.

Lifting our belongings and our tired and weeping children, dressed in
rumpled polyester, sagging nylons and our shiny shoes, we pulled our family into the bald man's line.

Because of a whirling storm, the kind the Mayans call a one-foot-rain,
Huraqan, or hurricane, that was pummeling the coastal waters off southern
California, our plane had been initially rerouted mid-flight to land in El
Paso, but finally turned west again to land several hours later than sched-
uled in Los Angeles in a thrashing turbulence so violent that none of us
would want to fly again for ten years.

Though still staggering from being whipped around and scared, not
knowing what might happen when we were on solid ground, our buzzed and
shaken nerves were strangely eased by the unceremonious bellowing and
shoulder pushing of the immigration shepherds as they separated us like

calves from mother cows into distinct human herds of American and Other.

Then a little over an hour later, with more and more people piling up behind us, we gradually made our way forward until finally we were allowed to drag our frazzled souls and bodies to stand before this shiny-headed, fifty-year-old California white man.

After examining our passports he stamped myself and the boys right in with no other comment than, "You could've gotten in quicker on the other side, son."

But after opening up the sealed packet containing communication from the consul and Yalur's passport, he motioned at first up to a central overlooking room, waving her passport in the air. Receiving no response from what I'd supposed to be his hidden superior who was most likely swamped with problems from the other booths, our bald-headed man turned back to us and showed me the damaging phrase written by the American counsel in Guatemala inquiring why, "Mr. You-know-who," referring to the consul, had written cryptically that, "both entrance or visa extension strongly not recommended," when he'd already issued a visitor's visa to that effect.

I couldn't risk explaining the subtleties of our situation to this man who I assumed followed only bureaucratic guidelines, not even that the consul was a racist and hated mixed marriages. Neither could I explain that our entire life hung in the balance of what to this officer was just a tiny portion of his daily job, for in those times because the States, terrified of the "communist threat," officially backed the Guatemalan Government, anyone trying to flee that government was sent back as an enemy of the U.S. Thousands of Central Americans were destroyed trying to legally enter the States forcing the remainder to enter anywhere they could, where they were branded as illegal aliens, deported and lost that way as well.

So, remembering the Story and how every mother animal practices some deception to draw what would eat her young away from the nest or den, I had to fabricate a tale to save my family from being eaten.

"Mr. You-know-who, the consul and myself, we used to be pretty good friends, but one night at an embassy going-away party for one of the boys we knew in the marine security guard, the consul's wife," and I whispered, "who is not a happy woman," then resuming my normal tone, "that night a little drunker than usual, began to solicit my attentions in such an explicit manner, that the consul who was right there lost his stirrups and commenced quarreling with his wife, during which she, at the top of her lungs, went on to elucidate how much better a man I must be than him, thereby starting a feud of which this passport comment is the direct result!"

To test me against what was written in the package, I suppose, the baldheaded man now looking down, not wanting me to see his losing battle with a smile that was verging on a full-out chuckle, inquired further as to the officially documented reasons we were visiting the States.

"We are attending an exhibition of my art in Honolulu," replying as if there were nothing on my mind.

"Does your family have to come along just for an art show?"

"Sir, take one look at me and ask yourself if you'd be inspired to buy paintings for a lot of money from the likes of me. Now look at my beautiful family and see that my wife is a pure-blooded Tzutujil Mayan Indian, who can explain all the stories and meanings behind my paintings so that everyone can understand the real meanings behind what I illustrate."

This was a bucket of toad piss of course. Yalur in those times had little or no interest in my paintings as art and through no fault of her own she wasn't well-versed in many of the stories. Having been raised as a Christian according to the narrow mores set down by the Oklahoma Catholics and her proselytized father, whose insistence, like Padre's, had been that the old stories and their deep understandings were best left forgotten and the foreign bible put in their place, Yalur had learned most of anything she knew of the old stories from her proximity to myself and the traditionalists with whom I'd served to keep alive the stories.

But for her survival, today I had to gamble, taking the chance that this Immigration man, like most of the people from this land whose memory of their own indigenous origins in ancient Europe and other places was now the prisoner of a very compartmentalized and literal kind of thinking that grossly associated a person's color and race to signify their culture and that people's appearances and dress-styles somehow equated social status with ability and merit.

"Does this mean you actually earn a living in Central America painting pictures?"

"Yes, I do."

"And you sell your artwork in various art galleries throughout Europe,

Middle East, Central and North America, is that correct?"

"That is true and correct," I replied.

Then removing a bent, well-used, big, black, over-wide wallet from his hip pocket, he loosed a strip of accordioned photos of some of the homeliest and most garish acrylic painting I'd ever seen in my life.

Holding them up to me for my inspection he began to explain, "My wife is a painter too, and I think she's very talented. The problem we have is that ... and we live over here in Long Beach ... is that we can't seem to find the right gallery for her to sell her art. What do you think of them, Mr. Prechtel? That's my daughter with my wife there at the bottom."

Though Mr. Prechtel the painter didn't think he'd ever seen so much consistency in style when it came to honest and ugly, for every one of the thirty photos of the paintings was more horrible and unfortunate than the next, when he came to the pictures of the man's little daughter and smiling, chubby wife with white-blonde hair and thick glasses, he could see how much they all loved each other and Mr. Prechtel the man started liking the lady's paintings as much as he loved life.

"These paintings are amazing," I said, "they've got a strange rare style and a forceful presence," not lying any more.

"Listen. Do you think you might be able, I mean with all your obvious connections, to find my wife a gallery or some place she could show her paintings?"

To cause the survival of my family I had to lie again, "It's inexplicable to me why such a talented painter as your wife should have any problem finding a gallery to represent her art. Sure. No problem, I'd certainly give it all my attention, but I'd need more time here in the States. I think for sure a gallery in San Francisco that I show in called the Patrick Gallery would probably be delighted to find such a good new artist, which is what they specialize in ..."

The other officers standing in the back were none too happy with the bald-headed fellow's friendly banter with the clients while so many people were backed up behind us. Their limits were pushed when I started writing down his address, telephone number and so forth.

After handing each other the other's information, he opened Yalur's passport to the page with all the unhappy ramblings of the American consul in Guatemala, then leaned over and whispered, "How long would you really like to have?"

"How long can you give us?" I whispered back, not daring to breathe.

"How does a year sound?"

"Sounds like just enough time to find your wife a gallery."

And with that said and a little adjustment to the writing he loudly stamped, then with something else stamped again, closed the passports and with a wink handed me the lot and pointed us to U.S. customs.

While trying to thank him, dazed by our luck, we were forcefully pulled away by other officers until we were finally bounced into another big concrete hall full of grinding conveyer belts. A sea of people we didn't know but with whom we vaguely felt a kinship for having stood together for hours in those traumatic moments in the waiting lines, were now scurrying about, yelling and fishing their belongings off the moving belts.

It took us a long time to find ours, but we did once the room cleared out a bit, for ours were the huge pile of things tied up in Guatemalan cloths, now left in the middle of the hall. Loading the entire affair onto various little carts that kept going crooked, we were shuffled and herded again into another mass of long lines of the same people in different order now waiting their inspection by customs officials.

All the sacred items, my bundles from Chiv and inherited bundles of my own, contained many ancient things, some of them centuries and centuries old. They had always appeared to me, when opened up at their appointed time, inside the ritual atmosphere of the village, as a breathtaking array of Gods, time counters and deified healing tools, which when gathered together in their respective coverings each became greater and more meaningful than the sum of their parts, for every single being inside, grand in its own right, was the deified particle of the story made into a whole story by its combination into a single bundle of which I had more than one.

Every bundle was to us a living story, a heavy piece of cultural DNA, out of which we could sprout a people, like a seed that contained a tree, to whom we could speak as a whole being or to the smallness of its parts. Each contained an immensity and they were heavy, beautiful, dense and revered by all who'd been initiated and knew them for what they were.

We needed our stories, so we fed them as bundles. But, as magnificent as they were, mine were now refugees like us, refugee seeds buried and tied into the soft things that we owned and which were soon to be inspected.

The bundles, our clothing and all we'd brought had looked magnificent back in the village, but staring at them here stacked upon the trolley, what we owned looked ragged and poor, especially the bundles which were hidden tied up inside an old tattered *uq*, or wraparound skirt of Yalur's. Panicking, I untied the package to see if they were still there. Seeing how miniscule and unimpressive they looked lying there, I lifted one. I could barely do it and realized as I did that they were still just as heavy, just as full, just as meaningful as before, but here in the land of forgetting they too had shrunk in size, altered in shape, although they still contained the Story. The Story, having a spirit of its own, was a refugee like us simply trying to hide to keep its depth and meaning alive.

I was very much afraid they'd take my bundles away from me as they contained so many things that to the uninitiated eye were simply antiquities and illegal to import. But, when our turn came for inspection some fracas broke out a couple of lanes over. All the agents started running about, little dogs on leashes came in sniffing, crowds gathered and people yelled.

When our flustered inspector had returned to his post, without opening even one of our bags, he looked at us with utter disgust and sounding a little like John Wayne, he blurted out. "Is all this shit yours?"

"Yes." I sheepishly replied.

"Then get it the hell out of here, it's holding up the line!"

Then forcibly pushing our carts out of the way we took it from there, wheeling ourselves forward with Jorge piled on top, following the signs without looking back straight out of the airport on to the street, up that street, still pushing the carts, past that street on to another street and into the late November smog of Los Angeles; into the bumbling loudness of a million cars speeding overhead on what we didn't know was the freeway alongside of which our little family walked exhausted, unfed and with only seven unspendable Guatemalan quetzales to our name into the land of forgetting, machines, concrete and bald-headed angels with wives that did bad art.

We wheeled and walked, wheeled and walked, at first unable to stop ourselves, out of a euphoria for the freedom of endless voluntary forward motion, somehow tangibly moving our muscles in a way the airplane had not, away from being so confined and so afraid for so very long.

But the air was too dense and poisonous and burnt our lungs, and in our exhausted condition Yalur finally crumbled onto the concrete, hysterically weeping, unwilling to stir another tired step toward what now seemed to be just an infinite rumbling wasteland, not the promised freedom she may have imagined, but the horrible endless anonymous existence I'd feared all along. There was no one here who cared, no one to meet us, or miss us, nowhere to go, no one to help us start up again from nothing. Not even anyone to flee.

Cajoling her and coaxing, finally pulling her to her feet, half carrying her in her weeping, the children screaming, I pushed our stolen airport cart filled with what this world saw as shabby goods towards the hopes of whatever my wits could scrounge.

A dark man came strolling up and out of one of the million concrete bridges that we passed and I stopped him to ask where the nearest hotel might be from there. Following what he'd said we came fairly soon upon an old-time looking place, almost fancy and somewhat underworldly, but into which I immediately ducked, setting my blubbering, over-heated family into the stuffed chairs of the cool foyer. I booked the most expensive room on the highest floor for an entire week, changing shapes again, hoping my imperious, unapproachable, unquestioned importance as a foreign dignitary would make the clerk feel exalted enough to be the one we looked toward during our stay, convincing him not to demand prepayment so as not to appear gauche and unfeeling for charging us when we were so exhausted from our international travel, needing to eat and sleep for the night without any pesky obstacles like bills to keep us from it.

The children had already fallen sound asleep in our arms as we pushed our stolen carts into the elevator and went up and into our top floor room.

After ordering from room service the most expensive and extensive of variety of food I could imagine, we ate and then hit the beds like four different-sized bars of gold bullion dropped onto sixteen miles of cat-tail fluff, sleeping and snoring like hibernating skunks for over twenty hours, waking again only to eat, clean and feed the children, dropping off again to dream about home and wandering.

On the second day in the unpaid hotel, with my family still puffing and sighing in their well-earned sleep, I searched through all my bundles to see if their contents had arrived intact; intending to make a divination for some guidance in our predicament. I'd never dared to think what we would do if we survived this far into the Story so I had to ask the Deities of Time, the

Goddess of the Story, the Lords and Ladies of Hills and Valleys about what direction we could take.

Whilst rummaging through the carrying clothes which had been our luggage I came upon a package wrapped in brown paper, tape and string addressed to a PO Box in New York City with an identical return address. Attached to it, dangling by a tape, was a small unsigned note asking if we could mail the package once inside the States.

Taking my small deer-headed ceremonial knife out from my bundles I cut into the package, only to find a couple of pounds of densely packed dried marijuana buds thickly wrapped inside.

My bundles and the spirits in them had made themselves small and insignificant, charming the guards, allowing us to pass through relatively unscathed past the drug-sniffing dogs. If the authorities had found this substance in those times, we would have been imprisoned, my bundles confiscated, my children put in foster homes, the little we had left to us taken and destroyed. Someone had jeopardized our lives and though I could have probably sold the stuff to get some cash, I flushed it all down the commode, humiliated that someone would do such a thing.

With no time to waste on my own boiling rage I had to find a way to feed and house my family, which I was doing from room service at this time, food for which I could never pay, reckoning at that point it was best to maintain the strength of all our bodies, especially Yalur's, for Santiago was still at the breast. Our life had been so much hardship for over a year, so much fright and uncertainty during the recent months, that the fact they could sleep so deeply, much less at all in the constant mechanical roar of that automobile-addicted city was a grand and blessed medicine.

Though the ancient story speech of my divination bundle had never been exposed to the tangled context of the big city and so-called progressive modern life, my interpretation of what I discovered there led me to spend my waking hours of the next three days piling up an immense, unpaid phone bill by calling every person and entity I could conjure from my memory throughout the U.S. who might have the capacity to give us the gift of a month or two at their home to acclimatize ourselves at least a hair's worth and maybe loan us enough money to live on until I could get going with a job to feed my family again myself.

As a painter no one really knew me in the States, Americans had never been among the most avid supporters of my art and as far as I could see through this smog and metallic thunder my medicine man existence would soon disappear into the fog. These realizations had me searching frantically through my assorted talents and proclivities for something that I could be paid money to perform, hopefully obtaining enough also to afford the service of an immigration attorney to arrange Yalur's alien residency with the immigration department, knowing that could take years and lots of cash.

Most people, when I called them, were not at home, while other phones were answered by children who didn't know us. Some of those people who did answer, for none of them called back, were either uninterested or unbelieving of our plight, thinking that I was making it all up, that I was too lazy to work and was conning them like a street beggar. If they had written letters of recommendation for us in the past, how in the world could I ask them for even more assistance after they'd gone out of their way already?

Others did not want their lives interrupted by any hard news that might cause them to doubt the isolated bubble of suburban reality that kept them safe from places like Latin America, with which I'd had no business getting tied up in the first place. Still others wouldn't listen, worried that bad luck might be contagious.

A couple of people who should have been very close to us, in some kind of unspoken feeling of Protestant revenge, actually felt victorious, gloating for having known all along that one could not safely follow the things that one truly loved without failing and falling into disgrace, as I obviously had, implying as well, that they'd prefer not to be associated any longer with the likes of me for if someone wanted me dead, I must have done something to deserve it and if someone in the Government thought I was immoral then they must've known something to cause them to think it. Therefore I would have to suffer the consequences of my arrogant flaunting of the rules, bend my spirit to the yoke, and begin living a stable, unadventurous, mediocre life like them and no, they couldn't spare the cash.

Certain academics who'd been very friendly to us as they'd made their ethnographic surveys back in the village before the all-out war and who had always said to contact them if we needed any help, now changed their tune once we were out of Guatemala.

One ethnographer even denied that he knew me or anything about my situation when contacted by the State Department for a character reference while we were pressing for Yalur's visa. Other anthropologists, some of whom had actually earned their degrees from my information and guidance, having been given exposure to rituals of which they would not have been aware, much less allowed to witness, without my credentials in the village, now did not want to be bothered, for they had gotten what they wanted out of us. One of these fellows in particular lived nine months in Atitlan supported by a lucrative grant, when I'd been a leader in the village. He had needed my permission to secure entrance into various ceremonies, get his recorded gleanings translated and permission to pursue his grant work and writing unhindered, which I'd arranged and helped him in many other ways.

When I called him from the unpaid hotel room explaining our situation, he stated in an irritated tone that we could visit for one day if we must, but he didn't want any screaming children running around his place.

Izzy and Vera Winer were the very first people I'd wanted to find, but I had lost my papers with their numbers somewhere in the airport shuffle and telephone information had no record of them. So I called Vera's brother's shoe store in Guatemala City leaving a message with a worker for Salo Harshov, saying that I was hoping to see the Winers and that we were in a hotel in Los Angeles.

A prisoner in the hotel room, crushed, betrayed, more educated in life, older, exhausted and broke, I fell back to sleep with my little family. Later that night, when awakened by a rude knocking, I unlocked the door and it was slammed open by the ponderous force of Izzy Winer's belly, who burst into the room, his hands up in the air, wearing the same suit I'd seen him in several years before.

"How did you find us?" I yelled over Izzy's yelling as he pulled up on my ears.

"Meshugenah, you crazy boy. What do you mean by calling my shivistezing mazik of a brother-in-law all the way in Guatemala? He calls us yelling all the way back from there telling us you're practically in our house. Did Vera call every hotel in town or what? Are we here, or what? Are you here? Yes, you are here. What? Are you a rich guy now, living it up on room service? Where are the dancing girls anyway?"

Vera came in with what turned out to be their pale young son and started chatting with Yalur, admiring the babies, who continued to sleep, pee and eat.

Sitting in that stuffy room I related the whole story to Izzy, who of course interrupted, "Why can't you come to our house, visit us a while, bring your stuff with you? What do you think? You don't have to check out until you need to, right?"

When I explained to him about the hotel bill, telephone bill and room service bill I couldn't pay, Izzy jumped back, but paid it, charging it of course to me later on.

He piled us into his big, beloved Buick, whose floor crinkled when we sat for all the discarded Italian hard-candy wrappers carpeting the entire floor.

Izzy traveled with candy in all the pockets of what I'd thought was the same suit, but which turned out to be one of sixty of the same exact suit, all of their pockets filled with the hard candy that all three hundred pounds of him crunched on all day long.

"You like candy?" He'd sort of yell every ten minutes or so, forcibly shoving one into your hand no matter what the reply.

We were taken generously into their home somewhere in a mostly Jewish suburb of Orange County during the Jewish holiday of Chanukah. We drank wine, prayed, sang, ate challah and wearing a yarmulkah and talus, we were feasted and watched Izzy light the menorah candles, while speaking beautiful Hebrew words that Vera translated for us about spirit versus power and strength, religious freedom and the restoration of the temple.

Some of their Polish neighbors came over with a lot of little kids and they all gave gifts and played a little divination game called dreidel in which Yalur and I got somewhat more engrossed than the other adults.

Later on, while sitting all together in the front room of the Winers' heavily carpeted house, Izzy, one of his big legs dangling and sort of rocking over the arm of a stuffed chair asked me, "So, Martín, tell me, what are you wanting to do? You've left your country; you've left your home. Now what are you planning to do?"

And just as I was going to reply he continued, "I think the best thing for you is to find a house close by here and begin to paint again. My wife says you're a good painter; you could be a great painter. We could make you famous. We could sell them for you right here. Who knows, Jerry Lewis could be auctioning them on TV someday! What do you say?"

And before I'd said a word in response, or could ask him a question, nodding his head he began again, his outstretched right hand going up and down with his words, "So, what you're saying, Martín, is that it's money you need and it's money we should like to give you for paintings."

"But, Izzy, I haven't got any paintings anywhere right now, I'm totally washed up."

"What, do you think I'm a schnook? Of course you don't have any paintings, but we could buy some paintings that aren't painted yet."

"How many paintings are we talking about, how many would you like to buy?"

At this point Izzy and Vera started talking in Yiddish and then in Polish and then back to Yiddish, during which time Yalur and I discussed the question in Tzutujil, then in Spanish then back to Tzutujil, all four of us converging at the same time back into English where very calmly Vera stated, "Since we've already got a promise of ten paintings from you for the thousand and a half bucks we already sent you, we thought we could use thirty more. We'd be willing to give you three thousand bucks for invisible paintings which you would make visible within the next year, what do you say, Martín?"

One hundred and ten dollars a painting?! A year previous I'd been receiving as much as three thousand dollars a painting, but this was not a year before and Yalur and I had absolutely not one centavo over seven Guatemalan quetzales, about five American dollars, between us and three thousand dollars was three thousand dollars we didn't have, so we agreed.

Izzy took me into another room and handed me thirty one-hundred-dollar bills, which looked far too clean and completely boring compared to Guatemalan money.

Returning to the front room we sat down with our wives and family again while Izzy, straddling the arm of his chair, began again, "Now what are you going to do Martín? What are your plans?"

And again before I could answer, Izzy continued, "So, what you're saying, Martín, is that you need a Buick?"

"Actually Izzy, I was thinking of a Ford pick-up truck."

"A Ford? What are you, a Catholic? No, what you need is a Buick, not a three-thousand-dollar Buick, but a good nine-hundred-dollar Buick."

But now I was in trouble with Yalur. Like many Tzutujil girls of her generation, Yalur was an epileptic. The young Tzutujil man to whom she had originally been attracted and married, returned her to her parents after only a week together when he witnessed her first grand mal seizure.

Her next love was a more honorable youth, a well-liked, handsome boy who'd been a close friend of mine, through whom Yalur and I had first met. But after being hauled off by the baker's troops to fulfill a terrible stint in the Guatemalan army, he became so embittered by the beatings and shame heaped upon him there, that like many of his fellow soldiers he joined a guerrilla group to fight the army and was killed very early on.

Yalur then married me mostly for convenience and security, not because she loved me or thought that I was cute, which in the village was not considered by women to be a disgrace of any sort; but as a result her loyalty was to her mother's family and not to the one we'd make.

In her mind, by giving up the village, though staying there would most certainly have meant her death, she reasoned that her coming to the United States would have to somehow monetarily compensate her for her losses. The U.S. to her was only a place to obtain money and someday to go home rich. As far as she was concerned, as she let everybody know, if it were anything other than that, she might as well have died in her village.

But in all that she was no more to blame than I, for though I thought I loved her when we began, what I really did love in her turned out to be the village itself. By marrying her I was marrying the town. Which to the Tzutujil was not only considered alright, but was in fact accepted as a tolerable reality experienced by many Mayan couples for whom true love was never found.

So, even when the honeymoon was over and another month of tortured mismatched marriage had ground past, during which I'd been physically beaten, pushed away and given every sign that this girl had no real love for me, through the heartbreak of my sad attempt I was still quite happily married to the village whose people held me better than Yalur would ever want to. This is not to say that over the years we didn't learn to have some affection for each other, mostly through the mutual joy of our children, but by then it was fairly clear that both of us were in love with being married in the village, not with one another.

Now that our village had been taken from both of us and the home and love that village had given us was gone, this togetherness in a land that neither of us understood was a togetherness of survival, where we functioned as comrades in a war we hadn't signed up for, bonded more by our losses than our loves; more sister and brother than husband and wife.

Despite all that and though she couldn't know how very distinct I was from most any other American, to her single-focused thinking I was from the U.S and the responsible party for taking her far away from her town. No matter how heroic, persistent, correct, patient and loyal I had been in the village and during our escape, I was, to her, totally responsible for compensating her monetarily for that heartbreak, of which I myself was a victim.

For this reason Yalur considered any cash I brought in to be her own. When Izzy and Vera advanced me the three thousand dollars, Yalur thought she was well on her way to becoming a rich woman and wouldn't speak to me for a week for my even considering to spend, in one afternoon, a third of "her" money, which granted, in Central America would have been six years' wages, on a car which we'd never before needed.

Though I understood and identified with the craziness and frustration that did the driving in her heart, I also knew that we would have to leave overly expensive California, not only because our three thousand dollars would be gone inside a month, but because in the local newspapers there had been reports of political executions carried out by extensions of the same groups that had been hunting us in Guatemala. I also longed to see the wild, unpopulated land of my upbringing again, wondering if the people there would not seem more welcoming to me now that I was grown and returning with children of my own.

Given the notorious dearth of accessible public transport in the western United States, for us to leave the toxic ground and poisoned choking air of overcrowded southern California and drive to New Mexico to negotiate the life of its wide spaces we would need a car just to function.

For me, who like my grandfather was suspicious of machines, it would simply be a tool for our family's survival. To Yalur a car was just a toy that I was buying for myself that would deplete what she would always see as "her cash," her nest egg that she was preparing to take back to the village with or without me. But after a week of not being able to go from the suburbs anywhere without a car, she began to understand that in order for me to make money for her, she needed to own a car, so I could drive her where she wanted to go and transport myself to where I could earn cash for her.

All of this landed Izzy and myself in the used car lot of a retail Chrysler/Buick outlet somewhere in that screeching and rumbling pot of concrete, cars and people of southern California.

For Izzy, bargaining was a manly sport; a semi-bloodless form of verbal fencing that showed he was a man without having to own a gun and a truck with big tires.

Bargaining was to me an ancient Native American art form, something I'd grown up with on the Reservation, which had gestated into an involuntary neurosis while participating in the penny capitalist atmosphere of the Tzutujil market place.

Izzy's method started by kicking cars right away, not the tires, though he kicked those too, but the fenders, the grills and the doors, and he kept kicking the cars like a gigantic three-year-old, much to the chagrin of the salesmen who tried to maintain their California cool.

"You call this a car?" Izzy sprayed as he grappled a Buick wheel well and started rocking the whole car like an angry gorilla with his intractable three hundred pounds, threatening to pull it completely off its fasteners.

"Every car in here, sir, we are proud to sell, all of them are checked over by our factory mechanics."

Pulling even harder than before, until you could hear the metal buckling a bit, to which the salesman forcefully hurried Izzy away from his mission to wreck the car.

"Please don't do that sir, you're going to ruin this vehicle."

"How much is this car anyway?" I asked.

"Twenty-eight hundred dollars, that's a thousand below what it's worth."

"Twenty-eight hundred dollars?" Izzy roared as he took another swipe at the fender, "Look, the fender's getting ready to fall off."

Having trouble controlling his frustration the salesman almost yelled, "That's because you're pulling on it."

Flopping his sausage-like arms and heavy short-fingered hands pretty close to the salesman's face, Izzy yelled, "Hey, if I can pull the fender off, I don't want to buy it."

Losing his stirrups, the salesman snapped back a bit, "If you pull anything off, you'll have to pay to get it fixed."

"Wow," Izzy replied, still shaking his hands along with his words, "what a guy! His car is falling apart, we walk in here and he wants us to pay him to fix it. How would you like to fix my car? What a schnook." And before any-one could say a thing Izzy continued, "If I could pull off this fender, then I'd go sell it to buy this wreck for what it's worth, seven hundred and fifty dollars. Which is what we will give you in cash right here in the car lot, right this minute. What do you say?"

It was then my turn to work on the poor man, who after a spell was so worn out that another guy who thought he could do better was sent out to relieve him, but we sent him back for cover within five minutes, when the manager arrived, who sold us the car for nine-hundred and fifty dollars, just to get us out of the lot before he started losing anymore fenders, then offered me a job as what he called a "grinder" buying used cars for the lot, which I didn't accept because I was buying this car to get out of there.

The car was a big, long, eight-year-old green Buick stationwagon that got seven miles to a gallon going down hill, with automatic buttons for everything, most of which would cease to function within three days of my children's concerted fascination, while Yalur's mysterious and immediate adaptation to riding in the car had her constantly adjusting the windows, the air vents, the mirrors, the antenna and the seats, with sunglasses on looking like the queen of Thailand in a suburban limousine of which, of course, I was the driver.

Izzy was disgusted with me for giving them a penny over nine hundred dollars, but then after signing all the papers as I was paying, we all discovered that I didn't have a driver's license!

Izzy was ecstatic. It was illegal for me to drive the car without a license and for this he badgered the beleaguered car people into issuing two days of collision insurance and delivering the car straight to his house for free, all of which was worth the fifty dollars he'd been brooding over. Mighty contented now, Izzy started singing Wayne Newton songs as he drove me to the Department of Motor Vehicles, where they gave me the written driver's test in Spanish on account of my heavy accent.

The written test I passed one-hundred percent three times in a row in Spanish over the next week on account of I'd failed the driving test until the last try. I hadn't driven in over a decade and the laws had changed. Now, strange ideas like center aisle turn lanes had been installed and that, combined with the fact that having grown up in the open roads and dusty tracks of New Mexico in a reservation pick-up truck, I was in no way prepared for the fast, crowded freeways of angry Los Angeles drivers, where cars were the exoskeleton of these people, who like grumpy crustaceans on wheels zoomed around thinking everybody else should move out of the way, where no one could merge and everybody was oblivious to what the other "moron" was doing. But I finally obtained my license and was glad we were leaving.

After placing my newly acquired driver's license into my hand-knotted man's string bag from the village with all our passports, documents and money, I wound it tightly like a bundle itself and pushed it under the front seat. Once we loaded up all our old village belongings and what the children needed for the ride, Vera handed Yalur a big shopping bag filled with sandwiches, sodas, fruit and Izzy's Italian candy, while Izzy himself sat on the hood and rocked the car about to the delight of my boys. Repaying Izzy for the hotel from the remaining cash from the sale of thirty unpainted paintings, we then hugged them all goodbye.

With the bundle of the "Village Heart" in the back, my other bundle strapped to its side, my little boys buckled into the seat behind and Yalur in the passenger seat, we drove away from Izzy and Vera, the hotel, the airport, customs, the killers, the bald-headed Immigration angel and thirty million frantic people.

Lumbering over the Sierra we headed into the beautiful clean, wide, unpeopled December desert straight toward the land I'd once fled, but this time with my babies under my arms and the pieces of my broken heart bound in place with the strong cords of memories of a majestic and magical existence whose face I most probably would never again be allowed to see, but whose weight and work I would carry through the story.

NEVER LOOKING DOWN, NEVER LOOKING BACK: ON A BLUE HORSE RIDING IN AT DAWN

I f what we experienced thereafter was our personal version of The Toe Bone and the Tooth, contrary to what some might have thought, our life in the United States would not be a descent into the Underworld, but rather a crossing over into the village of great forgetting, a place whose every detail wanted us to forget what we still carried and what we had left behind. Our arrival in Albuquerque, New Mexico, was simply a friendlier, second stage in our efforts to remember who we were under the sovereignty of that amnesia.

Though only nine-hundred miles away from Los Angeles by car, it took us a year and a half to get to Albuquerque, after a year and a half of struggle and poverty living outside Phoenix, Arizona, where we had been required to remain by ordinance of the Immigration and Naturalization Service until we had successfully trudged through the swamp of bureaucratic obstacles involved in straightening out Yalur's American residency permit. On the very day we received the long-awaited document in the mail and were officially free to move about again, we resumed our initial easterly rush for northern New Mexico, hoping to find a good place to live away from the cities along one of the streams north of Santa Fe.

Though never considering Albuquerque as anything more than a place to make a turn north, much less stay and make a nest, we, like spawning fish trying to swim farther north on the Rio Grande, got trapped like so many others in the silty dam of New Mexico's economic reality, where richer people from other places had bought up all the land and raised the cost of living. We were forced to live at poverty level in Albuquerque for over a year, then again south of town out in the desert, after which in a later burst of better luck we actually did find a way to stay alive in the northern part of the state in a variety of living situations that ran anywhere from furnished holes in cliffs to teepees in the sand, a cabin in the alpine wilderness, old adobe houses, a ranch house under a windmill and, God help us all, a series of apartments in Santa Fe itself.

But before we'd drifted north to better days, only two years out of Guatemala we were still quite indigent, held in an Albuquerque poverty trance, where we shivered through the blowing winter waiting for summer in a poorer section of an Albuquerque barrio in a house whose walls were as thin as the machine made tortillas that we were now forced to eat.

The old leaky truck we owned by then I couldn't afford to run, so I walked two miles toward Old Town where on a side street off of Central I'd found a job as a silversmith in a tiny jewelry shop that paid me a percentage of what they sold of anything I'd worked on, which most often was not enough.

On my twice-daily strolls through the cold there and back I met a homeless man who became my friend, whose name was Delbert Pope. Like Malip Qoquix, he was also a "great rememberer," but he had his own majestic style.

A middle aged Navaho, a Vietnam War veteran, this Diné man from the Chuska Mountains was, to hear him talk, more metal and nylon than bone, but despite it all he lived the entire cold winter months, both day and night, above a steam grate outside a freezer warehouse close by what the city called an undeveloped lot, but which was actually an overgrown chili field left over from when the place had been a village and every house an adobe home and a family farm.

Delbert called the field his lawn and the curb over the grate his throne, which he shared with a loyal old couple, Irma and Donanciano. Indeed, to me Delbert Pope was a friendly king, my only real friend in those uncertain days. He was full of stories, and always talking, always in the midst of telling a different one to his old friends every time we met and I learned a lot of things.

Back in the late 1600s one of Delbert's ancestors had been brought to New Mexico with several others, holding a position just a peg above a slave. He was part of a family of eastern Guatemalan Mayans of the Chortí people who were indentured in some way to a Spanish family now making their way north in the entourage of a Catholic priest reassigned from Guatemala, who was bringing the Black Christ of spring-side Esquipulas, Guatemala from the Chortí homeland to reside in the spring-side chapel of Chimayo, New Mexico where he was now the parish curate. This very image of the Black Christ still presides there today. At least that's what Delbert said.

This was not so strange, as I'd met several people descended from Mayans, like the Xiu family of Isleta, who were now culturally Pueblo Indians, but who were descended from the famous Xiu royal family of Mayans from Yucatan at the onset of the Spanish interruption of their culture.

In Colonial days numerous Mayan servants had arrived with their owners or employers in New Mexico attached to different families, eventually marrying locally, some of whom contributed generously to the development of the legendary weaving style still carried on, called by the collectors the Rio Grande style. Delbert's single Mayan ancestor, on the other hand, was not involved so much in weaving as in the making of the wool, meaning that like so many Indians imported in those days from the plains or way down south, he was charged with tending his owner's flocks out in the wild New Mexico hills. He was a shepherd.

One day some of Delbert's other ancestors came riding down out of the Chama Valley to borrow some sheep without asking. They drove away the entire flock this ten-year-old boy was overseeing and took the little boy along.

The boy became a favorite in the clan, grew up, married a Navaho lady from another clan and ended up as a prominent and happy Navaho man with a large flock of Spanish *churro* sheep, to which he continued to add by stealing liberally from the people by whom he'd been stolen from his home village in eastern Guatemala.

For this reason Delbert's last name was Pope.

Pop in all Mayan dialects is the word for a mat woven from tule rushes, as they are still called and used today. The Mayans piled these cushiony reed mats on top of one another to make thrones for their kings, queens and hierarchy, which is why all words for their positions contain the word *Pop* or reed mat. Even today there is not a Mayan village in Guatemala, which does not contain a family with the last name of *Pop*. The Tzutujil called their king the *Tzutujilpop*.

When the Americans, who took over where the Spanish left off, brutally massacred and forced the Navahos to settle, they registered their names, writing them as they were pronounced. The soldiers wrote Delbert's great grandfather's last name as Pope.

Delbert Pope and his friends would have been a king with his court no matter what. His handsome, gentlemanly manner and his regal patience with his suffering old friends made it obvious to anyone with a heart or any vision that his was what human dignity should be.

Her crinkly, dirt-colored hair bobbing at her slightest movement, making the illusion that she was always busy doing something more than listening, old Irma Candelaria never left Delbert's side. Just as loyal, her husband, bald Donanciano Leyba, though his sight was failing, was never seen very far away from her. Delbert was married as well, to a woman they all called YaYa who for some reason was never there on the street with them.

Our family was considered then to be truly poor by the standards of the place, but because these three residents of the steam grate, who were so much poorer than ourselves, considered themselves wealthy and lucky to have the warm steam rising from under the ground, they made us feel like princes and queens, not only by comparison but by the way they treated our visits to their grate as royalty visiting royalty.

Because they were, for that entire fall, winter and spring, the closest thing to a village we had in those demoralizing, lonely city times, we missed

Delbert and his friends in the summer when they disappeared with no farewell.

It would not be until fifteen years later when my life was very different, a little more moneyed, more controversial, more frantic, not necessarily happier, that I would discover where Delbert Pope and his court would disappear to in the summer.

One morning, after six years had clattered by since Yalur and I had been divorced, six years since she'd gone back to Guatemala to her town, converting to become a staunch follower of the American evangelical Christians that now utterly permeated her overcrowded village, there remarrying and giving birth to another child, that I, after flying back from London from teaching conferences and doctoring the public, was driving back from the airport in Albuquerque headed to my tiny, half underground adobe house in the old Tlaxcalan section of Santa Fe, that I saw Delbert trying to hitch a ride north with his old friends and this time with his wife.

My knees were seriously torn and swollen from an accident in Dorset and I could barely drive, much less walk. Though the boys had stayed with me when their mother returned, they'd already grown and gone off their separate ways and there was no one now in the house to be my friend and the sight of old Delbert, YaYa, Irma and Donanciano was a happy thing to me.

Sitting up front with me, Delbert looked like he hadn't aged a bit; his wife YaYa, who was tall and strong looking with a skunk stripe through her hair, was traveling with a very wolfy-looking dog. Irma and Donanciano looked the same way every year.

After giving each other the same royal welcome, I asked them where I could take them.

"We're all going to Delbert's summer home in Santa Fe."

"You have a summer home, Delbert?"

"Ya. I do. I have a two million dollar summer home right off the plaza in Santa Fe, across from where old Benjamin Rael used to graze his hundred goats. Where the DeVargas Mall now stands. You remember, don't you?"

"Yes, I do, I used to buy the goat cheese his daughter always brought around in those galvanized buckets."

"Anyway, that's where I spend my summers, for the last two decades."

When we arrived at Delbert's summer home in Santa Fe, it looked pretty much like what most people would have called a strong-looking concrete bridge spanning a dry arroyo.

"One time," Delbert explained, pointing to the mall and obeying his nature to always answer questions with a tale, "Irma fought a mob of dogs at a dumpster for a pile of pretty fresh steaks from the grocery store across the street.

"Like all the times before, I gathered up an armload of cottonwood branches, driftwood and roots and built a good fire to make hot coals to roast our meat in the new black barbecue grill that the pharmacist across the way," Delbert continued, still pointing toward the mall, "who lets Donanciano have his glaucoma medicine for nothing, had given us as a gift, when he realized the four of us were living out under the bridge."

A group of concerned, well-off, southern Californians recently relocated to New Mexico who didn't like the looks of homeless Navahos cooking meat under bridges so close to their new neighborhood came down to investigate in their SUV. They called the authorities.

The firemen, Delbert said, were very friendly when they saw the comfortable family situation the four of them had under the bridge and simply suggested to Delbert, who was an expert with fire, to move the brazier out farther so as not to asphyxiate themselves. When YaYa and Delbert promised to keep a bucket of water on hand they all shook hands and left, as was normal human behavior.

The policeman who came an hour later, on the other hand, informed Delbert that he could not cook under the bridge and that he was going to arrest them for vagrancy, as they had no permanent residence. Undaunted, Delbert had explained, "You'd be quite right officer, in any other circumstance, but in this one you are mistaken. I've lived here permanently every summer for as long as this bridge has been here. If you ask any of the other officers or any one on the street they'll tell you this bridge is called Delbert's Bridge and as permanence goes, this concrete bridge is as permanent as anything you're living in, if I'm not mistaken. Listen, this is a two-million-dollar bridge and I live here, it's my home; it has excellent views, a convenient location, and best of all it's paid for, by you and the same taxpayers who pay your salary, for which all of us here are very thankful. So, this evening I'm grilling some steaks out here on my deck where the fire department suggested, which you my friend are welcome to share, we have plenty for all."

The policeman had been so charmed by Delbert's intelligent tone and the well-spoken truth about his two-million-dollar paid-for summer home, that the four of them had been left in peace every summer since and the bridge from then on was called Delbert's Summer Home.

After leaving my friends under the bridge, I had intended to go to my house and sleep but when I arrived where I lived, half inside the ground in a snug little adobe house buried deep against the northern side of a hill, my damaged knees buckled as I entered and I careened down the steep, sandstone stairway, rolling into my lair, tumbling like a bird shot from the sky, the tendons behind my knees loudly snapping and coming unhinged as I dropped hard, crumpled to the floor in terrible pain and weeping, unable to get to my feet.

Realizing, as I lay immobilized in that timeless hole into which I'd finally tripped and crashed, that I was utterly alone, I wondered why in all my wild and precious forty-six years, I'd never found one single sweetheart who truly loved me, let alone liked me or let me love her back. Everyone had left for good, no village, no wife, no real friends, the children were grown and far away, there was no one to pull me to my feet or weep for my defeat for so many years of struggle to feed my children and keep the Story alive: I wondered if this were not a sign of things coming to an end for me.

For this and what happened after, I found myself loading every truly precious thing I owned onto my horses and riding to an underwater shrine out in the canyons to make a final gift to She who throughout my entire life I had served.

Three weeks after my spill, when I was strong enough to get around on sticks, with my legs tied beneath the kneecaps to keep them on their stumps, I filled my old painted rawhide saddlebags with every crumb of jade I had, every ancient Mayan necklace, every pre-European ax head, every banner stone and statue; every block, bead, lip-plug, and ear spool; every crumb of blue jade, green jade, clear jade, black jade, stripped jade, white jade, along with gold, turquoise, silver and serpentine, all of which was packed onto my old golden gelding's back, and with myself dangerously mounting my blue-eyed, silver-bridled paint, we made our way past where humans frequent the mountains, up to a little creek that ran uninterrupted down a basaltic canyon before it disappeared back into the ground, upon which, two miles from its spring-fed beginnings, a little cliff of ryolite hung in the willows over a pool, under whose surface inside an underwater cave at the roots of the stone overhang was my shrine to the Deer Woman, Daughter of the Mountain and Grandmother Growth, the Water Woman, the village-skirted woman, the mother of the corn woman, the forgotten woman, the can't-be-put-together woman, the woman-whose-look-I'd-seen-in-a-horse's-eye-that-saved-my-life woman, the Holy Female whose dismembered body was the diversity of all matter in all things in every life form. Toward that shrine I dove placing every precious thing I owned as a gift inside her cave.

After falling down the stairs, when I'd been finally able, I asked my old loyal divination bundle what the prospects were for my life, to which the bundle said that I was finished and that I should continue working even harder to do as much teaching and "planting of the seed" of the understandings that were in the bundles so I could leave the earth with a large explosive echo that I would become upon my departing, thereby spiritually feeding all the world as much as possible even in my passing.

I was sitting and weeping for what was now the unlikelihood of my ever finding someone who really loved and liked me before I disappeared when, like a great gorgeous fish, a realization leapt out of a pool of unseen possibility drenching my self-pitying mind with the cold clear water of the obvious, for which I began to laugh and then to weep again for all that I was worth.

Thousands of Native Mayans, Native Americans, Africans, Asians, Europeans, Siberians, Islanders, North, Central, South Americans, people of every kind had been coming to me for two and a half decades with every sort of condition, heartbreak, quandary and disease, and I'd served them all as a shaman, diviner and doctor through the power given to me by my initiation and my knowledge of the stories. At least half of all the people of every culture who came to seek my audience were hoping to find love and for this I'd always led them to my underwater shrines to give offerings to ritually feed and sustain the Great Suffering Mother of Life whose wombs give birth to all things, including sweethearts.

But despite all that, I, myself, had never in my entire life once petitioned this same lost Goddess in the tale, to see if she might be able to send me one of her "daughters" for me to love.

I had prayed and made grand offerings to the Female Deities on behalf of everybody else while praying only to the Sun and male Gods on my own behalf. Now when my life was divined to be at an end, I thought to give every precious thing I had to the Woman of the Water whose tears of grief for our forgetting were the blood in all our veins, and though I'd never forgotten her, I had forgotten to ask for myself.

Dismounting, then unloading all my gifts, I disrobed entirely and sunk into the freezing spring, dropping one by one each chunk and carving of jade into her liquid, hoping to feed her just a little. Then I let my tears roll into her watery eye while praying, explaining how my life was over and how I'd been so dense as not to come to her earlier on when I might have had time to actually learn to love, for until now I'd loved what hadn't loved me and therefore was still a novice.

With only my head sitting on the water, reflecting itself beneath, the horses watched sadly at the edge and seemed to weep with me as the day began to melt away.

At Delbert's summer mansion an unknown runaway teenager from the suburbs, a hungry street boy, poked his head under the bridge, carefully walked in and sat down next to Delbert in hopes of being asked to share whatever it was that smelled so good that Delbert had cooked in the embers and was now just rescuing from the ashes.

"Do you hear what I hear, Delbert?" Irma said, startled, looking up toward the mud swallow's nests in the dark upper recesses of the bridge columns.

Staring straight into the embers Delbert responded, "Yes, I do. He's finally coming up, he's coming to the surface."

Then they all stared concertedly at the ground from where they sat, as if seeing through it into another world.

"His body is worn and tired from all the struggle; he's had to throw so much of what he has gathered over his shoulder to survive. He doesn't think he can make it any further."

"Look," YaYa pointed to the ground, "the little deaths are piling up on him, they've cut the tendons at his knees."

Gazing with his glazed blind eyes, Donanciano saw quite clearly what the rest of them were looking at, "Delbert, his divination told him he was finished and now he's throwing everything he prizes into the spring."

Delbert sighed.

Then Delbert spoke, "My daughter, my daughter, my little girl whose eyes are the holy water. He feeds his gathered jade to the world to keep her heart. He's bringing it to the surface. He's kept the 'Heart of the Village' under his arms and the babies on his lap; he gathered everything to put what he lost back together again, to put her back together again and now he must throw it all away to feed his death. But, he still has her heart after he gambled so many times with the Lords of Death. He still has her heart fast in his arms."

"It's like this every time, ain't it, honey?" Irma said.

Long-haired ancient YaYa, looking long and hurt as if thinking five thoughts at once, stroked a broken-winged hawk she'd found and healed. "Delbert, do you think we could speak and sing him back to life? Though he's got only a few crumbs of the village left, he didn't lose the Heart. Do you think we could tell him back to life?"

The teenager, still hungry, was baffled, but asked, "Are you talking about me?"

"We might be, honey, but right now we are not," Irma cryptically explained, "We are talking about an old friend of ours who has kept us alive. By telling our story over and over for all these years, he alone had kept us from falling into nothing. He feeds us with delicious words and ritual gifts, just like you want us to feed you." Thumping off the ashes, Delbert handed the boy a cooled baked yam.

"Ever since we were pushed out of our mountains, out of the wild natural earth, we are now forced to live in any form we can, now in the city streets, right under the noses of those who say we do not exist, inside the lives and bodies of homeless human beings, unwanted, thrown away, unseen and forgotten. But thanks to those that tell the Story, we are still here just waiting ..."

"Who are you guys anyway?" the yam-gulping boy impatiently blurted out, pointing mostly at Delbert.

"I'm Delbert Pope."

"You're a Pope?"

"No, I'm not a Pope. I'm a God; the God of the Mountain."

"Yeah right," the humored boy replied through yam-muffled laughing, for he understood now that they were all just good-natured, crazy street people, like so many others he had seen before.

Then mocking them a little and still trying to participate a bit, he continued, "If that's true, then I'm the king of Spain."

Delbert got up and shook the boy's hand, "It's good to meet you, your majesty," then with a stern look on his face he asked the boy in a serious tone, "Are you the one that sent Columbus?"

"Delbert," YaYa called him away from the boy, "we've got to begin now, for if he ends, we end, our story ends, and this amnesia will have won; we have got to tell his story as he has so often told our own. Let's speak him into life."

Adding three sticks to the fire and making some motions with his hands, Delbert cleared his throat and began the story of how they met Swordfighter, then the story of The Toe Bone and the Tooth, then Martín's days as a child, then his days as a man in Swordfighter's village, then the story of his leaving the village, the mountain, to come across the line into the great forgetting where he never totally forgot...

"The Buick that he and Izzy bargained for didn't hold up very long. The engine block was warped, seized up one sunset and turned cherry red in the middle of the Painted Desert. Everything under the hood began to melt; ball bearings shot out like machine gun bullets, bing, plop, blang.

"Afraid the car would soon burst entirely into flames, Martín pulled his family off a-ways out into the rolling desert hills, to finally rest sitting in a stunned row atop a long, stone log of petrified wood, watching their car fully die whose engine had become so white hot that from where they sat out in the dark they could see clean through the steel until it cooled.

"Three years later, again the family stood gazing from a dark night into a second fire that they had set themselves, before they made their next move into a small apartment in Santa Fe, away from the desert tents, teepees and tornado that had buried their chili patch in drifting sand.

"They had moved from the poor and smoggy streets of the city where we all knew them as friends to that place thirty miles south of town in the rolling sandy hills, where living on the ground again, a tiny bit like back in the village, they were happy off and on. Martín made bows and arrows as he'd always known how, with which he shot and taught his boys to hunt the jack rabbits and cottontails they had for their meat. They grew gardens in the sand like they'd done before in the city, gathered wild mulberries along the Rio Grande and sold Yalur's weaving in the flea markets of Albuquerque on the weekends for a little cash. At the end of their stay, just before once again they would be made unwelcome, on one of the those chilly nights getting towards autumn, a strong tornado wind blew several distant houses away, but mysteriously left their teepee intact, which became a sanctuary then for several local children whose parents had gone out on the town, leaving the young people fending for themselves.

"By dawn the winds that raged on afterwards would bury their gardens two feet deep in a horizontal storm of biting sand, bowing in their teepee under four-foot drifts, against which the family and their little friends huddled through the night under sheepskins, sleeping bags, dogs and cats, trying not to breathe the blowing sand.

"Martín, like the others, rode the crashing sound of the relentless wind against the tent walls into a sleep in which he dreamt, visited again by his deceased friend and teacher from Atitlan, Old Nicolas Chiviliu Tacaxoy.

"*In that world there were only forested mountains, where perched on cliffs or hidden in valleys, tiny indigenous villages of every possible tribe from every country were found throughout. Climbing in and up, walking down and around, over the ridges and into every single village Martín dreamt that he was doctoring every sick person on the entire earth.*

"*He shouldered his bundles and healing tools, carried in a white* Nebaj, *men's string bag, hauling their heavy weight over cliff and valley for so many years and in such tireless dedication that he finally wandered off to find a warm sandy cliff to lie down and sleep for years to revive from sheer exhaustion.*

"*In every village he passed and from every hut into which he said hello on his way to find a rest, the people of every tribe now warned him to be careful because a scary and dangerous crazy man had been seen lurking in the forests of the world. He was lame, they said and walked with a stick. They didn't want Martín to be ambushed in his unwary, fatigued state.*

"*He found the cliff overlooking the world that he had doctored, where he thought he might lay and just as he was getting to the ground he noticed off to his left that old Chiviliu's widow Ya Chep Ski´ and his orphaned step-son, named Chiviliu as well, were kneeling with their back to him at the edge of the cliff praying to the rising sun, raising billows of fragrant incense smoke.*

"*Too overly fatigued to even say hello, Martín stretched out to sleep involuntarily, face down into the cool yellow sand, his body so heavy that he sunk straight into the earth until from his head to his toes he was flush with the surface of the ground.*

"*Unable to move or lift his head so much as the width of a termite, not even to get a breath, he would have suffocated where he lay, if he hadn't heard the shuffling, thumpity, clacking resonance of what he knew must be the highly feared madman of the mountains making his way toward him with his cane and lame right leg.*

"Then he heard the terrible high-pitched squeal of the man whom he was sure would kill him given that he had no strength to escape or resist, not to mention he couldn't inhale, at which point the end of the madman's walking stick came ramming forcefully into the ground just shy of his immobilized ears and cheekbone, coming to rest just under the end of his nose, which was then rapidly withdrawn thereby creating a little tunnel into which air rushed into his lungs and allowed Martín to breathe.

"Then he felt someone lay their fingers in some specific formation upon his back, straddling his spine which resulted in a wave of sweet sleep-like sap that oozed and channeled through places he didn't even know he had as if his body was the earth itself and was changing from hard frozen winter into the thawing ice of spring.

"This revived him just enough to make him able to speak out of the ground, 'Who are you anyway?'

"Though nobody answered, the hands returned to his back filling him with such a surging wall of warmth and vigor that the strength of his body was renewed beyond its original capacity and his understandings were made wider and more ably retained than ever before.

"Martín lifted his head a bit and tried looking up and back, where he saw a tall white man in his thirties, of great sinew and force, glowering down at him with short chestnut colored hair, dark sunglasses and a leather sheepskin bomber jacket.

"Looking forward again if only for a second to raise himself up out of the sand, he yelled it louder as he grunted to his feet, 'Who are you anyway?' and with that the voice of Old Chiviliu trumpeted out echoing off the cliffs with his famous chiding phrase. 'Bauga´ at biv atet?' 'Were you ever a lively child?'

"This of course was Chiv and by then he'd turned himself to Nicholas Chiviliu at the age of sixty years and in so doing pulled a young Martín fully to his feet, tousled his head and walked him away from the yellow dust down the gentle slope of the opposite side to a powerful shrine from Martín's childhood imbedded up in the red earth of the Jemez Mountains.

"Having him undress, Old Chiv then covered his body in colored earths after which he spoke from his perch up on a boulder.

"'Look,' pointing down the hill a bit, 'you must recognize that there is the House of the Morning Star,' referring to a four-cornered kjitchpop Tzajpen ch´at, or bed of the Gods, as the Tzutujil people called the large impermanent log structure of the

kind which Martín had many times helped and later directed the construction on behalf of numerous public ceremonies.

"'It's under there I would have you sit while I talk to you about some things. In there, no one can see you, and I want you invisible while I teach.'

And then Old Chiv began:

"'Lá, jujun aii y co waviera co kiachijab. Psanen nyon atet nugan.

Ja ruman kin bijchiwa camic majun chic nket naxibej chwach naq'omaj, ja vinaq natijoj ja vinaq jiera. Ktnxima´ rukux awqan, Ktnxima´ rukux awga´. Atet nqetba chpam ja chouj xtuscara kdta. Nketsbej trij jun nim quej nim raxrij. Nau qaxan?'

"'Son,' Chiv said, 'each of us here in this other world have our rainboy champions to struggle on our behalf in the living world, on the Flowering Earth. As for me, it's you I've got and you who I depend on to remember what I once remembered, to keep alive what I once knew. That's why I tell you, don't let people of any kind scare you away from teaching, especially now. Don't be scared to begin doctoring the people who can use it. Now, it's finally time to start. Tie up your wrists; tie up your ankles, and with that armor you must charge in at dawn, as the seed of the Father Sun sprouts his ray, riding well upon a deep blue horse. Do you hear me?'

"Before Martín could respond, two middle-aged Navaho women dressed in t-shirts, tennis shoes, sunglasses and jeans with sacred shoulder purses covered in silver buttons criss-crossing their chests, came puffing up the hill carrying between them in their outstretched arms an aged shima, a beautiful white-haired grandmother dressed in burgundy-colored traditional velvet skirts and blouses, old-time rawhide bottom Navaho boots, the tops died with mountain mahogany, and a lot of silver and coral around her waist, neck, wrists and fingers.

"The poor old lady could not place so much as one small toe to the ground without the most excruciating pain rising up into her ailing body, all of which caused her to moan and gasp and sometimes cry out so that the entire world could feel its depth and would weep out loud in sympathy.

"The younger woman hailed Old Chiv as they struggled to where he sat. Martín, naked and invisible, continued to breathe shallowly, sitting silently beneath the House of the Morning Star hiding from the world.

"'We are searching for Martín,' the ladies explained, 'as the two of us here have healed every sick person from every village, tribe and family in the entire Mountain Earth, but nonetheless we have failed to help Old Grandma who says only Martín can fix her if it is even possible at all. Do you know where we can find him?'

"Old Chiviliu, who even in the dead state retained his inimitable form, praised the beauty of the old lady's clothing and the obvious power of what was inside the other women's bags and anything else he could think up while avoiding at all cost speaking about Martín.

"Martín on the other hand was in a silent rage because he felt the women were lying about healing the Mountain people, taking credit for his work as soon as he disappeared to rest, foolishly not recognizing that the women were the same holy females who used his person to heal the people, who now came carrying what he carried, the old Story; the ailing but beautiful Grandmother Story, that needed not only to be carried as he always had but made so she could walk again. Like Chiviliu said, he had to teach and tell the Story to give her life as he had given life to us.

"But as he dreamed, he retained his ignorance, trying to remain calm and stay invisible when just as Chiv was getting ready to give in to those women's smooth pestering persistence, a blue wolf came carefully into the House of the Morning Star and started licking Martín's face with a big slobbering, warm, rasping tongue.

"Though trying not to make any noise to maintain his unseen state, Martín dearly wanted to help the old woman while fighting off the persistent mother wolf who was licking him all over his body as if he were her little cub, by whose commotion he was finally seen by all and awoke in the same instant, nearly buried in cold sand an hour before dawn.

"Some might have thought that after their highly blessed and unlikely getaway from wartime Guatemala, that their lives of being pursued should have eased upon their entry into the United States, but in the interim between the two fires, the little family was hardly ever settled and could never feel at home.

"The self-interested and incomprehensible abstraction of the use of money in the modern world and the impersonal nature of the people who promoted their television-minded story-less, synthetic, tribeless lives as something normal, was such that to the little family trying to stay alive and fed, the drowning environment of poverty and self-hatred in which they were forced to wade, where emotionless people from companies, banks and other entities cited laws they couldn't understand, always threatening them with one punishment or the next, seemed so identical in intention and tone to being chased and threatened by killers and political assailants that the momentum previously established in Guatemala of being pursued and harassed and forced by that into hiding, only to flee in the night the land friendless and broke in what they hoped was a better place to start all over again, became an unhappy cyclic tradition that continued in the U.S. for three harrowing years. Then one day Martín realized he didn't have to flee just because some maladjusted person, feeling small, got a momentary sense of power from their sadistic elation at seeing how terrified refugees could run, when for the last time someone was going to confiscate his family's rent-free teepee, which was at that time their only home, along with their stove, trunks, clothing and the few belongings they had finally succeeded in gathering, thereby leaving them without a home or possessions, Martín loaded up what they could carry once again, keeping the bundles and the precious things the little boys and Yalur couldn't leave behind. Making a pile of all the rest, they burnt the entire mound to the ground, leaving his antagonists with the ashes while they moved on, living out the story.

"The only thing the family had to leave that the little kids especially missed was their loyal mother cat who'd been nowhere to be found the night they left to start again in the town of Santa Fe.

"But six months later in May, while gathering medicinal desert plants to supply himself for the huge influx of people who'd begun to seek his cures, Martín had occasion to be gathering immortal roots close to where they used to live and where they had burnt up all their things. Unable to resist just a little peek at the old desert spot, he cautiously drove close, then stealthily crawled into the land where he found right in the perimeters of where the teepee used to stand, on the flat charcoal-impregnated sand, the mother cat as skinny and drawn up as a dry salted fish but still alive, just barely, curled up exactly in what would have been her old accustomed spot where the little boys used to sleep, still waiting for them to come back home.

"The old cat lived another eight years and made a lot of little kittens who also slept with the children, until overly befuddled from eating too much of a powerful variety of catnip that grew in the luxurious piney mountains where they were living by then, the tough old cat took on a sixty-pound raccoon, thinking in her inebriated mind that it was just a giant vole, and was bitten through the neck and killed.

"In concerted evening lessons, over the previous struggling year, Yalur had learned to speak and write an American English and a more ample Spanish from Martín, whose love of music and old village insistence on beautiful speech ensured that every member of his penniless little family was fluent in a minimum of the three distinct languages of Tzutujil, Spanish and English, while the boys were playing musical instruments by the age of six.

"For her ability with spoken English in such a predominantly monolingual land, Yalur could now accept a job demonstrating village back-strap weaving in a well-known import store in the capital of the state, Santa Fe, New Mexico, moving then from the wide open desert into a tiny, cramped apartment to be nearby so she could walk to her employment.

"During Martín's years in Guatemala, Santa Fe had grown from a well-established tourist stop and a place for local New Mexican villagers and ranchers to get supplies into a sprawling, highly stratified live-in commercial center where people from everywhere but New Mexico competed viciously to sell stuff to others of the same who were living out television-fed suburban fantasies of pioneer life, or rich folk from Dallas, New York or Los Angeles.

"The local Spanish speakers now referred to Santa Fe as Fanta Se. It was a city of unhappy elitists and the people who served them, all of whom drove around scowling at the crowds that they themselves were part of, oblivious to the original culture of the town, which their arrival had all but driven underground.

"Santa Fe chewed up and spat out more layers of hopeful newcomers than it kept, but it was for some a good place to sell things, but for everyone it was a hard town in which to live. It was a city of hope and frowns.

"Though economically life was a little better and food a steady thing, culturally it was difficult for the family to keep the pain of remembering what they all hoped to return to, alive, with no one there who could possibly share the weight of remembering.

"Yalur was in no way interested in what Martín was trying to keep alive, for she hadn't been witness to its entirety from the onset. She would've liked to go home to her village, but didn't care about the Story.

"Trying so hard then, all along, to keep alive such a magical, elusive thing as the language and vision of the Story, but without the culture or any comprehending soul who could hear it, he could not himself be sustained and was, as Martín's Swiss grandfather used to say, like a man carrying a newborn calf up a stairway for a year: the man grew strong and got better at carrying the load, but with no one to share the burden, the cow grew bigger than the man's capacity to lift it and the man was thereby crushed. The Story, like the cow, would have to walk on its own.

"The enormous physical strain and crushing sadness in his heart for all that he'd endured, when coupled with the depleting effects of all the animosity and paranoia these non-village people heaped upon him for their inability to understand why he stood so straight, spoke so strongly and for his village avocation as a priest, a shaman and a man, not to mention the fact, like all old-time village men in lean times, Martín, the last four years in hiding and in the States, when eating together, for only together did Mayans eat, he'd left all the protein for the children, thereby weakening considerably his joints and bones during all those tense and stressful times, making it so he was as a man who had been swimming for years in from a shipwreck, still holding his babies, his bundles and a wife that maybe didn't really love him, a man whose exhausted war-time spirit, at the first intimations that they had reached a shore reasonably beyond the storm, finally collapsed to take a breath when his over-burdened, malnutritioned body then twisted around in excruciating and unrelenting pain, until his navel was under his armpit and he could no longer stand or sit to eat or pee.

"No doctors could seem to fathom it or fix him. Every healer, except one, made him worse. Acupuncturists were baffled, the surgeons wanted to cut some muscles to straighten him enough for him to sit in a wheelchair, but like the old lady in the dream, his feet couldn't touch the ground without the moaning and screaming pain that he always grunted out both day and night.

"At first sign of this, Yalur packed all her belongings, got the cash and prepared to leave in a tearful huff, for she hadn't followed this man to live in hell where he was too weak to maintain her. She did this off and on every time Martín succumbed to an illness, but uncertain how to get to the village or where she might go that was any better and always missing her children and maybe sometimes even Martín, she would usually return the following day and go about things as if nothing had ever happened.

"Not yet in school, his children, though scared and sad for their prone, unmoving and moaning father, tried to help him by cooking up some inventive kinds of food, for they, like all Mayan boys, were experts with fire at an early age. They boiled some awfully strong coffee and prepared at Martín's direction small infusions of plant medicine, carefully balancing the little cups of the hot liquid faithfully to where he lay.

"After nine months of constant pain, one pre-light, snowy dawn Martín awoke from a rare two-hour sleep with a deep dream still rushing in his veins in which a magic animal had breathed lightning into him and said that within a year he would revive with more ability than ever.

"Two days later, he read an article about an indigenous painter from Santiago Atitlan who was going to be in town for an exhibition of his paintings in a prominent museum.

"The killings had continued fiercely in Guatemala, including Atitlan, and with such heart-sinking frequency that it was hard to even want to know about them, for every day or two, word came of another friend, acquaintance or a relative who had been tortured, raped, blown up, shot or disappeared until the count was so high that no one could keep it straight.

"How was it then that this young Tzutujil man could so casually come to the States to sell paintings, while the little family had been forced to struggle for years in hiding and in poverty?

"A new president in Guatemala, put in power by the U.S., had made Evangelical Christianity basically the state religion, and this young painter was a staunch adherent of the same.

"The young artist, for the fact he was an evangelical Christian, was given full consideration by the U.S. Immigration authorities as well as the official channels of state-supported museums such that he could easily travel and sell his work in the U.S.

"Though billed as a painter of scenes of *costumbrismo*, or what the museum advertised as "obsolete traditions" from our village, what he painted that the public bought in quantity were ceremonies over which Martín had once presided and Yalur had always seen since a child. With no actual comprehension, love or belief for the subtle magic of his own ancestral legacy, the very things Martín had tried to keep alive, this boy and his Christian sponsors were declaring its death and selling relics of a so-called bygone age which by its very act they were hastening to destroy, while strangely claiming this to be an indigenous event.

"Even so, such hypocrisy and complication could not override the desire of both Martín and Yalur to see, after several years, anyone at all from the home village, even this man whom they'd known before, who didn't know the Story. Though what happened there for Martín was hard and unexpected, it was all part of the Story he had to carry and most likely saved his life.

"Martín and family were driven to the exhibition and Martín was carried in. When the artist, whose wine glass had already been emptied several times, finally found him they bantered around in slang Tzutujil, pretending to like each other, discussing their lives and what each of them had done, when out of the fog of niceties the young painter flew into an unsolicited fury in which he clearly bellowed out in an alcohol-induced tone of braggadocio, to Yalur and Martín alike, that he, the painter of the show, was now a member of the Guatemalan government-sponsored civil militia that patrolled the village streets, and should Martín so much as show his face ever again in the village he would personally place a well-spent bullet in his stupid tradition-supporting head. After which the artist screamed that Martín could never, ever, ever, ever, never, ever return to Guatemala to live or even visit his old village because now his Christians were in charge and he personally would ensure that Martín would not survive.

"Why he said what he said in such an uncharacteristic and emphatic, un-Mayan manner, but still in Mayan language, no one could divine.

"The effect this had on Martín Prechtel, our friend who gave us life through his keeping of our story, was a devastating breaking of the dams behind which welled the turgid, churning grief-waters of his distant remembering.

"When they returned to where they lived, our friend's body went electric with pain from heel to head and then he commenced to remember everything he'd ever loved and the immensity of the life and village he now believed was utterly lost to him.

"For years he'd waited and hoped, like all of them, for the time when he could come back home and now the truth of that impossibility was a finality that started shaking in his feet and rose past his knees, into his belly, heart and hands, until his entire body quaked with the eminent arrival of a distantly originated sound.

"A weeping of the kind that turns bear bristles into rain and iron into water, a weeping that makes mud of entire dusty deserts, a weeping that rose and flooded the world with so much grieving water that the man trembled and thrashed in a sorrow so deep and wide his body couldn't hold it, a sorrow for the remembered deaths of all his friends whose names he yelled, streaming all the losses through his convulsing sobs; weeping all the waters of his eyes that would only stop long enough for him to drink more water with which to weep more tears and not dry his kidneys into little nuts.

"Martín did not cry out of rage or out of longing to go home, but out of sheer grief for his acceptance, now, of that impossibility, knowing that the living village he had left was now a thing of scattered bones, a place whose people could not remember how to gather up or articulate the crumbs. It had been the hope that had been killing him inside, whose impossibility was now a horrible relief.

"To him he wept three-thousand years, which to the neighbors seemed to be three solid days, throughout which the hoarse, relentless honesty of his sad and gushing sound made all that heard weep right along.

"That was when Yalur began to cry as well. Huddled all together the little family shook and wept. It would be the last time Yalur and Martín would nearly love each other, as they wept for what they both had lost.

"Though that initial flood of tears did not actually subside in only three days, springing forth over the years in more modest spurts to keep the profound sadness and remembrance a liquid instead of a hard, heart-killing thing, those first three days melted most of the ice-frozen grief that had bound up the rivers of his struggling veins, joints and dreaming heart. And though his eyes were crusted over, swollen and hardly able to see for a few days, in the year that followed after he remembered what he'd lost, Martín the maker of wet spots of remembrance on the earth, Martín the story man, Martín the carrier of the village heart, began slowly to walk again.

"Dreams came thundering in like herds of wild peccaries, flying in like flocks of cranes chased by hungry eagles. Dreams, some with Chiv directing, others we ourselves, dreams that pushed his speaking heart to feverishly rehearse his original prayers and songs, while tangibly refurbishing his healing tools from the village.

"His grief expenditure became as a molting of feathers on a bird whose wings were now renewed in more mature colors, flying more ably and somewhat adapted to the rarified air of the modern world.

"Some twenty miles to the east, on a tiny mountain creek beneath a forested yellow cliff where a million cinnamon colored bears did drift and grunt and dig for bugs all summer, Martín moved his family once again on to the wild land.

"For whatever reasons, life being what life will be, without one word of self-promotion, people of every tribe, nation, age, gender and situation started mysteriously streaming in to see Martín for advice and cures in the forms of divination, medicinal plants and ritual.

"At first, mostly Navahos came from Ganado, Chinle, Church Rock, Shiprock, Mexican Hat, Breadsprings, Crown Point, Kayenta, Gallup, Tuba City, some of them were Hatali, or medicine men themselves.

"Then Tibetan Lamas came, Tibetan people came, Taiwanese came, other Mayans came, Japanese came, New Mexican Raza came, Minnesotans came, Coloradoans, New Zealanders and French people came, Huicholes came, Turkish Laz came, Mongols came, Germans came, Maoris came, Aboriginal Australians came, Hindus came, Yoruba people came, Ashkenazi came, Pittsburgh Jews came, New York Jews came in droves, Ibos came, Mandingo speakers came, Housa came, scarred Mauritanian Moors came, displaced Tuareg came, Sephardim came, southern Blacks and southern Whites came, island mother Voodoon mistresses came, Brazilians came, Cubans came, Carrier Indians came, Dog Rib and Tanaina came, Salish people came, northern Cheyenne and Arapaho came, Assineboine came, Taos Indians came, Tlingit came, Nootka came, more Navahos came, Pueblo Indians came, Polish people came, Russians came, Kazakhi's came, Finns came, Todaodham came, one Sami came, two half Samis came, Californians came, wounded people came, sick people came, emergency room doctors came, psychologists came, broken-hearted women came, broken-hearted children came, angry youth came, unhappy wealthy people came, poor people came, cowboys came, game wardens came, gay people came, bureaucrats came, soldiers, merchants, old Italian winemakers came, crazed people came, sightless people came, handicapped people came, Vietnam war veterans came, little children came, old people came, sick animals were brought in, horses, dogs, wild birds, turkeys, cats, a snake, lizards, a young tiger, a sick spider, all of them came, every kind and every shape of misery, illness, mental hardship, hatred, aberration, unhappiness or oppression came into Martín's mountain tents every day for years, as many as twelve groups a day.

"Every day around 4 A.M. the two boys, now six and eight years old, before they went to school on the yellow bus that hauled them out of their forest and streams into another local town, would get the fires going in the woodstoves for their father who, preparing all his ritual tools for the morning, did one strenuous curing ceremony a day from 5 A.M. to 1 P.M.

"The inexhaustible possibilities of what he did were determined at some previous time during the ritual divinations he carried out for the sick and lost, every afternoon from 2 P.M. until sundown.

"When Yalur discovered that, unlike the Navahos, Mayans, Cubans, Yaqui, Africans, Chinese, Hindus and most of the world's people, who unrequested, always gave what they could for Martín's service and usually more than she could ever wish for, the suburban and big city supplicants considered themselves smart and lucky for getting away without paying, but that they would willingly pay if confronted, Yalur in great delight began collecting money from the crowds in such quantities that it soon became possible for the family to have six painted teepees with carpets, electric light, radios, sofas, stoves, beds and so on, until they considered themselves, though still living flat on the ground, to be quite well-off.

"Yalur would even chase people, running them down on foot over the forest road, throwing rocks and blocking in their cars with saplings if they refused or neglected to pay what she demanded. She would not allow anyone but herself to take, handle and hide the cash, which she squirreled away in jars, cans and woven Guatemalan wallets in places no one ever knew besides Yalur. Martín, who was terrified of her notorious rages and fits, had to petition the money he'd earned to purchase anything they might need, hoping she'd see the wisdom of it and not begin one of her tantrums that could last up to six hours of all-out vengeful screaming frenzy.

"But her tyranny took on a wider scope when her now very persuasive negotiating power convinced the regional phone company that her teepees were not like any other and should therefore be considered truly permanent structures, after which they were only too obliging to lay a mile of new cable free of charge to hitch up her private telephone.

"A village is not a pyramid with some lonely king on top, nor is it a flat horizontal mishmash where everyone is equal and therefore nothing. A village is made of beautiful failures and the fruit of the daily struggle, and though rooted in ancient story, its people's enduring beauty feeds an entangled spiritual immensity beyond the wants and needs of people.

"The particular brand of loneliness the village loss was for Yalur and Martín during their new stateside life, though ostensibly much relieved now that hundreds, and in some years over a thousand individuals came in to be healed, giving them some modicum of attention, honor and company beyond what either of them could provide the other, could in no way be construed to be what they had known as a tribe or village. Unfortunately it was a confusion that everybody fed.

"The American friends that Yalur incessantly now spoke to on the phone, because they were invisible as she talked, and spoke back like spirits from that same invisibility, became in her imagination a substitute village, an invisible town by whom she was quickly anointed as its unquestioned, witty and temperamental queen.

"Because of her history of grand mal epilepsy, which now, because of Martín's cures, only surfaced as cyclic rages, Yalur was still not allowed by law to drive an automobile. For this reason, in the beginning of Yalur's telephone era, those of her subjects whom she rang in town, in Santa Fe, were more than delighted to serve the requests of their new-found leader when asked to bring her little items she might need out in the hills, in the event they came by to visit.

"Not so gradually as one might imagine, this custom of polite petitions gestated into strong suggestions and then finally full-blown sovereign demands, to the point where no one could casually visit without calling first to determine what she desired.

"This was designed by Yalur the queen to teach the non-indigenous public the well-established village custom of visitors bringing little gifts, which of course had never been requested, but when she discovered it could be done successfully and just how far she could get, she extended her policy of material demands to the incoming clients as well, until nobody, including the sick and wounded who were already handing her their cash, was allowed to visit Martín in any capacity unless they passed first by her and were cradling at least a couple of frozen chickens and a dozen roses in a vase, which then incremented quickly to include bolts of velvet, radios, vacuum cleaners, blenders and the like, which they handed over graciously to the queen who then maintained a sweet demeanor as they further paid to see Martín, who was now beginning to feel like an enslaved court magician.

"It was another expansion of Yalur's vendetta to make the world pay for her injuries, confusing the personal losses she'd experienced as a girl and woman in the village with those she suffered by losing the village. She had wanted compensation, demanded it and received it, but it all backfired in a strange unexpected way.

"For the most part Americans were the descendants of a multitude of peoples, tribes and nations who had lost or fled their original homelands, usually losing in the process their languages, their stories, their food, their songs, their etiquette, their clothing styles and their identities, all of which made these first immigrants feel alone and powerless. The possession of money became one of the prime tools that all displaced people could use to gain a feeling of power in such a villageless society where little else was ultimately respected. But the hollow place of their loneliness and lost identities were never filled by the percentage of people that finally achieved a full bank account.

"The generations that followed of what could now be called Americans, though distant from their ancestral losses, still carried that emptiness, but never lost the habit of thinking money made them valuable.

"Thus, accustomed to paying for everything they had, assuming as well that by paying they could obtain anything they wanted, they needed money, like soldiers needed guns, to equalize their power by its possession, money which did not reflect the possessors' abilities, strength or experience and which in the end did nothing but anesthetize the rancoring desire for home, village and a spiritual purpose.

"Underestimating the insatiable and vacuous hunger in the amnesia in which they were ensconced, that desired the same feeling of belonging, tribe and village that the presence of Martín, Yalur and their young sons, who kept the eagles off the ducks, fed the horses, sang village songs, spoke their language and still followed their parents everywhere, momentarily provided to the lonely hordes that wandered in, it was implied in the minds of these hungry suburban exiles that with their demanded "gifts," they were paying to be received into the courteous arms and graces of what to them was the regal bearing and village intactness of Martín and Yalur's family camp out in the woods. When that habit was established by Yalur's exuberant demands, those with money came and went in droves, inundating the place, fantasizing that they were the children of this four-person village.

"Because of this, the telephone, Yalur's taxing and the times, Martín's clientele began to shift until it consisted of mostly unhappy, wealthy yuppie men and modern women who held Yalur to be a wise indigenous mother and Martín the subject of a combination of confused desires; some hungry for a man to love vicariously just through proximity, others wanted him to be their father, or maybe a brother and sometimes even hoping to be him, for his relentless service to the wild, Holy Female in the Earth, Water and the Story, which he still carried close, none of which they could see, but they could smell and sense from the look upon his face.

"The people's desire for a village did not equal their ability to understand what that might mean and their desire never equaled love and in the end, their desire which was born of the very hunger whose politics had killed the village in the first place, their ancestors and everyone else's, now ate up again what they were hungry for. Instead of becoming the thing they were looking for, learning like villagers how to suffer beautifully and cultivate life, they amplified their unframed tribeless appetites, leaving everyone hungry, including Yalur and Martín.

"It cannot be said that Martín and Yalur were not trying as well to somehow reassemble the village they had lost, with the bits they had retained. It cannot be said that Martín was not trying to bring back alive, in some new kind of way, a complete village from the understandings, rituals and the clear love he had in the mountains for the same Holy Female, my daughter, the daughter of Grandmother Growth and the Mountain, trying as Chiv had said to regrow in the soil of modern America, whose exported legacy had been the cause of village loss worldwide, a new version of the village whose fruit might hold seeds that could be regrown again in Atitlan when their loss was finally as complete as in the States.

"But the sum of these pieces of desire did not equal the worth of the missing heart, for a village built from desire with a skeleton of memories of only losses, without a living indigenous heart that flowers, innovates, imagines, weeps, laughs and loves, becomes only a devouring monster with a hunger greater than the sum of its parts."

Delbert, the Mountain God, stood up, pulled up his jeans, put three more cottonwood sticks onto the embers and fanned them into flames.

Then he began again.

"When the war eased up a little in Santiago Atitlan following the massacre of December 1991, after which the permanently stationed Guatemalan army had been officially removed out of the town, its people were so utterly changed and the spiritual life of the village he had known had become so completely refugeed, like a tiny forgotten fish hiding beneath a rock of bitter memories, that Martín could not do more than visit, without living every day in a teary bog of waiting for what could never be again, and continued to reside in the States with his two teenage sons.

"Yalur, on the other hand, had always intended to return to the village, to make up and to live back with her only moderately elated kin. After a lot of turbulent squabbling with Martín, heartrending sobs and months of noisy back and forth, all of which appeared to her subjects like marital strife, Yalur finally dug up her hidden money and returned alone to Atitlan.

"Her abandoned subjects, those who had thought that sitting at the couple's feet in their living room somehow made a village, wanted their money's worth and accustomed in their talk show-indoctrinated minds to sacrificing their leaders to their own inadequacies and losses, leaders they themselves had pedestaled, instead of seeing that their feeling of loss was itself a sacrifice of grief to what is holy in life, which had already given them so much, now felt betrayed by Martín who they held totally responsible for the break up of a village they never had and proceeded to punish him in a heartless way beyond the proportion of his supposed crime.

"If Yalur had always been heading for home, Martín had always been heading for life, toward the heart of She in whose eyes he'd once seen the Holy and finally found a home only to lose it again. It was this heart of Life for which he was now forced to gamble against the judgmental tide of this embittered and outraged segment of the population's ability to comprehend what he was still clutching to his chest.

"He would be chased, not by big deaths, for they are noble, but by little dishonorable deaths, who this time weren't soldiers, hit-men or guerrillas, but those same insatiable, otherwise reasonable-appearing individuals who had claimed to be his 'new village' in the States.

"These people were strongly determined through their well-organized, thorough and concerted program of creative slander that Martín would never heal another soul or make another penny, hoping by their efforts that not one crumb of his former respected position, or any of the possessions his family had accrued by then, should remain.

"A very detailed gnashing of unforgiving and resentful teeth carried out by a certain more zealous clique of this heartless village took the form of a series of harassments of a bizarre character and dimension, designed to stop Martín's movement away from them in his now constant pursuit of life, hoping he'd look back and get mortally entangled in the petty hatreds of these well-funded and persistent servants of deaths' hunger that pursued him snapping their jaws behind his back.

"Martín the jumper of walls, the racer with my daughter's heart clutched to his chest, the thief of Benefacio's roses, Martín, having been chased repeatedly in the past in the cause of what he loved, knew all too well by now that loss is the root of the tooth of gain, set in the hungry jaws of what chases humans through their lives and that there was no shame in loss nor pride in gain that was as important as what life-giving thing you did with what you are left when that tooth has gnawed off from your life what it can grab.

"Remembering from the Story that one did not burn or spend one's memories of what had been loved in order to move toward life and away from death, but rather after wrestling death with the beauty of one's creations, learned from gathering up the bones of one's losses, that one should spend the bones of gathered losses and grief, thereby retaining the wild hope, the spiritual knowledge and the eloquent behavior of a person who now knows how to gather such bones, then as the bones were spent, the memories were retained, and the living heart one earns in that diligent endeavor, is then taken toward life.

"But the Story also said that he should never look back at the little deaths devouring the material bones of all his losses and that he should not let go of what he loved and the Heart of Life no matter how maddening and hard the biting from the back did get, always moving along toward that little hole in the underworld sky, out of which the heart he held, like a seed, would sprout him into life like the Sun sprouts into day, or die trying because otherwise one's life would be just an endless shouldering of resentments about the losses.

"So he remembered that he shouldn't look down and he shouldn't look back, as he clutched to his chest the heart of what he loved as he moved forward toward the light.

"So when the electric lines to his house were cut and his water pipes were sawn through,
He didn't look down,
And he didn't look back,
And he kept the heart of Her held close as he moved away from death's little bites, forward into life.

"And when every single client abandoned him, cutting off his income with which to feed his boys and someone stole his refrigerator,
He didn't look down,
And he didn't look back,
And he kept the heart clutched to his chest, moving forward into life.

"And when because of this he was forced to sell all but five of their forty beloved, many-colored horses to have enough food to eat,
He didn't look down,
He didn't look back,
But just kept loving what he loved and kept moving toward more life.

"And as they were being paid for all the horses that were leaving, all the windows in their house were being smashed and every one of his magic-filled trunks and boxes, rare fans and feathers, hides, knives and several extravagant-looking minor bundles with a lot of sacred equipment were stolen,
He didn't look down,
And he didn't look back,
But dug up his real bundles where they'd been safely hidden and kept them clutched close to his chest and kept moving toward life.

"And when immediately after that their two loyal wolf dogs and their friendly wooly malamute were murdered and a three-year-old bay gelding named in Tzutujil *Chay 'Snic*, or Obsidian Ant, lay killed by a malicious injection of chlorine bleach in the neck, a fast, beautiful horse that had just been put under saddle and was intended as a gift to the eldest boy,
He didn't look down,
He didn't look back,
He skinned the horse, made a drum out of his hide and a drum stick of his tail and began to sing and weep, as always, swearing to the fast little horse's windy soul that he'd always ride him toward life like a little unforgotten horse of song.

"And before the hide could dry, when his remaining dogs and two remaining horses, a strawberry roan and a line back dun, were stolen, leaving them now with only two geldings and a herd stallion with no herd,

He didn't look down,

He didn't look back,

But clutched the heart of Her whose eyes had pulled him here and kept moving straight into life.

"And the night he was shot at in the dark and a thief took his three silver-covered saddles of which he'd crafted every particle himself,

He didn't look down,

He didn't look back,

But clutching the heart of his love tight,

Kept moving toward the light.

"When not a single friend remained, no one who would wave or say hello, and to save his boys and three remaining horses he moved to another state where a year before he'd been well-received and repeatedly petitioned to return;

He didn't look down,

He didn't look back,

But just kept moving forward toward life.

"And upon their arrival to this new area when they discovered that the defamation squad had already been there and no one would hire him for anything whatsoever, so he and the boys could eat;

He didn't look down,

He didn't look back,

But clutching the heart of what he knew

Kept moving toward life.

"And when they had only illegally-gotten deer meat dried and stewed with pinto beans to eat for weeks on end,

He didn't look down,

He didn't look back,

Just kept tightly to his chest what he believed and kept walking into life.

"And when the dust had settled and the world thought they'd been ground to dust and they were still standing,

He didn't look down,

He didn't look back,

But just kept moving into life.

"And when a white-haired poet from a northern state who'd been a former client, but who he hadn't seen for years invited Martín to teach a bit in a conference, well-paid, in front of two-hundred white men he didn't know,

He didn't look down,

And he didn't look back,

And finding more goodness than he expected

Continued moving toward life.

"And when, as a result of that, within three years he was teaching twenty conferences for men and women a year and could finally feed his boys,

He didn't look down,

And he didn't look back,

But kept clutching to his chest the heart of Her, for whom he moved toward life.

"And returning unannounced to live in a little adobe hole in Santa Fe, his children each gone their way, Martín, who now told the story of the Toe Bone and the Tooth during fifty conferences worldwide a year, still,

Didn't look down,

And didn't look back,

But just kept carrying that story and her heart as he continued moving into life.

"When after several years of teaching and traveling so intense that he came home less than three months of the year, on his third visit to England where he found himself in Dorset sprinting up a grassy hill with a mob of Irishmen, English fellows, Welshmen and Scots chased by fifty desire-crazed, lady milk cows who'd been dazzled by a very secret and holy sound which Martín had taught the boys, who'd misbehaved and dishonored the oath they'd sworn to never utter the sound outside a ritual context, but which they'd blurted out in a hazel thicket whilst cutting switches with a terrified Martín, thereby causing, in their disbelief, every female animal for two miles about to come crashing wildly toward the sound looking mighty hopeful, all of which caused the men to pile up on the fence stiles scrambling to get across during which Martín's knees were damaged and snapped, causing him to walk with a carved hazel stick and still,

He didn't look down,

And he didn't look back,
But kept moving into life.

"Then on the following night after being driven back to London through the murky damp of a December drizzle, for having previously agreed to do so, Martín hobbled with his hazel cane, tired and hurting through slippery catwalks, over cold steel girders and scabbing irons, down scaffolding and into the soon-to-be paved, ghost-filled muck of an expansive, unlit, underground chamber that echoed as he sloshed through its muddy puddles toward a meeting in the center of this hollow place, over which a magical and hopeful structure, a kind of rebuilt temple of spoken English, where words like an ancient breed of horses of every color, height, bone and speed could be stabled and kept alive and let out to walk, run, balk or buck, change and even with dignity die, but never lost and always fed, and on occasions, even added to, a place of spoken plays called Shakespeare's Globe Theatre would soon be raised, for which Martín, in his capacity as a diviner and a spirit lawyer had been called in to assist the directors in disentangling the spiritual sources of an ongoing string of identical accidents plaguing the construction which hadn't responded to the approaches they had tried.

"Though what Martín suggested took some months to carry out, when it was effected the state of affairs was much alleviated.

"When asked what he should like as compensation for his efforts, expertise, prayers and time, Martín responded that the only thing he wanted was to sit with the Queen on opening night, during the presentation of the first play when the theatre was dedicated, so as to be present to bless the theatre properly in the way Old Chiv had taught him and for which he was now himself well-known.

"Everyone laughed a lot and thought that he must be joking, for the likelihood of such a thing ever happening would be less than impossible to arrange. When further pressed for a more reasonable and serious reply, he explained that since there were so many ghosts whose centuries-old grief and bitterness still resided in the mud beneath the stage and indeed the entire town, their historical unhappiness could be mollified and healed by the sight of an indigenous, earth-oriented person blessing the theatre seated with the Queen, who could both be blessed in turn by the magic of Shakespeare.

"Ghosts, Martín continued to explain, could bring a people down, accounting for all the wars, and when left unregarded and unfed, devour people's imagination. The stage and the efforts of all actors throughout time worked like a spiritual engine whose imaginative outpourings fed the ghosts beneath them that the rest of the world created, left behind and forgot. The artists' imaginations kept the nation's ghosts from eating the people and maintained the culture despite itself.

"Martín, when assured that no one with the wherewithal to make his sitting with the Queen a reality could even imagine such a preposterous event, Martín went on to say he was quite satisfied to simply donate his time to assist with the little that he could, to help the artists maintain their imaginations and love of beautiful, ghost-healing speech as represented in the old plays, against the cultural amnesia of the times. Then limping off to his waiting airplane,

He didn't look down,

He didn't look back,

And though during the strain of too much work, little deaths found ways to cut hard at his knees,

He kept beating life's rhythm out with the little horse tail on the little horsehide drum, singing the stories and the songs that kept us alive and speaking while he clutched the heart of our daughter to his chest,

And continued moving into life.

"And returning from his fourth English visit still limping from his injury from the cows, he picked us up thumbing north and delivered us to our Santa Fe bridge after which he tumbled hard, down the stony stairs to the bottom of his lair, onto his back. There, after so many years of struggle forward toward the little hole of day, life and the hope of understanding hands reaching toward him, having already spent most of the pieces of what he'd gathered and the little he still had from the village, all to keep ourselves, the God of Mountain, Stone, Fire, the stories, Grandmother Growth, the Heart of Life and himself alive, he now stared out of his fatigue, wondering why it was he'd been forced to live his entire life loving the heart he carried without having its love to hold, without the one and only person whose own heart though separate and all her own, could fit perfectly on the now empty throne of the kingdom of his life.

"When, for all of this, he inquired of the deities within his divination bundle, who we Gods know so well as the two hundred sixty separate deities of cyclic Time who articulate together as pin-bones in the great scaly fish of Life's movement through the liquid matrix of Now, he was told by them in no uncertain terms that Martín's days of lonely heart carrying were soon over and his struggles to remake the village of his heart and his struggles to keep our story alive were almost over, all of which this forty-six-year-old half-blood, lover of the heart and singer of the Story interpreted to mean what the exhaustion in his bones seemed to say, that his life would soon be done.

"But done does not always mean dead; it sometimes means cooked, or mature, or ready.

"He wept to think how he had never had a sweetheart he could kiss, to listen to and to talk with, to search and marvel together at the smallest miracle of the ground and air, to see the caddis fly hatch rising from the streams, watching raccoons scared of growling desert frogs. Though surrounded in his public work with admirers and people by the droves, he'd always been alone in their midst and wept again to think how he should leave this time around without ever having known that kind of earthly height. But then he accepted the hard truth of it and,
He didn't look down,
He didn't look back,
Always singing and speaking the story, holding
Its heart close to his chest and
Kept moving into life.

"And in this, and particularly now, still maintaining the village customs and spiritual principles with which he'd always lived and been imbued, within which humans are not on this earth for their own sake, understanding that Nature is big and holy and can not ultimately be successfully plundered without the plunderers being consumed, nor can Nature be imitated without Her permission, where humans have to feel the grief of the awareness of the strangeness of such acts, Martín gathered together all his remaining precious items, natural treasures altered by human hands, carved and polished jades and gold and gave them with a delicious word offering to Our Daughter's heart as a final gift to the Story he'd lived out and to what he'd always carried.

"In a turnaround that often affects the courageous and good hearted, Martín had in the past often prayed to Our Daughter, the Goddess of the

Water and the Possibility of Life, on behalf of the crowds of suffering people that he now served, but though he caringly protected and fed Her Heart with rituals, feasts, delicious words and the telling of Her tale, he never had asked the Heart, the Mother of Life, for anything himself.

"So, comprehending that though Our Daughter, the Mother of Life, lives dismembered, distributed in all living things, she was most easily approached by him in the clear pools of unpeopled mountains, where like the wide eyes of deer and the loyal gaze of an untiring mare, they were the watery eyes of earth, of Her, to whom he now beseeched, asking her for the first time in his life to make a gift of one of her daughters, a living human being to have and hold before he was finished with his life, for which effect, he settled into the pool and left his gifts inside, his weeping head floating on top of the water where his tears rained into his reflection and
He didn't look down,
He didn't look back,
Coming up to the surface of his life."

Delbert sighed, and put his breath into his hands, "That's when we heard the weeping of his voice and the sound of jade filling up our daughter's heart."

And Irma spoke, "It's like this every time, isn't it, honey?"

"That's true, Irma, like this every time," Donanciano agreed.

"He is still praying to us for life, still floating in that pool, as we, having been fed and kept alive by his losses, his storytelling and his jade, have continued remembering him alive," said tall, skunk-haired YaYa, who, misty-eyed, kept on speaking.

"We are alive and talking because of that lonely man. If we are to continue, we must keep telling him into life. Though he has not lived any more than this moment, the sum of all his gifts to us is a seed beyond the Now and from that we must remember what hasn't happened yet."

At this point the entranced, hungry street boy shook his much awakened head and uttered out clearly and suddenly, "How can you remember what hasn't happened, to continue speaking him into life? If he hasn't lived it yet, how can it be remembered?"

"What we as Gods remember," YaYa responded, "is how hard we tried so long ago to bring our poor, dismembered daughter's bones back to life, attempting with the little bits another boy brought back with the living heart he'd saved by spending all her gathered bones; which, through our efforts meant that two humans were made to live, love and walk, whose existence made us, the Gods of the Mountain and Goddess of all Growth, into blood relatives to those same forgetful humans that now have us living, forgotten, under their bridges, but blood relatives as well to others yet who are capable of loving what is divine in one another if it appears small enough to grasp.

"As Delbert is the Lord of Mountains, of clay, soil, sand and stones, and the fire that hides in minerals and mountains, he is the Lord and maker of the ground and because of that he is the Lord of what has already been, in which the sum of all the past is added up and becomes what we call the Now. The story of this collected past is the story-ground, the spoken earth in which I, YaYa, the Benefactress of Growth, make seeds to sprout and take root in the past that Delbert speaks into view. The possibilities of any of the things that could happen, that haven't happened yet, are carried in the seed of divine speech, unseen, that my talking makes to sprout and grow and fruit beyond the Now, but deeply rooted in it.

"Every tree, plant, animal, person, everything that lives, makes seeds, dies and comes back to life, is the fruit of Grandmother Growth doing her remembering, which is rooted in the Mountain Maker's tale. My remembering brings trees out of seeds and what hasn't happened come into view."

Then, standing, she called the Air and the Breath of Day and Night, to whom she made a promise to her lost daughter, the most powerful Goddess who lives dispersed beyond the Mountain Maker's story and Grandmother Growth's Time, to be seen whole only in unexpected moments of ecstasy and hope; to her YaYa spoke in such a way that none might interrupt.

"Ajni jaura rax kotzejal ruchiuliu juyu taqaj oqnaq vuuq´, anen kin ripaj chwach ja acha xuquina xucam rukux ruchiuleu chwach ruiyaj, rutí rukmstaniel ruchieleu vinaaq, anen xtikinnatax jarukaslimaal majan ta vinaqira ruman ja acha majun oqxtquramastaj joj batsra kayon ka qan, ka qá.

"As this green flowering world, its animals and its tear-watered soil, is my own skirt, I spread it over what this floating man has salvaged from amnesia's hungry jaws and I will remember what has not happened yet into view for the life of this man because he never allowed the Story of us in which all of us are rooted to be forgotten."

The homeless Goddess of Growth, YaYa, the wife of the homeless God of the Mountain, from beneath their beloved bridge, began to speak Martín into life; pulling him out of the pool and beyond the story he'd already lived:

"Not eight days had come and gone since my daughter, whose heart has ears, heard him crying for life and love, after he had sacrificed every single treasure he had left, when Martín, who was determined now to teach more ferociously and beautifully than he'd ever done before so as to flare brightly and echo loudly in his final efforts to keep alive the Story and die worthy of the heart, in the course of bringing that to bear, on the very day and exact moment he had wanted to be sitting with the Queen, while teaching instead in a summer conference in Wisconsin, was just about to mount the stage in front of an expectant crowd when he felt a tiny touch upon his shoulder just like the caress that brought him back to life in his dream, and in that very instant a voice behind him spoke, whose content he didn't comprehend for its being overridden so completely by the beauty of its sound, whose tone mercilessly staggered him, having waited millions of years for this sound, which he recognized from a time before time, that he could feel but no longer recollect, whose voice was like the untroubled bubbling and clear liquid song of an otter-filled brook, carving lace from ice beneath rounded hummocks of guarding snow.

"When he turned to look he was stunned and unable to speak in any language whatsoever, something that had never happened before in his history, not only because a beautiful, young, curly-headed woman was standing there, not only because a Goddess-eyed woman was speaking to him in her gorgeous liquid tones, but because her eyes could actually see him and in her seeing caused him to see her heart, the heart that she had struggled as well to keep alive, instead of just his own reflection in her eyes.

"Concentric layers of warm liquid recognition thawed their hope into ecstatic sight in which each remembered how many thousand years of mutual searching through every age both of them had walked, each thinking the other to be irrevocably lost, but now the both of them held out the very grief-washed heart in their hand that the other sought, each fitting perfectly onto the other's empty throne. She had the heart of a Goddess, at least two teeth of a Goddess for having such a smile, and the grace of her walk that only two toe bones of a Goddess could give. Now the world could have the Story, and these two people could have human lives, these two sweethearts who found a way to live the story of ordinary people, extraordinarily in love. And the story of the struggle of what it takes to be graced with such love is the story from which all humans are descended."

Irma looked up and said, "It's like this every time, isn't it, honey?"

"Yes, it is, Irma," Donanciano said. "Yes, it is."

Delbert wept beneath the bridge and started a fire for the evening meal.

The young street boy wandered off telling the story of the Toe Bone and the Tooth to whomsoever would listen.

And YaYa, weeping for their lost daughter, just kept on remembering and talking everything into life.

Kiil utziil
Utzlaj bey
Utzlaj colo
Nimlajtaq kaslimaal
Majun loulo
Oxlajuj Matioxiil.

MAYAN, GUATEMALAN SPANISH AND NEW MEXICAN SPANISH WORDS

L ike indigenous languages throughout the world, Tzutujil Maya is a rich oral institution. In the recent past those who have decided to commit Tzutujil words to written symbols have composed as many orthographies as there were people wanting to write them.

Because the greatness of a language is in its speaking, its sounds cannot be truly written, they must be heard. The glossary that follows is only here as an attempt to show a little bit of the subtle depth and vast beauty of indigenous thought contained in the spoken Tzutujil. Though approximate, it uses symbols that have come to be commonly accepted for writing highland Mayan words.

The letter *x* is pronounced as "sh". Letters such as *q´, c´, tz, t´, a´*, etc., represent beautiful Tzutujil sounds not present in any European language. All other consonants and vowels are pronounced as in Spanish. Spanish words are spelled each according to Guatemalan and New Mexico custom and pronounced according to the rules followed in modern Spanish.

ajcun: *Tzutujil Mayan*. Literally, he or she who searches, a tracker and therefore a catch-all term for all types of shaman.

Aj Q´ij: *Tzutujil Mayan*. Literally, he or she of the Sun or Day. Signifies a diviner who employs the ancient Mesoamerican calendar to diagnose social dilemmas and illness.

aldea: *Spanish*. An outlying hamlet or satellite settlement adjacent to a larger town.

amate: *Nahuat adopted into Spanish*. A tree of the mulberry family called *Pov´* in Tzutujil Maya from whose bark hammered paper was made which, before the Europeans, comprised most of the people's clothing and offering material, as well as paper for writing and painting.

anona: *Nahuat adopted into Spanish*. A Central American tree whose fruit is shaped and scaled like a pine cone and is sweet, tart and delicious and full of black seeds. Called *qwash* by the Tzutujil.

baboso: *Guatemalan Spanish*. From *babas*, meaning saliva; literally, a drooler, a fool.

bayh: *Tzutujil Mayan*. Gopher.

berrinche: *Guatemalan Spanish*. An all-out glazed-eyed tantrum.

beyal: See *ru beyal*

biis: *Tzutujil Mayan*. Grief, sorrow, the substance of sadness that must remain liquid or it solidifies into bitterness or pathological sickness.

boj chij: *Tzutujil Mayan*. Literally, to spin fine cotton thread, but used to mean to cajole, court or talk somebody into doing something.

buak: *Tzutujil Mayan*. A big head-sized mass of corn dough steamed in leaves, then sliced and toasted on a griddle.

caballeria(s): *Old Spanish*. Still in common use in Guatemala and Latin America, referring to a very large expanse of land. From the word for a knight or gentleman, originally the royally-distributed inheritance of an aristocrat, which included the local people, from which the "gentleman" received all his support. Now a land measurement that varies from country to country.

cacao: *Nahuat adopted into Spanish and English*. From Mayan *Cacav*, the chocolate bean tree, originally the "gold standard" and money of all Mayan societies and the sacred currency of marriages and initiations among the Tzutujil. There are both wild and domesticated varieties, of which the later has been much changed since becoming the source of modern chocolate.

cacomistle: *Nahuat*. A shy, big-eyed tree fox called in the U.S a ring-tailed cat, in Tzutujil, *xiwaan*.

cafetal: *Spanish*. Coffee plantation or grove.

calawala: *Spanish*. A tropical plant with large, shady leaves, whose hairy root is much used in Native Medicine.

casueleja: *Guatemalan Spanish*. A sweet cake made with egg yolks, customarily soaked in honey then eaten by the entire populace on Good Friday.

cedula: *Spanish*. In Guatemala an internal passport required of all citizens and alien residents for travel within the country.

ceviche: *Spanish*. A cocktail of finely chopped raw shellfish, fish or various other creatures mixed with chopped mints, parsleys, limes, chilies and tomatoes, eaten fresh, cold and uncooked; delicious.

charlada, charla: *Guatemalan Spanish.* A talk, a lecture, conversation.

chicharron: *Spanish.* Golden planks of slowly rendered pork skins.

chichicaste: *Nahuat adopted into Guatemalan Spanish.* The giant nettle, which can grow ten feet tall.

chipilin: *Nahuat adopted into Guatemalan Spanish.* A cultivated and wild-growing leguminous native plant called *much* in Mayan; the leaves are eaten in a myriad different forms. Said to produce relaxation and sleep.

chirmoal: *Tzutujil from Toltec.* Any of the various tomato-based sauces and roasted chilis forming the basis of half of most villagers' everyday fare, along with hand-slapped corn cakes.

choreque: *Nahuat-Spanish.* Leguminous tree much like a mimosa with a profusion of orange snapdragon-like flowers.

choza: *Guatemalan Spanish.* A thatched hut or cabin.

churro: *Spanish.* An ancient breed of very hardy Middle Eastern sheep brought to Spain by early Phonecians and Sephardic Jews and again to the American Southwest by Spanish colonists, where they have been prized ever since by the Diné or Navaho people for their ability to thrive in rugged conditions while producing an ideal wool for the weaving of rugs. The male sheep often have between four and six horns that sometimes curl and ripple in wild forms around their heads forming almost a cage. From the shape of their horns comes their name, "churro", which is a kind of long tubular Spanish doughnut, still made throughout Spain and all Latin America. Considered by some to be a subspecies of Jacob's sheep.

cieba: *Spanish.* The Holy Kapok tree of lowland Central America. Some were so big that whole towns were established around a single tree whose spreading branches could shade a circle a hundred feet in diameter. Called *Inup* in Tzutujil Mayan.

clantun: *Tzutujil Mayan.* The giant datura or belladonna plant. They reach the height of fifteen feet and have enormous white flowers that open only at night and whose powerful intoxicating fragrance is narcotic in itself. Though poisonous taken internally, it is much used in healing. She is the wife of Holy Boy.

coati: Abbreviation for coatimundi. *Nahuat adopted into English.* In Guatemalan Spanish: *Pizote.* In Tzutujil Mayan: *Ziis.* The famous one-third raccoon, one-third monkey, one-third badger, skinny-nosed, clownish beasts who go about in family packs with their tails straight up. The males turn solid black and become solitary animals in their later years.

cofradia(s): *Spanish from Latin*. Literally, brotherhood. Originally a lay organization charged with caring for the cult of the image of an Iberian *santo* (see *santo*), but eventually altered by the Tzutujil into a native spiritual institution where their ancient Gods and their versions of Catholic saints were housed. Refers to the officials of these sacred houses.

comal: *Spanish from Nahuat*. Literally, a clay tortilla griddle about an inch thick and usually two feet across which is placed on three stones over a fire. Some people nowadays use oil drum lids. Called *xot* in most Mayan dialects, it is one of the most ancient cooking implements in continuous use in the world.

comedor: *Spanish*. Literally, eatery; a diner, an informal restaurant.

corozo palm: A very large, majestic, lowland palm tree whose torpedo-like buds can measure up to six feet in length. The profusion of tiny light green and cream colored flowers contained within have a powerful smell and are used in initiation and sacred-house rituals as well as Mayanized Catholic ceremonies. Formerly bows and arrows were made from its springy wood.

costumbre: *Spanish*. Literally, custom. In Guatemalan Spanish refers to any kind of Native American spiritual ritual, usually with a shaman, as differentiated from those of the American or European churches.

cotinga: *Spanish*. Mayan, *raxon*. A beautiful red-chested, turquoise-blue bird, prized by all ancient Mesoamerican peoples for its feathers and spiritual significance.

criada: *Spanish*. A maid. From the word *criar*, to cultivate, raise or care for. In Guatemala since colonial times certain Mayan villages have supplied resident non-Indians and city families with cooks, parlor maids, washerwomen and so on. The Tzutujil were noteworthy for their unwillingness to do so.

cuerda(s): *Spanish*. Twine or cord, but also refers to the antique Spanish measurement of land still in use in Guatemala. Official dimensions vary from district to district. A *cuerda* was originally measured off by squaring a length of cord.

curassow: *South American Spanish*. A large, black, tropical forest ground bird with curly head feathers. Called *Pajuil* in Guatemalan Spanish, Chuy in Tzutujil Maya.

cuxa: *Guatemalan Spanish*. A homemade liquor of very high alcohol content distilled usually from fermented tropical fruits, but in some districts made from wheat and others corn. Called *Psiwanya*, or canyon water, by the Tzutujil and Tzam, or *snot*, by the Quiché.

delantale(s): *Spanish*. An apron.

derrumbre: *Spanish*. A landslide.

encomendero: *Spanish*. A holder of an *encomienda* or a royal Spanish land grant which after the so-called conquest were awarded to certain aristocratic and military families as pay. This included the indigenous people residing within those zones who were forced to produce an annual quota of rent and tribute to the *encomendero*, who in turn was required to pay a percentage to the crown and in some cases the church as well.

encino: *Spanish*. In New Mexico Spanish denotes any of several varieties of scrub oaks.

guanacaste: See *ocuy*.

guerrillero: *Spanish*. Literally, a maker of small war or guerrilla. A specialist in using minimal means and vital strategy to fight for a big cause against a large, well-established military force.

huipil: *Nahuat adopted into Spanish*. An indigenous blouse, called *pot* in Tzutujil. See *pot*.

huraqan: *Tzutujil Mayan and most Mayan languages*. Literally, One Foot, meaning hurricane. The word in English comes directly from the Mayan.

immortal: *Spanish*. Literally, immortal. A rare medicinal plant of the American Southwest.

ixoc (ee-shuck): *Tzutujil Mayan*. Grown woman.

Ixoc Juo: *Tzutujil Mayan*. Literally, Lady Five. The Goddess of gambling and luck, invoked by men wagering in Mayan corn dice. Five is a winning roll.

jaguarundi: *Nahuat*. A rare, very shy, nocturnal Central American wild cat who can have a red, gray or dark coat, a flattened sort of otter-like whiskery face and who usually crawls very low to the ground, likes to swim and climbs trees. Otherwise looks like a miniature cougar.

jaspeado: *Spanish*. The textile-dying method of *ikat*, where the threads are tie-dyed before weaving to produce a complexity of forms going in every direction.

jocote: *Spanish from Nahuat.* A delicious Guatemalean tropical plum. In Tzutujil: *kinoum.*

joron cotón: *Tzutujil Mayan.* An ancient form of man's shirt.

kiem: *Tzutujil Mayan.* A woman's backstrap weaving loom on which all the family's clothing is produced using an ingenious arrangement of polished sticks of different shapes.

kinkajou: *South American Spanish.* A tree-dwelling, furry, long-tailed, wide-eyed animal, looking lemur-like and marsupial-like, who is always worried. Called *micoleon* in Spanish or lion-monkey, aptly describing its appearance.

kiq: *Tzutujil Mayan.* Literally, blood; refers to the coagulated sap of rubber trees used to make the world's first rubber balls. Very large significance in shamanism and the ancient Mayan ritual ballgame.

kixwuuch: *Tzutujil Mayan.* Literally, thorn opossum; the porcupine.

kuk: *Tzutujil Mayan.* Squirrel.

la´: *Tzutujil Mayan.* Evocative; boy, son, child.

mangax: *Mayanized Spanish.* From *mangas*, or sleeve, see *q´u.*

matones: *Guatemalan Spanish.* Killers, hitmen.

mestiza(o): *Spanish.* A person of mixed ancestry.

metate: *Spanish and English from Nahuat.* Grinding stone.

morosos: *Spanish.* Literally, morons, but with a slightly more negative meaning.

mos, mosí: *Mayan.* From the antique Spanish *mozo*, meaning a peasant under an aristocrat, which to the Mayans meant a non-Mayan person who carried out the biddings of their *encomiendero* or colonial overlords. In modern Tzutujil *mos* or the plural *mosí* signifies any non-Tzutujil.

motmot: *Spanish from Nahuat.* A beautiful bird who strips the feathers off the quill of its two long tail feathers, save the very end, forming two rackets which they clip back and forth like scissors as they sing. Called *Doq Doq* in Tzutujil Mayan in imitation of their song.

Najbey Jal: *Tzutujil Mayan.* The original corn.

nimchoy: *Tzutujil Mayan.* Literally, big mouse; a wood rat.

nu jii: *Tzutujil Mayan.* My son-in-law.

ocuy: *Tzutujil Mayan.* Differing varieties of beautiful yellow-wooded *guanacaste* trees.

ollin: *Nahuat*. Native latex rubber from the sap of the rubber tree. Also signifies movement because of its use for making rubber balls that were sacred paraphernalia in the Mesoamerican ritual ballgame. See *kiq*.

pan dulce: *Spanish*. Literally, sweet bread; a sweet, beautiful egg bread made in creative shapes with a little sugar on top.

pas: *Tzutujil Mayan*. A man's highly ornamented sash that holds up his *scav* pants.

pericon: *Spanish*. Literally, big parrot; a cultivated medicinal plant with a strong anesthetic flavor.

paquan: *Tzutujilized Nahuat*. A short, black, herringbone wool jacket worn by old traditional men.

pataxte: *Nahuat*. Wild cacao; the uncultivated, more fragrant, strangely convoluted tree and pod of the wild chocolate fruit whose larger seeds are toasted and ground up with domesticated cacoa beans, or chocolate, to make various ceremonial drinks. The smell of this wild *cacav* fruit, flowers and tree is indescribably wild, melancholy, delicious, sweet, musty and narcotic and it can be eaten as a fruit. Called *peq'* by the Tzutujil. A holy plant.

pila: *Spanish*. Public fountain with many pools and slanting troughs usually in the middle of Latin American villages or in courtyards where women traditionally bring their clothing and little children to wash.

pixnic: *Tzutujil Mayan*. A very popular edible wild green plant of the nightshade family.

pom (rhymes with Rome): *Tzutujil Mayan*. Any of several varieties of very specific tree resins used ritually as incense and called generically by the Nahuat name in English: copal.

pot (rhymes with coat): *Tzutujil Mayan*. A woman's handwoven blouse that extends to the knees and sometimes to the ankles over which is wrapped the *uuq*, wraparound skirt.

puub: *Tzutujil Mayan*. Blowgun. Mayan blowguns shoot pellets, not darts, and were used anciently for hunting birds high up in the forest canopy. Most tribes used fired clay pellets as ammunition, but the Tzutujil were famous for their use of giant iris seeds, which are very hard and perfectly round and can be shot at very high speeds.

q´ijibal: *Tzutujil Mayan*. Literally, sun tool; a shaman or shamaness's gathering of deities and tools used in healing and divination.

qu´: *Tzutujil Mayan.* The thick blanket-like shawl of working men used like a saddle blanket under the loads they carry on their backs and the same cloth made into the ceremonial black-sleeved robes worn by male hierarchy members, sometimes called *mangax.*

quej ic´: *Tzutujil Mayan.* Literally, deer chili. A potent wild pepper so powerful no living person can eat a whole one.

quetzal: *Nahuat; Guatemalan Spanish.* The rare, magnificent *trogon* whose long iridescent tail and red and green body feathers were prized ceremonially by all Mesoamerican peoples. The feathers were a sacred currency among the ancient hierarchy and subsequently so highly levied by the European invaders as tribute, that the bird became extinct in most of its former range, surviving in only a few pockets where its natural habitat still exists.

Because of its ancient use as indigenous currency, along with *cacav*, the modern Guatemalan banknote is called a *quetzal.* Plural *quetzales.*

qumarcah: *Quiché and Tzutujil Mayan.* Literally, decayed vernal cane; the place name of the pre-European Quiché cultural center.

rax c´aam: *Tzutujil Mayan.* Literally, green vine; the wild forest morning glory flower. A tree climbing plant.

raza: *Spanish; New Mexico Spanish.* Literally, the race; a native-born, Spanish-speaking New Mexico resident whose ancestors were pioneers from Spain.

ru beyal: *Tzutujil Mayan.* Literally, one's road or direction. Signifies how something should be done; the stroking of the fur in the direction in which it lies is the *beyal*; doing what is good for the community is the *beyal.*

Rumuxux Ruchiuleu: *Tzutujil Mayan.* Literally, the navel of the soil's edge, the Umbilicus of the Earth, the center of the world. Tzutujil ceremonial name for their home town.

santo(s): *Spanish.* Literally, holy or saint. The cult of *santos* brought to all Latin America from Spain as characterized by grand statues of saints who are still venerated as miraculous, and as gods and goddesses by the Mayans who superimposed their own deities onto them. A *santo* would be one of the holy statues.

sabino: *New Mexico Spanish.* The tree and fragrant wood of the one-seed juniper.

scav: *Tzutujil Mayan*. A man's and boy's pocketless, handwoven purple-striped knee pants, held up by the use of a *pas*, or sash, often highly embroidered just like a woman's *pot*.

siwan: *Tzutujil Mayan*. Literally, ravine. The place where Santiago Atitlan sits is called Siwan Tnamit, or ravine village.

ta´: *Tzutujil Mayan*. Literally, father; evocative.

tamandua: *South American Spanish*. The smaller, golden ant bear, as distinguished from the giant anteater.

tepiscuintle: *Nahuat*. Literally, hill dog. A delicate spotted deer-like rodent widely hunted for its meat. In Tzutujil Mayan *lalav*.

tie´: *Tzutujil Mayan*. Literally, mother; evocative.

tinaja: *Spanish*. Water jar.

tjoy snic: *Tzutujil Mayan*. Literally, eater of ants; the *tamandua*.

traje: *Spanish*. Clothing outfit or suit; in Guatemalan Spanish refers to native dress versus non-Indian clothing, for women in particular.

tramatista: *Guatamalan Spanish*. A negotiator, trouble-shooter or a broker who by means of shortcuts and under-the-table deals causes a desired effect for pay, usually in the realm of bureaucracy.

trampa: *Spanish*. Literally, a trap. Guatemalan slang for a small one-owner store or diner.

tule: *Spanish from Nahuat*. The tule reed plant, a tall, beautiful three-sided lake rush which is much employed to make reed mats and highly revered by the Tzutujil for making sacred door coverings as thresholds to the other worlds in order to reach the Holy. The Tzutujil call it *tzok*.

tut: *Tzutujil Mayan*. A large woven, straw hat no longer in use. At one time a crown.

tzan tzuy: *Tzutujil Mayan*. Literally, gourd tendrils. A tree whose velvety leaves are widely eaten as stewed greens, called *siete camisas* or seven shirts in Guatemalan Spanish.

umul: *Tzutujil Mayan*. Literally, rabbit.

uuq: *Tzutujil Mayan*. A woman's wraparound skirt. Santiago Atitlan has always been one of the few Mayan villages where the women fasten their skirts without the use of a sash.

vinaaq: *Tzutujil Mayan*. Literally, named. The word for the number twenty and simultaneously meaning a human being on account of having ten fingers and ten toes. Tzutujil shamans and midwives, when praying for the positive outcome of a child's gestation in the womb, invoke the Deities to give the child "a complete number of heads on his/her hands (fingers), a complete number of heads on his/her feet (toes)" and thereby coming together as a "complete" twenty or human being.

xcajcoj: *Tzutujil Mayan*. Literally, the native, undyed, golden colored cotton; in ritual context refers to a man's ceremonial headcloth, which must contain prescribed stripes of this brown cotton.

xcap: *Tzutujil Mayan*. The red circular headdress of the women of Santiago Atitlan consisting of a long, two-inch wide, thick handwoven ribbon wound into the hair and around and around the head until a halo protruding out from the head two to five inches is formed. Usually highly ornamented with tassels hanging off to one side.

xeca: *Mayanized Guatemalan Spanish*. A hollow, sweet, wholewheat natural starter, lens-shaped bread that can stay fresh for weeks.

xoy xjap: *Tzutujil Mayan*. A simple, homemade, one-piece man's work sandal originally made of various tough barks of trees but now mostly from thin rubber tire tread. Their form is seen in ancient Mayan carvings and writings.

xe che xe caam: *Tzutujil Mayan*. Literally, under trees, under vines. Refers to hiding homeless in the bush to avoid an epidemic or pursuit by killers.

xejuyu: *Tzutujil Mayan*. Literally, under hills. Refers to the flat, hot, low-altitude coast south of the Mayan volcanic mountain highlands.

xq´e´ ch´oy: *Tzutujil Mayan*. Literally, boundary mouse; a large deer mouse with silver fur and white belly.

yaxtan: *Tzutujil Mayan*. *Ya* precedes every woman's name and refers to water. *Xtan* means little girl. A woman's word used amongst them when addressing each other.

yerba buena: *Spanish*. Literally, good herb. The spearmint plant. Tzutujil Mayan; *panzut*. A lot of ceremonial food is cooked with *yerba buena,* as are medicines.

yuquillo: *Spanish*. Little *yuca*. A tuberous starchy root. Refers usually to arrowroot flour or other similar root flours.

zotz: *Tzutujil Mayan*. Bat: the animal.